OECD Transfer Pricing Guidelines for Multinational Enterprises and Tax Administrations

22 JULY 2010

OECD

ORGANISATION FOR ECONOMIC CO-OPERATION AND DEVELOPMENT

The OECD is a unique forum where governments work together to address the economic, social and environmental challenges of globalisation. The OECD is also at the forefront of efforts to understand and to help governments respond to new developments and concerns, such as corporate governance, the information economy and the challenges of an ageing population. The Organisation provides a setting where governments can compare policy experiences, seek answers to common problems, identify good practice and work to co-ordinate domestic and international policies.

The OECD member countries are: Australia, Austria, Belgium, Canada, Chile, the Czech Republic, Denmark, Finland, France, Germany, Greece, Hungary, Iceland, Ireland, Italy, Japan, Korea, Luxembourg, Mexico, the Netherlands, New Zealand, Norway, Poland, Portugal, the Slovak Republic, Slovenia, Spain, Sweden, Switzerland, Turkey, the United Kingdom and the United States. The Commission of the European Communities takes part in the work of the OECD.

OECD Publishing disseminates widely the results of the Organisation's statistics gathering and research on economic, social and environmental issues, as well as the conventions, guidelines and standards agreed by its members.

ISBN 978-92-64-09033-0 (print)
ISBN 978-92-64-09018-7 (PDF)

Also available in French: *Principes de l'OCDE applicables en matière de prix de transfert à l'intention des entreprises multinationales et des administrations fiscales*

Corrigenda to OECD publications may be found on line at: *www.oecd.org/publishing/corrigenda*.
© OECD 2010

Foreword

These Guidelines are a revision of the OECD Report *Transfer Pricing and Multinational Enterprises* (1979). They were approved in their original version by the Committee on Fiscal Affairs on 27 June 1995 and by the OECD Council for publication on 13 July 1995.

Since their original version, these Guidelines have been supplemented:

- By the report on intangible property and services, adopted by the Committee on Fiscal Affairs on 23 January 1996 [DAFFE/CFA(96)2] and noted by the Council on 11 April 1996 [C(96)46], incorporated in Chapters VI and VII;

- By the report on cost contribution arrangements, adopted by the Committee on Fiscal Affairs on 25 June 1997 [DAFFE/CFA(97)27] and noted by the Council on 24 July 1997 [C(97)144], incorporated in Chapter VIII;

- By the report on the guidelines for monitoring procedures on the OECD Transfer Pricing Guidelines and the involvement of the business community [DAFFE/CFA/WD(97)11/REV1], adopted by the Committee on Fiscal Affairs on 24 June 1997 and noted by the Council on 23 October 1997 [C(97)196], incorporated in the annexes;

- By the report on the guidelines for conducting advance pricing arrangements under the mutual agreement procedure, adopted by the Committee on Fiscal Affairs on 30 June 1999 [DAFFE/CFA(99)31] and noted by the Council on 28 October 1999 [C(99)138], incorporated in the annexes;

- By the report on the transfer pricing aspects of business restructurings, adopted by the Committee on Fiscal Affairs on 22 June 2010 [CTPA/CFA(2010)46] and approved by the Council on 22 July 2010 [Annex I to C(2010)99], incorporated in Chapter IX.

In addition, these Guidelines have been modified:

- By an update of Chapter IV, adopted by the Committee on Fiscal Affairs on 6 June 2008 [CTPA/CFA(2008)30/REV1] and an update of the Foreword and of the Preface, adopted by the Committee on Fiscal Affairs on 22 June 2009 [CTPA/CFA(2009)51/REV1], approved by the Council on 16 July 2009 [C(2009)88];

- By a revision of Chapters I-III, adopted by the Committee on Fiscal Affairs on 22 June 2010 [CTPA/CFA(2010)55] and approved by the Council on 22 July 2010 [Annex I to C(2010)99]; and

- By an update of the Foreword, of the Preface, of the Glossary, of Chapters IV-VIII and of the annexes, adopted by the Committee on Fiscal Affairs on 22 June 2010 [CTPA/CFA(2010)47] and approved by the Council on 22 July 2010 [Annex I to C(2010)99].

These Guidelines will continue to be supplemented with additional guidance addressing other aspects of transfer pricing and will be periodically reviewed and revised on an ongoing basis.

Table of Contents

Chapter I

The Arm's Length Principle

Chapter II

Transfer Pricing Methods

Chapter III

Comparability Analysis

Chapter IV

**Administrative Approaches to Avoiding and
Resolving Transfer Pricing Disputes**

Chapter V

Documentation

Chapter VI

Special Considerations for Intangible Property

Chapter VII

Special Considerations for Intra-Group Services

Chapter VIII

Cost Contribution Arrangements

Chapter IX

Transfer Pricing Aspects of Business Restructurings

Preface

1.   The role of multinational enterprises (MNEs) in world trade has increased dramatically over the last 20 years. This in part reflects the increased integration of national economies and technological progress, particularly in the area of communications. The growth of MNEs presents increasingly complex taxation issues for both tax administrations and the MNEs themselves since separate country rules for the taxation of MNEs cannot be viewed in isolation but must be addressed in a broad international context.

2.   These issues arise primarily from the practical difficulty, for both MNEs and tax administrations, of determining the income and expenses of a company or a permanent establishment that is part of an MNE group that should be taken into account within a jurisdiction, particularly where the MNE group's operations are highly integrated.

3.   In the case of MNEs, the need to comply with laws and administrative requirements that may differ from country to country creates additional problems. The differing requirements may lead to a greater burden on an MNE, and result in higher costs of compliance, than for a similar enterprise operating solely within a single tax jurisdiction.

4.   In the case of tax administrations, specific problems arise at both policy and practical levels. At the policy level, countries need to reconcile their legitimate right to tax the profits of a taxpayer based upon income and expenses that can reasonably be considered to arise within their territory with the need to avoid the taxation of the same item of income by more than one tax jurisdiction. Such double or multiple taxation can create an impediment to cross-border transactions in goods and services and the movement of capital. At a practical level, a country's determination of such income and expense allocation may be impeded by difficulties in obtaining pertinent data located outside its own jurisdiction.

5.   At a primary level, the taxing rights that each country asserts depend on whether the country uses a system of taxation that is residence-based, source-based, or both. In a residence-based tax system, a country will include in its tax base all or part of the income, including income from

sources outside that country, of any person (including juridical persons such as corporations) who is considered resident in that jurisdiction. In a source-based tax system, a country will include in its tax base income arising within its tax jurisdiction, irrespective of the residence of the taxpayer. As applied to MNEs, these two bases, often used in conjunction, generally treat each enterprise within the MNE group as a separate entity. OECD member countries have chosen this separate entity approach as the most reasonable means for achieving equitable results and minimising the risk of unrelieved double taxation. Thus, each individual group member is subject to tax on the income arising to it (on a residence or source basis).

6.   In order to apply the separate entity approach to intra-group transactions, individual group members must be taxed on the basis that they act at arm's length in their transactions with each other. However, the relationship among members of an MNE group may permit the group members to establish special conditions in their intra-group relations that differ from those that would have been established had the group members been acting as independent enterprises operating in open markets. To ensure the correct application of the separate entity approach, OECD member countries have adopted the arm's length principle, under which the effect of special conditions on the levels of profits should be eliminated.

7.   These international taxation principles have been chosen by OECD member countries as serving the dual objectives of securing the appropriate tax base in each jurisdiction and avoiding double taxation, thereby minimising conflict between tax administrations and promoting international trade and investment. In a global economy, coordination among countries is better placed to achieve these goals than tax competition. The OECD, with its mission to contribute to the expansion of world trade on a multilateral, non-discriminatory basis and to achieve the highest sustainable economic growth in member countries, has continuously worked to build a consensus on international taxation principles, thereby avoiding unilateral responses to multilateral problems.

8.   The foregoing principles concerning the taxation of MNEs are incorporated in the *OECD Model Tax Convention on Income and on Capital* (OECD Model Tax Convention), which forms the basis of the extensive network of bilateral income tax treaties between OECD member countries and between OECD member and non-member countries. These principles also are incorporated in the Model United Nations Double Taxation Convention between Developed and Developing Nations.

9.   The main mechanisms for resolving issues that arise in the application of international tax principles to MNEs are contained in these bilateral treaties. The Articles that chiefly affect the taxation of MNEs are:

Article 4, which defines residence; Articles 5 and 7, which determine the taxation of permanent establishments; Article 9, which relates to the taxation of the profits of associated enterprises and applies the arm's length principle; Articles 10, 11, and 12, which determine the taxation of dividends, interest, and royalties, respectively; and Articles 24, 25, and 26, which contain special provisions relating to non-discrimination, the resolution of disputes, and exchange of information.

10.   The Committee on Fiscal Affairs, which is the main tax policy body of the OECD, has issued a number of reports relating to the application of these Articles to MNEs and to others. The Committee has encouraged the acceptance of common interpretations of these Articles, thereby reducing the risk of inappropriate taxation and providing satisfactory means of resolving problems arising from the interaction of the laws and practices of different countries.

11.   In applying the foregoing principles to the taxation of MNEs, one of the most difficult issues that has arisen is the establishment for tax purposes of appropriate transfer prices. Transfer prices are the prices at which an enterprise transfers physical goods and intangible property or provides services to associated enterprises. For purposes of these Guidelines, an "associated enterprise" is an enterprise that satisfies the conditions set forth in Article 9, sub-paragraphs 1a) and 1b) of the OECD Model Tax Convention. Under these conditions, two enterprises are associated if one of the enterprises participates directly or indirectly in the management, control, or capital of the other or if "the same persons participate directly or indirectly in the management, control, or capital" of both enterprises (*i.e.* if both enterprises are under common control). The issues discussed in these Guidelines also arise in the treatment of permanent establishments as discussed in the *Report on the Attribution of Profits to Permanent Establishments* that was adopted by the OECD Council in July 2008, which supersedes the OECD Report *Model Tax Convention: Attribution of Income to Permanent Establishments* (1994). Some relevant discussion may also be found in the OECD Report *International Tax Avoidance and Evasion* (1987).

12.   Transfer prices are significant for both taxpayers and tax administrations because they determine in large part the income and expenses, and therefore taxable profits, of associated enterprises in different tax jurisdictions. Transfer pricing issues originally arose in transactions between associated enterprises operating within the same tax jurisdiction. The domestic issues are not considered in these Guidelines, which focus on the international aspects of transfer pricing. These international aspects are more difficult to deal with because they involve more than one tax jurisdiction and therefore any adjustment to the transfer price in one

jurisdiction implies that a corresponding change in another jurisdiction is appropriate. However, if the other jurisdiction does not agree to make a corresponding adjustment the MNE group will be taxed twice on this part of its profits. In order to minimise the risk of such double taxation, an international consensus is required on how to establish for tax purposes transfer prices on cross-border transactions.

13.   These Guidelines are intended to be a revision and compilation of previous reports by the OECD Committee on Fiscal Affairs addressing transfer pricing and other related tax issues with respect to multinational enterprises. The principal report is *Transfer Pricing and Multinational Enterprises* (1979) (the "1979 Report") which was repealed by the OECD Council in 1995. Other reports address transfer pricing issues in the context of specific topics. These reports are *Transfer Pricing and Multinational Enterprises -- Three Taxation Issues* (1984) (the "1984 Report"), and *Thin Capitalisation* (the "1987 Report"). A list of amendments made to these Guidelines is included in the Foreword.

14.   These Guidelines also draw upon the discussion undertaken by the OECD on the proposed transfer pricing regulations in the United States [see the OECD Report *Tax Aspects of Transfer Pricing within Multinational Enterprises: The United States Proposed Regulations* (1993)]. However, the context in which that Report was written was very different from that in which these Guidelines have been undertaken, its scope was far more limited, and it specifically addressed the United States proposed regulations.

15.   OECD member countries continue to endorse the arm's length principle as embodied in the OECD Model Tax Convention (and in the bilateral conventions that legally bind treaty partners in this respect) and in the 1979 Report. These Guidelines focus on the application of the arm's length principle to evaluate the transfer pricing of associated enterprises. The Guidelines are intended to help tax administrations (of both OECD member countries and non-member countries) and MNEs by indicating ways to find mutually satisfactory solutions to transfer pricing cases, thereby minimising conflict among tax administrations and between tax administrations and MNEs and avoiding costly litigation. The Guidelines analyse the methods for evaluating whether the conditions of commercial and financial relations within an MNE satisfy the arm's length principle and discuss the practical application of those methods. They also include a discussion of global formulary apportionment.

16.   OECD member countries are encouraged to follow these Guidelines in their domestic transfer pricing practices, and taxpayers are encouraged to follow these Guidelines in evaluating for tax purposes whether their transfer pricing complies with the arm's length principle. Tax

administrations are encouraged to take into account the taxpayer's commercial judgement about the application of the arm's length principle in their examination practices and to undertake their analyses of transfer pricing from that perspective.

17.   These Guidelines are also intended primarily to govern the resolution of transfer pricing cases in mutual agreement proceedings between OECD member countries and, where appropriate, arbitration proceedings. They further provide guidance when a corresponding adjustment request has been made. The Commentary on paragraph 2 of Article 9 of the OECD Model Tax Convention makes clear that the State from which a corresponding adjustment is requested should comply with the request only if that State "considers that the figure of adjusted profits correctly reflects what the profits would have been if the transactions had been at arm's length". This means that in competent authority proceedings the State that has proposed the primary adjustment bears the burden of demonstrating to the other State that the adjustment "is justified both in principle and as regards the amount." Both competent authorities are expected to take a cooperative approach in resolving mutual agreement cases.

18.   In seeking to achieve the balance between the interests of taxpayers and tax administrators in a way that is fair to all parties, it is necessary to consider all aspects of the system that are relevant in a transfer pricing case. One such aspect is the allocation of the burden of proof. In most jurisdictions, the tax administration bears the burden of proof, which may require the tax administration to make a *prima facie* showing that the taxpayer's pricing is inconsistent with the arm's length principle. It should be noted, however, that even in such a case a tax administration might still reasonably oblige the taxpayer to produce its records to enable the tax administration to undertake its examination of the controlled transactions. In other jurisdictions the taxpayer may bear the burden of proof in some respects. Some OECD member countries are of the view that Article 9 of the OECD Model Tax Convention establishes burden of proof rules in transfer pricing cases which override any contrary domestic provisions. Other countries, however, consider that Article 9 does not establish burden of proof rules (cf. paragraph 4 of the Commentary on Article 9 of the OECD Model Tax Convention). Regardless of which party bears the burden of proof, an assessment of the fairness of the allocation of the burden of proof would have to be made in view of the other features of the jurisdiction's tax system that have a bearing on the overall administration of transfer pricing rules, including the resolution of disputes. These features include penalties, examination practices, administrative appeals processes, rules regarding payment of interest with respect to tax assessments and refunds, whether

proposed tax deficiencies must be paid before protesting an adjustment, the statute of limitations, and the extent to which rules are made known in advance. It would be inappropriate to rely on any of these features, including the burden of proof, to make unfounded assertions about transfer pricing. Some of these issues are discussed further in Chapter IV.

19.   These Guidelines focus on the main issues of principle that arise in the transfer pricing area. The Committee on Fiscal Affairs intends to continue its work in this area. A revision of Chapters I-III and a new Chapter IX were approved in 2010, reflecting work undertaken by the Committee on comparability, on transactional profit methods and on the transfer pricing aspects of business restructurings. Future work will address such issues as the application of the arm's length principle to transactions involving intangible property, services, cost contribution arrangements, permanent establishments, and thin capitalisation. The Committee intends to have regular reviews of the experiences of OECD member and selected non-member countries in the use of the methods used to apply the arm's length principle, with particular emphasis on difficulties encountered in the application of transactional profit methods (as defined in Chapter II) and the ways in which these problems have been resolved between countries.

Glossary

Advance pricing arrangement ("APA")

An arrangement that determines, in advance of controlled transactions, an appropriate set of criteria (*e.g.* method, comparables and appropriate adjustments thereto, critical assumptions as to future events) for the determination of the transfer pricing for those transactions over a fixed period of time. An advance pricing arrangement may be unilateral involving one tax administration and a taxpayer or multilateral involving the agreement of two or more tax administrations.

Arm's length principle

The international standard that OECD member countries have agreed should be used for determining transfer prices for tax purposes. It is set forth in Article 9 of the OECD Model Tax Convention as follows: where "conditions are made or imposed between the two enterprises in their commercial or financial relations which differ from those which would be made between independent enterprises, then any profits which would, but for those conditions, have accrued to one of the enterprises, but, by reason of those conditions, have not so accrued, may be included in the profits of that enterprise and taxed accordingly".

Arm's length range

A range of figures that are acceptable for establishing whether the conditions of a controlled transaction are arm's length and that are derived either from applying the same transfer pricing method to multiple comparable data or from applying different transfer pricing methods.

Associated enterprises

Two enterprises are associated enterprises with respect to each other if one of the enterprises meets the conditions of Article 9, sub-paragraphs 1*a)* or 1*b)* of the OECD Model Tax Convention with respect to the other enterprise.

Balancing payment

A payment, normally from one or more participants to another, to adjust participants' proportionate shares of contributions, that increases the value of the contributions of the payer and decreases the value of the contributions of the payee by the amount of the payment.

Buy-in payment

A payment made by a new entrant to an already active CCA for obtaining an interest in any results of prior CCA activity.

Buy-out payment

Compensation that a participant who withdraws from an already active CCA may receive from the remaining participants for an effective transfer of its interests in the results of past CCA activities.

Commercial intangible

An intangible that is used in commercial activities such as the production of a good or the provision of a service, as well as an intangible right that is itself a business asset transferred to customers or used in the operation of business.

Comparability analysis

A comparison of a controlled transaction with an uncontrolled transaction or transactions. Controlled and uncontrolled transactions are comparable if none of the differences between the transactions could materially affect the factor being examined in the methodology (*e.g.* price or margin), or if reasonably accurate adjustments can be made to eliminate the material effects of any such differences.

Comparable uncontrolled transaction

A comparable uncontrolled transaction is a transaction between two independent parties that is comparable to the controlled transaction under examination. It can be either a comparable transaction between one party to the controlled transaction and an independent party ("internal comparable") or between two independent parties, neither of which is a party to the controlled transaction ("external comparable").

Comparable uncontrolled price (CUP) method

A transfer pricing method that compares the price for property or services transferred in a controlled transaction to the price charged for property or services transferred in a comparable uncontrolled transaction in comparable circumstances.

Compensating adjustment

An adjustment in which the taxpayer reports a transfer price for tax purposes that is, in the taxpayer's opinion, an arm's length price for a controlled transaction, even though this price differs from the amount actually charged between the associated enterprises. This adjustment would be made before the tax return is filed.

Contribution analysis

An analysis used in the profit split method under which the combined profits from controlled transactions are divided between the associated enterprises based upon the relative value of the functions performed (taking into account assets used and risks assumed) by each of the associated enterprises participating in those transactions, supplemented as much as possible by external market data that indicate how independent enterprises would have divided profits in similar circumstances.

Controlled transactions

Transactions between two enterprises that are associated enterprises with respect to each other.

Corresponding adjustment

An adjustment to the tax liability of the associated enterprise in a second tax jurisdiction made by the tax administration of that jurisdiction, corresponding to a primary adjustment made by the tax administration in a first tax jurisdiction, so that the allocation of profits by the two jurisdictions is consistent.

Cost contribution arrangement ("CCA")

A CCA is a framework agreed among enterprises to share the costs and risks of developing, producing, or obtaining assets, services, or rights, and to determine the nature and extent of the interests of each participant in the results of the activity of developing, producing, or obtaining those assets, services, or rights.

Cost plus mark up

A mark up that is measured by reference to margins computed after the direct and indirect costs incurred by a supplier of property or services in a transaction.

Cost plus method

A transfer pricing method using the costs incurred by the supplier of property (or services) in a controlled transaction. An appropriate cost plus mark up is added to this cost, to make an appropriate profit in light of the functions performed (taking into account assets used and risks assumed) and the market conditions. What is arrived at after adding the cost plus mark up to the above costs may be regarded as an arm's length price of the original controlled transaction.

Direct-charge method

A method of charging directly for specific intra-group services on a clearly identified basis.

Direct costs

Costs that are incurred specifically for producing a product or rendering service, such as the cost of raw materials.

Functional analysis

An analysis of the functions performed (taking into account assets used and risks assumed) by associated enterprises in controlled transactions and by independent enterprises in comparable uncontrolled transactions.

Global formulary apportionment

An approach to allocate the global profits of an MNE group on a consolidated basis among the associated enterprises in different countries on the basis of a predetermined formula.

Gross profits

The gross profits from a business transaction are the amount computed by deducting from the gross receipts of the transaction the allocable purchases or production costs of sales, with due adjustment for increases or decreases in inventory or stock-in-trade, but without taking account of other expenses.

Independent enterprises

Two enterprises are independent enterprises with respect to each other if they are not associated enterprises with respect to each other.

Indirect-charge method

A method of charging for intra-group services based upon cost allocation and apportionment methods.

Indirect costs

Costs of producing a product or service which, although closely related to the production process, may be common to several products or services (for example, the costs of a repair department that services equipment used to produce different products).

Intra-group service

An activity (*e.g.* administrative, technical, financial, commercial, etc.) for which an independent enterprise would have been willing to pay or perform for itself.

Intentional set-off

A benefit provided by one associated enterprise to another associated enterprise within the group that is deliberately balanced to some degree by different benefits received from that enterprise in return.

Marketing intangible

An intangible that is concerned with marketing activities, which aids in the commercial exploitation of a product or service and/or has an important promotional value for the product concerned.

Multinational enterprise group (MNE group)

A group of associated companies with business establishments in two or more countries.

Multinational enterprise (MNE)

A company that is part of an MNE group.

Mutual agreement procedure

A means through which tax administrations consult to resolve disputes regarding the application of double tax conventions. This procedure, described and authorised by Article 25 of the OECD Model Tax Convention, can be used to eliminate double taxation that could arise from a transfer pricing adjustment.

Net profit indicator

The ratio of net profit to an appropriate base (*e.g.* costs, sales, assets). The transactional net margin method relies on a comparison of an appropriate net profit indicator for the controlled transaction with the same net profit indicator in comparable uncontrolled transactions.

"On call" services

Services provided by a parent company or a group service centre, which are available at any time for members of an MNE group.

Primary adjustment

An adjustment that a tax administration in a first jurisdiction makes to a company's taxable profits as a result of applying the arm's length principle to transactions involving an associated enterprise in a second tax jurisdiction.

Profit potential

The expected future profits. In some cases it may encompass losses. The notion of "profit potential" is often used for valuation purposes, in the determination of an arm's length compensation for a transfer of intangibles or of an ongoing concern, or in the determination of an arm's length indemnification for the termination or substantial renegotiation of existing arrangements, once it is found that such compensation or indemnification would have taken place between independent parties in comparable circumstances.

Profit split method

A transactional profit method that identifies the combined profit to be split for the associated enterprises from a controlled transaction (or controlled transactions that it is appropriate to aggregate under the principles of Chapter III) and then splits those profits between the associated enterprises based upon an economically valid basis that approximates the division of profits that would have been anticipated and reflected in an agreement made at arm's length.

Resale price margin

A margin representing the amount out of which a reseller would seek to cover its selling and other operating expenses and, in the light of the functions performed (taking into account assets used and risks assumed), make an appropriate profit.

Resale price method

A transfer pricing method based on the price at which a product that has been purchased from an associated enterprise is resold to an independent enterprise. The resale price is reduced by the resale price margin. What is left after subtracting the resale price margin can be regarded, after adjustment for other costs associated with the purchase of the product (*e.g.* custom duties), as an arm's length price of the original transfer of property between the associated enterprises.

Residual analysis

An analysis used in the profit split method which divides the combined profit from the controlled transactions under examination in two stages. In the first stage, each participant is allocated sufficient profit to provide it with a basic return appropriate for the type of transactions in which it is engaged. Ordinarily this basic return would be determined by reference to the market returns achieved for similar types of transactions by independent enterprises. Thus, the basic return would generally not account for the return that would be generated by any unique and valuable assets possessed by the participants. In the second stage, any residual profit (or loss) remaining after the first stage division would be allocated among the parties based on an analysis of the facts and circumstances that might indicate how this residual would have been divided between independent enterprises.

Secondary adjustment

An adjustment that arises from imposing tax on a secondary transaction.

Secondary transaction

A constructive transaction that some countries will assert under their domestic legislation after having proposed a primary adjustment in order to make the actual allocation of profits consistent with the primary adjustment. Secondary transactions may take the form of constructive dividends, constructive equity contributions, or constructive loans.

Shareholder activity

An activity which is performed by a member of an MNE group (usually the parent company or a regional holding company) solely because of its ownership interest in one or more other group members, *i.e.* in its capacity as shareholder.

Simultaneous tax examinations

A simultaneous tax examination, as defined in Part A of the OECD Model Agreement for the Undertaking of Simultaneous Tax Examinations, means an "arrangement between two or more parties to examine simultaneously and independently, each on its own territory, the tax affairs of (a) taxpayer(s) in which they have a common or related interest with a view to exchanging any relevant information which they so obtain".

Trade intangible

A commercial intangible other than a marketing intangible.

Traditional transaction methods

The comparable uncontrolled price method, the resale price method, and the cost plus method.

Transactional net margin method

A transactional profit method that examines the net profit margin relative to an appropriate base (*e.g.* costs, sales, assets) that a taxpayer realises from a controlled transaction (or transactions that it is appropriate to aggregate under the principles of Chapter III).

Transactional profit method

A transfer pricing method that examines the profits that arise from particular controlled transactions of one or more of the associated enterprises participating in those transactions.

Uncontrolled transactions

Transactions between enterprises that are independent enterprises with respect to each other.

Chapter I

The Arm's Length Principle

A. Introduction

1.1   This Chapter provides a background discussion of the arm's length principle, which is the international transfer pricing standard that OECD member countries have agreed should be used for tax purposes by MNE groups and tax administrations. The Chapter discusses the arm's length principle, reaffirms its status as the international standard, and sets forth guidelines for its application.

1.2   When independent enterprises transact with each other, the conditions of their commercial and financial relations (*e.g.* the price of goods transferred or services provided and the conditions of the transfer or provision) ordinarily are determined by market forces. When associated enterprises transact with each other, their commercial and financial relations may not be directly affected by external market forces in the same way, although associated enterprises often seek to replicate the dynamics of market forces in their transactions with each other, as discussed in paragraph 1.5 below. Tax administrations should not automatically assume that associated enterprises have sought to manipulate their profits. There may be a genuine difficulty in accurately determining a market price in the absence of market forces or when adopting a particular commercial strategy. It is important to bear in mind that the need to make adjustments to approximate arm's length transactions arises irrespective of any contractual obligation undertaken by the parties to pay a particular price or of any intention of the parties to minimize tax. Thus, a tax adjustment under the arm's length principle would not affect the underlying contractual obligations for non-tax purposes between the associated enterprises, and may be appropriate even where there is no intent to minimize or avoid tax. The consideration of transfer pricing should not be confused with the consideration of problems of tax fraud or tax avoidance, even though transfer pricing policies may be used for such purposes.

1.3   When transfer pricing does not reflect market forces and the arm's length principle, the tax liabilities of the associated enterprises and the tax revenues of the host countries could be distorted.   Therefore, OECD member countries have agreed that for tax purposes the profits of associated enterprises may be adjusted as necessary to correct any such distortions and thereby ensure that the arm's length principle is satisfied.   OECD member countries consider that an appropriate adjustment is achieved by establishing the conditions of the commercial and financial relations that they would expect to find between independent enterprises in comparable transactions under comparable circumstances.

1.4   Factors other than tax considerations may distort the conditions of commercial and financial relations established between associated enterprises. For example, such enterprises may be subject to conflicting governmental pressures (in the domestic as well as foreign country) relating to customs valuations, anti-dumping duties, and exchange or price controls. In addition, transfer price distortions may be caused by the cash flow requirements of enterprises within an MNE group. An MNE group that is publicly held may feel pressure from shareholders to show high profitability at the parent company level, particularly if shareholder reporting is not undertaken on a consolidated basis. All of these factors may affect transfer prices and the amount of profits accruing to associated enterprises within an MNE group.

1.5   It should not be assumed that the conditions established in the commercial and financial relations between associated enterprises will invariably deviate from what the open market would demand. Associated enterprises in MNEs sometimes have a considerable amount of autonomy and can often bargain with each other as though they were independent enterprises. Enterprises respond to economic situations arising from market conditions, in their relations with both third parties and associated enterprises. For example, local managers may be interested in establishing good profit records and therefore would not want to establish prices that would reduce the profits of their own companies. Tax administrations should keep these considerations in mind to facilitate efficient allocation of their resources in selecting and conducting transfer pricing examinations. Sometimes, it may occur that the relationship between the associated enterprises may influence the outcome of the bargaining. Therefore, evidence of hard bargaining alone is not sufficient to establish that the transactions are at arm's length.

B. Statement of the arm's length principle

B.1   Article 9 of the OECD Model Tax Convention

1.6   The authoritative statement of the arm's length principle is found in paragraph 1 of Article 9 of the OECD Model Tax Convention, which forms the basis of bilateral tax treaties involving OECD member countries and an increasing number of non-member countries. Article 9 provides:

> [Where] conditions are made or imposed between the two [associated] enterprises in their commercial or financial relations which differ from those which would be made between independent enterprises, then any profits which would, but for those conditions, have accrued to one of the enterprises, but, by reason of those conditions, have not so accrued, may be included in the profits of that enterprise and taxed accordingly.

By seeking to adjust profits by reference to the conditions which would have obtained between independent enterprises in comparable transactions and comparable circumstances (*i.e.* in "comparable uncontrolled transactions"), the arm's length principle follows the approach of treating the members of an MNE group as operating as separate entities rather than as inseparable parts of a single unified business. Because the separate entity approach treats the members of an MNE group as if they were independent entities, attention is focused on the nature of the transactions between those members and on whether the conditions thereof differ from the conditions that would be obtained in comparable uncontrolled transactions. Such an analysis of the controlled and uncontrolled transactions, which is referred to as a "comparability analysis", is at the heart of the application of the arm's length principle. Guidance on the comparability analysis is found in Section D below and in Chapter III.

1.7   It is important to put the issue of comparability into perspective in order to emphasise the need for an approach that is balanced in terms of, on the one hand, its reliability and, on the other, the burden it creates for taxpayers and tax administrations. Paragraph 1 of Article 9 of the OECD Model Tax Convention is the foundation for comparability analyses because it introduces the need for:

- A comparison between conditions (including prices, but not only prices) made or imposed between associated enterprises and those which would be made between independent enterprises, in order to determine whether a re-writing of the accounts for the purposes of calculating tax liabilities of associated enterprises is authorised under Article 9 of the OECD Model Tax Convention (see paragraph 2 of the Commentary on Article 9); and

- A determination of the profits which would have accrued at arm's length, in order to determine the quantum of any re-writing of accounts.

1.8   There are several reasons why OECD member countries and other countries have adopted the arm's length principle. A major reason is that the arm's length principle provides broad parity of tax treatment for members of MNE groups and independent enterprises.   Because the arm's length principle puts associated and independent enterprises on a more equal footing for tax purposes, it avoids the creation of tax advantages or disadvantages that would otherwise distort the relative competitive positions of either type of entity.   In so removing these tax considerations from economic decisions, the arm's length principle promotes the growth of international trade and investment.

1.9   The arm's length principle has also been found to work effectively in the vast majority of cases. For example, there are many cases involving the purchase and sale of commodities and the lending of money where an arm's length price may readily be found in a comparable transaction undertaken by comparable independent enterprises under comparable circumstances. There are also many cases where a relevant comparison of transactions can be made at the level of financial indicators such as mark-up on costs, gross margin, or net profit indicators. Nevertheless, there are some significant cases in which the arm's length principle is difficult and complicated to apply, for example, in MNE groups dealing in the integrated production of highly specialised goods, in unique intangibles, and/or in the provision of specialised services. Solutions exist to deal with such difficult cases, including the use of the transactional profit split method described in Chapter II, Part III of these Guidelines in those situations where it is the most appropriate method in the circumstances of the case.

1.10   The arm's length principle is viewed by some as inherently flawed because the separate entity approach may not always account for the economies of scale and interrelation of diverse activities created by integrated businesses. There are, however, no widely accepted objective criteria for allocating the economies of scale or benefits of integration between associated enterprises. The issue of possible alternatives to the arm's length principle is discussed in Section C below.

1.11   A practical difficulty in applying the arm's length principle is that associated enterprises may engage in transactions that independent enterprises would not undertake. Such transactions may not necessarily be motivated by tax avoidance but may occur because in transacting business with each other, members of an MNE group face different commercial circumstances than would independent enterprises. Where independent enterprises seldom undertake transactions of the type entered into by associated enterprises, the arm's length principle is difficult to apply because there is little or no direct evidence of what conditions would have been established by independent enterprises. The mere fact that a transaction may not be found between independent parties does not of itself mean that it is not arm's length.

1.12   In certain cases, the arm's length principle may result in an administrative burden for both the taxpayer and the tax administrations of evaluating significant numbers and types of cross-border transactions. Although associated enterprises normally establish the conditions for a transaction at the time it is undertaken, at some point the enterprises may be required to demonstrate that these are consistent with the arm's length principle. (See discussion of timing and compliance issues at Sections B and C of Chapter III and at Chapter V on Documentation). The tax administration may also have to engage in this verification process perhaps some years after the transactions have taken place. The tax administration would review any supporting documentation prepared by the taxpayer to show that its transactions are consistent with the arm's length principle, and may also need to gather information about comparable uncontrolled transactions, the market conditions at the time the transactions took place, etc., for numerous and varied transactions. Such an undertaking usually becomes more difficult with the passage of time.

1.13   Both tax administrations and taxpayers often have difficulty in obtaining adequate information to apply the arm's length principle. Because the arm's length principle usually requires taxpayers and tax administrations to evaluate uncontrolled transactions and the business activities of independent enterprises, and to compare these with the transactions and activities of associated enterprises, it can demand a substantial amount of data. The information that is accessible may be incomplete and difficult to interpret; other information, if it exists, may be difficult to obtain for reasons of its geographical location or that of the parties from whom it may have to be acquired. In addition, it may not be possible to obtain information from independent enterprises because of confidentiality concerns. In other cases information about an independent enterprise which could be relevant may simply not exist, or there may be no comparable independent enterprises, *e.g.* if that industry has reached a high level of vertical integration. It is important not to lose sight of the objective to find a reasonable estimate of an arm's length outcome based on reliable information. It should also be recalled at this point that transfer pricing is not an exact science but does require the exercise of judgment on the part of both the tax administration and taxpayer.

B.2 Maintaining the arm's length principle as the international consensus

1.14 While recognizing the foregoing considerations, the view of OECD member countries continues to be that the arm's length principle should govern the evaluation of transfer prices among associated enterprises. The arm's length principle is sound in theory since it provides the closest approximation of the workings of the open market in cases where property (such as goods, other types of tangible assets, or intangible assets) is transferred or services are rendered between associated enterprises. While it may not always be straightforward to apply in practice, it does generally produce appropriate levels of income between members of MNE groups, acceptable to tax administrations. This reflects the economic realities of the controlled taxpayer's particular facts and circumstances and adopts as a benchmark the normal operation of the market.

1.15 A move away from the arm's length principle would abandon the sound theoretical basis described above and threaten the international consensus, thereby substantially increasing the risk of double taxation. Experience under the arm's length principle has become sufficiently broad and sophisticated to establish a substantial body of common understanding among the business community and tax administrations. This shared understanding is of great practical value in achieving the objectives of securing the appropriate tax base in each jurisdiction and avoiding double taxation. This experience should be drawn on to elaborate the arm's length principle further, to refine its operation, and to improve its administration by providing clearer guidance to taxpayers and more timely examinations. In sum, OECD member countries continue to support strongly the arm's length principle. In fact, no legitimate or realistic alternative to the arm's length principle has emerged. Global formulary apportionment, sometimes mentioned as a possible alternative, would not be acceptable in theory, implementation, or practice. (See Section C, immediately below, for a discussion of global formulary apportionment).

C. A non-arm's-length approach: global formulary apportionment

C.1   Background and description of approach

1.16   Global formulary apportionment has sometimes been suggested as an alternative to the arm's length principle as a means of determining the proper level of profits across national taxing jurisdictions. The approach has not been applied as between countries although it has been attempted by some local taxing jurisdictions.

1.17   Global formulary apportionment would allocate the global profits of an MNE group on a consolidated basis among the associated enterprises in different countries on the basis of a predetermined and mechanistic formula. There would be three essential components to applying global formulary apportionment: determining the unit to be taxed, *i.e.* which of the subsidiaries and branches of an MNE group should comprise the global taxable entity; accurately determining the global profits; and establishing the formula to be used to allocate the global profits of the unit. The formula would most likely be based on some combination of costs, assets, payroll, and sales.

1.18   Global formulary apportionment should not be confused with the transactional profit methods discussed in Part III of Chapter II. Global formulary apportionment would use a formula that is predetermined for all taxpayers to allocate profits whereas transactional profit methods compare, on a case-by-case basis, the profits of one or more associated enterprises with the profit experience that comparable independent enterprises would have sought to achieve in comparable circumstances. Global formulary apportionment also should not be confused with the selected application of a formula developed by both tax administrations in cooperation with a specific taxpayer or MNE group after careful analysis of the particular facts and circumstances, such as might be used in a mutual agreement procedure, advance pricing agreement, or other bilateral or multilateral determination. Such a formula is derived from the particular facts and circumstances of the taxpayer and thus avoids the globally pre-determined and mechanistic nature of global formulary apportionment.

C.2   Comparison with the arm's length principle

1.19   Global formulary apportionment has been promoted as an alternative to the arm's length principle by advocates who claim that it would provide greater administrative convenience and certainty for taxpayers. These advocates also take the position that global formulary apportionment is more in keeping with economic reality. They argue that an MNE group must be considered on a group-wide or consolidated basis to reflect the business realities of the relationships among the associated enterprises in the group. They assert that the separate accounting method is inappropriate for highly integrated groups because it is difficult to determine what contribution each associated enterprise makes to the overall profit of the MNE group.

1.20   Apart from these arguments, advocates contend that global formulary apportionment reduces compliance costs for taxpayers since in principle only one set of accounts would be prepared for the group for domestic tax purposes.

1.21   OECD member countries do not accept these propositions and do not consider global formulary apportionment a realistic alternative to the arm's length principle, for the reasons discussed below.

1.22   The most significant concern with global formulary apportionment is the difficulty of implementing the system in a manner that both protects against double taxation and ensures single taxation. To achieve this would require substantial international coordination and consensus on the predetermined formulae to be used and on the composition of the group in question. For example, to avoid double taxation there would have to be common agreement to adopt the approach in the first instance, followed by agreement on the measurement of the global tax base of an MNE group, on the use of a common accounting system, on the factors that should be used to apportion the tax base among different jurisdictions (including non-member countries), and on how to measure and weight those factors. Reaching such agreement would be time-consuming and extremely difficult. It is far from clear that countries would be willing to agree to a universal formula.

1.23   Even if some countries were willing to accept global formulary apportionment, there would be disagreements because each country may want to emphasize or include different factors in the formula based on the activities or factors that predominate in its jurisdiction. Each country would have a strong incentive to devise formulae or formula weights that would maximise that country's own revenue. In addition, tax administrations would have to consider jointly how to address the potential for artificially shifting the production factors used in the formula (*e.g.* sales, capital) to low tax countries. There could be tax avoidance to the extent that the components of the relevant formula can be manipulated, *e.g.* by entering into unnecessary financial transactions, by the deliberate location of mobile assets, by requiring that particular companies within an MNE group maintain inventory levels in excess of what normally would be encountered in an uncontrolled company of that type, and so on.

1.24   The transition to a global formulary apportionment system therefore would present enormous political and administrative complexity and require a level of international cooperation that is unrealistic to expect in the field of international taxation. Such multilateral coordination would require the inclusion of all major countries where MNEs operate. If all the major countries failed to agree to move to global formulary apportionment, MNEs would be faced with the burden of complying with two totally different systems. In other words, for the same set of transactions they would be forced to calculate the profits accruing to their members under two completely different standards. Such a result would create the potential for double taxation (or under-taxation) in every case.

1.25   There are other significant concerns in addition to the double taxation issues discussed above. One such concern is that predetermined formulae are arbitrary and disregard market conditions, the particular circumstances of the individual enterprises, and management's own allocation of resources, thus producing an allocation of profits that may bear no sound relationship to the specific facts surrounding the transaction. More specifically, a formula based on a combination of cost, assets, payroll, and sales implicitly imputes a fixed rate of profit per currency unit (*e.g.* dollar, euro, yen) of each component to every member of the group and in every tax jurisdiction, regardless of differences in functions, assets, risks, and efficiencies and among members of the MNE group. Such an approach could potentially assign profits to an entity that would incur losses if it were an independent enterprise.

1.26   Another issue for global formulary apportionment is dealing with exchange rate movements. Although exchange rate movements can complicate application of the arm's length principle they do not have the same impact as for global formulary apportionment; the arm's length principle is better equipped to deal with the economic consequences of exchange rate movements because it requires the analysis of the specific facts and circumstances of the taxpayer. If the formula relies on costs, the result of applying a global formulary apportionment would be that as a particular currency strengthens in one country consistently against another currency in which an associated enterprise keeps its accounts, a greater share of the profit would be attributed to the enterprise in the first country to reflect the costs of its payroll nominally increased by the currency fluctuation. Thus, under a global formulary apportionment, the exchange rate movement in this example would lead to increasing the profits of the associated enterprise operating with the stronger currency whereas in the long run a strengthening currency makes exports less competitive and leads to a downward pressure on profits.

1.27   Contrary to the assertions of its advocates, global formulary apportionment may in fact present intolerable compliance costs and data requirements because information would have to be gathered about the entire MNE group and presented in each jurisdiction on the basis of the currency and the book and tax accounting rules of that particular jurisdiction. Thus, the documentation and compliance requirements for an application of global formulary apportionment would generally be more burdensome than under the separate entity approach of the arm's length principle. The costs of a global formulary apportionment would be further magnified if not all countries could agree on the components of the formula or on the way the components are measured.

1.28   Difficulties also would arise in determining the sales of each member and in the valuation of assets (*e.g.* historic cost versus market value), especially in the valuation of intangible property. These difficulties would be compounded by the existence across taxing jurisdictions of different accounting standards and of multiple currencies. Accounting standards among all countries would have to be conformed in order to arrive at a meaningful measure of profit for the entire MNE group. Of course, some of these difficulties, for example the valuation of assets and intangibles, also exist under the arm's length principle, although significant progress in respect of the latter has been made, whereas no credible solutions have been put forward under global formulary apportionment.

1.29   Global formulary apportionment would have the effect of taxing an MNE group on a consolidated basis and therefore abandons the separate entity approach. As a consequence, global formulary apportionment cannot, as a practical matter, recognize important geographical differences, separate company efficiencies, and other factors specific to one company or sub-grouping within the MNE group that may legitimately play a role in determining the division of profits between enterprises in different tax jurisdictions. The arm's length principle, in contrast, recognizes that an associated enterprise may be a separate profit or loss centre with individual characteristics and economically may be earning a profit even when the rest of the MNE group is incurring a loss. Global formulary apportionment does not have the flexibility to account properly for this possibility.

1.30   By disregarding intra-group transactions for the purpose of computing consolidated profits, global formulary apportionment would raise questions about the relevance of imposing withholding taxes on cross-border payments between group members and would involve a rejection of a number of rules incorporated in bilateral tax treaties.

1.31   Unless global formulary apportionment includes every member of an MNE group, it must retain a separate entity rule for the interface between that part of the group subject to global formulary apportionment and the rest of the MNE group. Global formulary apportionment could not be used to value the transactions between the global formulary apportionment group and the rest of the MNE group. Thus, a clear disadvantage with global formulary apportionment is that it does not provide a complete solution to the allocation of profits of an MNE group unless global formulary apportionment is applied on the basis of the whole MNE group. This exercise would be a serious undertaking for a single tax administration given the size and scale of operations of major MNE groups and the information that would be required. The MNE group would also be required, in any event, to maintain separate accounting for corporations that are not members of the MNE group for global formulary apportionment tax purposes but that are still associated enterprises of one or more members of the MNE group. In fact, many domestic commercial and accountancy rules would still require the use of arm's length prices (*e.g.* customs rules), so that irrespective of the tax provisions a taxpayer would have to book properly every transaction at arm's length prices.

C.3   *Rejection of non-arm's-length methods*

1.32   For the foregoing reasons, OECD member countries reiterate their support for the consensus on the use of the arm's length principle that has emerged over the years among member and non-member countries and agree that the theoretical alternative to the arm's length principle represented by global formulary apportionment should be rejected.

D. Guidance for applying the arm's length principle

D.1   *Comparability analysis*

D.1.1   *Significance of the comparability analysis and meaning of "comparable"*

1.33   Application of the arm's length principle is generally based on a comparison of the conditions in a controlled transaction with the conditions in transactions between independent enterprises.   In order for such comparisons to be useful, the economically relevant characteristics of the situations being compared must be sufficiently comparable. To be comparable means that none of the differences (if any) between the situations being compared could materially affect the condition being examined in the methodology (*e.g.* price or margin), or that reasonably accurate adjustments can be made to eliminate the effect of any such differences. In determining the degree of comparability, including what adjustments are necessary to establish it, an understanding of how independent enterprises evaluate potential transactions is required. Detailed guidance on performing a comparability analysis is set forth in Chapter III.

1.34   Independent enterprises, when evaluating the terms of a potential transaction, will compare the transaction to the other options realistically available to them, and they will only enter into the transaction if they see no alternative that is clearly more attractive. For example, one enterprise is unlikely to accept a price offered for its product by an independent enterprise if it knows that other potential customers are willing to pay more under similar conditions. This point is relevant to the question of comparability, since independent enterprises would generally take into account any economically relevant differences between the options realistically available to them (such as differences in the level of risk or other comparability factors discussed below) when valuing those options. Therefore, when making the comparisons entailed by application of the arm's length principle, tax administrations should also take these differences into account when establishing whether there is comparability between the situations being compared and what adjustments may be necessary to achieve comparability.

1.35   All methods that apply the arm's length principle can be tied to the concept that independent enterprises consider the options available to them and in comparing one option to another they consider any differences between the options that would significantly affect their value. For instance, before purchasing a product at a given price, independent enterprises normally would be expected to consider whether they could buy the same product on otherwise comparable terms and conditions but at a lower price from another party. Therefore, as discussed in Chapter II, Part II, the comparable uncontrolled price method compares a controlled transaction to similar uncontrolled transactions to provide a direct estimate of the price the parties would have agreed to had they resorted directly to a market alternative to the controlled transaction. However, the method becomes a less reliable substitute for arm's length transactions if not all the characteristics of these uncontrolled transactions that significantly affect the price charged between independent enterprises are comparable. Similarly, the resale price and cost plus methods compare the gross profit margin earned in the controlled transaction to gross profit margins earned in similar uncontrolled transactions. The comparison provides an estimate of the gross profit margin one of the parties could have earned had it performed the same functions for independent enterprises and therefore provides an estimate of the payment that party would have demanded, and the other party would have been willing to pay, at arm's length for performing those functions. Other methods, as discussed in Chapter II, Part III, are based on comparisons of net profit indicators (such as profit margins) between independent and associated enterprises as a means to estimate the profits that one or each of the associated enterprises could have earned had they dealt solely with independent enterprises, and therefore the payment those enterprises would have demanded at arm's length to compensate them for using their resources in the controlled transaction. Where there are differences between the situations being compared that could materially affect the comparison, comparability adjustments must be made, where possible, to improve the reliability of the comparison. Therefore, in no event can unadjusted industry average returns themselves establish arm's length conditions.

1.36   As noted above, in making these comparisons, material differences between the compared transactions or enterprises should be taken into account. In order to establish the degree of actual comparability and then to make appropriate adjustments to establish arm's length conditions (or a range thereof), it is necessary to compare attributes of the transactions or enterprises that would affect conditions in arm's length transactions. Attributes or "comparability factors" that may be important when determining comparability include the characteristics of the property or services transferred, the functions performed by the parties (taking into account assets used and risks assumed), the contractual terms, the economic circumstances of the parties, and the business strategies pursued by the parties. These comparability factors are discussed in more detail at Section D.1.2 below.

1.37   The extent to which each of these factors matters in establishing comparability will depend upon the nature of the controlled transaction and the pricing method adopted. For a discussion of the relevance of these factors for the application of particular pricing methods, see the consideration of those methods in Chapter II.

D.1.2   Factors determining comparability

1.38   Paragraph 1.36 refers to five factors that may be important when determining comparability. As part of a comparison exercise, the examination of the five comparability factors is by nature two-fold, *i.e.* it includes an examination of the factors affecting the taxpayer's controlled transactions and an examination of the factors affecting uncontrolled transactions. Both the nature of the controlled transaction and the transfer pricing method adopted (see Chapter II for a discussion of transfer pricing methods) should be taken into account when evaluating the relative importance of any missing piece of information on possible comparables, which can vary on a case-by-case basis. Information on product characteristics might be more important if the method applied is a comparable uncontrolled price method than if it is a transactional net margin method. If it can be reasonably assumed that the unadjusted difference is not likely to have a material effect on the comparability, the uncontrolled transaction at issue should not be rejected as potentially comparable, despite some pieces of information being missing.

D.1.2.1 Characteristics of property or services

1.39   Differences in the specific characteristics of property or services often account, at least in part, for differences in their value in the open market.   Therefore, comparisons of these features may be useful in determining the comparability of controlled and uncontrolled transactions. Characteristics that may be important to consider include the following: in the case of transfers of tangible property, the physical features of the property, its quality and reliability, and the availability and volume of supply; in the case of the provision of services, the nature and extent of the services; and in the case of intangible property, the form of transaction (*e.g.* licensing or sale), the type of property (*e.g.* patent, trademark, or know-how), the duration and degree of protection, and the anticipated benefits from the use of the property.

1.40   Depending on the transfer pricing method, this factor must be given more or less weight. Among the methods described at Chapter II of these Guidelines, the requirement for comparability of property or services is the strictest for the comparable uncontrolled price method. Under the comparable uncontrolled price method, any material difference in the characteristics of property or services can have an effect on the price and would require an appropriate adjustment to be considered (see in particular paragraph 2.15). Under the resale price method and cost plus method, some differences in the characteristics of property or services are less likely to have a material effect on the gross profit margin or mark-up on costs (see in particular paragraphs 2.23 and 2.41). Differences in the characteristics of property or services are also less sensitive in the case of the transactional profit methods than in the case of traditional transaction methods (see in particular paragraph 2.69). This however does not mean that the question of comparability in characteristics of property or services can be ignored when applying these methods, because it may be that product differences entail or reflect different functions performed, assets used and/or risks assumed by the tested party. See paragraphs 3.18-3.19 for a discussion of the notion of tested party.

1.41   In practice, it has been observed that comparability analyses for methods based on gross or net profit indicators often put more emphasis on functional similarities than on product similarities. Depending on the facts and circumstances of the case, it may be acceptable to broaden the scope of the comparability analysis to include uncontrolled transactions involving products that are different, but where similar functions are undertaken. However, the acceptance of such an approach depends on the effects that the product differences have on the reliability of the comparison and on whether or not more reliable data are available. Before broadening the search to include a larger number of potentially comparable uncontrolled transactions based on similar functions being undertaken, thought should be given to whether such transactions are likely to offer reliable comparables for the controlled transaction.

D.1.2.2   Functional analysis

1.42   In   transactions   between   two   independent   enterprises, compensation usually will reflect the functions that each enterprise performs (taking into account assets used and risks assumed). Therefore, in determining whether controlled and uncontrolled transactions or entities are comparable, a functional analysis is necessary. This functional analysis seeks to identify and compare the economically significant activities and responsibilities undertaken, assets used and risks assumed by the parties to the transactions. For this purpose, it may be helpful to understand the structure and organisation of the group and how they influence the context in which the taxpayer operates. It will also be relevant to determine the legal rights and obligations of the taxpayer in performing its functions.

1.43   The functions that taxpayers and tax administrations might need to identify and compare include, *e.g.* design, manufacturing, assembling, research and development, servicing, purchasing, distribution, marketing, advertising, transportation, financing and management. The principal functions performed by the party under examination should be identified. Adjustments should be made for any material differences from the functions undertaken by any independent enterprises with which that party is being compared. While one party may provide a large number of functions relative to that of the other party to the transaction, it is the economic significance of those functions in terms of their frequency, nature, and value to the respective parties to the transactions that is important.

1.44   The functional analysis should consider the type of assets used, such as plant and equipment, the use of valuable intangibles, financial assets, etc., and the nature of the assets used, such as the age, market value, location, property right protections available, etc.

1.45 Controlled and uncontrolled transactions and entities are not comparable if there are significant differences in the risks assumed for which appropriate adjustments cannot be made. Functional analysis is incomplete unless the material risks assumed by each party have been considered since the assumption or allocation of risks would influence the conditions of transactions between the associated enterprises. Usually, in the open market, the assumption of increased risk would also be compensated by an increase in the expected return, although the actual return may or may not increase depending on the degree to which the risks are actually realised.

1.46 The types of risks to consider include market risks, such as input cost and output price fluctuations; risks of loss associated with the investment in and use of property, plant, and equipment; risks of the success or failure of investment in research and development; financial risks such as those caused by currency exchange rate and interest rate variability; credit risks; and so forth.

1.47 The functions carried out (taking into account the assets used and the risks assumed) will determine to some extent the allocation of risks between the parties, and therefore the conditions each party would expect in arm's length transactions. For example, when a distributor takes on responsibility for marketing and advertising by risking its own resources in these activities, its expected return from the activity would usually be commensurately higher and the conditions of the transaction would be different from when the distributor acts merely as an agent, being reimbursed for its costs and receiving the income appropriate to that activity. Similarly, a contract manufacturer or a contract research provider that takes on no meaningful risk would usually expect only a limited return.

1.48 In line with the discussion below in relation to contractual terms, it may be considered whether a purported allocation of risk is consistent with the economic substance of the transaction. In this regard, the parties' conduct should generally be taken as the best evidence concerning the true allocation of risk. If, for example, a manufacturer sells property to an associated distributor in another country and the taxpayer's contract indicates that the distributor assumes all exchange rate risks in relation to this controlled transaction, but the transfer price appears in fact to be adjusted so as to insulate the distributor from the effects of exchange rate movements, then the tax administrations may wish to challenge the purported allocation of exchange rate risk for this particular controlled transaction.

1.49   An additional factor to consider in examining the economic substance of a purported risk allocation is the consequence of such an allocation in arm's length transactions. In arm's length transactions it generally makes sense for parties to be allocated a greater share of those risks over which they have relatively more control. For example, suppose that Company A contracts to produce and ship goods to Company B, and the level of production and shipment of goods are to be at the discretion of Company B. In such a case, Company A would be unlikely to agree to take on substantial inventory risk, since it exercises no control over the inventory level while Company B does. Of course, there are many risks, such as general business cycle risks, over which typically neither party has significant control and which at arm's length could therefore be allocated to one or the other party to a transaction. Analysis is required to determine to what extent each party bears such risks in practice.

1.50   When evaluating the extent to which a party to a transaction bears currency exchange and/or interest rate risk, it will ordinarily be necessary to determine whether the taxpayer and/or the MNE group have in place a business strategy which deals with the minimisation or management of such risks. Hedging arrangements, forward contracts, put and call options, swaps, etc., both over-the-counter and special purpose, are common. Members of an MNE may also make use of hedges with other associated enterprises, particularly in the financial sector. If a party that bears a significant market risk declines to hedge its exposure, this may reflect a decision that it will assume the risk, or it may reflect a decision to have the risk hedged by another enterprise within the MNE group. These or other strategies with regard to the hedging or non-hedging of risks, if not accounted for in the transfer pricing analysis, could lead to an inaccurate determination of the profits in a particular jurisdiction.

1.51   In some cases, it has been argued that the relative lack of accuracy of the functional analysis of possible external comparables (as defined in paragraph 3.24) might be counterbalanced by the size of the sample of third party data; however quantity does not make up for poor quality of data in producing a sufficiently reliable analysis. See paragraphs 3.2, 3.38 and 3.46.

D.1.2.3   Contractual terms

1.52   In arm's length transactions, the contractual terms of a transaction generally define explicitly or implicitly how the responsibilities, risks and benefits are to be divided between the parties. As such, an analysis of contractual terms should be a part of the functional analysis discussed above.   The   terms   of   a   transaction   may   also   be   found   in correspondence/communications between the parties other than a written contract. Where no written terms exist, the contractual relationships of the parties must be deduced from their conduct and the economic principles that generally govern relationships between independent enterprises.

1.53   In transactions between independent enterprises, the divergence of interests between the parties ensures that they will ordinarily seek to hold each other to the terms of the contract, and that contractual terms will be ignored or modified after the fact generally only if it is in the interests of both parties. The same divergence of interests may not exist in the case of associated enterprises, and it is therefore important to examine whether the conduct of the parties conforms to the terms of the contract or whether the parties' conduct indicates that the contractual terms have not been followed or are a sham. In such cases, further analysis is required to determine the true terms of the transaction.

1.54   In practice, information concerning the contractual terms of potentially comparable uncontrolled transactions may be either limited or unavailable, particularly where external comparables provide the basis for the analysis. The effect of deficiencies in information in establishing comparability will differ depending on the type of transaction being examined and the transfer pricing method applied, see paragraph 1.38. For instance, if the controlled transaction is a licence agreement for the exploitation of intellectual property rights and the transfer pricing method is the comparable uncontrolled price method, information on the key contractual terms of uncontrolled licences, such as the licence's duration, geographic area, exclusivity, etc., can be assumed to be critical to assessing whether such uncontrolled licences provide reliable comparables for the controlled transaction.

D.1.2.4   Economic circumstances

1.55   Arm's length prices may vary across different markets even for transactions involving the same property or services; therefore, to achieve comparability requires that the markets in which the independent and associated enterprises operate do not have differences that have a material effect on price or that appropriate adjustments can be made. As a first step, it is essential to identify the relevant market or markets taking account of available substitute goods or services. Economic circumstances that may be relevant to determining market comparability include the geographic location; the size of the markets; the extent of competition in the markets and the relative competitive positions of the buyers and sellers; the availability (risk thereof) of substitute goods and services; the levels of supply and demand in the market as a whole and in particular regions, if relevant; consumer purchasing power; the nature and extent of government regulation of the market; costs of production, including the costs of land, labour, and capital; transport costs; the level of the market (*e.g.* retail or wholesale); the date and time of transactions; and so forth. The facts and circumstances of the particular case will determine whether differences in economic circumstances have a material effect on price and whether reasonably accurate adjustments can be made to eliminate the effects of such differences, see paragraph 1.38.

1.56   The existence of a cycle (economic, business, or product cycle) is one of the economic circumstances that may affect comparability. See paragraph 3.77 in relation to the use of multiple year data where there are cycles.

1.57   The geographic market is another economic circumstance that can affect comparability. The identification of the relevant market is a factual question. For a number of industries, large regional markets encompassing more than one country may prove to be reasonably homogeneous, while for others, differences among domestic markets (or even within domestic markets) are very significant.

1.58   In cases where similar controlled transactions are carried out by an MNE group in several countries and where the economic circumstances in these countries are in effect reasonably homogeneous, it may be appropriate for this MNE group to rely on a multiple-country comparability analysis to support its transfer pricing policy towards this group of countries. But there are also numerous situations where an MNE group offers significantly different ranges of products or services in each country, and/or performs significantly different functions in each of these countries (using significantly different assets and assuming significantly different risks), and/or where its business strategies and/or economic circumstances are found to be significantly different. In these latter situations, the recourse to a multiple-country approach may reduce reliability.

D.1.2.5   Business strategies

1.59   Business strategies must also be examined in determining comparability for transfer pricing purposes. Business strategies would take into account many aspects of an enterprise, such as innovation and new product development, degree of diversification, risk aversion, assessment of political changes, input of existing and planned labour laws, duration of arrangements, and other factors bearing upon the daily conduct of business. Such business strategies may need to be taken into account when determining the comparability of controlled and uncontrolled transactions and enterprises.

1.60   Business strategies also could include market penetration schemes. A taxpayer seeking to penetrate a market or to increase its market share might temporarily charge a price for its product that is lower than the price charged for otherwise comparable products in the same market. Furthermore, a taxpayer seeking to enter a new market or expand (or defend) its market share might temporarily incur higher costs (*e.g.* due to start-up costs or increased marketing efforts) and hence achieve lower profit levels than other taxpayers operating in the same market.

1.61   Timing issues can pose particular problems for tax administrations when evaluating whether a taxpayer is following a business strategy that distinguishes it from potential comparables. Some business strategies, such as those involving market penetration or expansion of market share, involve reductions in the taxpayer's current profits in anticipation of increased future profits. If in the future those increased profits fail to materialize because the purported business strategy was not actually followed by the taxpayer, legal constraints may prevent re-examination of earlier tax years by the tax administrations. At least in part for this reason, tax administrations may wish to subject the issue of business strategies to particular scrutiny.

1.62   When evaluating whether a taxpayer was following a business strategy that temporarily decreased profits in return for higher long-run profits, several factors should be considered. Tax administrations should examine the conduct of the parties to determine if it is consistent with the purported business strategy. For example, if a manufacturer charges its associated distributor a below-market price as part of a market penetration strategy, the cost savings to the distributor may be reflected in the price charged to the distributor's customers or in greater market penetration expenses incurred by the distributor. A market penetration strategy of an MNE group could be put in place by the manufacturer or by the distributor acting separately from the manufacturer (and the resulting cost borne by either of them). Furthermore, unusually intensive marketing and advertising efforts would often accompany a market penetration or market share expansion strategy. Another factor to consider is whether the nature of the relationship between the parties to the controlled transaction would be consistent with the taxpayer bearing the costs of the business strategy. For example, in arm's length transactions a company acting solely as a sales agent with little or no responsibility for long-term market development would generally not bear the costs of a market penetration strategy. Where a company has undertaken market development activities at its own risk and enhances the value of a product through a trademark or trade name or increases goodwill associated with the product, this situation should be reflected in the analysis of functions for the purposes of establishing comparability.

1.63   An additional consideration is whether there is a plausible expectation that following the business strategy will produce a return sufficient to justify its costs within a period of time that would be acceptable in an arm's length arrangement. It is recognised that a business strategy such as market penetration may fail, and the failure does not of itself allow the strategy to be ignored for transfer pricing purposes. However, if such an expected outcome was implausible at the time of the transaction, or if the business strategy is unsuccessful but nonetheless is continued beyond what an independent enterprise would accept, the arm's length nature of the business strategy may be doubtful. In determining what period of time an independent enterprise would accept, tax administrations may wish to consider evidence of the commercial strategies evident in the country in which the business strategy is being pursued. In the end, however, the most important consideration is whether the strategy in question could plausibly be expected to prove profitable within the foreseeable future (while recognising that the strategy might fail), and that a party operating at arm's length would have been prepared to sacrifice profitability for a similar period under such economic circumstances and competitive conditions.

D.2   *Recognition of the actual transactions undertaken*

1.64   A tax administration's examination of a controlled transaction ordinarily should be based on the transaction actually undertaken by the associated enterprises as it has been structured by them, using the methods applied by the taxpayer insofar as these are consistent with the methods described in Chapter II.   In other than exceptional cases, the tax administration should not disregard the actual transactions or substitute other transactions for them.   Restructuring of legitimate business transactions would be a wholly arbitrary exercise the inequity of which could be compounded by double taxation created where the other tax administration does not share the same views as to how the transaction should be structured.

1.65   However, there are two particular circumstances in which it may, exceptionally, be both appropriate and legitimate for a tax administration to consider disregarding the structure adopted by a taxpayer in entering into a controlled transaction. The first circumstance arises where the economic substance of a transaction differs from its form.   In such a case the tax administration may disregard the parties' characterisation of the transaction and re-characterise it in accordance with its substance.   An example of this circumstance would be an investment in an associated enterprise in the form of interest-bearing debt when, at arm's length, having regard to the economic circumstances of the borrowing company, the investment would not be expected to be structured in this way.   In this case it might be appropriate for a tax administration to characterise the investment in accordance with its economic substance with the result that the loan may be treated as a subscription of capital. The second circumstance arises where, while the form and substance of the transaction are the same, the arrangements made in relation to the transaction, viewed in their totality, differ from those which would have been adopted by independent enterprises behaving in a commercially rational manner and the actual structure practically impedes the tax administration from determining an appropriate transfer price. An example of this circumstance would be a sale under a long-term contract, for a lump sum payment, of unlimited entitlement to the intellectual property rights arising as a result of future research for the term of the contract (as indicated in paragraph 1.11). While in this case it may be proper to respect the transaction as a transfer of commercial property, it would nevertheless be appropriate for a tax administration to conform the terms of that transfer in their entirety (and not simply by reference to pricing) to those that might reasonably have been expected had the transfer of property been the subject of a transaction involving independent enterprises. Thus, in the case described above it might be appropriate for the tax administration, for example, to adjust the conditions of the agreement in a commercially rational manner as a continuing research agreement.

1.66   In both sets of circumstances described above, the character of the transaction may derive from the relationship between the parties rather than be determined by normal commercial conditions and may have been structured by the taxpayer to avoid or minimise tax. In such cases, the totality of its terms would be the result of a condition that would not have been made if the parties had been engaged in arm's length transactions. Article 9 would thus allow an adjustment of conditions to reflect those which the parties would have attained had the transaction been structured in accordance with the economic and commercial reality of parties transacting at arm's length.

1.67   Associated enterprises are able to make a much greater variety of contracts and arrangements than can independent enterprises because the normal conflict of interest which would exist between independent parties is often absent. Associated enterprises may and frequently do conclude arrangements of a specific nature that are not or are very rarely encountered between independent parties. This may be done for various economic, legal, or fiscal reasons dependent on the circumstances in a particular case. Moreover, contracts within an MNE could be quite easily altered, suspended, extended, or terminated according to the overall strategies of the MNE as a whole, and such alterations may even be made retroactively. In such instances tax administrations would have to determine what the underlying reality is behind a contractual arrangement in applying the arm's length principle.

1.68   In addition, tax administrations may find it useful to refer to alternatively structured transactions between independent enterprises to determine whether the controlled transaction as structured satisfies the arm's length principle. Whether evidence from a particular alternative can be considered will depend on the facts and circumstances of the particular case, including the number and accuracy of the adjustments necessary to account for differences between the controlled transaction and the alternative and the quality of any other evidence that may be available.

1.69   The difference between restructuring the controlled transaction under review which, as stated above, generally is inappropriate, and using alternatively structured transactions as comparable uncontrolled transactions is demonstrated in the following example. Suppose a manufacturer sells goods to a controlled distributor located in another country and the distributor accepts all currency risk associated with these transactions. Suppose further that similar transactions between independent manufacturers and distributors are structured differently in that the manufacturer, and not the distributor, bears all currency risk. In such a case, the tax administration should not disregard the controlled taxpayer's purported assignment of risk unless there is good reason to doubt the economic substance of the controlled distributor's assumption of currency risk. The fact that independent enterprises do not structure their transactions in a particular fashion might be a reason to examine the economic logic of the structure more closely, but it would not be determinative. However, the uncontrolled transactions involving a differently structured allocation of currency risk could be useful in pricing the controlled transaction, perhaps employing the comparable uncontrolled price method if sufficiently accurate adjustments to their prices could be made to reflect the difference in the structure of the transactions.

D.3   Losses

1.70   When an associated enterprise consistently realizes losses while the MNE group as a whole is profitable, the facts could trigger some special scrutiny of transfer pricing issues. Of course, associated enterprises, like independent enterprises, can sustain genuine losses, whether due to heavy start-up costs, unfavourable economic conditions, inefficiencies, or other legitimate business reasons. However, an independent enterprise would not be prepared to tolerate losses that continue indefinitely. An independent enterprise that experiences recurring losses will eventually cease to undertake business on such terms. In contrast, an associated enterprise that realizes losses may remain in business if the business is beneficial to the MNE group as a whole.

1.71   The fact that there is an enterprise making losses that is doing business with profitable members of its MNE group may suggest to the taxpayers or tax administrations that the transfer pricing should be examined. The loss enterprise may not be receiving adequate compensation from the MNE group of which it is a part in relation to the benefits derived from its activities. For example, an MNE group may need to produce a full range of products and/or services in order to remain competitive and realize an overall profit, but some of the individual product lines may regularly lose revenue. One member of the MNE group might realize consistent losses because it produces all the loss-making products while other members produce the profit-making products. An independent enterprise would perform such a service only if it were compensated by an adequate service charge. Therefore, one way to approach this type of transfer pricing problem would be to deem the loss enterprise to receive the same type of service charge that an independent enterprise would receive under the arm's length principle.

1.72   A factor to consider in analysing losses is that business strategies may differ from MNE group to MNE group due to a variety of historic, economic, and cultural reasons. Recurring losses for a reasonable period may be justified in some cases by a business strategy to set especially low prices to achieve market penetration. For example, a producer may lower the prices of its goods, even to the extent of temporarily incurring losses, in order to enter new markets, to increase its share of an existing market, to introduce new products or services, or to discourage potential competitors. However, especially low prices should be expected for a limited period only, with the specific object of improving profits in the longer term. If the pricing strategy continues beyond a reasonable period, a transfer pricing adjustment may be appropriate, particularly where comparable data over several years show that the losses have been incurred for a period longer than that affecting comparable independent enterprises. Further, tax administrations should not accept especially low prices (*e.g.* pricing at marginal cost in a situation of underemployed production capacities) as arm's length prices unless independent enterprises could be expected to have determined prices in a comparable manner.

D.4   The effect of government policies

1.73   There are some circumstances in which a taxpayer will consider that an arm's length price must be adjusted to account for government interventions such as price controls (even price cuts), interest rate controls,

controls over payments for services or management fees, controls over the payment of royalties, subsidies to particular sectors, exchange control, anti-dumping duties, or exchange rate policy. As a general rule, these government interventions should be treated as conditions of the market in the particular country, and in the ordinary course they should be taken into account in evaluating the taxpayer's transfer price in that market. The question then presented is whether in light of these conditions the transactions undertaken by the controlled parties are consistent with transactions between independent enterprises.

1.74   One issue that arises is determining the stage at which a price control affects the price of a product or service. Often the direct impact will be on the final price to the consumer, but there may nonetheless be an impact on prices paid at prior stages in the supply of goods to the market. MNEs in practice may make no adjustment in their transfer prices to take account of such controls, leaving the final seller to suffer any limitation on profit that may occur, or they may charge prices that share the burden in some way between the final seller and the intermediate supplier. It should be considered whether or not an independent supplier would share in the costs of the price controls and whether an independent enterprise would seek alternative product lines and business opportunities. In this regard, it is unlikely that an independent enterprise would be prepared to produce, distribute, or otherwise provide products or services on terms that allowed it no profit. Nevertheless, it is quite obvious that a country with price controls must take into account that those price controls will affect the profits that can be realised by enterprises selling goods subject to those controls.

1.75   A special problem arises when a country prevents or "blocks" the payment of an amount which is owed by one associated enterprise to another or which in an arm's length arrangement would be charged by one associated enterprise to another. For example, exchange controls may effectively prevent an associated enterprise from transferring interest payments abroad on a loan made by another associated enterprise located in a different country. This circumstance may be treated differently by the two countries involved: the country of the borrower may or may not regard the untransferred interest as having been paid, and the country of the lender may or may not treat the lender as having received the interest. As a general rule, where the government intervention applies equally to transactions between associated enterprises and transactions between independent enterprises (both in law and in fact), the approach to this problem where it occurs between associated enterprises should be the same for tax purposes as that adopted for transactions between independent enterprises. Where the government intervention applies only to transactions between associated enterprises, there is no simple solution to the problem. Perhaps one way to deal with the issue is to apply the arm's length principle viewing the intervention as a condition affecting the terms of the transaction. Treaties may specifically address the approaches available to the treaty partners where such circumstances exist.

1.76   A difficulty with this analysis is that often independent enterprises simply would not enter into a transaction in which payments were blocked. An independent enterprise might find itself in such an arrangement from time to time, most likely because the government interventions were imposed subsequent to the time that the arrangement began. But it seems unlikely that an independent enterprise would willingly subject itself to a substantial risk of non-payment for products or services rendered by entering into an arrangement when severe government interventions already existed unless the profit projections or anticipated return from the independent enterprise's proposed business strategy are sufficient to yield it an acceptable rate of return notwithstanding the existence of the government intervention that may affect payment.

1.77   Because independent enterprises might not engage in a transaction subject to government interventions, it is unclear how the arm's length principle should apply. One possibility is to treat the payment as having been made between the associated enterprises, on the assumption that an independent enterprise in a similar circumstance would have insisted on payment by some other means. This approach would treat the party to whom the blocked payment is owed as performing a service for the MNE group. An alternative approach that may be available in some countries would be to defer both the income and the relevant expenses of the taxpayer. In other words, the party to whom this blocked payment was due would not be allowed to deduct expenses, such as additional financing costs, until the blocked payment was made. The concern of tax administrations in these situations is mainly their respective tax bases. If an associated enterprise claims a deduction in its tax computations for a blocked payment, then there should be corresponding income to the other party. In any case, a taxpayer should not be permitted to treat blocked payments due from an associated enterprise differently from blocked payments due from an independent enterprise.

D.5   Use of customs valuations

1.78   The arm's length principle is applied, broadly speaking, by many customs administrations as a principle of comparison between the value attributable to goods imported by associated enterprises, which may be affected by the special relationship between them, and the value for similar goods imported by independent enterprises. Valuation methods for customs purposes however may not be aligned with the OECD's recognised transfer pricing methods. That being said, customs valuations may be useful to tax administrations in evaluating the arm's length character of a controlled transaction transfer price and vice versa. In particular, customs officials may have contemporaneous information regarding the transaction that could be relevant for transfer pricing purposes, especially if prepared by the taxpayer, while tax authorities may have transfer pricing documentation which provides detailed information on the circumstances of the transaction.

1.79   Taxpayers may have competing incentives in setting values for customs and tax purposes. In general, a taxpayer importing goods may be interested in setting a low price for the transaction for customs purposes so that the customs duty imposed will be low. (There could be similar considerations arising with respect to value added taxes, sales taxes, and excise taxes.) For tax purposes, however, a higher price paid for those same goods would increase the deductible costs in the importing country (although this would also increase the sales revenue of the seller in the country of export). Cooperation between income tax and customs administrations within a country in evaluating transfer prices is becoming more common and this should help to reduce the number of cases where customs valuations are found unacceptable for tax purposes or vice versa. Greater cooperation in the area of exchange of information would be particularly useful, and should not be difficult to achieve in countries that already have integrated administrations for income taxes and customs duties. Countries that have separate administrations may wish to consider modifying the exchange of information rules so that the information can flow more easily between the different administrations.

Chapter II

Transfer Pricing Methods

Part I: Selection of the transfer pricing method

A. Selection of the most appropriate transfer pricing method to the circumstances of the case

2.1   Parts II and III of this chapter respectively describe "traditional transaction methods" and "transactional profit methods" that can be used to establish whether the conditions imposed in the commercial or financial relations between associated enterprises are consistent with the arm's length principle. Traditional transaction methods are the comparable uncontrolled price method or CUP method, the resale price method, and the cost plus method. Transactional profit methods are the transactional net margin method and the transactional profit split method.

2.2   The selection of a transfer pricing method always aims at finding the most appropriate method for a particular case. For this purpose, the selection process should take account of the respective strengths and weaknesses of the OECD recognised methods; the appropriateness of the method considered in view of the nature of the controlled transaction, determined in particular through a functional analysis; the availability of reliable information (in particular on uncontrolled comparables) needed to apply the selected method and/or other methods; and the degree of comparability between controlled and uncontrolled transactions, including the reliability of comparability adjustments that may be needed to eliminate material differences between them. No one method is suitable in every possible situation, nor is it necessary to prove that a particular method is not suitable under the circumstances.

2.3   Traditional transaction methods are regarded as the most direct means of establishing whether conditions in the commercial and financial relations between associated enterprises are arm's length. This is because any difference in the price of a controlled transaction from the price in a comparable uncontrolled transaction can normally be traced directly to the commercial and financial relations made or imposed between the enterprises, and the arm's length conditions can be established by directly substituting the price in the comparable uncontrolled transaction for the price of the controlled transaction. As a result, where, taking account of the criteria described at paragraph 2.2, a traditional transaction method and a transactional profit method can be applied in an equally reliable manner, the traditional transaction method is preferable to the transactional profit method. Moreover, where, taking account of the criteria described at paragraph 2.2, the comparable uncontrolled price method (CUP) and another transfer pricing method can be applied in an equally reliable manner, the CUP method is to be preferred. See paragraphs 2.13-2.20 for a discussion of the CUP method.

2.4   There are situations where transactional profit methods are found to be more appropriate than traditional transaction methods. For example, cases where each of the parties makes valuable and unique contributions in relation to the controlled transaction, or where the parties engage in highly integrated activities, may make a transactional profit split more appropriate than a one-sided method. As another example, where there is no or limited publicly available reliable gross margin information on third parties, traditional transaction methods might be difficult to apply in cases other than those where there are internal comparables, and a transactional profit method might be the most appropriate method in view of the availability of information.

2.5   However, it is not appropriate to apply a transactional profit method merely because data concerning uncontrolled transactions are difficult to obtain or incomplete in one or more respects. The same criteria listed in paragraph 2.2 that were used to reach the initial conclusion that none of the traditional transactional methods could be reliably applied under the circumstances must be considered again in evaluating the reliability of the transactional profit method.

2.6   Methods that are based on profits can be accepted only insofar as they are compatible with Article 9 of the OECD Model Tax Convention, especially with regard to comparability. This is achieved by applying the methods in a manner that approximates arm's length pricing. The application of the arm's length principle is generally based on a comparison of the price, margin or profits from particular controlled transactions with the price, margin or profits from comparable transactions between independent enterprises. In the case of a transactional profit split method, it is based on an approximation of the division of profits that independent enterprises would have expected to realise from engaging in the transaction(s) (see paragraph 2.108).

2.7   In no case should transactional profit methods be used so as to result in over-taxing enterprises mainly because they make profits lower than the average, or in under-taxing enterprises that make higher than average profits. There is no justification under the arm's length principle for imposing additional tax on enterprises that are less successful than average or, conversely, for under-taxing enterprises that are more successful than average, when the reason for their success or lack thereof is attributable to commercial factors.

2.8   The guidance at paragraph 2.2 that the selection of a transfer pricing method always aims at finding the most appropriate method for each particular case does not mean that all the transfer pricing methods should be analysed in depth or tested in each case in arriving at the selection of the most appropriate method. As a matter of good practice, the selection of the most appropriate method and comparables should be evidenced and can be part of a typical search process as proposed at paragraph 3.4.

2.9   Moreover, MNE groups retain the freedom to apply methods not described in these Guidelines (hereafter "other methods") to establish prices provided those prices satisfy the arm's length principle in accordance with these Guidelines. Such other methods should however not be used in substitution for OECD-recognised methods where the latter are more appropriate to the facts and circumstances of the case. In cases where other methods are used, their selection should be supported by an explanation of why OECD-recognised methods were regarded as less appropriate or non-workable in the circumstances of the case and of the reason why the selected other method was regarded as providing a better solution. A taxpayer should maintain and be prepared to provide documentation regarding how its transfer prices were established. For a discussion of documentation, see Chapter V.

2.10   It is not possible to provide specific rules that will cover every case. Tax administrators should hesitate from making minor or marginal adjustments. In general, the parties should attempt to reach a reasonable accommodation keeping in mind the imprecision of the various methods and the preference for higher degrees of comparability and a more direct and closer relationship to the transaction. It should not be the case that useful information, such as might be drawn from uncontrolled transactions that are not identical to the controlled transactions, should be dismissed simply because some rigid standard of comparability is not fully met. Similarly, evidence from enterprises engaged in controlled transactions with associated enterprises may be useful in understanding the transaction under review or as a pointer to further investigation. Further, any method should be permitted where its application is agreeable to the members of the MNE group involved with the transaction or transactions to which the methodology applies and also to the tax administrations in the jurisdictions of all those members.

B. Use of more than one method

2.11   The arm's length principle does not require the application of more than one method for a given transaction (or set of transactions that are appropriately aggregated following the standard described at paragraph 3.9), and in fact undue reliance on such an approach could create a significant burden for taxpayers. Thus, these Guidelines do not require either the tax examiner or taxpayer to perform analyses under more than one method. While in some cases the selection of a method may not be straightforward and more than one method may be initially considered, generally it will be possible to select one method that is apt to provide the best estimation of an arm's length price. However, for difficult cases, where no one approach is conclusive, a flexible approach would allow the evidence of various methods to be used in conjunction. In such cases, an attempt should be made to reach a conclusion consistent with the arm's length principle that is satisfactory from a practical viewpoint to all the parties involved, taking into account the facts and circumstances of the case, the mix of evidence available, and the relative reliability of the various methods under consideration. See paragraphs 3.58-3.59 for a discussion of cases where a range of figures results from the use of more than one method.

Part II: Traditional transaction methods

A. Introduction

2.12   This part provides a detailed description of traditional transaction methods that are used to apply the arm's length principle. These methods are the comparable uncontrolled price method or CUP method, the resale price method, and the cost plus method.

B. Comparable uncontrolled price method

B.1   In general

2.13   The CUP method compares the price charged for property or services transferred in a controlled transaction to the price charged for property or services transferred in a comparable uncontrolled transaction in comparable circumstances. If there is any difference between the two prices, this may indicate that the conditions of the commercial and financial relations of the associated enterprises are not arm's length, and that the price in the uncontrolled transaction may need to be substituted for the price in the controlled transaction.

2.14   Following the principles in Chapter I, an uncontrolled transaction is comparable to a controlled transaction (*i.e.* it is a comparable uncontrolled transaction) for purposes of the CUP method if one of two conditions is met: a) none of the differences (if any) between the transactions being compared or between the enterprises undertaking those transactions could materially affect the price in the open market; or, b) reasonably accurate adjustments can be made to eliminate the material effects of such differences. Where it is possible to locate comparable uncontrolled transactions, the CUP method is the most direct and reliable way to apply the arm's length principle. Consequently, in such cases the CUP method is preferable over all other methods.

2.15   It may be difficult to find a transaction between independent enterprises that is similar enough to a controlled transaction such that no differences have a material effect on price. For example, a minor difference in the property transferred in the controlled and uncontrolled transactions could materially affect the price even though the nature of the business activities undertaken may be sufficiently similar to generate the same overall profit margin. When this is the case, some adjustments will be appropriate. As discussed below in paragraph 2.16, the extent and reliability of such adjustments will affect the relative reliability of the analysis under the CUP method.

2.16   In considering whether controlled and uncontrolled transactions are comparable, regard should be had to the effect on price of broader business functions other than just product comparability (*i.e.* factors relevant to determining comparability under Chapter I). Where differences exist between the controlled and uncontrolled transactions or between the enterprises undertaking those transactions, it may be difficult to determine reasonably accurate adjustments to eliminate the effect on price. The difficulties that arise in attempting to make reasonably accurate adjustments should not routinely preclude the possible application of the CUP method. Practical considerations dictate a more flexible approach to enable the CUP method to be used and to be supplemented as necessary by other appropriate methods, all of which should be evaluated according to their relative accuracy. Every effort should be made to adjust the data so that it may be used appropriately in a CUP method. As for any method, the relative reliability of the CUP method is affected by the degree of accuracy with which adjustments can be made to achieve comparability.

B.2   Examples of the application of the CUP method

2.17   The following examples illustrate the application of the CUP method, including situations where adjustments may need to be made to uncontrolled transactions to make them comparable uncontrolled transactions.

2.18   The CUP method is a particularly reliable method where an independent enterprise sells the same product as is sold between two associated enterprises. For example, an independent enterprise sells unbranded Colombian coffee beans of a similar type, quality, and quantity as those sold between two associated enterprises, assuming that the controlled and uncontrolled transactions occur at about the same time, at the same stage in the production/distribution chain, and under similar conditions. If the only available uncontrolled transaction involved unbranded Brazilian coffee beans, it would be appropriate to inquire whether the difference in the coffee beans has a material effect on the price. For example, it could be asked whether the source of coffee beans commands a premium or requires a discount generally in the open market. Such information may be obtainable from commodity markets or may be deduced from dealer prices. If this difference does have a material effect on price, some adjustments would be appropriate. If a reasonably accurate adjustment cannot be made, the reliability of the CUP method would be reduced, and it might be necessary to select another less direct method instead.

2.19   One illustrative case where adjustments may be required is where the circumstances surrounding controlled and uncontrolled sales are identical, except for the fact that the controlled sales price is a delivered price and the uncontrolled sales are made f.o.b. factory. The differences in terms of transportation and insurance generally have a definite and reasonably ascertainable effect on price. Therefore, to determine the uncontrolled sales price, adjustment should be made to the price for the difference in delivery terms.

2.20   As another example, assume a taxpayer sells 1,000 tons of a product for $80 per ton to an associated enterprise in its MNE group, and at the same time sells 500 tons of the same product for $100 per ton to an independent enterprise. This case requires an evaluation of whether the different volumes should result in an adjustment of the transfer price. The relevant market should be researched by analysing transactions in similar products to determine typical volume discounts.

C. Resale price method

C.1   In general

2.21   The resale price method begins with the price at which a product that has been purchased from an associated enterprise is resold to an independent enterprise. This price (the resale price) is then reduced by an appropriate gross margin on this price (the "resale price margin") representing the amount out of which the reseller would seek to cover its selling and other operating expenses and, in the light of the functions performed (taking into account assets used and risks assumed), make an appropriate profit. What is left after subtracting the gross margin can be regarded, after adjustment for other costs associated with the purchase of the product (*e.g.* customs duties), as an arm's length price for the original transfer of property between the associated enterprises. This method is probably most useful where it is applied to marketing operations.

2.22   The resale price margin of the reseller in the controlled transaction may be determined by reference to the resale price margin that the same reseller earns on items purchased and sold in comparable uncontrolled transactions ("internal comparable"). Also, the resale price margin earned by an independent enterprise in comparable uncontrolled transactions may serve as a guide ("external comparable"). Where the reseller is carrying on a general brokerage business, the resale price margin may be related to a brokerage fee, which is usually calculated as a percentage of the sales price of the product sold. The determination of the resale price margin in such a case should take into account whether the broker is acting as an agent or a principal.

2.23   Following the principles in Chapter I, an uncontrolled transaction is comparable to a controlled transaction (*i.e.* it is a comparable uncontrolled transaction) for purposes of the resale price method if one of two conditions is met: a) none of the differences (if any) between the transactions being compared or between the enterprises undertaking those transactions could materially affect the resale price margin in the open market; or, b) reasonably accurate adjustments can be made to eliminate the material effects of such differences. In making comparisons for purposes of the resale price method, fewer adjustments are normally needed to account for product differences than under the CUP method, because minor product differences are less likely to have as material an effect on profit margins as they do on price.

2.24   In a market economy, the compensation for performing similar functions would tend to be equalized across different activities. In contrast, prices for different products would tend to equalize only to the extent that those products were substitutes for one another. Because gross profit margins represent gross compensation, after the cost of sales for specific functions performed (taking into account assets used and risks assumed), product differences are less significant. For example, the facts may indicate that a distribution company performs the same functions (taking into account assets used and risks assumed) selling toasters as it would selling blenders, and hence in a market economy there should be a similar level of compensation for the two activities. However, consumers would not consider toasters and blenders to be particularly close substitutes, and hence there would be no reason to expect their prices to be the same.

2.25   Although broader product differences can be allowed in the resale price method, the property transferred in the controlled transaction must still be compared to that being transferred in the uncontrolled transaction. Broader differences are more likely to be reflected in differences in functions performed between the parties to the controlled and uncontrolled transactions. While less product comparability may be required in using the resale price method, it remains the case that closer comparability of products will produce a better result. For example, where there is a valuable or unique intangible involved in the transaction, product similarity may assume greater importance and particular attention should be paid to it to ensure that the comparison is valid.

2.26   It may be appropriate to give more weight to other attributes of comparability discussed in Chapter I (*i.e.* functions performed, economic circumstances, etc.) when the profit margin relates primarily to those other attributes and only secondarily to the particular product being transferred. This circumstance will usually exist where the profit margin is determined for an associated enterprise that has not used unique assets (such as valuable, unique intangibles) to add significant value to the product being transferred. Thus, where uncontrolled and controlled transactions are comparable in all characteristics other than the product itself, the resale price method might produce a more reliable measure of arm's length conditions than the CUP method, unless reasonably accurate adjustments could be made to account for differences in the products transferred. The same point is true for the cost plus method, discussed below.

2.27   When the resale price margin used is that of an independent enterprise in a comparable transaction, the reliability of the resale price method may be affected if there are material differences in the ways the associated enterprises and independent enterprises carry out their businesses. Such differences could include those that affect the level of costs taken into account (*e.g.* the differences could include the effect of management efficiency on levels and ranges of inventory maintenance), which may well have an impact on the profitability of an enterprise but which may not necessarily affect the price at which it buys or sells its goods or services in the open market. These types of characteristics should be analyzed in determining whether an uncontrolled transaction is comparable for purposes of applying the resale price method.

2.28   The resale price method also depends on comparability of functions performed (taking into account assets used and risks assumed). It may become less reliable when there are differences between the controlled and uncontrolled transactions and the parties to the transactions, and those differences have a material effect on the attribute being used to measure arm's length conditions, in this case the resale price margin realised. Where there are material differences that affect the gross margins earned in the controlled and uncontrolled transactions (*e.g.* in the nature of the functions performed by the parties to the transactions), adjustments should be made to account for such differences. The extent and reliability of those adjustments will affect the relative reliability of the analysis under the resale price method in any particular case.

2.29   An appropriate resale price margin is easiest to determine where the reseller does not add substantially to the value of the product. In contrast, it may be more difficult to use the resale price method to arrive at an arm's length price where, before resale, the goods are further processed or incorporated into a more complicated product so that their identity is lost or transformed (*e.g.* where components are joined together in finished or semi-finished goods). Another example where the resale price margin requires particular care is where the reseller contributes substantially to the creation or maintenance of intangible property associated with the product (*e.g.* trademarks or trade names) which are owned by an associated enterprise. In such cases, the contribution of the goods originally transferred to the value of the final product cannot be easily evaluated.

2.30   A resale price margin is more accurate where it is realised within a short time of the reseller's purchase of the goods. The more time that elapses between the original purchase and resale the more likely it is that other factors – changes in the market, in rates of exchange, in costs, etc. – will need to be taken into account in any comparison.

2.31   It should be expected that the amount of the resale price margin will be influenced by the level of activities performed by the reseller. This level of activities can range widely from the case where the reseller performs only minimal services as a forwarding agent to the case where the reseller takes on the full risk of ownership together with the full responsibility for and the risks involved in advertising, marketing, distributing and guaranteeing the goods, financing stocks, and other connected services. If the reseller in the controlled transaction does not carry on a substantial commercial activity but only transfers the goods to a third party, the resale price margin could, in light of the functions performed, be a small one. The resale price margin could be higher where it can be demonstrated that the reseller has some special expertise in the marketing of such goods, in effect bears special risks, or contributes substantially to the creation or maintenance of intangible property associated with the product. However, the level of activity performed by the reseller, whether minimal or substantial, would need to be well supported by relevant evidence. This would include justification for marketing expenditures that might be considered unreasonably high; for example, when part or most of the promotional expenditure was clearly incurred as a service performed in favour of the legal owner of the trademark. In such a case the cost plus method may well supplement the resale price method.

2.32   Where the reseller is clearly carrying on a substantial commercial activity in addition to the resale activity itself, then a reasonably substantial resale price margin might be expected. If the reseller in its activities employs valuable and possibly unique assets (*e.g.* intangible property of the reseller, such as its marketing organisation), it may be inappropriate to evaluate the arm's length conditions in the controlled transaction using an unadjusted resale price margin derived from uncontrolled transactions in which the uncontrolled reseller does not employ similar assets. If the reseller possesses valuable marketing intangibles, the resale price margin in the uncontrolled transaction may underestimate the profit to which the reseller in the controlled transaction is entitled, unless the comparable uncontrolled transaction involves the same reseller or a reseller with similarly valuable marketing intangibles.

2.33   In a case where there is a chain of distribution of goods through an intermediate company, it may be relevant for tax administrations to look not only at the resale price of goods that have been purchased from the intermediate company but also at the price that such company pays to its own supplier and the functions that the intermediate company undertakes. There could well be practical difficulties in obtaining this information and the true function of the intermediate company may be difficult to determine. If it cannot be demonstrated that the intermediate company either bears a real risk or performs an economic function in the chain that has increased the value of the goods, then any element in the price that is claimed to be attributable to the activities of the intermediate company would reasonably be attributed elsewhere in the MNE group, because independent enterprises would not normally have allowed such a company to share in the profits of the transaction.

2.34   The resale price margin should also be expected to vary according to whether the reseller has the exclusive right to resell the goods. Arrangements of this kind are found in transactions between independent enterprises and may influence the margin. Thus, this type of exclusive right should be taken into account in any comparison. The value to be attributed to such an exclusive right will depend to some extent upon its geographical scope and the existence and relative competitiveness of possible substitute goods. The arrangement may be valuable to both the supplier and the reseller in an arm's length transaction. For instance, it may stimulate the reseller to greater efforts to sell the supplier's particular line of goods. On the other hand, such an arrangement may provide the reseller with a kind of monopoly with the result that the reseller possibly can realize a substantial turn over without great effort. Accordingly, the effect of this factor upon the appropriate resale price margin must be examined with care in each case.

2.35   Where the accounting practices differ from the controlled transaction to the uncontrolled transaction, appropriate adjustments should be made to the data used in calculating the resale price margin in order to ensure that the same types of costs are used in each case to arrive at the gross margin. For example, costs of R&D may be reflected in operating expenses or in costs of sales. The respective gross margins would not be comparable without appropriate adjustments.

C.2 Examples of the application of the resale price method

2.36 Assume that there are two distributors selling the same product in the same market under the same brand name. Distributor A offers a warranty; Distributor B offers none. Distributor A is not including the warranty as part of a pricing strategy and so sells its product at a higher price resulting in a higher gross profit margin (if the costs of servicing the warranty are not taken into account) than that of Distributor B, which sells at a lower price. The two margins are not comparable until a reasonably accurate adjustment is made to account for that difference.

2.37 Assume that a warranty is offered with respect to all products so that the downstream price is uniform. Distributor C performs the warranty function but is, in fact, compensated by the supplier through a lower price. Distributor D does not perform the warranty function which is performed by the supplier (products are sent back to the factory). However, Distributor D's supplier charges D a higher price than is charged to Distributor C. If Distributor C accounts for the cost of performing the warranty function as a cost of goods sold, then the adjustment in the gross profit margins for the differences is automatic. However, if the warranty expenses are accounted for as operating expenses, there is a distortion in the margins which must be corrected. The reasoning in this case would be that, if D performed the warranty itself, its supplier would reduce the transfer price, and therefore, D's gross profit margin would be greater.

2.38 A company sells a product through independent distributors in five countries in which it has no subsidiaries. The distributors simply market the product and do not perform any additional work. In one country, the company has set up a subsidiary. Because this particular market is of strategic importance, the company requires its subsidiary to sell only its product and to perform technical applications for the customers. Even if all other facts and circumstances are similar, if the margins are derived from independent enterprises that do not have exclusive sales arrangements or perform technical applications like those undertaken by the subsidiary, it is necessary to consider whether any adjustments must be made to achieve comparability.

D. Cost plus method

D.1 In general

2.39 The cost plus method begins with the costs incurred by the supplier of property (or services) in a controlled transaction for property transferred or services provided to an associated purchaser. An appropriate cost plus mark up is then added to this cost, to make an appropriate profit in light of the functions performed and the market conditions. What is arrived at after adding the cost plus mark up to the above costs may be regarded as an arm's length price of the original controlled transaction. This method probably is most useful where semi finished goods are sold between associated parties, where associated parties have concluded joint facility agreements or long-term buy-and-supply arrangements, or where the controlled transaction is the provision of services.

2.40   The cost plus mark up of the supplier in the controlled transaction should ideally be established by reference to the cost plus mark up that the same supplier earns in comparable uncontrolled transactions ("internal comparable"). In addition, the cost plus mark up that would have been earned in comparable transactions by an independent enterprise may serve as a guide ("external comparable").

2.41   Following the principles in Chapter I, an uncontrolled transaction is comparable to a controlled transaction (*i.e.* it is a comparable uncontrolled transaction) for purposes of the cost plus method if one of two conditions is met: a) none of the differences (if any) between the transactions being compared or between the enterprises undertaking those transactions materially affect the cost plus mark up in the open market; or, b) reasonably accurate adjustments can be made to eliminate the material effects of such differences. In determining whether a transaction is a comparable uncontrolled transaction for the purposes of the cost plus method, the same principles apply as described in paragraphs 2.23-2.28 for the resale price method. Thus, fewer adjustments may be necessary to account for product differences under the cost plus method than the CUP method, and it may be appropriate to give more weight to other factors of comparability described in Chapter I, some of which may have a more significant effect on the cost plus mark up than they do on price. As under the resale price method (see paragraph 2.28), where there are differences that materially affect the cost plus mark ups earned in the controlled and uncontrolled transactions (for example in the nature of the functions performed by the parties to the transactions), reasonably accurate adjustments should be made to account for such differences. The extent and reliability of those adjustments will affect the relative reliability of the analysis under the cost plus method in particular cases.

2.42   For example, assume that Company A manufactures and sells toasters to a distributor that is an associated enterprise, that Company B manufactures and sells irons to a distributor that is an independent enterprise, and that the profit margins on the manufacture of basic toasters and irons are generally the same in the small household appliance industry.

(The use of the cost plus method here presumes that there are no highly similar independent toaster manufacturers). If the cost plus method were being applied, the mark ups being compared in the controlled and uncontrolled transactions would be the difference between the selling price by the manufacturer to the distributor and the costs of manufacturing the product, divided by the costs of manufacturing the product. However, Company A may be much more efficient in its manufacturing processes than Company B thereby enabling it to have lower costs. As a result, even if Company A were making irons instead of toasters and charging the same price as Company B is charging for irons (*i.e.* no special condition were to exist), it would be appropriate for Company A's profit level to be higher than that of Company B. Thus, unless it is possible to adjust for the effect of this difference on the profit, the application of the cost plus method would not be wholly reliable in this context.

2.43   The cost plus method presents some difficulties in proper application, particularly in the determination of costs. Although it is true that an enterprise must cover its costs over a period of time to remain in business, those costs may not be the determinant of the appropriate profit in a specific case for any one year. While in many cases companies are driven by competition to scale down prices by reference to the cost of creating the relevant goods or providing the relevant service, there are other circumstances where there is no discernible link between the level of costs incurred and a market price (*e.g.* where a valuable discovery has been made and the owner has incurred only small research costs in making it).

2.44   In addition, when applying the cost plus method one should pay attention to apply a comparable mark up to a comparable cost basis. For instance, if the supplier to which reference is made in applying the cost plus method in carrying out its activities employs leased business assets, the cost basis might not be comparable without adjustment if the supplier in the controlled transaction owns its business assets. The cost plus method relies upon a comparison of the mark up on costs achieved in a controlled transaction and the mark up on costs achieved in one or more comparable uncontrolled transactions. Therefore, differences between the controlled and uncontrolled transactions that have an effect on the size of the mark up must be analyzed to determine what adjustments should be made to the uncontrolled transactions' respective mark up.

2.45   For this purpose, it is particularly important to consider differences in the level and types of expenses – operating expenses and non-operating expenses including financing expenditures – associated with functions performed and risks assumed by the parties or transactions being compared. Consideration of these differences may indicate the following:

a) If expenses reflect a functional difference (taking into account assets used and risks assumed) which has not been taken into account in applying the method, an adjustment to the cost plus mark up may be required.

b) If the expenses reflect additional functions that are distinct from the activities tested by the method, separate compensation for those functions may need to be determined. Such functions may for example amount to the provision of services for which an appropriate reward may be determined. Similarly, expenses that are the result of capital structures reflecting non-arm's length arrangements may require separate adjustment.

c) If differences in the expenses of the parties being compared merely reflect efficiencies or inefficiencies of the enterprises, as would normally be the case for supervisory, general, and administrative expenses, then no adjustment to the gross margin may be appropriate.

In any of the above circumstances it may be appropriate to supplement the cost plus and resale price methods by considering the results obtained from applying other methods (see paragraph 2.11).

2.46   Another important aspect of comparability is accounting consistency. Where the accounting practices differ in the controlled transaction and the uncontrolled transaction, appropriate adjustments should be made to the data used to ensure that the same type of costs are used in each case to ensure consistency. The gross profit mark ups must be measured consistently between the associated enterprise and the independent enterprise. In addition, there may be differences across enterprises in the treatment of costs that affect gross profit mark ups that would need to be accounted for in order to achieve reliable comparability. In some cases it may be necessary to take into account certain operating expenses in order to achieve consistency and comparability; in these circumstances the cost plus method starts to approach a net rather than gross profit analysis. To the extent that the analysis takes into account operating expenses, its reliability may be adversely affected for the reasons set forth in paragraphs 2.64-2.67. Thus, the safeguards described in paragraphs 2.68-2.75 may be relevant in assessing the reliability of such analyses.

2.47   While precise accounting standards and terms may vary, in general the costs and expenses of an enterprise are understood to be divisible into three broad categories. First, there are the direct costs of producing a product or service, such as the cost of raw materials. Second, there are indirect costs of production, which although closely related to the production process may be common to several products or services (*e.g.* the costs of a repair department that services equipment used to produce different products). Finally, there are the operating expenses of the enterprise as a whole, such as supervisory, general, and administrative expenses.

2.48   The distinction between gross and net profit analyses may be understood in the following terms. In general, the cost plus method will use mark ups computed after direct and indirect costs of production, while a net profit method will use profits computed after operating expenses of the enterprise as well. It must be recognised that because of the variations in practice among countries, it is difficult to draw any precise lines between the three categories described above. Thus, for example, an application of the cost plus method may in a particular case include the consideration of some expenses that might be considered operating expenses, as discussed in paragraph 2.46. Nevertheless, the problems in delineating with mathematical precision the boundaries of the three categories described above do not alter the basic practical distinction between the gross and net profit approaches.

2.49   In principle historical costs should be attributed to individual units of production, although admittedly the cost plus method may over-emphasize historical costs. Some costs, for example costs of materials, labour, and transport will vary over a period and in such a case it may be appropriate to average the costs over the period. Averaging also may be appropriate across product groups or over a particular line of production. Further, averaging may be appropriate with respect to the costs of fixed assets where the production or processing of different products is carried on simultaneously and the volume of activity fluctuates. Costs such as replacement costs and marginal costs also may need to be considered where these can be measured and they result in a more accurate estimate of the appropriate profit.

2.50   The costs that may be considered in applying the cost plus method are limited to those of the supplier of goods or services. This limitation may raise a problem of how to allocate some costs between suppliers and purchasers. There is a possibility that some costs will be borne by the purchaser in order to diminish the supplier's cost base on which the mark up will be calculated. In practice, this may be achieved by not allocating to the supplier an appropriate share of overheads and other costs borne by the purchaser (often the parent company) for the benefit of the supplier (often a subsidiary). The allocation should be undertaken based on an analysis of functions performed (taking into account assets used and risks assumed) by the respective parties as provided in Chapter I. A related problem is how overhead costs should be apportioned, whether by reference to turnover, number or cost of employees, or some other criterion. The issue of cost allocation is also discussed in Chapter VIII on cost contribution arrangements.

2.51   In some cases, there may be a basis for using only variable or incremental (*e.g.* marginal) costs, because the transactions represent a disposal of marginal production. Such a claim could be justified if the goods could not be sold at a higher price in the relevant foreign market (see also the discussion of market penetration in Chapter I). Factors that could be taken into account in evaluating such a claim include information on whether the taxpayer has any other sales of the same or similar products in that particular foreign market, the percentage of the taxpayers' production (in both volume and value terms) that the claimed "marginal production" represents, the term of the arrangement, and details of the marketing analysis that was undertaken by the taxpayer or MNE group which led to the conclusion that the goods could not be sold at a higher price in that foreign market.

2.52   No general rule can be set out that deals with all cases. The various methods for determining costs should be consistent as between the controlled and uncontrolled transactions and consistent over time in relation to particular enterprises. For example, in determining the appropriate cost plus mark up, it may be necessary to take into account whether products can be supplied by various sources at widely differing costs. Associated enterprises may choose to calculate their cost plus basis on a standardised basis. An independent party probably would not accept to pay a higher price resulting from the inefficiency of the other party. On the other hand, if the other party is more efficient than can be expected under normal circumstances, this other party should benefit from that advantage. The associated enterprise may agree in advance which costs would be acceptable as a basis for the cost plus method.

D.2   *Examples of the application of the cost plus method*

2.53   A is a domestic manufacturer of timing mechanisms for mass-market clocks. A sells this product to its foreign subsidiary B. A earns a 5 percent gross profit mark up with respect to its manufacturing operation. X, Y, and Z are independent domestic manufacturers of timing mechanisms for mass-market watches. X, Y, and Z sell to independent foreign purchasers. X, Y, and Z earn gross profit mark ups with respect to their manufacturing operations that range from 3 to 5 percent. A accounts for supervisory, general, and administrative costs as operating expenses, and thus these costs are not reflected in cost of goods sold. The gross profit mark ups of X, Y, and Z, however, reflect supervisory, general, and administrative costs as part of costs of goods sold. Therefore, the gross profit mark ups of X, Y, and Z must be adjusted to provide accounting consistency.

2.54   Company C in country D is a 100% subsidiary of company E, located in country F. In comparison with country F, wages are very low in country D. At the expense and risk of company E, television sets are assembled by company C. All the necessary components, know-how, etc. are provided by company E. The purchase of the assembled product is guaranteed by company E in case the television sets fail to meet a certain quality standard. After the quality check the television sets are brought – at the expense and risk of company E – to distribution centres company E has in several countries. The function of company C can be described as a purely contract manufacturing function. The risks company C could bear are eventual differences in the agreed quality and quantity. The basis for applying the cost plus method will be formed by all the costs connected to the assembling activities.

2.55   Company A of an MNE group agrees with company B of the same MNE group to carry out contract research for company B. All risks of a failure of the research are born by company B. This company also owns all the intangibles developed through the research and therefore has also the profit chances resulting from the research. This is a typical setup for applying a cost plus method. All costs for the research, which the associated parties have agreed upon, have to be compensated. The additional cost plus may reflect how innovative and complex the research carried out is.

Part III: Transactional profit methods

A. Introduction

2.56   This Part provides a discussion of transactional profit methods that may be used to approximate arm's length conditions where such methods are the most appropriate to the circumstances of the case, see paragraphs 2.1-2.11. Transactional profit methods examine the profits that arise from particular transactions among associated enterprises. The only profit methods that satisfy the arm's length principle are those that are consistent with Article 9 of the OECD Model Tax Convention and follow the requirement for a comparability analysis as described in these Guidelines. In particular, so-called "comparable profits methods" or "modified cost plus/resale price methods" are acceptable only to the extent that they are consistent with these Guidelines.

2.57   A transactional profit method examines the profits that arise from particular controlled transactions. The transactional profit methods for purposes of these Guidelines are the transactional profit split method and the transactional net margin method. Profit arising from a controlled transaction can be a relevant indicator of whether the transaction was affected by conditions that differ from those that would have been made by independent enterprises in otherwise comparable circumstances.

B. Transactional net margin method

B.1   In general

2.58   The transactional net margin method examines the net profit relative to an appropriate base (*e.g.* costs, sales, assets) that a taxpayer realises from a controlled transaction (or transactions that are appropriate to aggregate under the principles of paragraphs 3.9-3.12). Thus, a transactional net margin method operates in a manner similar to the cost plus and resale price methods. This similarity means that in order to be applied reliably, the transactional net margin method must be applied in a manner consistent with the manner in which the resale price or cost plus method is applied. This means in particular that the net profit indicator of the taxpayer from the controlled transaction (or transactions that are appropriate to aggregate under the principles of paragraphs 3.9-3.12) should ideally be established by reference to the net profit indicator that the same taxpayer earns in comparable uncontrolled transactions, *i.e.* by reference to "internal comparables" (see paragraphs 3.27-3.28). Where this is not possible, the net margin that would have been earned in comparable transactions by an independent enterprise ("external comparables") may serve as a guide (see paragraphs 3.29-3.35). A functional analysis of the controlled and uncontrolled transactions is required to determine whether the transactions are comparable and what adjustments may be necessary to obtain reliable results. Further, the other requirements for comparability, and in particular those of paragraphs 2.68 -2.75, must be applied.

2.59   A transactional net margin method is unlikely to be reliable if each party to a transaction makes valuable, unique contributions, see paragraph 2.4. In such a case, a transactional profit split method will generally be the most appropriate method, see paragraph 2.109. However, a one-sided method (traditional transaction method or transactional net margin method) may be applicable in cases where one of the parties makes all the unique contributions involved in the controlled transaction, while the other party does not make any unique contribution. In such a case, the tested party should be the less complex one. See paragraphs 3.18-3.19 for a discussion of the notion of tested party.

2.60   There are also many cases where a party to a transaction makes contributions that are not unique – *e.g.* uses non-unique intangibles such as non-unique business processes or non-unique market knowledge. In such cases, it may be possible to meet the comparability requirements to apply a traditional transaction method or a transactional net margin method because the comparables would also be expected to use a comparable mix of non-unique contributions.

2.61   Finally, the lack of valuable and unique contributions involved in a particular transaction does not automatically imply that the transactional net margin method is the most appropriate method.

B.2   Strengths and weaknesses[1]

2.62   One strength of the transactional net margin method is that net profit indicators (*e.g.* return on assets, operating income to sales, and possibly other measures of net profit) are less affected by transactional differences than is the case with price, as used in the CUP method. Net

---

[1]   An example illustrating the sensitivity of gross and net profit margin indicators is found in Annex I to Chapter II.

profit indicators also may be more tolerant to some functional differences between the controlled and uncontrolled transactions than gross profit margins. Differences in the functions performed between enterprises are often reflected in variations in operating expenses. Consequently, this may lead to a wide range of gross profit margins but still broadly similar levels of net operating profit indicators. In addition, in some countries the lack of clarity in the public data with respect to the classification of expenses in the gross or operating profits may make it difficult to evaluate the comparability of gross margins, while the use of net profit indicators may avoid the problem.

2.63   Another practical strength of the transactional net margin method is that, as with any one-sided method, it is necessary to examine a financial indicator for only one of the associated enterprises (the "tested" party). Similarly, it is often not necessary to state the books and records of all participants in the business activity on a common basis or to allocate costs for all participants as is the case with the transactional profit split method. This can be practically advantageous when one of the parties to the transaction is complex and has many interrelated activities or when it is difficult to obtain reliable information about one of the parties. However, a comparability (including functional) analysis must always be performed in order to appropriately characterise the transaction between the parties and choose the most appropriate transfer pricing method, and this analysis generally necessitates that some information on the five comparability factors in relation to the controlled transaction be collected on both the tested and the non-tested parties. See paragraphs 3.20-3.23.

2.64   There are also a number of weaknesses to the transactional net margin method. The net profit indicator of a taxpayer can be influenced by some factors that would either not have an effect, or have a less substantial or direct effect, on price or gross margins between independent parties. These aspects may make accurate and reliable determinations of arm's length net profit indicators difficult. Thus, it is important to provide some detailed guidance on establishing comparability for the transactional net margin method, as set forth in paragraphs 2.68-2.75 below.

2.65   Application of any arm's length method requires information on uncontrolled transactions that may not be available at the time of the controlled transactions. This may make it particularly difficult for taxpayers that attempt to apply the transactional net margin method at the time of the controlled transactions (although use of multiple year data as discussed in paragraphs 3.75-3.79 may mitigate this concern). In addition, taxpayers may not have access to enough specific information on the profits attributable to comparable uncontrolled transactions to make a valid application of the method. It also may be difficult to ascertain revenue and operating expenses related to the controlled transactions to establish the net profit indicator used as the profit measure for the transactions. Tax administrators may have more information available to them from examinations of other taxpayers. See paragraph 3.36 for a discussion of information available to tax administrators that may not be disclosed to the taxpayer, and paragraphs 3.67-3.79 for a discussion of timing issues.

2.66   Like the resale price and cost plus methods, the transactional net margin method is applied to only one of the associated enterprises. The fact that many factors unrelated to transfer prices may affect net profits, in conjunction with the one-sided nature of the analysis under this method, can affect the overall reliability of the transactional net margin method if an insufficient standard of comparability is applied. Detailed guidance on establishing comparability for the transactional net margin method is given in section B.3.1 below.

2.67   There may also be difficulties in determining an appropriate corresponding adjustment when applying the transactional net margin method, particularly where it is not possible to work back to a transfer price. This could be the case, for example, where the taxpayer deals with associated enterprises on both the buying and the selling sides of the controlled transaction. In such a case, if the transactional net margin method indicates that the taxpayer's profit should be adjusted upwards, there may be some uncertainty about which of the associated enterprises' profits should be reduced.

B.3   Guidance for application

B.3.1   The comparability standard to be applied to the transactional net margin method

2.68   A comparability analysis must be performed in all cases in order to select and apply the most appropriate transfer pricing method, and the process for selecting and applying a transactional net margin method should not be less reliable than for other methods. As a matter of good practice, the typical process for identifying comparable transactions and using data so obtained which is described at paragraph 3.4 or any equivalent process designed to ensure robustness of the analysis should be followed when applying a transactional net margin method, just as with any other method. That being said, it is recognised that in practice the level of information available on the factors affecting external comparable transactions is often limited. Determining a reliable estimate of an arm's length outcome requires flexibility and the exercise of good judgment. See paragraph 1.13.

2.69   Prices are likely to be affected by differences in products, and gross margins are likely to be affected by differences in functions, but net profit indicators are less adversely affected by such differences. As with the resale price and cost plus methods that the transactional net margin method resembles, this, however, does not mean that a mere similarity of functions between two enterprises will necessarily lead to reliable comparisons. Assuming similar functions can be isolated from among the wide range of functions that enterprises may exercise, in order to apply the method, the net profit indicators related to such functions may still not be automatically comparable where, for instance, the enterprises concerned carry on those functions in different economic sectors or markets with different levels of profitability. When the comparable uncontrolled transactions being used are those of an independent enterprise, a high degree of similarity is required in a number of aspects of the associated enterprise and the independent enterprise involved in the transactions in order for the controlled transactions to be comparable; there are various factors other than products and functions that can significantly influence net profit indicators.

2.70   The use of net profit indicators can potentially introduce a greater element of volatility into the determination of transfer prices for two reasons. First, net profit indicators can be influenced by some factors that do not have an effect (or have a less substantial or direct effect) on gross margins and prices, because of the potential for variation of operating expenses across enterprises. Second, net profit indicators can be influenced by some of the same factors, such as competitive position, that can influence price and gross margins, but the effect of these factors may not be as readily eliminated. In the traditional transaction methods, the effect of these factors may be eliminated as a natural consequence of insisting upon greater product and function similarity. Depending on the facts and circumstances of the case and in particular on the effect of the functional differences on the cost structure and on the revenue of the potential comparables, net profit indicators can be less sensitive than gross margins to differences in the extent and complexity of functions and to differences in the level of risks (assuming the contractual allocation of risks is arm's length). On the other hand, depending on the facts and circumstances of the case and in particular on the proportion of fixed and variable costs, the transactional net margin method may be more sensitive than the cost plus or resale price methods to differences in capacity utilisation, because differences in the levels of absorption of indirect fixed costs (*e.g.* fixed manufacturing costs or fixed distribution costs) would affect the net profit indicator but may not affect the gross margin or gross mark-up on costs if not reflected in price differences. See Annex I to Chapter II "Sensitivity of gross and net profit indicators".

2.71   Net profit indicators may be directly affected by such forces operating in the industry as follows: threat of new entrants, competitive position, management efficiency and individual strategies, threat of substitute products, varying cost structures (as reflected, for example, in the age of plant and equipment), differences in the cost of capital (*e.g.* self financing versus borrowing), and the degree of business experience (*e.g.* whether the business is in a start-up phase or is mature). Each of these factors in turn can be influenced by numerous other elements. For example, the level of the threat of new entrants will be determined by such elements as product differentiation, capital requirements, and government subsidies and regulations. Some of these elements also may impact the application of the traditional transaction methods.

2.72   Assume, for example, that a taxpayer sells top quality audio players to an associated enterprise, and the only profit information available on comparable business activities is on generic medium quality audio player sales. Assume that the top quality audio player market is growing in its sales, has a high entry barrier, has a small number of competitors, and is with wide possibilities for product differentiation. All of the differences are likely to have material effect on the profitability of the examined activities and compared activities, and in such a case would require adjustment. As with other methods, the reliability of the necessary adjustments will affect the reliability of the analysis. It should be noted that even if two enterprises are in exactly the same industry, the profitability may differ depending on their market shares, competitive positions, etc.

2.73   It might be argued that the potential inaccuracies resulting from the above types of factors can be reflected in the size of the arm's length range. The use of a range may to some extent mitigate the level of inaccuracy, but may not account for situations where a taxpayer's profits are increased or reduced by a factor unique to that taxpayer. In such a case, the range may not include points representing the profits of independent enterprises that are affected in a similar manner by a unique factor. The use of a range, therefore, may not always solve the difficulties discussed above. See discussion of arm's length ranges at paragraphs 3.55-3.66.

2.74   The transactional net margin method may afford a practical solution to otherwise insoluble transfer pricing problems if it is used sensibly and with appropriate adjustments to account for differences of the type referred to above. The transactional net margin method should not be used unless the net profit indicators are determined from uncontrolled transactions of the same taxpayer in comparable circumstances or, where the comparable uncontrolled transactions are those of an independent enterprise, the differences between the associated enterprises and the independent enterprises that have a material effect on the net profit indicator being used are adequately taken into account. Many countries are concerned that the safeguards established for the traditional transaction methods may be overlooked in applying the transactional net margin method. Thus where differences in the characteristics of the enterprises being compared have a material effect on the net profit indicators being used, it would not be appropriate to apply the transactional net margin method without making adjustments for such differences. The extent and reliability of those adjustments will affect the relative reliability of the analysis under the transactional net margin method. See discussion of comparability adjustments at paragraphs 3.47-3.54.

2.75   Another important aspect of comparability is measurement consistency. The net profit indicators must be measured consistently between the associated enterprise and the independent enterprise. In addition, there may be differences in the treatment across enterprises of operating expenses and non-operating expenses affecting the net profits such as depreciation and reserves or provisions that would need to be accounted for in order to achieve reliable comparability.

B.3.2   Selection of the net profit indicator

2.76   In applying the transactional net margin method, the selection of the most appropriate net profit indicator should follow the guidance at paragraphs 2.2 and 2.8 in relation to the selection of the most appropriate method to the circumstances of the case. It should take account of the respective strengths and weaknesses of the various possible indicators; the appropriateness of the indicator considered in view of the nature of the controlled transaction, determined in particular through a functional analysis; the availability of reliable information (in particular on uncontrolled comparables) needed to apply the transactional net margin method based on that indicator; and the degree of comparability between controlled and uncontrolled transactions, including the reliability of comparability adjustments that may be needed to eliminate differences between them, when applying the transactional net margin method based on that indicator. These factors are discussed below in relation to both the determination of the net profit and its weighting.

B.3.3   Determination of the net profit

2.77   As a matter of principle, only those items that (a) directly or indirectly relate to the controlled transaction at hand and (b) are of an operating nature should be taken into account in the determination of the net profit indicator for the application of the transactional net margin method.

2.78   Costs and revenues that are not related to the controlled transaction under review should be excluded where they materially affect comparability with uncontrolled transactions. An appropriate level of segmentation of the taxpayer's financial data is needed when determining or testing the net profit it earns from a controlled transaction (or from transactions that are appropriately aggregated according to the guidance at paragraphs 3.9-3.12). Therefore, it would be inappropriate to apply the transactional net margin method on a company-wide basis if the company engages in a variety of different controlled transactions that cannot be appropriately compared on an aggregate basis with those of an independent enterprise.

2.79   Similarly, when analysing the transactions between the independent enterprises to the extent they are needed, profits attributable to transactions that are not similar to the controlled transactions under examination should be excluded from the comparison. Finally, when net profit indicators of an independent enterprise are used, the profits attributable to the transactions of the independent enterprise must not be distorted by controlled transactions of that enterprise. See paragraphs 3.9-3.12 on the evaluation of a taxpayer's separate and combined transactions and paragraph 3.37 on the use of non-transactional third party data.

2.80   Non-operating items such as interest income and expenses and income taxes should be excluded from the determination of the net profit indicator. Exceptional and extraordinary items of a non-recurring nature should generally also be excluded. This however is not always the case as there may be situations where it would be appropriate to include them, depending on the circumstances of the case and on the functions being undertaken and risks being borne by the tested party. Even where exceptional and extraordinary items are not taken into account in the determination of the net profit indicator, it may be useful to review them because they can provide valuable information for the purpose of comparability analysis (for instance by reflecting that the tested party bears a given risk).

2.81   In those cases where there is a correlation between the credit terms and the sales prices, it could be appropriate to reflect interest income in respect of short-term working capital within the calculation of the net profit indicator and/or to proceed with a working capital adjustment, see paragraphs 3.47-3.54. An example would be where a large retail business benefits from long credit terms with its suppliers and from short credit terms with its customers, thus making it possible to derive excess cash that in turn may make it possible to have lower sales prices to customers than if such advantageous credit terms were not available.

2.82   Whether foreign exchange gains and losses should be included or excluded from the determination of the net profit indicator raises a number of difficult comparability issues. First, it needs to be considered whether the foreign exchange gains and losses are of a trading nature (*e.g.* exchange gain or loss on a trade receivable or payable) and whether or not the tested party is responsible for them. Second, any hedging of the foreign currency exposure on the underlying trade receivable or payable also needs to be considered and treated in the same way in determining the net profit. In effect, if a transactional net margin is applied to a transaction in which the foreign exchange risk is borne by the tested party, foreign exchange gains or losses should be consistently accounted for (either in the calculation of the net profit indicator or separately).

2.83   For financial activities where the making and receiving of advances constitutes the ordinary business of the taxpayer, it will generally be appropriate to consider the effect of interest and amounts in the nature of interest when determining the net profit indicator.

2.84   Difficult comparability issues can arise where the accounting treatment of some items by potential third party comparables is unclear or does not allow reliable measurement or adjustment (see paragraph 2.75). This can be the case in particular for depreciation, amortisation, stock option and pension costs. The decision whether or not to include such items in the determination of the net profit indicator for applying the transactional net margin method will depend on a weighing of their expected effects on the appropriateness of the net profit indicator to the circumstances of the transaction and on the reliability of the comparison (see paragraph 3.50).

2.85   Whether start-up costs and termination costs should be included in the determination of the net profit indicator depends on the facts and circumstances of the case and on whether in comparable circumstances, independent parties would have agreed either for the party performing the functions to bear the start-up costs and possible termination costs; or for part or all of these costs to be recharged with no mark-up, e.g. to the customer or a principal; or for part or all of these costs to be recharged with a mark-up, e.g. by including them in the calculation of the net profit indicator of the party performing the functions. See Chapter IX, Part II, Section E for a discussion of termination costs in the context of a business restructuring.

B.3.4   Weighting the net profit

2.86   The selection of the denominator should be consistent with the comparability (including functional) analysis of the controlled transaction, and in particular it should reflect the allocation of risks between the parties (provided said allocation of risks is arm's length, see paragraphs 1.47-1.50).

For instance, capital-intensive activities such as certain manufacturing activities may involve significant investment risk, even in those cases where the operational risks (such as market risks or inventory risks) might be limited. Where a transactional net margin method is applied to such cases, the investment-related risks are reflected in the net profit indicator if the latter is a return on investment (*e.g.* return on assets or return on capital employed). Such indicator might need to be adjusted (or a different net profit indicator selected) depending on what party to the controlled transaction bears that risk, as well as on the degree of differences in risk that may be found in the taxpayer's controlled transaction and in comparables. See paragraphs 3.47-3.54 for a discussion of comparability adjustments.

2.87   The denominator should be focussed on the relevant indicator(s) of the value of the functions performed by the tested party in the transaction under review, taking account of its assets used and risks assumed. Typically, and subject to a review of the facts and circumstances of the case, sales or distribution operating expenses may be an appropriate base for distribution activities, full costs or operating expenses may be an appropriate base for a service or manufacturing activity, and operating assets may be an appropriate base for capital-intensive activities such as certain manufacturing activities or utilities. Other bases can also be appropriate depending on the circumstances of the case.

2.88   The denominator should be reasonably independent from controlled transactions, otherwise there would be no objective starting point. For instance, when analysing a transaction consisting in the purchase of goods by a distributor from an associated enterprise for resale to independent customers, one could not weight the net profit indicator against the cost of goods sold because these costs are the controlled costs for which consistency with the arm's length principle is being tested. Similarly, for a controlled transaction consisting in the provision of services to an associated enterprise, one could not weight the net profit indicator against the revenue from the sale of services because these are the controlled sales for which consistency with the arm's length principle is being tested. Where the denominator is materially affected by controlled transaction costs that are not the object of the testing (such as head office charges, rental fees or royalties paid to an associated enterprise), caution should be exercised to ensure that said controlled transaction costs do not materially distort the analysis and in particular that they are in accordance with the arm's length principle.

2.89   The denominator should be one that is capable of being measured in a reliable and consistent manner at the level of the taxpayer's controlled transactions. In addition, the appropriate base should be one that is capable of being measured in a reliable and consistent manner at the level of the comparable uncontrolled transactions. This in practice limits the ability to use certain indicators, as discussed at paragraph 2.99 below. Further, the taxpayer's allocation of indirect expenses to the transaction under review should be appropriate and consistent over time.

B.3.4.1   Cases where the net profit is weighted to sales

2.90   A net profit indicator of net profit divided by sales, or net profit margin, is frequently used to determine the arm's length price of purchases from an associated enterprise for resale to independent customers. In such cases, the sales figure at the denominator should be the re-sales of items purchased in the controlled transaction under review. Sales revenue that is derived from uncontrolled activities (purchase from independent parties for re-sale to independent parties) should not be included in the determination or testing of the remuneration for controlled transactions, unless the uncontrolled transactions are such that they do not materially affect the comparison; and/or the controlled and uncontrolled transactions are so closely linked that they cannot be evaluated adequately on a separate basis. One example of the latter situation can sometimes occur in relation to uncontrolled after-sales services or sales of spare parts provided by a distributor to independent end-user customers where they are closely linked to controlled purchase transactions by the distributor for resale to the same independent end-user customers, for instance because the service activity is performed using rights or other assets that are granted under the distribution arrangement. See also discussion of portfolio approaches in paragraph 3.10.

2.91   One question that arises in cases where the net profit indicator is weighted against sales is how to account for rebates and discounts that may be granted to customers by the taxpayer or the comparables. Depending on the accounting standards, rebates and discounts may be treated as a reduction of sales revenue or as an expense. Similar difficulties can arise in relation to foreign exchange gains or losses. Where such items materially affect the comparison, the key is to compare like with like and follow the same accounting principles for the taxpayer and for the comparables.

B.3.4.2   Cases where the net profit is weighted to costs

2.92   Cost-based indicators should only be used in those cases where costs are a relevant indicator of the value of the functions performed, assets used and risks assumed by the tested party. In addition, the determination of what costs should be included in the cost base should derive from a careful review of the facts and circumstances of the case. Where the net profit indicator is weighted against costs, only those costs that directly or indirectly relate to the controlled transaction under review (or transactions aggregated in accordance to the principle at paragraphs 3.9-3.12) should be taken into account. Accordingly, an appropriate level of segmentation of a taxpayer's accounts is needed in order to exclude from the denominator costs that relate to other activities or transactions and materially affect comparability with uncontrolled transactions. Moreover, in most cases only those costs which are of an operating nature should be included in the denominator. The discussion at paragraphs 2.80-2.85 above also applies to costs as denominator.

2.93   In applying a cost-based transactional net margin method, fully loaded costs are often used, including all the direct and indirect costs attributable to the activity or transaction, together with an appropriate allocation in respect of the overheads of the business. The question can arise whether and to what extent it is acceptable at arm's length to treat a significant portion of the taxpayer's costs as pass-through costs to which no profit element is attributed (*i.e.* as costs which are potentially excludable from the denominator of the net profit indicator). This depends on the extent to which an independent party in comparable circumstances would agree not to earn a mark-up on part of the costs it incurs. The response should not be based on the classification of costs as "internal" or "external" costs, but rather on a comparability (including functional) analysis. See paragraph 7.36.

2.94   Where treating costs as pass-through costs is found to be arm's length, a second question arises as to the consequences on comparability and on the determination of the arm's length range. Because it is necessary to compare like with like, if pass-through costs are excluded from the denominator of the taxpayer's net profit indicator, comparable costs should also be excluded from the denominator of the comparable net profit indicator. Comparability issues may arise in practice where limited information is available on the breakdown of the costs of the comparables.

2.95   Depending on the facts and circumstances of the case, actual costs, as well as standard or budgeted costs, may be appropriate to use as the cost base. Using actual costs may raise an issue because the tested party may have no incentive to carefully monitor the costs. In arrangements between independent parties, it is not rare that a cost savings objective is factored into the remuneration method. It can also happen in manufacturing arrangements between independent parties that prices are set on the basis of standard costs, and that any decrease or increase in actual costs compared to standard costs is attributed to the manufacturer. Where they reflect the arrangements that would be taken between independent parties, similar mechanisms could be taken into account in the application of the cost-based transactional net margin method. See paragraph 2.52 for a discussion of the same issue in relation to the cost plus method.

2.96   The use of budgeted costs can also raise a number of concerns where large differences between actual costs and budgeted costs result. Independent parties are not likely to set prices on the basis of budgeted costs without agreeing on what factors are to be taken into account in setting the budget, without having regard to how budgeted costs have compared with actual costs in previous years and without addressing how unforeseen circumstances are to be treated.

B.3.4.3   Cases where the net profit is weighted to assets

2.97   Returns on assets (or on capital) can be an appropriate base in cases where assets (rather than costs or sales) are a better indicator of the value added by the tested party, *e.g.* in certain manufacturing or other asset-intensive activities and in capital-intensive financial activities. Where the indicator is a net profit weighted to assets, operating assets only should be used. Operating assets include tangible operating fixed assets, including land and buildings, plant and equipment, operating intangible assets used in the business, such as patents and know-how, and working capital assets such as inventory and trade receivables (less trade payables). Investments and cash balances are generally not operating assets outside the financial industry sector.

2.98   In cases where the net profit is weighted to assets, the question arises how to value the assets, *e.g.* at book value or market value. Using book value could possibly distort the comparison, *e.g.* between those enterprises that have depreciated their assets and those that have more recent assets with on-going depreciation, and between enterprises that use acquired intangibles and others that use self-developed intangibles. Using market value could possibly alleviate this concern, although it can raise other reliability issues where valuation of assets is uncertain and can also prove to be extremely costly and burdensome, especially for intangible assets. Depending on the facts and circumstances of the case, it may be possible to perform adjustments to improve the reliability of the comparison. The choice between book value, adjusted book value, market value and other possibly available options should be made with a view to finding the most reliable measure, taking account of the size and complexity of the transaction and of the costs and burden involved, see Chapter III, Section C.

B.3.4.4   Other possible net profit indicators

2.99   Other net profit indicators may be appropriate depending on the facts and circumstances of the transactions. For instance, depending on the industry and on the controlled transaction under review, it may be useful to look at other denominators where independent data may exist, such as: floor area of retail points, weight of products transported, number of employees, time, distance, etc. While there is no reason to rule out the use of such bases where they provide a reasonable indication of the value added by the tested party to the controlled transaction, they should only be used where it is possible to obtain reliable comparable information to support the application of the method with such a net profit indicator.

B.3.5   Berry ratios

2.100   "Berry ratios" are defined as ratios of gross profit to operating expenses. Interest and extraneous income are generally excluded from the gross profit determination; depreciation and amortisation may or may not be included in the operating expenses, depending in particular on the possible uncertainties they can create in relation to valuation and comparability.

2.101   The selection of the appropriate financial indicator depends on the facts and circumstances of the case, see paragraph 2.76. Concerns have been expressed that Berry ratios are sometimes used in cases where they are not appropriate without the caution that is necessary in the selection and determination of any transfer pricing method and financial indicator. See paragraph 2.92 in relation to the use of cost-based indicators in general. One common difficulty in the determination of Berry ratios is that they are very sensitive to classification of costs as operating expenses or not, and therefore can pose comparability issues. In addition, the issues raised at paragraphs 2.93-2.94 above in relation to pass-through costs equally arise in the application of Berry ratios. In order for a Berry ratio to be appropriate to test the remuneration of a controlled transaction (*e.g.* consisting in the distribution of products), it is necessary that:

- The value of the functions performed in the controlled transaction (taking account of assets used and risks assumed) is proportional to the operating expenses,

- The value of the functions performed in the controlled transaction (taking account of assets used and risks assumed) is not materially affected by the value of the products distributed, *i.e.* it is not proportional to sales, and

- The taxpayer does not perform, in the controlled transactions, any other significant function (*e.g.* manufacturing function) that should be remunerated using another method or financial indicator.

2.102   A situation where Berry ratios can prove useful is for intermediary activities where a taxpayer purchases goods from an associated enterprise and on-sells them to other associated enterprises. In such cases, the resale price method may not be applicable given the absence of uncontrolled sales, and a cost plus method that would provide for a mark-up on the cost of goods sold might not be applicable either where the cost of goods sold consists in controlled purchases. By contrast, operating expenses in the case of an intermediary may be reasonably independent from transfer pricing formulation, unless they are materially affected by controlled transaction costs such as head office charges, rental fees or royalties paid to an associated enterprise, so that, depending on the facts and circumstances of the case, a Berry ratio may be an appropriate indicator, subject to the comments above.

B.3.6   Other guidance

2.103   While it is not specific to the transactional net margin method, the issue of the use of non-transactional third party data is in practice more acute when applying this method due to the heavy reliance on external comparables. The problem arises because there are often insufficient public data to allow for third party net profit indicators to be determined at transactional level. This is why there needs to be sufficient comparability between the controlled transaction and the comparable uncontrolled transactions. Given that often the only data available for the third parties are company-wide data, the functions performed by the third party in its total operations must be closely aligned to those functions performed by the tested party with respect to its controlled transactions in order to allow the former to be used to determine an arm's length outcome for the latter. The overall objective is to determine a level of segmentation that provides reliable comparables for the controlled transaction, based on the facts and circumstances of the particular case. In case it is impossible in practice to achieve the transactional level set out as the ideal by these Guidelines, it is still important to try to find the most reliable comparables as discussed at paragraph 3.2, through making suitable adjustments based on the evidence that is available.

2.104   See in particular paragraphs 3.18-3.19 for guidance on the tested party, paragraphs 3.55-3.66 for guidance on the arm's length range, and paragraphs 3.75-3.79 for guidance on multiple year data.

B.4 Examples of the application of the transactional net margin method

2.105 By way of illustration, the example of cost plus at paragraph 2.53 demonstrates the need to adjust the gross mark up arising from transactions in order to achieve consistent and reliable comparison. Such adjustments may be made without difficulty where the relevant costs can be readily analyzed. Where, however, it is known that an adjustment is required, but it is not possible to identify the particular costs for which an adjustment is required, it may, nevertheless, be possible to identify the net profit arising on the transaction and thereby ensure that a consistent measure is used. For example, if the supervisory, general, and administrative costs that are treated as part of costs of goods sold for the independent enterprises X, Y and Z cannot be identified so as to adjust the mark up in a reliable application of cost plus, it may be necessary to examine net profit indicators in the absence of more reliable comparisons.

2.106 A similar approach may be required when there are differences in functions performed by the parties being compared. Assume that the facts are the same as in the example at paragraph 2.38 except that it is the comparable independent enterprises that perform the additional function of technical support and not the associated enterprise, and that these costs are reported in the cost of goods sold but cannot be separately identified. Because of product and market differences it may not be possible to find a CUP, and a resale price method would be unreliable since the gross margin of the independent enterprises would need to be higher than that of the associated enterprise in order to reflect the additional function and to cover the unknown additional costs. In this example, it may be more reliable to examine net margins in order to assess the difference in the transfer price that would reflect the difference in function. The use of net margins in such a case needs to take account of comparability and may not be reliable if there would be a material effect on net margin as a result of the additional function or as a result of market differences.

2.107 The facts are the same as in paragraph 2.36. However, the amount of the warranty expenses incurred by Distributor A proves impossible to ascertain so that it is not possible to reliably adjust the gross profit of A to make the gross profit margin properly comparable with that of B. However, if there are no other material functional differences between A and B and the net profit of A relative to its sales is known, it might be possible to apply the transactional net margin method to B by comparing the margin relative to A's sales to net profits with the margin calculated on the same basis for B.

C. Transactional profit split method

C.1 In general

2.108   The transactional profit split method seeks to eliminate the effect on profits of special conditions made or imposed in a controlled transaction (or in controlled transactions that are appropriate to aggregate under the principles of paragraphs 3.9-3.12) by determining the division of profits that independent enterprises would have expected to realise from engaging in the transaction or transactions. The transactional profit split method first identifies the profits to be split for the associated enterprises from the controlled transactions in which the associated enterprises are engaged (the "combined profits"). References to "profits" should be taken as applying equally to losses. See paragraphs 2.124-2.131 for a discussion of how to measure the profits to be split. It then splits those combined profits between the associated enterprises on an economically valid basis that approximates the division of profits that would have been anticipated and reflected in an agreement made at arm's length.   See paragraphs 2.132–2.145 for a discussion of how to split the combined profits.

C.2 Strengths and weaknesses

2.109   The main strength of the transactional profit split method is that it can offer a solution for highly integrated operations for which a one-sided method would not be appropriate. For example, see the discussion of the appropriateness and application of profit split methods to the global trading of financial instruments between associated enterprises in Part III, Section C of the Report on the Attribution of Profits to Permanent Establishments.[2] A transactional profit split method may also be found to be the most appropriate method in cases where both parties to a transaction make unique and valuable contributions (*e.g.* contribute unique intangibles) to the transaction, because in such a case independent parties might wish to share the profits of the transaction in proportion to their respective contributions and a two-sided method might be more appropriate in these circumstances than a one-sided method. In addition, in the presence of unique and valuable

---

[2]   See Report on the Attribution of Profits to Permanent Establishments, approved by the Committee on Fiscal Affairs on 24 June 2008 and by the Council for publication on 17 July 2008 and the 2010 Sanitised Version of the Report on the Attribution of Profits to Permanent Establishments, approved by the Committee on Fiscal Affairs on 22 June 2010 and by the Council for publication on 22 July 2010.

contributions, reliable comparables information might be insufficient to apply another method. On the other hand, a transactional profit split method would ordinarily not be used in cases where one party to the transaction performs only simple functions and does not make any significant unique contribution (*e.g.* contract manufacturing or contract service activities in relevant circumstances), as in such cases a transactional profit split method typically would not be appropriate in view of the functional analysis of that party. See paragraphs 3.38-3.39 for a discussion of limitations in available comparables.

2.110   Where comparables data are available, they can be relevant in the profit split analysis to support the division of profits that would have been achieved between independent parties in comparable circumstances. Comparables data can also be relevant in the profit split analysis to assess the value of the contributions that each associated enterprise makes to the transactions. In effect, the assumption is that independent parties would have split the combined profits in proportion to the value of their respective contributions to the generation of profit in the transaction. On the other hand, the external market data considered in valuing the contribution each associated enterprise makes to the controlled transactions will be less closely connected to those transactions than is the case with the other available methods.

2.111   However, in those cases where there is no more direct evidence of how independent parties in comparable circumstances would have split the profit in comparable transactions, the allocation of profits may be based on the division of functions (taking account of the assets used and risks assumed) between the associated enterprises themselves.

2.112   Another strength of the transactional profit split method is that it offers flexibility by taking into account specific, possibly unique, facts and circumstances of the associated enterprises that are not present in independent enterprises, while still constituting an arm's length approach to the extent that it reflects what independent enterprises reasonably would have done if faced with the same circumstances.

2.113   A further strength of the transactional profit split method is that it is less likely that either party to the controlled transaction will be left with an extreme and improbable profit result, since both parties to the transaction are evaluated. This aspect can be particularly important when analysing the contributions by the parties in respect of the intangible property employed in the controlled transactions. This two-sided approach may also be used to achieve a division of the profits from economies of scale or other joint efficiencies that satisfies both the taxpayer and tax administrations.

2.114   A weakness of the transactional profit split method relates to difficulties in its application. On first review, the transactional profit split method may appear readily accessible to both taxpayers and tax administrations because it tends to rely less on information about independent enterprises.   However, associated enterprises and tax administrations alike may have difficulty accessing information from foreign affiliates. In addition, it may be difficult to measure combined revenue and costs for all the associated enterprises participating in the controlled transactions, which would require stating books and records on a common basis and making adjustments in accounting practices and currencies. Further, when the transactional profit split method is applied to operating profit, it may be difficult to identify the appropriate operating expenses associated with the transactions and to allocate costs between the transactions and the associated enterprises' other activities.

C.3   Guidance for application

C.3.1   In general

2.115   These Guidelines do not seek to provide an exhaustive catalogue of ways in which the transactional profit split method may be applied. Application of the method will depend on the circumstances of the case and the information available, but the overriding objective should be to approximate as closely as possible the split of profits that would have been realised had the parties been independent enterprises.

2.116   Under the transactional profit split method, the combined profits are to be split between the associated enterprises on an economically valid basis that approximates the division of profits that would have been anticipated and reflected in an agreement made at arm's length. In general, the determination of the combined profits to be split and of the splitting factors should:

- Be consistent with the functional analysis of the controlled transaction under review, and in particular reflect the allocation of risks among the parties,

- Be consistent with the determination of the combined profits to be split and of the splitting factors which would have been agreed between independent parties,

- Be consistent with the type of profit split approach (*e.g.* contribution analysis, residual analysis, or other; *ex ante* or *ex post* approach, as discussed at paragraphs 2.118-2.145 below), and

- Be capable of being measured in a reliable manner.

2.117   In addition,

- If a transactional profit split method is used to set transfer pricing in controlled transactions (*ex ante* approach), it would be reasonable to expect the life-time of the arrangement and the criteria or allocation keys to be agreed in advance of the transaction,

- The person using a transactional profit split method (taxpayer or tax administration) should be prepared to explain why it is regarded as the most appropriate method to the circumstances of the case, as well as the way it is implemented, and in particular the criteria or allocation keys used to split the combined profits, and

- The determination of the combined profits to be split and of the splitting factors should generally be used consistently over the life-time of the arrangement, including during loss years, unless independent parties in comparable circumstances would have agreed otherwise and the rationale for using differing criteria or allocation keys is documented, or if specific circumstances would have justified a re-negotiation between independent parties.

C.3.2   *Various approaches for splitting the profits*

2.118   There are a number of approaches for estimating the division of profits, based on either projected or actual profits, as may be appropriate, to which independent enterprises would have agreed, two of which are discussed in the following paragraphs. These approaches – contribution analysis and residual analysis – are not necessarily exhaustive or mutually exclusive.

C.3.2.1   Contribution analysis

2.119   Under a contribution analysis, the combined profits, which are the total profits from the controlled transactions under examination, would be divided between the associated enterprises based upon a reasonable approximation of the division of profits that independent enterprises would have expected to realize from engaging in comparable transactions. This division can be supported by comparables data where available. In the absence thereof, it is often based on the relative value of the functions performed by each of the associated enterprises participating in the controlled transactions, taking account of their assets used and risks assumed. In cases where the relative value of the contributions can be measured directly, it may not be necessary to estimate the actual market value of each participant's contributions.

2.120   It can be difficult to determine the relative value of the contribution that each of the associated enterprises makes to the controlled transactions, and the approach will often depend on the facts and circumstances of each case.   The determination might be made by comparing the nature and degree of each party's contribution of differing types (for example, provision of services, development expenses incurred, capital invested) and assigning a percentage based upon the relative comparison and external market data. See paragraphs 2.132-2.145 for a discussion of how to split the combined profits.

C.3.2.2   Residual analyses[3]

2.121   A residual analysis divides the combined profits from the controlled transactions under examination in two stages. In the first stage, each participant is allocated an arm's length remuneration for its non-unique contributions in relation to the controlled transactions in which it is engaged. Ordinarily this initial remuneration would be determined by applying one of the traditional transaction methods or a transactional net margin method, by reference to the remuneration of comparable transactions between independent enterprises. Thus, it would generally not account for the return that would be generated by any unique and valuable contribution by the participants.   In the second stage, any residual profit (or loss) remaining after the first stage division would be allocated among the parties based on an analysis of the facts and circumstances, following the guidance as described at paragraphs 2.132-2.145 for splitting the combined profits.

2.122   An alternative approach to how to apply a residual analysis could seek to replicate the outcome of bargaining between independent enterprises in the free market. In this context, in the first stage, the initial remuneration provided to each participant would correspond to the lowest price an independent seller reasonably would accept in the circumstances and the highest price that the buyer would be reasonably willing to pay. Any

---

[3]   An example illustrating the application of the residual profit split is found in Annex II to Chapter II.

discrepancy between these two figures could result in the residual profit over which independent enterprises would bargain. In the second stage, the residual analysis therefore could divide this pool of profit based on an analysis of any factors relevant to the associated enterprises that would indicate how independent enterprises might have split the difference between the seller's minimum price and the buyer's maximum price.

2.123   In some cases an analysis could be performed, perhaps as part of a residual profit split or as a method of splitting profits in its own right, by taking into account the discounted cash flow to the parties to the controlled transactions over the anticipated life of the business. One of the situations in which this may be an effective method could be where a start-up is involved, cash flow projections were carried out as part of assessing the viability of the project, and capital investment and sales could be estimated with a reasonable degree of certainty. However, the reliability of such an approach will depend on the use of an appropriate discount rate, which should be based on market benchmarks. In this regard, it should be noted that industry-wide risk premiums used to calculate the discount do not distinguish between particular companies let alone segments of businesses, and estimates of the relative timing of receipts can be problematic. Such an approach, therefore, would require considerable caution and should be supplemented where possible by information derived from other methods.

C.3.3   Determining the combined profits to be split

2.124   The combined profits to be split in a transactional profit split method are the profits of the associated enterprises from the controlled transactions in which the associated enterprises are engaged. The combined profits to be split should only be those arising from the controlled transaction(s) under review. In determining those profits, it is essential to first identify the relevant transactions to be covered by the transactional profit split. It is also essential to identify the level of aggregation, see paragraphs 3.9-3.12. Where a taxpayer has controlled transactions with more than one associated enterprise, it is also necessary to identify the parties in relation to those transactions and the profits to be split among them.

2.125   In order to determine the combined profits to be split, the accounts of the parties to the transaction to which a transactional profit split is applied need to be put on a common basis as to accounting practice and currency, and then combined. Because accounting standards can have significant effects on the determination of the profits to be split, accounting standards should be selected in advance of applying the method and applied consistently over the lifetime of the arrangement. See paragraphs 2.115-

2.117 for general guidance on the consistency of the determination of the combined profits to be split.

2.126   Financial accounting may provide the starting point for determining the profit to be split in the absence of harmonized tax accounting standards. The use of other financial data (*e.g.* cost accounting) should be permitted where such accounts exist, are reliable, auditable and sufficiently transactional. In this context, product-line income statements or divisional accounts may prove to be the most useful accounting records.

C.3.3.1   Actual or projected profits

2.127   If the profit split method were to be used by associated enterprises to set transfer pricing in controlled transactions (*i.e.* an *ex ante* approach), then each associated enterprise would seek to achieve the division of profits that independent enterprises would have expected to realize from engaging in comparable transactions. Depending on the facts and circumstances, profit splits using either actual or projected profits are observed in practice.

2.128   When a tax administration examines the application of the method used *ex ante* to evaluate whether the method has reliably approximated arm's length transfer pricing, it is critical for the tax administration to acknowledge that the taxpayer could not have known what the actual profit experience of the business activity would be at the time that the conditions of the controlled transaction were established.   Without such an acknowledgement, the application of the transactional profit split method could penalize or reward a taxpayer by focusing on circumstances that the taxpayer could not reasonably have foreseen.   Such an application would be contrary to the arm's length principle, because independent enterprises in similar circumstances could only have relied upon projections and could not have known the actual profit experience. See also paragraph 3.74.

2.129   In using the transactional profit split method to establish the conditions of controlled transactions, the associated enterprises would seek to achieve the division of profit that independent enterprises would have realized. The evaluation of the conditions of the controlled transactions of associated enterprises using a transactional profit split method will be easiest for a tax administration where the associated enterprises have originally determined such conditions on the same basis.   The evaluation may then begin on the same basis to verify whether the division of actual profits is in accordance with the arm's length principle.

2.130   Where the associated enterprises have determined the conditions in their controlled transactions on a basis other than the transactional profit split method, the tax administration would evaluate such conditions on the basis of the actual profit experience of the enterprise. However, care would need to be exercised to ensure that the application of a transactional profit split method is performed in a context that is similar to what the associated enterprises would have experienced, *i.e.* on the basis of information known or reasonably foreseeable by the associated enterprises at the time the transactions were entered into, in order to avoid the use of hindsight. See paragraphs 2.11 and 3.74.

C.3.3.2   Different measures of profits[4]

2.131   Generally, the combined profits to be split in a transactional profit split method are operating profits. Applying the transactional profit split in this manner ensures that both income and expenses of the MNE are attributed to the relevant associated enterprise on a consistent basis. However, occasionally, it may be appropriate to carry out a split of gross profits and then deduct the expenses incurred in or attributable to each relevant enterprise (and excluding expenses taken into account in computing gross profits). In such cases, where different analyses are being applied to divide the gross income and the deductions of the MNE among associated enterprises, care must be taken to ensure that the expenses incurred in or attributable to each enterprise are consistent with the activities and risks undertaken there, and that the allocation of gross profits is likewise consistent with the placement of activities and risks. For example, in the case of an MNE that engages in highly integrated worldwide trading operations, involving various types of property, it may be possible to determine the enterprises in which expenses are incurred (or attributed), but not to accurately determine the particular trading activities to which those expenses relate. In such a case, it may be appropriate to split the gross profits from each trading activity and then deduct from the resulting overall gross profits the expenses incurred in or attributable to each enterprise, bearing in mind the caution noted above.

C.3.4   How to split the combined profits

C.3.4.1   In general

2.132   The relevance of comparable uncontrolled transactions or internal data and the criteria used to achieve an arm's length division of the profits depend on the facts and circumstances of the case. It is therefore not

---

[4]   An example illustrating different measures of profits when applying a transactional profit split method can be found in Annex III to Chapter II.

desirable to establish a prescriptive list of criteria or allocation keys. See paragraphs 2.115-2.117 for general guidance on the consistency of the determination of the splitting factors. In addition, the criteria or allocation keys used to split the profit should:

- Be reasonably independent of transfer pricing policy formulation, *i.e.* they should be based on objective data (*e.g.* sales to independent parties), not on data relating to the remuneration of controlled transactions (*e.g.* sales to associated enterprises), and

- Be supported by comparables data, internal data, or both.

C.3.4.2 Reliance on data from comparable uncontrolled transactions

2.133 One possible approach is to split the combined profits based on the division of profits that actually results from comparable uncontrolled transactions. Examples of possible sources of information on uncontrolled transactions that might usefully assist the determination of criteria to split the profits, depending on the facts and circumstances of the case, include joint-venture arrangements between independent parties under which profits are shared, such as development projects in the oil and gas industry; pharmaceutical collaborations, co-marketing or co-promotion agreements; arrangements between independent music record labels and music artists; uncontrolled arrangements in the financial services sector; etc.

C.3.4.3 Allocation keys

2.134 In practice, the division of the combined profits under a transactional profit split method is generally achieved using one or more allocation keys. Depending on the facts and circumstances of the case, the allocation key can be a figure (*e.g.* a 30%-70% split based on evidence of a similar split achieved between independent parties in comparable transactions), or a variable (*e.g.* relative value of participant's marketing expenditure or other possible keys as discussed below). Where more than one allocation key is used, it will also be necessary to weight the allocation keys used to determine the relative contribution that each allocation key represents to the earning of the combined profits.

2.135 In practice, allocation keys based on assets/capital (operating assets, fixed assets, intangible assets, capital employed) or costs (relative spending and/or investment in key areas such as research and development, engineering, marketing) are often used. Other allocation keys based for instance on incremental sales, headcounts (number of individuals involved in the key functions that generate value to the transaction), time spent by a certain group of employees if there is a strong correlation between the time spent and the creation of the combined profits, number of servers, data storage, floor area of retail points, etc. may be appropriate depending on the facts and circumstances of the transactions.

Asset-based allocation keys

2.136   Asset-based or capital-based allocation keys can be used where there is a strong correlation between tangible or intangible assets or capital employed and creation of value in the context of the controlled transaction. See paragraph 2.145 for a brief discussion of splitting the combined profits by reference to capital employed. In order for an allocation key to be meaningful, it should be applied consistently to all the parties to the transaction. See paragraph 2.98 for a discussion of comparability issues in relation to asset valuation in the context of the transactional net margin method, which is also valid in the context of the transactional profit split method.

2.137   One particular circumstance where the transactional profit split method may be found to be the most appropriate method is the case where each party to the transaction contributes valuable, unique intangibles. Intangible assets pose difficult issues in relation both to their identification and to their valuation. Identification of intangibles can be difficult because not all valuable intangible assets are legally protected and registered and not all valuable intangible assets are recorded in the accounts. An essential part of a transactional profit split analysis is to identify what intangible assets are contributed by each associated enterprise to the controlled transaction and their relative value. Guidance on intangible property is found at Chapter VI of these Guidelines. See also the examples in the Annex to Chapter VI "Examples to illustrate the Transfer Pricing Guidelines on intangible property and highly uncertain valuation".

Cost-based allocation keys

2.138   An allocation key based on expenses may be appropriate where it is possible to identify a strong correlation between relative expenses incurred and relative value added. For example, marketing expenses may be an appropriate key for distributors-marketers if advertising generates material marketing intangibles, *e.g.* in consumer goods where the value of marketing intangibles is affected by advertising. Research and development expenses may be suitable for manufacturers if they relate to the development of significant trade intangibles such as patents. However, if, for instance, each party contributes different valuable intangibles, then it is not appropriate to use a cost-based allocation key unless cost is a reliable measure of the relative value of those intangibles. Remuneration is frequently used in situations where people functions are the primary factor in generating the combined profits.

2.139   Cost-based allocation keys have the advantage of simplicity. It is however not always the case that a strong correlation exists between relative expenses and relative value, as discussed in paragraph 6.27. One possible issue with cost-based allocation keys is that they can be very sensitive to accounting classification of costs. It is therefore necessary to clearly identify in advance what costs will be taken into account in the determination of the allocation key and to determine the allocation key consistently among the parties.

Timing issues

2.140   Another important issue is the determination of the relevant period of time from which the elements of determination of the allocation key (*e.g.* assets, costs, or others) should be taken into account. A difficulty arises because there can be a time lag between the time when expenses are incurred and the time when value is created, and it is sometimes difficult to decide which period's expenses should be used. For example, in the case of a cost-based allocation key, using the expenditure on a single-year basis may be suitable for some cases, while in some other cases it may be more suitable to use accumulated expenditure (net of depreciation or amortization, where appropriate in the circumstances) incurred in the previous as well as the current years. Depending on the facts and circumstances of the case, this determination may have a significant effect on the allocation of profits amongst the parties. As noted at paragraphs 2.116-2.117 above, the selection of the allocation key should be appropriate to the particular circumstances of the case and provide a reliable approximation of the division of profits that would have been agreed between independent parties.

C.3.4.4   Reliance on data from the taxpayer's own operations ("internal data")

2.141   Where comparable uncontrolled transactions of sufficient reliability are lacking to support the division of the combined profits, consideration should be given to internal data, which may provide a reliable means of establishing or testing the arm's length nature of the division of profits. The types of such internal data that are relevant will depend on the facts and circumstances of the case and should satisfy the conditions outlined in this Section and in particular at paragraphs 2.116-2.117 and 2.132. They will frequently be extracted from the taxpayers' cost accounting or financial accounting.

2.142   For instance, where an asset-based allocation key is used, it may be based on data extracted from the balance sheets of the parties to the transaction. It will often be the case that not all the assets of the taxpayers relate to the transaction at hand and that accordingly some analytical work is needed for the taxpayer to draw a "transactional" balance sheet that will be used for the application of the transactional profit split method. Similarly, where cost-based allocation keys are used that are based on data extracted from the taxpayers' profit and loss accounts, it may be necessary to draw transactional accounts that identify those expenses that are related to the controlled transaction at hand and those that should be excluded from the determination of the allocation key. The type of expenditure that is taken into account (*e.g.* salaries, depreciation, etc.) as well as the criteria used to determine whether a given expense is related to the transaction at hand or is rather related to other transactions of the taxpayer (*e.g.* to other lines of products not subject to this profit split determination) should be applied consistently to all the parties to the transaction. See also paragraph 2.98 for a discussion of valuation of assets in the context of the transactional net margin method where the net profit is weighted to assets, which is also relevant to the valuation of assets in the context of a transactional profit split where an asset-based allocation key is used.

2.143   Internal data may also be helpful where the allocation key is based on a cost accounting system, *e.g.* headcounts involved in some aspects of the transaction, time spent by a certain group of employees on certain tasks, number of servers, data storage, floor area of retail points, etc.

2.144   Internal data are essential to assess the values of the respective contributions of the parties to the controlled transaction. The determination of such values should rely on a functional analysis that takes into account all the economically significant functions, assets and risks contributed by the parties to the controlled transaction. In those cases where the profit is split on the basis of an evaluation of the relative importance of the functions, assets and risks to the value added to the controlled transaction, such evaluation should be supported by reliable objective data in order to limit arbitrariness. Particular attention should be given to the identification of the relevant contributions of valuable intangibles and the assumption of significant risks and the importance, relevance and measurement of the factors which gave rise to these valuable intangibles and significant risks.

2.145   One possible approach not discussed above is to split the combined profits so that each of the associated enterprises participating in the controlled transactions earns the same rate of return on the capital it employs in that transaction. This method assumes that each participant's capital investment in the transaction is subject to a similar level of risk, so that one might expect the participants to earn similar rates of return if they were operating in the open market. However, this assumption may not be realistic. For example, it would not account for conditions in capital markets and could ignore other relevant aspects that would be revealed by a functional analysis and that should be taken into account in a transactional profit split.

D. Conclusions on transactional profit methods

2.146   Paragraphs 2.1-2.11 provide guidance on the selection of the most appropriate transfer pricing method to the circumstances of the case.

2.147   As discussed in these Guidelines, there are concerns regarding the use of the transactional net margin method, in particular that it is sometimes applied without adequately taking into account the relevant differences between the controlled and uncontrolled transactions being compared. Many countries are concerned that the safeguards established for the traditional transaction methods may be overlooked in applying the transactional net margin method. Thus, where differences in the characteristics of the transactions being compared have a material effect on the net profit indicators being used, it would not be appropriate to apply the transactional net margin method without making adjustments for such differences. See paragraphs 2.68-2.75 (the comparability standard to be applied to the transactional net margin method).

2.148   The recognition that the use of transactional profit methods may be necessary is not intended to suggest that independent enterprises would use these methods to set prices. As with any method, it is important that it be possible to calculate appropriate corresponding adjustments when transactional profit methods are used, recognising that in certain cases corresponding adjustments may be determined on an aggregate basis consistent with the aggregation principles in paragraphs 3.9-3.12.

2.149   In all cases, caution must be used to determine whether a transactional profit method as applied to a particular aspect of a case can produce an arm's length answer, either in conjunction with a traditional transaction method or on its own. The question ultimately can be resolved only on a case-by-case basis taking into account the strengths and weaknesses set forth above for a particular transactional profit method to be applied, the comparability (including functional) analysis of the parties to the transaction, and the availability and reliability of comparable data. In addition, these conclusions assume that countries will have a certain degree of sophistication in their underlying tax systems before applying these methods.

Chapter III

Comparability Analysis

A. Performing a comparability analysis

3.1 General guidance on comparability is found in Section D of Chapter I. By definition, a comparison implies examining two terms: the controlled transaction under review and the uncontrolled transactions that are regarded as potentially comparable. The search for comparables is only part of the comparability analysis. It should be neither confused with nor separated from the comparability analysis. The search for information on potentially comparable uncontrolled transactions and the process of identifying comparables is dependent upon prior analysis of the taxpayer's controlled transaction and of the relevant comparability factors (see paragraphs 1.38-1.63). A methodical, consistent approach should provide some continuity or linkage in the whole analytical process, thereby maintaining a constant relationship amongst the various steps: from the preliminary analysis of the conditions of the controlled transaction, to the selection of the transfer pricing method, through to the identification of potential comparables and ultimately a conclusion about whether the controlled transactions being examined are consistent with the arm's length principle as described in paragraph 1 of Article 9 of the OECD Model Tax Convention.

3.2 As part of the process of selecting the most appropriate transfer pricing method (see paragraph 2.2) and applying it, the comparability analysis always aims at finding the most reliable comparables. Thus, where it is possible to determine that some uncontrolled transactions have a lesser degree of comparability than others, they should be eliminated (see also paragraph 3.56). This does not mean that there is a requirement for an exhaustive search of all possible sources of comparables as it is acknowledged that there are limitations in availability of information and that searches for comparables data can be burdensome. See also discussion of compliance efforts at paragraphs 3.80-3.83.

3.3   In order for the process to be transparent, it is considered a good practice for a taxpayer that uses comparables to support its transfer pricing, or a tax administration that uses comparables to support a transfer pricing adjustment, to provide appropriate supporting information for the other interested party (*i.e.* tax auditor, taxpayer or foreign competent authorities) to be able to assess the reliability of the comparables used. See paragraph 3.36 for a discussion of information available to tax administrations that is not disclosed to taxpayers. General guidance on documentation requirements is found at Chapter V of these Guidelines. See also the Annex to Chapter IV "Guidelines for conducting Advance Pricing Arrangements under the Mutual Agreement Procedure ("MAP APAs")".

A.1   Typical process

3.4   Below is a description of a typical process that can be followed when performing a comparability analysis. This process is considered an accepted good practice but it is not a compulsory one, and any other search process leading to the identification of reliable comparables may be acceptable as reliability of the outcome is more important than process (*i.e.* going through the process does not provide any guarantee that the outcome will be arm's length, and not going through the process does not imply that the outcome will not be arm's length).

Step 1:   Determination of years to be covered.

Step 2:   Broad-based analysis of the taxpayer's circumstances.

Step 3:   Understanding the controlled transaction(s) under examination, based in particular on a functional analysis, in order to choose the tested party (where needed), the most appropriate transfer pricing method to the circumstances of the case, the financial indicator that will be tested (in the case of a transactional profit method), and to identify the significant comparability factors that should be taken into account.

Step 4:   Review of existing internal comparables, if any.

Step 5:   Determination of available sources of information on external comparables where such external comparables are needed taking into account their relative reliability.

Step 6:   Selection of the most appropriate transfer pricing method and, depending on the method, determination of the relevant financial indicator (*e.g.* determination of the relevant net profit indicator in case of a transactional net margin method).

Step 7:   Identification of potential comparables: determining the key characteristics to be met by any uncontrolled transaction in order to be regarded as potentially comparable, based on the relevant factors identified in Step 3 and in accordance with the comparability factors set forth at paragraphs 1.38-1.63.

Step 8: Determination of and making comparability adjustments where appropriate.

Step 9: Interpretation and use of data collected, determination of the arm's length remuneration.

3.5   In practice, this process is not a linear one. Steps 5 to 7 in particular might need to be carried out repeatedly until a satisfactory conclusion is reached, *i.e.* the most appropriate method is selected, especially because the examination of available sources of information may in some instances influence the selection of the transfer pricing method. For instance, in cases where it is not possible to find information on comparable transactions (step 7) and/or to make reasonably accurate adjustments (step 8), taxpayers might have to select another transfer pricing method and repeat the process starting from step 4.

3.6   See paragraph 3.82 for a discussion of a process to establish, monitor and review transfer prices.

A.2   *Broad-based analysis of the taxpayer's circumstances*

3.7   The "broad-based analysis" is an essential step in the comparability analysis. It can be defined as an analysis of the industry, competition, economic and regulatory factors and other elements that affect the taxpayer and its environment, but not yet within the context of looking at the specific transactions in question. This step helps understand the conditions in the taxpayer's controlled transaction as well as those in the uncontrolled transactions to be compared, in particular the economic circumstances of the transaction (see paragraphs 1.55-1.58).

A.3   *Review of the controlled transaction and choice of the tested party*

3.8   The review of the controlled transaction(s) under examination aims at identifying the relevant factors that will influence the selection of the tested party (where needed), the selection and application of the most appropriate transfer pricing method to the circumstances of the case, the financial indicator that will be tested (in the case of a transactional profit method), the selection of comparables and where relevant the determination of comparability adjustments.

A.3.1 Evaluation of a taxpayer's separate and combined transactions

3.9   Ideally, in order to arrive at the most precise approximation of arm's length conditions, the arm's length principle should be applied on a transaction-by-transaction basis. However, there are often situations where separate transactions are so closely linked or continuous that they cannot be evaluated adequately on a separate basis. Examples may include *1.* some long-term contracts for the supply of commodities or services, *2.* rights to use intangible property, and *3.* pricing a range of closely-linked products (*e.g.* in a product line) when it is impractical to determine pricing for each individual product or transaction. Another example would be the licensing of manufacturing know-how and the supply of vital components to an associated manufacturer; it may be more reasonable to assess the arm's length terms for the two items together rather than individually. Such transactions should be evaluated together using the most appropriate arm's length method. A further example would be the routing of a transaction through another associated enterprise; it may be more appropriate to consider the transaction of which the routing is a part in its entirety, rather than consider the individual transactions on a separate basis.

3.10   Another example where a taxpayer's transactions may be combined is related to portfolio approaches. A portfolio approach is a business strategy consisting of a taxpayer bundling certain transactions for the purpose of earning an appropriate return across the portfolio rather than necessarily on any single product within the portfolio. For instance, some products may be marketed by a taxpayer with a low profit or even at a loss, because they create a demand for other products and/or related services of the same taxpayer that are then sold or provided with high profits (*e.g.* equipment and captive aftermarket consumables, such as vending coffee machines and coffee capsules, or printers and cartridges). Similar approaches can be observed in various industries. Portfolio approaches are an example of a business strategy that may need to be taken into account in the comparability analysis and when examining the reliability of comparables. See paragraphs 1.59-1.63 on business strategies. However, as discussed in paragraphs 1.70-1.72, these considerations will not explain continued overall losses or poor performance over time. Moreover, in order to be acceptable, portfolio approaches must be reasonably targeted as they should not be used to apply a transfer pricing method at the taxpayer's company-wide level in those cases where different transactions have different economic logic and should be segmented. See paragraphs 2.78-2.79. Finally, the above comments should not be misread as implying that it would be acceptable for one entity within an MNE group to have a below arm's length return in order to provide benefits to another entity of the MNE group, see in particular paragraph 1.71.

3.11   While some separately contracted transactions between associated enterprises may need to be evaluated together in order to determine whether the conditions are arm's length, other transactions contracted between such enterprises as a package may need to be evaluated separately. An MNE may package as a single transaction and establish a single price for a number of benefits such as licences for patents, know-how, and trademarks, the provision of technical and administrative services, and the lease of production facilities. This type of arrangement is often referred to as a package deal. Such comprehensive packages would be unlikely to include sales of goods, however, although the price charged for sales of goods may cover some accompanying services. In some cases, it may not be feasible to evaluate the package as a whole so that the elements of the package must be segregated. In such cases, after determining separate transfer pricing for the separate elements, the tax administration should nonetheless consider whether in total the transfer pricing for the entire package is arm's length.

3.12   Even in uncontrolled transactions, package deals may combine elements that are subject to different tax treatment under domestic law or an income tax convention. For example, royalty payments may be subject to withholding tax but lease payments may be subject to net taxation. In such circumstances, it may still be appropriate to determine the transfer pricing on a package basis, and the tax administration could then determine whether for other tax reasons it is necessary to allocate the price to the elements of the package. In making this determination, tax administrations should examine the package deal between associated enterprises in the same way that they would analyze similar deals between independent enterprises. Taxpayers should be prepared to show that the package deal reflects appropriate transfer pricing.

A.3.2   Intentional set-offs

3.13   An intentional set-off is one that associated enterprises incorporate knowingly into the terms of the controlled transactions. It occurs when one associated enterprise has provided a benefit to another associated enterprise within the group that is balanced to some degree by different benefits received from that enterprise in return. These enterprises may indicate that the benefit each has received should be set off against the benefit each has provided as full or part payment for those benefits so that only the net gain or loss (if any) on the transactions needs to be considered for purposes of assessing tax liabilities. For example, an enterprise may license another enterprise to use a patent in return for the provision of know-how in another connection and indicate that the transactions result in no profit or loss to either party. Such arrangements may sometimes be encountered between independent enterprises and should be assessed in accordance with the arm's length principle in order to quantify the value of the respective benefits presented as set-offs.

3.14   Intentional set-offs may vary in size and complexity. Such set-offs may range from a simple balance of two transactions (such as a favourable selling price for manufactured goods in return for a favourable purchase price for the raw material used in producing the goods) to an arrangement for a general settlement balancing all benefits accruing to both parties over a period. Independent enterprises would be very unlikely to consider the latter type of arrangement unless the benefits could be sufficiently accurately quantified and the contract is created in advance. Otherwise, independent enterprises normally would prefer to allow their receipts and disbursements to flow independently of each other, taking any profit or loss resulting from normal trading.

3.15   Recognition of intentional set-offs does not change the fundamental requirement that for tax purposes the transfer prices for controlled transactions must be consistent with the arm's length principle. It would be a good practice for taxpayers to disclose the existence of set-offs intentionally built into two or more transactions between associated enterprises and demonstrate (or acknowledge that they have relevant supporting information and have undertaken sufficient analysis to be able to show) that, after taking account of the set-offs, the conditions governing the transactions are consistent with the arm's length principle.

3.16   It may be necessary to evaluate the transactions separately to determine whether they each satisfy the arm's length principle. If the transactions are to be analysed together, care should be taken in selecting comparable transactions and regard had to the discussion at paragraphs 3.9-3.12. The terms of set-offs relating to international transactions between associated enterprises may not be fully consistent with those relating to purely domestic transactions between independent enterprises because of the differences in tax treatment of the set-off under different national tax systems or differences in the treatment of the payment under a bilateral tax treaty. For example, withholding tax would complicate a set-off of royalties against sales receipts.

3.17   A taxpayer may seek on examination a reduction in a transfer pricing adjustment based on an unintentional over-reporting of taxable income. Tax administrations in their discretion may or may not grant this request. Tax administrations may also consider such requests in the context of mutual agreement procedures and corresponding adjustments (see Chapter IV).

A.3.3   Choice of the tested party

3.18   When applying a cost plus, resale price or transactional net margin method as described in Chapter II, it is necessary to choose the party to the transaction for which a financial indicator (mark-up on costs, gross margin, or net profit indicator) is tested. The choice of the tested party should be consistent with the functional analysis of the transaction. As a general rule, the tested party is the one to which a transfer pricing method can be applied in the most reliable manner and for which the most reliable comparables can be found, *i.e.* it will most often be the one that has the less complex functional analysis.

3.19   This can be illustrated as follows. Assume that company A manufactures two types of products, P1 and P2, that it sells to company B, an associated enterprise in another country. Assume that A is found to manufacture P1 products using valuable, unique intangibles that belong to B and following technical specifications set by B. Assume that in this P1 transaction, A only performs simple functions and does not make any valuable, unique contribution in relation to the transaction. The tested party for this P1 transaction would most often be A. Assume now that A is also manufacturing P2 products for which it owns and uses valuable unique intangibles such as valuable patents and trademarks, and for which B acts as a distributor. Assume that in this P2 transaction, B only performs simple functions and does not make any valuable, unique contribution in relation to the transaction. The tested party for the P2 transaction would most often be B.

A.3.4   Information on the controlled transaction

3.20   In order to select and apply the most appropriate transfer pricing method to the circumstances of the case, information is needed on the comparability factors in relation to the controlled transaction under review and in particular on the functions, assets and risks of all the parties to the controlled transaction, including the foreign associated enterprise(s). Specifically, while one-sided methods (*e.g.* cost plus, resale price or transactional net margin method which are discussed in detail in Chapter II) only require examining a financial indicator or profit level indicator for one of the parties to the transaction (the "tested party" as discussed in paragraphs 3.18-3.19), some information on the comparability factors of the controlled transaction and in particular on the functional analysis of the non-tested party is also needed in order to appropriately characterise the controlled transaction and select the most appropriate transfer pricing method.

3.21   Where the most appropriate transfer pricing method in the circumstances of the case, determined following the guidance at paragraphs 2.1-2.11, is a transactional profit split, financial information on all the parties to the transaction, domestic and foreign, is needed. Given the two-sided nature of this method, the application of a transactional profit split necessitates particularly detailed information on the foreign associated enterprise party to the transaction. This includes information on the five comparability factors in order to appropriately characterise the relationship between the parties and demonstrate the appropriateness of the transactional profit split method, as well as financial information (the determination of the combined profits to be split and the splitting of the profits both rely on financial information pertaining to all the parties to the transaction, including the foreign associated enterprise). Accordingly, where the most appropriate transfer pricing method in the circumstances of the case is a transactional profit split, it would be reasonable to expect that taxpayers be ready to provide tax administrations with the necessary information on the foreign associated enterprise party to the transaction, including the financial data necessary to calculate the profit split.

3.22   Where the most appropriate transfer pricing method in the circumstances of the case, determined following the guidance at paragraphs 2.1-2.11, is a one-sided method, financial information on the tested party is needed in addition to the information referred to in paragraph 3.20 – irrespective of whether the tested party is a domestic or foreign entity. So if the most appropriate method is a cost plus, resale price or transactional net margin method and the tested party is the foreign entity, sufficient information is needed to be able to reliably apply the selected method to the foreign tested party and to enable a review by the tax administration of the country of the non-tested party of the application of the method to the foreign tested party. On the other hand, once a particular one-sided method is chosen as the most appropriate method and the tested party is the domestic taxpayer, the tax administration generally has no reason to further ask for financial data of the foreign associated enterprise.

3.23   As explained above, transfer pricing analysis necessitates some information to be available about foreign associated enterprises, the nature and extent of which depends especially on the transfer pricing method used. However, as noted at paragraph 5.11, gathering such information may present a taxpayer with difficulties that it does not encounter in producing its own information. These difficulties should be taken into account in developing rules and/or procedures on documentation.

A.4   Comparable uncontrolled transactions

A.4.1   In general

3.24   A comparable uncontrolled transaction is a transaction between two independent parties that is comparable to the controlled transaction under examination. It can be either a comparable transaction between one party to the controlled transaction and an independent party ("internal comparable") or between two independent enterprises, neither of which is a party to the controlled transaction ("external comparable").

3.25   Comparisons of a taxpayer's controlled transactions with other controlled transactions carried out by the same or another MNE group are irrelevant to the application of the arm's length principle and therefore should not be used by a tax administration as the basis for a transfer pricing adjustment or by a taxpayer to support its transfer pricing policy.

3.26   The presence of minority shareholders may be one factor leading to the outcomes of a taxpayer's controlled transactions being closer to arm's length, but it is not determinative in and of itself. The influence of minority shareholders depends on a number of factors, including whether the minority shareholder has a participation in the capital of the parent company or in the capital of a subsidiary, and whether it has and actually exercises some influence on the pricing of intra-group transactions.

A.4.2   Internal comparables

3.27   Step 4 of the typical process described at paragraph 3.4 is a review of existing internal comparables, if any. Internal comparables may have a more direct and closer relationship to the transaction under review than external comparables. The financial analysis may be easier and more reliable as it will presumably rely on identical accounting standards and practices for the internal comparable and for the controlled transaction. In addition, access to information on internal comparables may be both more complete and less costly.

3.28   On the other hand, internal comparables are not always more reliable and it is not the case that any transaction between a taxpayer and an independent party can be regarded as a reliable comparable for controlled transactions carried on by the same taxpayer. Internal comparables where they exist must satisfy the five comparability factors in the same way as external comparables, see paragraphs 1.38-1.63. Guidance on comparability adjustments also applies to internal comparables, see paragraphs 3.47-3.54. Assume for instance that a taxpayer manufactures a particular product, sells a significant volume thereof to its foreign associated retailer and a marginal volume of the same product to an independent party. In such a case, the difference in volumes is likely to materially affect the comparability of the two transactions. If it is not possible to make a reasonably accurate adjustment to eliminate the effects of such difference, the transaction between the taxpayer and its independent customer is unlikely to be a reliable comparable.

A.4.3   *External comparables and sources of information*

3.29   There are various sources of information that can be used to identify potential external comparables. This sub-section discusses particular issues that arise with respect to commercial databases, foreign comparables and information undisclosed to taxpayers. Additionally, whenever reliable internal comparables exist, it may be unnecessary to search for external ones, see paragraphs 3.27-3.28.

A.4.3.1   Databases

3.30   A common source of information is commercial databases, which have been developed by editors who compile accounts filed by companies with the relevant administrative bodies and present them in an electronic format suitable for searches and statistical analysis. They can be a practical and sometimes cost-effective way of identifying external comparables and may provide the most reliable source of information, depending on the facts and circumstances of the case.

3.31   A number of limitations to commercial databases are frequently identified. Because these commercial databases rely on publicly available information, they are not available in all countries, since not all countries have the same amount of publicly available information about their companies. Moreover, where they are available, they do not include the same type of information for all the companies operating in a given country because disclosure and filing requirements may differ depending on the legal form of the company and on whether or not it is listed. Care must be exercised with respect to whether and how these databases are used, given that they are compiled and presented for non-transfer pricing purposes. It is not always the case that commercial databases provide information that is detailed enough to support the chosen transfer pricing method. Not all databases include the same level of detail and can be used with similar assurance. Importantly, it is the experience in many countries that commercial databases are used to compare the results of companies rather than of transactions because third party transactional information is rarely available. See paragraph 3.37 for a discussion of the use of non-transactional third party data.

3.32   It may be unnecessary to use a commercial database if reliable information is available from other sources, *e.g.* internal comparables. Where they are used, commercial databases should be used in an objective manner and genuine attempts should be made to use the databases to identify reliable comparable information.

3.33   Use of commercial databases should not encourage quantity over quality. In practice, performing a comparability analysis using a commercial database alone may give rise to concerns about the reliability of the analysis, given the quality of the information relevant to assessing comparability that is typically obtainable from a database. To address these concerns, database searches may need to be refined with other publicly available information, depending on the facts and circumstances. Such a refinement of the database search with other sources of information is meant to promote quality over standardised approaches and is valid both for database searches made by taxpayers/practitioners and for those made by tax administrations. It should be understood in light of the discussion of the costs and compliance burden created for the taxpayer at paragraphs 3.80-3.83.

3.34   There are also proprietary databases that are developed and maintained by some advisory firms. In addition to the issues raised above for commercial databases that are more broadly commercialised, proprietary databases also raise a further concern with respect to their coverage of data if they are based on a more limited portion of the market than commercial databases. When a taxpayer has used a proprietary database to support its transfer prices, the tax administration may request access to the database to review the taxpayer's results, for obvious transparency reasons.

A.4.3.2   Foreign source or non-domestic comparables

3.35   Taxpayers do not always perform searches for comparables on a country-by-country basis, *e.g.* in cases where there are insufficient data available at the domestic level and/or in order to reduce compliance costs where several entities of an MNE group have comparable functional analyses. Non-domestic comparables should not be automatically rejected just because they are not domestic. A determination of whether non-domestic comparables are reliable has to be made on a case-by-case basis and by reference to the extent to which they satisfy the five comparability factors. Whether or not one regional search for comparables can be reliably used for several subsidiaries of an MNE group operating in a given region of the world depends on the particular circumstances in which each of those subsidiaries operates. See paragraphs 1.57-1.58 on market differences and multi-country analyses. Difficulties may also arise from differing accounting standards.

A.4.3.3 Information undisclosed to taxpayers

3.36 Tax administrators may have information available to them from examinations of other taxpayers or from other sources of information that may not be disclosed to the taxpayer. However, it would be unfair to apply a transfer pricing method on the basis of such data unless the tax administration was able, within the limits of its domestic confidentiality requirements, to disclose such data to the taxpayer so that there would be an adequate opportunity for the taxpayer to defend its own position and to safeguard effective judicial control by the courts.

A.4.4   Use of non-transactional third party data

3.37 The transactional focus of transfer pricing methods and the question of a possible aggregation of the taxpayer's controlled transactions are discussed at paragraphs 3.9-3.12. A different question is whether non-transactional third party data can provide reliable comparables for a taxpayer's controlled transactions (or set of transactions aggregated consistently with the guidance at paragraphs 3.9-3.12). In practice, available third party data are often aggregated data, at a company-wide or segment level, depending on the applicable accounting standards. Whether such non-transactional third party data can provide reliable comparables for the taxpayer's controlled transaction or set of transactions aggregated consistently with the guidance at paragraphs 3.9-3.12 depends in particular on whether the third party performs a range of materially different transactions. Where segmented data are available, they can provide better comparables than company-wide, non-segmented data, because of a more transactional focus, although it is recognised that segmented data can raise issues in relation to the allocation of expenses to various segments. Similarly, company-wide third party data may provide better comparables than third party segmented data in certain circumstances, such as where the activities reflected in the comparables correspond to the set of controlled transactions of the taxpayer.

A.4.5   Limitations in available comparables

3.38 The identification of potential comparables has to be made with the objective of finding the most reliable data, recognising that they will not always be perfect. For instance, independent transactions may be scarce in certain markets and industries. A pragmatic solution may need to be found, on a case-by-case basis, such as broadening the search and using information on uncontrolled transactions taking place in the same industry and a comparable geographical market, but performed by third parties that may have different business strategies, business models or other slightly different economic circumstances; information on uncontrolled transactions taking place in the same industry but in other geographical markets; or information on uncontrolled transactions taking place in the same geographical market but in other industries. The choice among these various options will depend on the facts and circumstances of the case, and in particular on the significance of the expected effects of comparability defects on the reliability of the analysis.

3.39   A transactional profit split method might in appropriate circumstances be considered without comparable data, *e.g.* where the absence of comparable data is due to the presence of valuable, unique intangibles contributed by each party to the transaction (see paragraph 2.109). However, even in cases where comparable data are scarce and imperfect, the selection of the most appropriate transfer pricing method should be consistent with the functional analysis of the parties, see paragraph 2.2.

A.5   *Selecting or rejecting potential comparables*

3.40   There are basically two ways in which the identification of potentially comparable third party transactions can be conducted.

3.41   The first one, which can be qualified as the "additive" approach, consists of the person making the search drawing up a list of third parties that are believed to carry out potentially comparable transactions. Information is then collected on transactions conducted by these third parties to confirm whether they are in effect acceptable comparables, based on the pre-determined comparability criteria. This approach arguably gives well-focused results – all the transactions retained in the analysis are carried out by well-known players in the taxpayer's market. As indicated above, in order to ensure a sufficient degree of objectivity it is important that the process followed be transparent, systematic and verifiable. The "additive" approach may be used as the sole approach where the person making the search has knowledge of a few third parties that are engaged in transactions that are comparable to the examined controlled transaction. It is worth noting that the "additive" approach presents similarities with the approach followed when identifying internal comparables. In practice, an "additive" approach may encompass both internal and external comparables.

3.42   The second possibility, the "deductive" approach, starts with a wide set of companies that operate in the same sector of activity, perform similar broad functions and do not present economic characteristics that are obviously different. The list is then refined using selection criteria and publicly available information (*e.g.* from databases, Internet sites, information on known competitors of the taxpayer). In practice, the "deductive" approach typically starts with a search on a database. It is therefore important to follow the guidance on internal comparables and on the sources of information on external comparables, see paragraphs 3.24-3.39. In addition, the "deductive" approach is not appropriate to all cases and all methods and the discussion in this section should not be interpreted as affecting the criteria for selecting a transfer pricing method set out in paragraphs 2.1-2.11.

3.43   In practice, both quantitative and qualitative criteria are used to include or reject potential comparables. Examples of qualitative criteria are found in product portfolios and business strategies. The most commonly observed quantitative criteria are:

- Size criteria in terms of Sales, Assets or Number of Employees. The size of the transaction in absolute value or in proportion to the activities of the parties might affect the relative competitive positions of the buyer and seller and therefore comparability.

- Intangible-related criteria such as ratio of Net Value of Intangibles/Total Net Assets Value, or ratio of Research and Development ("R&D")/Sales where available: they may be used for instance to exclude companies with valuable intangibles or significant R&D activities when the tested party does not use valuable intangible assets nor participate in significant R&D activities.

- Criteria related to the importance of export sales (Foreign Sales/Total Sales), where relevant.

- Criteria related to inventories in absolute or relative value, where relevant.

- Other criteria to exclude third parties that are in particular special situations such as start-up companies, bankrupted companies, etc. when such peculiar situations are obviously not appropriate comparisons.

The choice and application of selection criteria depends on the facts and circumstances of each particular case and the above list is neither limitative nor prescriptive.

3.44   One advantage of the "deductive" approach is that it is more reproducible and transparent than the "additive". It is also easier to verify because the review concentrates on the process and on the relevance of the selection criteria retained. On the other hand, it is acknowledged that the quality of the outcome of a "deductive" approach depends on the quality of the search tools on which it relies (*e.g.* quality of the database where a database is used and possibility to obtain detailed enough information). This can be a practical limitation in some countries where the reliability and usefulness of databases in comparability analyses are questionable.

3.45   It would not be appropriate to give systematic preference to one approach over the other because, depending on the circumstances of the case, there could be value in either the "additive" or the "deductive" approach, or in a combination of both. The "additive" and "deductive" approaches are often not used exclusively. In a typical "deductive" approach, in addition to searching public databases it is common to include third parties, for instance known competitors (or third parties that are known to carry out transactions potentially comparable to those of the taxpayer), which may otherwise not be found following a purely deductive approach, *e.g.* because they are classified under a different industry code. In such cases, the "additive" approach operates as a tool to refine a search that is based on a "deductive" approach.

3.46   The process followed to identify potential comparables is one of the most critical aspects of the comparability analysis and it should be transparent, systematic and verifiable. In particular, the choice of selection criteria has a significant influence on the outcome of the analysis and should reflect the most meaningful economic characteristics of the transactions compared. Complete elimination of subjective judgments from the selection of comparables would not be feasible, but much can be done to increase objectivity and ensure transparency in the application of subjective judgments. Ensuring transparency of the process may depend on the extent to which the criteria used to select potential comparables are able to be disclosed and the reasons for excluding some of the potential comparables are able to be explained. Increasing objectivity and ensuring transparency of the process may also depend on the extent to which the person reviewing the process (whether taxpayer or tax administration) has access to information regarding the process followed and to the same sources of data. Issues of documentation of the process of identifying comparables are discussed in Chapter V.

A.6 Comparability adjustments

3.47 The need to adjust comparables and the requirement for accuracy and reliability are pointed out in these Guidelines on several occasions, both for the general application of the arm's length principle and more specifically in the context of each method. As noted at paragraph 1.33, to be comparable means that none of the differences (if any) between the situations being compared could materially affect the condition being examined in the methodology or that reasonably accurate adjustments can be made to eliminate the effect of any such differences. Whether comparability adjustments should be performed (and if so, what adjustments should be performed) in a particular case is a matter of judgment that should be evaluated in light of the discussion of costs and compliance burden at Section C.

A.6.1 Different types of comparability adjustments

3.48 Examples of comparability adjustments include adjustments for accounting consistency designed to eliminate differences that may arise from differing accounting practices between the controlled and uncontrolled transactions; segmentation of financial data to eliminate significant non-comparable transactions; adjustments for differences in capital, functions, assets, risks.

3.49 An example of a working capital adjustment designed to reflect differing levels of accounts receivable, accounts payable and inventory is provided in the Annex to Chapter III. The fact that such adjustments are found in practice does not mean that they should be performed on a routine or mandatory basis. Rather, the improvement to comparability should be shown when proposing these types of adjustments (as for any type of adjustment). Further, a significantly different level of relative working capital between the controlled and uncontrolled parties may result in further investigation of the comparability characteristics of the potential comparable.

A.6.2 Purpose of comparability adjustments

3.50 Comparability adjustments should be considered if (and only if) they are expected to increase the reliability of the results. Relevant considerations in this regard include the materiality of the difference for which an adjustment is being considered, the quality of the data subject to adjustment, the purpose of the adjustment and the reliability of the approach used to make the adjustment.

3.51   It bears emphasis that comparability adjustments are only appropriate for differences that will have a material effect on the comparison. Some differences will invariably exist between the taxpayer's controlled transactions and the third party comparables. A comparison may be appropriate despite an unadjusted difference, provided that the difference does not have a material effect on the reliability of the comparison. On the other hand, the need to perform numerous or substantial adjustments to key comparability factors may indicate that the third party transactions are in fact not sufficiently comparable.

3.52   It is not always the case that adjustments are warranted. For instance, an adjustment for differences in accounts receivable may not be particularly useful if major differences in accounting standards were also present that could not be resolved. Likewise, sophisticated adjustments are sometimes applied to create the false impression that the outcome of the comparables search is "scientific", reliable and accurate.

A.6.3   Reliability of the adjustment performed

3.53   It is not appropriate to view some comparability adjustments, such as for differences in levels of working capital, as "routine" and uncontroversial, and to view certain other adjustments, such as for country risk, as more subjective and therefore subject to additional requirements of proof and reliability. The only adjustments that should be made are those that are expected to improve comparability.

A.6.4   Documenting and testing comparability adjustments

3.54   Ensuring the needed level of transparency of comparability adjustments may depend upon the availability of an explanation of any adjustments performed, the reasons for the adjustments being considered appropriate, how they were calculated, how they changed the results for each comparable and how the adjustment improves comparability. Issues regarding documentation of comparability adjustments are discussed in Chapter V.

A.7   Arm's length range

A.7.1   In general

3.55   In some cases it will be possible to apply the arm's length principle to arrive at a single figure (e.g. price or margin) that is the most reliable to establish whether the conditions of a transaction are arm's length.

However, because transfer pricing is not an exact science, there will also be many occasions when the application of the most appropriate method or methods produces a range of figures all of which are relatively equally reliable. In these cases, differences in the figures that comprise the range may be caused by the fact that in general the application of the arm's length principle only produces an approximation of conditions that would have been established between independent enterprises. It is also possible that the different points in a range represent the fact that independent enterprises engaged in comparable transactions under comparable circumstances may not establish exactly the same price for the transaction.

3.56   In some cases, not all comparable transactions examined will have a relatively equal degree of comparability. Where it is possible to determine that some uncontrolled transactions have a lesser degree of comparability than others, they should be eliminated.

3.57   It may also be the case that, while every effort has been made to exclude points that have a lesser degree of comparability, what is arrived at is a range of figures for which it is considered, given the process used for selecting comparables and limitations in information available on comparables, that some comparability defects remain that cannot be identified and/or quantified, and are therefore not adjusted. In such cases, if the range includes a sizeable number of observations, statistical tools that take account of central tendency to narrow the range (*e.g.* the interquartile range or other percentiles) might help to enhance the reliability of the analysis.

3.58   A range of figures may also result when more than one method is applied to evaluate a controlled transaction. For example, two methods that attain similar degrees of comparability may be used to evaluate the arm's length character of a controlled transaction. Each method may produce an outcome or a range of outcomes that differs from the other because of differences in the nature of the methods and the data, relevant to the application of a particular method, used. Nevertheless, each separate range potentially could be used to define an acceptable range of arm's length figures. Data from these ranges could be useful for purposes of more accurately defining the arm's length range, for example when the ranges overlap, or for reconsidering the accuracy of the methods used when the ranges do not overlap. No general rule may be stated with respect to the use of ranges derived from the application of multiple methods because the conclusions to be drawn from their use will depend on the relative reliability of the methods employed to determine the ranges and the quality of the information used in applying the different methods.

3.59   Where the application of the most appropriate method (or, in relevant circumstances, of more than one method, see paragraph 2.11), produces a range of figures, a substantial deviation among points in that range may indicate that the data used in establishing some of the points may not be as reliable as the data used to establish the other points in the range or that the deviation may result from features of the comparable data that require adjustments. In such cases, further analysis of those points may be necessary to evaluate their suitability for inclusion in any arm's length range.

A.7.2   Selecting the most appropriate point in the range

3.60   If the relevant condition of the controlled transaction (*e.g.* price or margin) is within the arm's length range, no adjustment should be made.

3.61   If the relevant condition of the controlled transaction (*e.g.* price or margin) falls outside the arm's length range asserted by the tax administration, the taxpayer should have the opportunity to present arguments that the conditions of the controlled transaction satisfy the arm's length principle, and that the result falls within the arm's length range (*i.e.* that the arm's length range is different from the one asserted by the tax administration). If the taxpayer is unable to establish this fact, the tax administration must determine the point within the arm's length range to which it will adjust the condition of the controlled transaction.

3.62   In determining this point, where the range comprises results of relatively equal and high reliability, it could be argued that any point in the range satisfies the arm's length principle. Where comparability defects remain as discussed at paragraph 3.57, it may be appropriate to use measures of central tendency to determine this point (for instance the median, the mean or weighted averages, etc., depending on the specific characteristics of the data set), in order to minimise the risk of error due to unknown or unquantifiable remaining comparability defects.

A.7.3   Extreme results: comparability considerations

3.63   Extreme results might consist of losses or unusually high profits. Extreme results can affect the financial indicators that are looked at in the chosen method (*e.g.* the gross margin when applying a resale price, or a net profit indicator when applying a transactional net margin method). They can also affect other items, *e.g.* exceptional items which are below the line but nonetheless may reflect exceptional circumstances. Where one or more of the potential comparables have extreme results, further examination would be needed to understand the reasons for such extreme results. The reason might be a defect in comparability, or exceptional conditions met by an otherwise comparable third party. An extreme result may be excluded on the basis that a previously overlooked significant comparability defect has been brought to light, not on the sole basis that the results arising from the proposed "comparable" merely appear to be very different from the results observed in other proposed "comparables".

3.64   An independent enterprise would not continue loss-generating activities unless it had reasonable expectations of future profits. See paragraphs 1.70 to 1.72. Simple or low risk functions in particular are not expected to generate losses for a long period of time. This does not mean however that loss-making transactions can never be comparable. In general, all relevant information should be used and there should not be any overriding rule on the inclusion or exclusion of loss-making comparables. Indeed, it is the facts and circumstances surrounding the company in question that should determine its status as a comparable, not its financial result.

3.65   Generally speaking, a loss-making uncontrolled transaction should trigger further investigation in order to establish whether or not it can be a comparable. Circumstances in which loss-making transactions/ enterprises should be excluded from the list of comparables include cases where losses do not reflect normal business conditions, and where the losses incurred by third parties reflect a level of risks that is not comparable to the one assumed by the taxpayer in its controlled transactions. Loss-making comparables that satisfy the comparability analysis should not however be rejected on the sole basis that they suffer losses.

3.66   A similar investigation should be undertaken for potential comparables returning abnormally large profits relative to other potential comparables.

B. Timing issues in comparability

3.67   There are timing issues in comparability with respect to the time of origin, collection and production of information on comparability factors and comparable uncontrolled transactions that are used in a comparability analysis. See paragraphs 5.3, 5.4, 5.5, 5.9 and 5.14 of Chapter V for indications with respect to timing issues in the context of transfer pricing documentation requirements.

B.1   Timing of origin

3.68   In principle, information relating to the conditions of comparable uncontrolled transactions undertaken or carried out during the same period of time as the controlled transaction ("contemporaneous uncontrolled transactions") is expected to be the most reliable information to use in a comparability analysis, because it reflects how independent parties have behaved in an economic environment that is the same as the economic environment of the taxpayer's controlled transaction. Availability of information on contemporaneous uncontrolled transactions may however be limited in practice, depending on the timing of collection.

B.2   Timing of collection

3.69   In some cases, taxpayers establish transfer pricing documentation to demonstrate that they have made reasonable efforts to comply with the arm's length principle at the time their intra-group transactions were undertaken, *i.e.* on an *ex ante* basis (hereinafter "the arm's length price-setting" approach), based on information that was reasonably available to them at that point. Such information includes not only information on comparable transactions from previous years, but also information on economic and market changes that may have occurred between those previous years and the year of the controlled transaction. In effect, independent parties in comparable circumstances would not base their pricing decision on historical data alone.

3.70   In other instances, taxpayers might test the actual outcome of their controlled transactions to demonstrate that the conditions of these transactions were consistent with the arm's length principle, *i.e.* on an *ex post* basis (hereinafter "the arm's length outcome-testing" approach). Such test typically takes place as part of the process for establishing the tax return at year-end.

3.71   Both the arm's length price-setting and the arm's length outcome-testing approaches, as well as combinations of these two approaches, are found among OECD member countries. The issue of double taxation may arise where a controlled transaction takes place between two associated enterprises where different approaches have been applied and lead to different outcomes, for instance because of a discrepancy between market expectations taken into account in the arm's length price-setting approach and actual outcomes observed in the arm's length outcome-testing approach. See paragraphs 4.38 and 4.39. Competent authorities are encouraged to use their best efforts to resolve any double taxation issues that may arise from different country approaches to year-end adjustments and that may be submitted to them under a mutual agreement procedure (Article 25 of the OECD Model Tax Convention).

B.3   Valuation highly uncertain at the outset and unpredictable events

3.72   The question arises whether and if so how to take account in the transfer pricing analysis of future events that were unpredictable at the time of the testing of a controlled transaction, in particular where valuation at that time was highly uncertain. The question should be resolved, both by taxpayers and tax administrations, by reference to what independent enterprises would have done in comparable circumstances to take account of the valuation uncertainty in the pricing of the transaction.

3.73   The reasoning that is found at paragraphs 6.28-6.32 and in Annex to Chapter VI "Examples to illustrate the Transfer Pricing Guidelines on intangible property and highly uncertain valuation" for transactions involving intangibles for which valuation is uncertain applies by analogy to other types of transactions with valuation uncertainties. The main question is to determine whether the valuation was sufficiently uncertain at the outset that the parties at arm's length would have required a price adjustment mechanism, or whether the change in value was so fundamental a development that it would have led to a renegotiation of the transaction. Where this is the case, the tax administration would be justified in determining the arm's length price for the transaction on the basis of the adjustment clause or re-negotiation that would be provided at arm's length in a comparable uncontrolled transaction. In other circumstances, where there is no reason to consider that the valuation was sufficiently uncertain at the outset that the parties would have required a price adjustment clause or would have renegotiated the terms of the agreement, there is no reason for tax administrations to make such an adjustment as it would represent an inappropriate use of hindsight. The mere existence of uncertainty should not require an *ex post* adjustment without a consideration of what independent enterprises would have done or agreed between them.

B.4   Data from years following the year of the transaction

3.74   Data from years following the year of the transaction may also be relevant to the analysis of transfer prices, but care must be taken to avoid the use of hindsight. For example, data from later years may be useful in comparing product life cycles of controlled and uncontrolled transactions for the purpose of determining whether the uncontrolled transaction is an appropriate comparable to use in applying a particular method. Subsequent conduct by the parties will also be relevant in ascertaining the actual terms and conditions that operate between the parties.

B.5   Multiple year data

3.75   In practice, examining multiple year data is often useful in a comparability analysis, but it is not a systematic requirement. Multiple year data should be used where they add value to the transfer pricing analysis. It would not be appropriate to set prescriptive guidance as to the number of years to be covered by multiple year analyses.

3.76   In order to obtain a complete understanding of the facts and circumstances surrounding the controlled transaction, it generally might be useful to examine data from both the year under examination and prior years. The analysis of such information might disclose facts that may have influenced (or should have influenced) the determination of the transfer price. For example, the use of data from past years will show whether a taxpayer's reported loss on a transaction is part of a history of losses on similar transactions, the result of particular economic conditions in a prior year that increased costs in the subsequent year, or a reflection of the fact that a product is at the end of its life cycle. Such an analysis may be particularly useful where a transactional profit method is applied. See paragraph 1.72 on the usefulness of multiple year data in examining loss situations. Multiple year data can also improve the understanding of long term arrangements.

3.77   Multiple year data will also be useful in providing information about the relevant business and product life cycles of the comparables. Differences in business or product life cycles may have a material effect on transfer pricing conditions that needs to be assessed in determining comparability. The data from earlier years may show whether the independent enterprise engaged in a comparable transaction was affected by comparable economic conditions in a comparable manner, or whether different conditions in an earlier year materially affected its price or profit so that it should not be used as a comparable.

3.78   Multiple year data can also improve the process of selecting third party comparables *e.g.* by identifying results that may indicate a significant variance from the underlying comparability characteristics of the controlled transaction being reviewed, in some cases leading to the rejection of the comparable, or to detect anomalies in third party information.

3.79   The use of multiple year data does not necessarily imply the use of multiple year averages. Multiple year data and averages can however be used in some circumstances to improve reliability of the range. See paragraphs 3.57-3.62 for a discussion of statistical tools.

C. Compliance issues

3.80   One question that arises when putting the need for comparability analyses into perspective is the extent of the burden and costs that should be borne by a taxpayer to identify possible comparables and obtain detailed information thereon. It is recognised that the cost of information can be a real concern, especially for small to medium sized operations, but also for those MNEs that deal with a very large number of controlled transactions in many countries. Paragraphs 4.28, 5.6, 5.7 and 5.28 contain explicit recognition of the need for a reasonable application of the requirement to document comparability.

3.81   When undertaking a comparability analysis, there is no requirement for an exhaustive search of all possible relevant sources of information. Taxpayers and tax administrations should exercise judgment to determine whether particular comparables are reliable.

3.82   It is a good practice for taxpayers to set up a process to establish, monitor and review their transfer prices, taking into account the size of the transactions, their complexity, level of risk involved, and whether they are performed in a stable or changing environment. Such a practical approach would conform to a pragmatic risk assessment strategy or prudent business management principle. In practice, this means that it may be reasonable for a taxpayer to devote relatively less effort to finding information on comparables supporting less significant or less material controlled transactions. For simple transactions that are carried out in a stable environment and the characteristics of which remain the same or similar, a detailed comparability (including functional) analysis may not be needed every year.

3.83   Small to medium sized enterprises are entering into the area of transfer pricing and the number of cross-border transactions is ever increasing. Although the arm's length principle applies equally to small and medium sized enterprises and transactions, pragmatic solutions may be appropriate in order to make it possible to find a reasonable response to each transfer pricing case.

Chapter IV

Administrative Approaches to Avoiding and Resolving Transfer Pricing Disputes

A. Introduction

4.1   This chapter examines various administrative procedures that could be applied to minimise transfer pricing disputes and to help resolve them when they do arise between taxpayers and their tax administrations, and between different tax administrations. Such disputes may arise even though the guidance in these Guidelines is followed in a conscientious effort to apply the arm's length principle. It is possible that taxpayers and tax administrations may reach differing determinations of the arm's length conditions for the controlled transactions under examination given the complexity of some transfer pricing issues and the difficulties in interpreting and evaluating the circumstances of individual cases.

4.2   Where two or more tax administrations take different positions in determining arm's length conditions, double taxation may occur. Double taxation means the inclusion of the same income in the tax base by more than one tax administration, when either the income is in the hands of different taxpayers (economic double taxation, for associated enterprises) or the income is in the hands of the same juridical entity (juridical double taxation, for permanent establishments). Double taxation is undesirable and should be eliminated whenever possible, because it constitutes a potential barrier to the development of international trade and investment flows. The double inclusion of income in the tax base of more than one jurisdiction does not always mean that the income will actually be taxed twice.

4.3   This chapter discusses several administrative approaches to resolving disputes caused by transfer pricing adjustments and for avoiding double taxation. Section B discusses transfer pricing compliance practices by tax administrations, in particular examination practices, the burden of proof, and penalties. Section C discusses corresponding adjustments

(Paragraph 2 of Article 9 of the OECD Model Tax Convention) and the mutual agreement procedure (Article 25). Section D describes the use of simultaneous tax examinations by two (or more) tax administrations to expedite the identification, processing, and resolution of transfer pricing issues (and other international tax issues). Sections E and F describe some possibilities for minimising transfer pricing disputes between taxpayers and their tax administrations. Section E addresses the possibility of developing safe harbours for certain taxpayers, and Section F deals with advance pricing arrangements, which address the possibility of determining in advance a transfer pricing methodology or conditions for the taxpayer to apply to specified controlled transactions. Section G considers briefly the use of arbitration procedures to resolve transfer pricing disputes between countries.

B. Transfer pricing compliance practices

4.4   Tax compliance practices are developed and implemented in each member country according to its own domestic legislation and administrative procedures. Many domestic tax compliance practices have three main elements: a) to reduce opportunities for non-compliance (*e.g.* through withholding taxes and information reporting); b) to provide positive assistance for compliance (*e.g.* through education and published guidance); and, c) to provide disincentives for non-compliance. As a matter of domestic sovereignty and to accommodate the particularities of widely varying tax systems, tax compliance practices remain within the province of each country. Nevertheless a fair application of the arm's length principle requires clear procedural rules to ensure adequate protection of the taxpayer and to make sure that tax revenue is not shifted to countries with overly harsh procedural rules. However, when a taxpayer under examination in one country is a member of an MNE group, it is possible that the domestic tax compliance practices in a country examining a taxpayer will have consequences in other tax jurisdictions. This may be particularly the case when cross-border transfer pricing issues are involved, because the transfer pricing has implications for the tax collected in the tax jurisdictions of the associated enterprises involved in the controlled transaction. If the same transfer pricing is not accepted in the other tax jurisdictions, the MNE group may be subject to double taxation as explained in paragraph 4.2. Thus, tax administrations should be conscious of the arm's length principle when applying their domestic compliance practices and the potential implications of their transfer pricing compliance rules for other tax jurisdictions, and seek to facilitate both the equitable allocation of taxes between jurisdictions and the prevention of double taxation for taxpayers.

4.5   This section describes three aspects of transfer pricing compliance that should receive special consideration to help tax jurisdictions administer their transfer pricing rules in a manner that is fair to taxpayers and other jurisdictions. While other tax law compliance practices are in common use in OECD member countries – for example, the use of litigation and evidentiary sanctions where information may be sought by a tax administration but is not provided – these three aspects will often impact on how tax administrations in other jurisdictions approach the mutual agreement procedure process and determine their administrative response to ensuring compliance with their own transfer pricing rules. The three aspects are: examination practices, the burden of proof, and penalty systems. The evaluation of these three aspects will necessarily differ depending on the characteristics of the tax system involved, and so it is not possible to describe a uniform set of principles or issues that will be relevant in all cases. Instead, this section seeks to provide general guidance on the types of problems that may arise and reasonable approaches for achieving a balance of the interests of the taxpayers and tax administrations involved in a transfer pricing inquiry.

B.1   *Examination practices*

4.6   Examination practices vary widely among OECD member countries. Differences in procedures may be prompted by such factors as the system and the structure of the tax administration, the geographic size and population of the country, the level of domestic and international trade, and cultural and historical influences.

4.7   Transfer pricing cases can present special challenges to the normal audit or examination practices, both for the tax administration and for the taxpayer. Transfer pricing cases are fact-intensive and may involve difficult evaluations of comparability, markets, and financial or other industry information. Consequently, a number of tax administrations have examiners who specialise in transfer pricing, and transfer pricing examinations themselves may take longer than other examinations and follow separate procedures.

4.8   Because transfer pricing is not an exact science, it will not always be possible to determine the single correct arm's length price; rather, as Chapter III recognises, the correct price may have to be estimated within a range of acceptable figures. Also, the choice of methodology for establishing arm's length transfer pricing will not often be unambiguously clear. Taxpayers may experience particular difficulties when the tax administration proposes to use a methodology, for example a transactional profit method, that is not the same as that used by the taxpayer.

4.9   In a difficult transfer pricing case, because of the complexity of the facts to be evaluated, even the best-intentioned taxpayer can make an honest mistake. Moreover, even the best-intentioned tax examiner may draw the wrong conclusion from the facts. Tax administrations are encouraged to take this observation into account in conducting their transfer pricing examinations. This involves two implications. First, tax examiners are encouraged to be flexible in their approach and not demand from taxpayers in their transfer pricing a precision that is unrealistic under all the facts and circumstances. Second, tax examiners are encouraged to take into account the taxpayer's commercial judgment about the application of the arm's length principle, so that the transfer pricing analysis is tied to business realities. Therefore, tax examiners should undertake to begin their analyses of transfer pricing from the perspective of the method that the taxpayer has chosen in setting its prices. The guidance provided in Chapter II, Part I dealing with the selection of the most appropriate transfer pricing method also may assist in this regard.

4.10   A tax administration should keep in mind in allocating its audit resources the taxpayer's process of setting prices, for example whether the MNE group operates on a profit centre basis. See paragraph 1.5.

B.2   *Burden of proof*

4.11   Like examination practices, the burden of proof rules for tax cases also differ among OECD member countries. In most jurisdictions, the tax administration bears the burden of proof both in its own internal dealings with the taxpayer (*e.g.* assessment and appeals) and in litigation. In some of these countries, the burden of proof can be reversed, allowing the tax administration to estimate taxable income, if the taxpayer is found not to have acted in good faith, for example, by not cooperating or complying with reasonable documentation requests or by filing false or misleading returns. In other countries, the burden of proof is on the taxpayer. In this respect, however, the conclusions of paragraphs 4.16 and 4.17 should be noted.

4.12   The implication for the behaviour of the tax administration and the taxpayer of the rules governing burden of proof should be taken into account. For example, where as a matter of domestic law the burden of proof is on the tax administration, the taxpayer may not have any legal obligation to prove the correctness of its transfer pricing unless the tax administration makes a *prima facie* showing that the pricing is inconsistent with the arm's length principle. Even in such a case, of course, the tax administration might still reasonably oblige the taxpayer to produce its records that would enable the tax administration to undertake its examination. In some countries, taxpayers have a duty to cooperate with the tax administration imposed on them by law. In the event that a taxpayer fails to cooperate, the tax administration may be given the authority to estimate the taxpayer's income and to assume relevant facts based on experience. In these cases, tax administrations should not seek to impose such a high level of cooperation that would make it too difficult for reasonable taxpayers to comply.

4.13   In jurisdictions where the burden of proof is on the taxpayer, tax administrations are generally not at liberty to raise assessments against taxpayers which are not soundly based in law. A tax administration in an OECD member country, for example, could not raise an assessment based on a taxable income calculated as a fixed percentage of turnover and simply ignore the arm's length principle. In the context of litigation in countries where the burden of proof is on the taxpayer, the burden of proof is often seen as a shifting burden. Where the taxpayer presents to a court a reasonable argument and evidence to suggest that its transfer pricing was arm's length, the burden of proof may legally or *de facto* shift to the tax administration to counter the taxpayer's position and to present argument and evidence as to why the taxpayer's transfer pricing was not arm's length and why the assessment is correct. On the other hand, where a taxpayer makes little effort to show that its transfer pricing was arm's length, the burden imposed on the taxpayer would not be satisfied where a tax administration raised an assessment which was soundly based in law.

4.14   When transfer pricing issues are present, the divergent rules on burden of proof among OECD member countries will present serious problems if the strict legal rights implied by those rules are used as a guide for appropriate behaviour. For example, consider the case where the controlled transaction under examination involves one jurisdiction in which the burden of proof is on the taxpayer and a second jurisdiction in which the burden of proof is on the tax administration. If the burden of proof is guiding behaviour, the tax administration in the first jurisdiction might make an unsubstantiated assertion about the transfer pricing, which the taxpayer might accept, and the tax administration in the second jurisdiction would have the burden of disproving the pricing. It could be that neither the taxpayer in the second jurisdiction nor the tax administration in the first jurisdiction would be making efforts to establish an acceptable arm's length price. This type of behaviour would set the stage for significant conflict as well as double taxation.

4.15   Consider the same facts as in the example in the preceding paragraph. If the burden of proof is again guiding behaviour, a taxpayer in the first jurisdiction being a subsidiary of a taxpayer in the second jurisdiction (notwithstanding the burden of proof and these Guidelines), may be unable or unwilling to show that its transfer prices are arm's length. The tax administration in the first jurisdiction after examination makes an adjustment in good faith based on the information available to it. The parent company in the second jurisdiction is not obliged to provide to its tax administration any information to show that the transfer pricing was arm's length as the burden of proof rests with the tax administration. This will make it difficult for the two tax administrations to reach agreement in competent authority proceedings.

4.16   In practice, neither countries nor taxpayers should misuse the burden of proof in the manner described above. Because of the difficulties with transfer pricing analyses, it would be appropriate for both taxpayers and tax administrations to take special care and to use restraint in relying on the burden of proof in the course of the examination of a transfer pricing case. More particularly, as a matter of good practice, the burden of proof should not be misused by tax administrations or taxpayers as a justification for making groundless or unverifiable assertions about transfer pricing. A tax administration should be prepared to make a good faith showing that its determination of transfer pricing is consistent with the arm's length principle even where the burden of proof is on the taxpayer, and taxpayers similarly should be prepared to make a good faith showing that their transfer pricing is consistent with the arm's length principle regardless of where the burden of proof lies.

4.17   The Commentary on paragraph 2 of Article 9 of the OECD Model Tax Convention makes clear that the State from which a corresponding adjustment is requested should comply with the request only if that State "considers that the figure of adjusted profits correctly reflects what the profits would have been if the transactions had been at arm's length". This means that in competent authority proceedings the State that has proposed the primary adjustment bears the burden of demonstrating to the other State that the adjustment "is justified both in principle and as regards the amount." Both competent authorities are expected to take a cooperative approach in resolving mutual agreement cases.

B.3   Penalties

4.18   Penalties are most often directed toward providing disincentives for non-compliance, where the compliance at issue may relate to procedural requirements such as providing necessary information or filing returns, or to the substantive determination of tax liability. Penalties are generally designed to make tax underpayments and other types of non-compliance more costly than compliance. The Committee on Fiscal Affairs has recognised that promoting compliance should be the primary objective of civil tax penalties. OECD Report *Taxpayers' Rights and Obligations* (1990).

If a mutual agreement between two countries results in a withdrawal or reduction of an adjustment, it is important that there exist possibilities to cancel or mitigate a penalty imposed by the tax administrations.

4.19   Care should be taken in comparing different national penalty practices and policies with one another. First, any comparison needs to take into account that there may be different names used in the various countries for penalties that accomplish the same purposes. Second, the overall compliance measures of an OECD member country should be taken into account. National tax compliance practices depend, as indicated above, on the overall tax system in the country, and they are designed on the basis of domestic need and balance, such as the choice between the use of taxation measures that remove or limit opportunities for noncompliance (*e.g.* imposing a duty on taxpayers to cooperate with the tax administration or reversing the burden of proof in situations where a taxpayer is found not to have acted in good faith) and the use of monetary deterrents (*e.g.* additional tax imposed as a consequence of underpayments of tax in addition to the amount of the underpayment). The nature of tax penalties may also be affected by the judicial system of a country. Most countries do not apply no-fault penalties; in some countries, for example, the imposition of a no-fault penalty would be against the underlying principles of their legal system.

4.20   There are a number of different types of penalties that tax jurisdictions have adopted. Penalties can involve either civil or criminal sanctions – criminal penalties are virtually always reserved for cases of very significant fraud, and they usually carry a very high burden of proof for the party asserting the penalty (*i.e.* the tax administration). Criminal penalties are not the principal means to promote compliance in any of the OECD member countries. Civil (or administrative) penalties are more common, and they typically involve a monetary sanction (although as discussed above there may be a non-monetary sanction such as a shifting of the burden of proof when, *e.g.* procedural requirements are not met or the taxpayer is uncooperative and an effective penalty results from a discretionary adjustment).

4.21   Some civil penalties are directed towards procedural compliance, such as timely filing of returns and information reporting. The amount of such penalties is often small and based on a fixed amount that may be assessed for each day in which, *e.g.* the failure to file continues. The more significant civil penalties are those directed at the understatement of tax liability.

4.22   Although some countries may refer to a "penalty", the same or similar imposition by another country may be classified as "interest". Some countries'' "penalty" regimes may therefore include an "additional tax", or "interest", for understatements which result in late payments of tax beyond the due date. This is often designed to ensure the revenue recovers at least the real time value of money (taxes) lost.

4.23   Civil monetary penalties for tax understatement are frequently triggered by one or more of the following: an understatement of tax liability exceeding a threshold amount, negligence of the taxpayer, or wilful intent to evade tax (and also fraud, although fraud can trigger much more serious criminal penalties). Many OECD member countries impose civil monetary penalties for negligence or wilful intent, while only a few countries penalise "no-fault" understatements of tax liability.

4.24   It is difficult to evaluate in the abstract whether the amount of a civil monetary penalty is excessive. Among OECD member countries, civil monetary penalties for tax understatement are frequently calculated as a percentage of the tax understatement, where the percentage most often ranges from 10 percent to 200 percent. In most OECD member countries, the rate of the penalty increases as the conditions for imposing the penalty increase. For instance, the higher rate penalties often can be imposed only by showing a high degree of taxpayer culpability, such as a wilful intent to evade. "No-fault" penalties, where used, tend to be at lower rates than those triggered by taxpayer culpability (see paragraph 4.28).

4.25   Improved compliance in the transfer pricing area is of some concern to OECD member countries and the appropriate use of penalties may play a role in addressing this concern. However, owing to the nature of transfer pricing problems, care should be taken to ensure that the administration of a penalty system as applied in such cases is fair and not unduly onerous for taxpayers.

4.26   Because cross-border transfer pricing issues implicate the tax base of two jurisdictions, an overly harsh penalty system in one jurisdiction may give taxpayers an incentive to overstate taxable income in that jurisdiction contrary to Article 9. If this happens, the penalty system fails in its primary objective to promote compliance and instead leads to non-compliance of a different sort – non-compliance with the arm's length principle and under-reporting in the other jurisdiction. Each OECD member country should ensure that its transfer pricing compliance practices are not enforced in a manner inconsistent with the objectives of the OECD Model Tax Convention, avoiding the distortions noted above.

4.27   It is generally regarded by OECD member countries that the fairness of the penalty system should be considered by reference to whether the penalties are proportionate to the offence. This would mean, for example, that the severity of a penalty would be balanced against the conditions under which it would be imposed, and that the harsher the penalty the more limited the conditions in which it would apply.

4.28   Since penalties are only one of many administrative and procedural aspects of a tax system, it is difficult to conclude whether a particular penalty is fair or not without considering the other aspects of the tax system. Nonetheless, OECD member countries agree that the following conclusions can be drawn regardless of the other aspects of the tax system in place in a particular country. First, imposition of a sizable "no-fault" penalty based on the mere existence of an understatement of a certain amount would be unduly harsh when it is attributable to good faith error rather than negligence or an actual intent to avoid tax. Second, it would be unfair to impose sizable penalties on taxpayers that made a reasonable effort in good faith to set the terms of their transactions with associated enterprises in a manner consistent with the arm's length principle. In particular, it would be inappropriate to impose a transfer pricing penalty on a taxpayer for failing to consider data to which it did not have access, or for failure to apply a transfer pricing method that would have required data that was not available to the taxpayer. Tax administrations are encouraged to take these observations into account in the implementation of their penalty provisions.

C. Corresponding adjustments and the mutual agreement procedure: Articles 9 and 25 of the OECD Model Tax Convention

C.1   The mutual agreement procedure

4.29   The mutual agreement procedure is a well-established means through which tax administrations consult to resolve disputes regarding the application of double tax conventions. This procedure, described and authorised by Article 25 of the OECD Model Tax Convention, can be used to eliminate double taxation that could arise from a transfer pricing adjustment.

4.30   Article 25 sets out three different areas where mutual agreement procedures are generally used. The first area includes instances of "taxation not in accordance with the provisions of the Convention" and is covered in paragraphs 1 and 2 of the Article. Procedures in this area are typically initiated by the taxpayer. The other two areas, which do not necessarily involve the taxpayer, are dealt with in paragraph 3 and involve questions of "interpretation or application of the Convention" and the elimination of double taxation in cases not otherwise provided for in the Convention. Paragraph 9 of the Commentary on Article 25 makes clear that Article 25 is intended to be used by competent authorities in resolving not only problems of juridical double taxation but also those of economic double taxation arising from transfer pricing adjustments made pursuant to paragraph 1 of Article 9.

4.31   Paragraph 5 of Article 25, which was incorporated in the OECD Model Tax Convention in 2008, provides that, in the cases where the competent authorities are unable to reach an agreement within two years of the initiation of a case under paragraph 1 of Article 25, the unresolved issues will, at the request of the person who presented the case, be solved through an arbitration process. This extension of the mutual agreement procedure ensures that where the competent authorities cannot reach an agreement on one or more issues that prevent the resolution of a case, a resolution of the case will still be possible by submitting those issues to arbitration. Where one or more issues have been submitted to arbitration in accordance with such a provision, and unless a person directly affected by the case does not accept the mutual agreement that implements the arbitration decision, that decision shall be binding on both States, the taxation of any person directly affected by the case will have to conform with the decision reached on the issues submitted to arbitration and the decisions reached in the arbitral process will be reflected in the mutual agreement that will be presented to these persons. Where a particular bilateral treaty does not contain an arbitration clause similar to the one of paragraph 5 of Article 25, the mutual agreement procedure does not compel competent authorities to reach an agreement and resolve their tax disputes and competent authorities are obliged only to endeavour to reach an agreement. The competent authorities may be unable to come to an agreement because of conflicting domestic laws or restrictions imposed by domestic law on the tax administration's power of compromise. Note however that even in the absence of an arbitration clause similar to the one of paragraph 5 of Article 25 in a particular bilateral treaty, the competent authorities of the contracting States may by mutual agreement establish a similar binding arbitration procedure (see paragraph 69 of the Commentary on Article 25 of the OECD Model Tax Convention). Note, too, that the member States of the European Communities signed on 23 July 1990 their multilateral Arbitration Convention, which entered into force on 1 January 1995, to resolve transfer pricing disputes among them.

C.2   *Corresponding adjustments: Paragraph 2 of Article 9*

4.32   To eliminate double taxation in transfer pricing cases, tax administrations may consider requests for corresponding adjustments as described in paragraph 2 of Article 9. A corresponding adjustment, which in practice may be undertaken as part of the mutual agreement procedure, can mitigate or eliminate double taxation in cases where one tax administration increases a company's taxable profits (*i.e.* makes a primary adjustment) as a result of applying the arm's length principle to transactions involving an associated enterprise in a second tax jurisdiction. The corresponding adjustment in such a case is a downward adjustment to the tax liability of that associated enterprise, made by the tax administration of the second jurisdiction, so that the allocation of profits between the two jurisdictions is consistent with the primary adjustment and no double taxation occurs. It is also possible that the first tax administration will agree to decrease (or eliminate) the primary adjustment as part of the consultative process with the second tax administration, in which case the corresponding adjustment would be smaller (or perhaps unnecessary). It should be noted that a corresponding adjustment is not intended to provide a benefit to the MNE group greater than would have been the case if the controlled transactions had been undertaken at arm's length conditions in the first instance.

4.33   Paragraph 2 of Article 9 specifically recommends that the competent authorities consult each other if necessary to determine corresponding adjustments. This demonstrates that the mutual agreement procedure of Article 25 may be used to consider corresponding adjustment requests. However, the overlap between the two Articles has caused OECD member countries to consider whether the mutual agreement procedure can be used to achieve corresponding adjustments where the bilateral income tax convention between two Contracting States does not include a provision comparable to paragraph 2 of Article 9. Paragraphs 11 and 12 of the Commentary on Article 25 of the OECD Model Tax Convention now expressly state the view of most OECD member countries that the mutual agreement procedure is considered to apply to transfer pricing adjustment cases even in the absence of a provision comparable to paragraph 2 of Article 9. Paragraph 12 also notes that those OECD member countries that do not agree with this view in practice apply domestic laws in most cases to alleviate double taxation of *bona fide* enterprises.

4.34   Under paragraph 2 of Article 9, a corresponding adjustment may be made by a contracting state either by recalculating the profits subject to tax for the associated enterprise in that country using the relevant revised price or by letting the calculation stand and giving the associated enterprise relief against its own tax paid in that State for the additional tax charged to the associated enterprise by the adjusting State as a consequence of the revised transfer price. The former method is by far the more common among OECD member countries.

4.35   In the absence of an arbitration decision arrived at pursuant to an arbitration procedure comparable to that provided for under paragraph 5 of Article 25 which provides for a corresponding adjustment, corresponding adjustments are not mandatory, mirroring the rule that tax administrations are not required to reach agreement under the mutual agreement procedure. Under paragraph 2 of Article 9, a tax administration should make a corresponding adjustment only insofar as it considers the primary adjustment to be justified both in principle and in amount. The non-mandatory nature of corresponding adjustments is necessary so that one tax administration is not forced to accept the consequences of an arbitrary or capricious adjustment by another State. It also is important to maintaining the fiscal sovereignty of each OECD member country.

4.36   Once a tax administration has agreed to make a corresponding adjustment it is necessary to establish whether the adjustment is to be attributed to the year in which the controlled transactions giving rise to the adjustment took place or to an alternative year, such as the year in which the primary adjustment is determined. This issue also often raises the question of a taxpayer's entitlement to interest on the overpayment of tax in the jurisdiction which has agreed to make the corresponding adjustment (discussed in paragraphs 4.63-4.65). The first approach is more appropriate because it achieves a matching of income and expenses and better reflects the economic situation as it would have been if the controlled transactions had been at arm's length. However, in cases involving lengthy delays between the year covered by the adjustment and the year of its acceptance of by the taxpayer or a final court decision, the tax administration should have the flexibility to agree to make corresponding adjustments for the year of acceptance of or decision on the primary adjustment. This approach would need to rely on domestic law for implementation. While not ordinarily preferred, it could be appropriate as an equitable measure in exceptional cases to facilitate implementation and to avoid time limit barriers.

4.37   Corresponding adjustments can be a very effective means of obtaining relief from double taxation resulting from transfer pricing adjustments. OECD member countries generally strive in good faith to reach agreement whenever the mutual agreement procedure is invoked. Through the mutual agreement procedure, tax administrations can address issues in a non-adversarial proceeding, often achieving a negotiated settlement in the interests of all parties. It also allows tax administrations to take into account other taxing rights issues, such as withholding taxes.

4.38   At least one OECD member country has a procedure that may reduce the need for primary adjustments by allowing the taxpayer to report a transfer price for tax purposes that is, in the taxpayer's opinion, an arm's length price for a controlled transaction, even though this price differs from the amount actually charged between the associated enterprises. This adjustment, sometimes known as a "compensating adjustment", would be made before the tax return is filed. Compensating adjustments may facilitate the reporting of taxable income by taxpayers in accordance with the arm's length principle, recognising that information about comparable uncontrolled transactions may not be available at the time associated enterprises establish the prices for their controlled transactions. Thus, for the purpose of lodging a correct tax return, a taxpayer would be permitted to make a compensating adjustment that would record the difference between the arm's length price and the actual price recorded in its books and records.

4.39   However, compensating adjustments are not recognised by most OECD member countries, on the grounds that the tax return should reflect the actual transactions. If compensating adjustments are permitted (or required) in the country of one associated enterprise but not permitted in the country of the other associated enterprise, double taxation may result because corresponding adjustment relief may not be available if no primary adjustment is made. The mutual agreement procedure is available to resolve difficulties presented by compensating adjustments, and competent authorities are encouraged to use their best efforts to resolve any double taxation which may arise from different country approaches to such year-end adjustments.

C.3   Concerns with the procedures

4.40   While corresponding adjustment and mutual agreement procedures have proved to be able to resolve most transfer pricing conflicts, serious concerns have been expressed by taxpayers. For example, because transfer pricing issues are so complex, taxpayers have expressed concerns that there may not be sufficient safeguards in the procedures against double taxation. These concerns are mainly addressed with the introduction in the 2008 update of the OECD Model Tax Convention of a new paragraph 5 to Article 25 which introduces a mechanism that allows taxpayers to request arbitration of unresolved issues that have prevented competent authorities from reaching a mutual agreement within two years. There is also in the Commentary on Article 25 a favourable discussion of the use of supplementary dispute resolution mechanisms in addition to arbitration, including mediation and the referral of factual disputes to third party experts.

4.41   Taxpayers have also expressed fears that their cases may be settled not on their individual merits but by reference to a balance of the results in other cases. An established good practice is that, in the resolution of mutual agreement cases, a competent authority should engage in discussions with other competent authorities in a principled, fair, and objective manner, with each case being decided on its own merits and not by reference to any balance of results in other cases. To the extent applicable, these Guidelines are an appropriate basis for the development of a principled approach. Similarly, there may be a fear of retaliation or offsetting adjustments by the country from which the corresponding adjustment has been requested. It is not the intention of tax administrations to take retaliatory action; the fears of taxpayers may be a result of inadequate communication of this fact. Tax administrations should take steps to assure taxpayers that they need not fear retaliatory action and that, consistent with the arm's length principle, each case is resolved on its own merits. Taxpayers should not be deterred from initiating mutual agreement procedures where Article 25 is applicable.

4.42   Perhaps the most significant concerns that have been expressed with the mutual agreement procedure, as it affects corresponding adjustments, are the following, which are discussed separately in the sections below:

1.   Time limits under domestic law may make corresponding adjustments unavailable if those limits are not waived in the relevant tax treaty.

2.   Mutual agreement procedures may take too long to complete.

3.   Taxpayer participation may be limited.

4.   Published procedures may not be readily available to instruct taxpayers on how the procedure may be used; and

5.   There may be no procedures to suspend the collection of tax deficiencies or the accrual of interest pending resolution of the mutual agreement procedure.

C.4   Recommendations to address concerns

C.4.1   Time limits

4.43   Relief under paragraph 2 of Article 9 may be unavailable if the time limit provided by treaty or domestic law for making corresponding adjustments has expired. Paragraph 2 of Article 9 does not specify whether there should be a time limit after which corresponding adjustments should not be made. Some countries prefer an open-ended approach so that double taxation may be mitigated. Other countries consider the open-ended approach to be unreasonable for administrative purposes. Thus, relief may depend on whether the applicable treaty overrides domestic time limitations, establishes other time limits, or has no effect on domestic time limits.

4.44   Time limits for finalising a taxpayer's tax liability are necessary to provide certainty for taxpayers and tax administrations. In a transfer pricing case a country may be legally unable to make a corresponding adjustment if the time has expired for finalising the tax liability of the relevant associated enterprise. Thus, the existence of such time limits and the fact that they vary from country to country should be considered in order to minimise double taxation.

4.45   Paragraph 2 of Article 25 of the OECD Model Tax Convention addresses the time limit issue by requiring that an agreement reached pursuant to the mutual agreement procedure be implemented regardless of any time limits in the domestic law of the Contracting States. Time limits therefore do not impede the making of corresponding adjustments where a bilateral treaty includes this provision. Some countries, however, may be unwilling or unable to override their domestic time limits in this way and have entered explicit reservations on this point. OECD member countries therefore are encouraged as far as possible to extend domestic time limits for purposes of making corresponding adjustments when mutual agreement procedures have been invoked.

4.46   Where a bilateral treaty does not override domestic time limits for the purposes of the mutual agreement procedure, tax administrations should be ready to initiate discussions quickly upon the taxpayer's request, well before the expiration of any time limits that would preclude the making of an adjustment. Furthermore, OECD member countries are encouraged to adopt domestic law that would allow the suspension of time limits on determining tax liability until the discussions have been concluded.

4.47   The time limit issue might also be addressed through rules governing primary adjustments rather than corresponding adjustments. The problem of time limits on corresponding adjustments is at times due to the fact that the initial assessments for primary adjustments for a taxable year are not made until many years later. Thus, one proposal favoured by some countries is to incorporate in bilateral treaties a provision that would prohibit the issuance of an initial assessment after the expiration of a specified period. Many countries, however, have objected to this approach. Tax administrations may need a long time to make the necessary investigations to establish an adjustment. It would be difficult for many tax administrations to ignore the need for an adjustment, regardless of when it becomes apparent, provided that they were not prevented by their domestic time limits from making the adjustment. While it is not possible at this stage to recommend generally a time limit on initial assessments, tax administrations are encouraged to make these assessments within their own domestic time limits without extension. If the complexity of the case or lack of cooperation from the taxpayer necessitates an extension, the extension should be made for a minimum and specified time period. Further, where domestic time limits can be extended with the agreement of the taxpayer, such an extension should be made only when the taxpayer's consent is truly voluntary. Tax examiners are encouraged to indicate to taxpayers at an early stage their intent to make an assessment based on cross-border transfer pricing, so that the taxpayer can, if it so chooses, inform the tax administration in the other interested state so it can begin considering the issue in the context of a prospective mutual agreement procedure.

4.48   Another time limit that must be considered is the three year time limit within which a taxpayer must invoke the mutual agreement procedure under Article 25 of the OECD Model Tax Convention. The three year period begins to run from the first notification of the action resulting in taxation not in accordance with the provisions of the Convention, which can be the time when the tax administration first notifies the taxpayer of the proposed adjustment, described as the "adjustment action" or "act of taxation", or an earlier date as discussed at paragraphs 21-24 of the Commentary on Article 25. Although some countries consider three years too short a period for invoking the procedure, other countries consider it too long and have entered reservations on this point. The Commentary on Article 25 indicates that the time limit "must be regarded as a minimum so that Contracting States are left free to agree in their bilateral conventions upon a longer period in the interests of taxpayers".

4.49   The three year time limit raises an issue about determining its starting date, which is addressed at paragraphs 21-24 of the Commentary on Article 25. In particular, paragraph 21 states that the three year time period "should be interpreted in the way most favourable to the taxpayer". Paragraph 22 contains guidance on the determination of the date of the act of taxation. Paragraph 23 discusses self-assessment cases. Paragraph 24 clarifies that "where it is the combination of decisions or actions taken in both Contracting States resulting in taxation not in accordance with the Convention, it begins to run only from the first notification of the most recent decision or action."

4.50   In order to minimise the possibility that time limits may prevent the mutual agreement procedure from effectively ensuring relief from or avoidance of double taxation, taxpayers should be permitted to avail themselves of the procedure at the earliest possible stage, which is as soon as an adjustment appears likely. If this were done, the process of consultation could be begun before any irrevocable steps were taken by either tax administration, with the prospect that there would be as few procedural obstacles as possible in the way of achieving a mutually acceptable conclusion to the discussions. However, some competent authorities may not like to be involved at such an early stage because a proposed adjustment may not result in final action or may not trigger a claim for a corresponding adjustment. Consequently, too early an invocation of the mutual agreement process may create unnecessary work.

4.51   Nevertheless, the competent authorities should be prepared to enter into discussions under the mutual agreement procedure relating to transfer pricing issues at as early a stage as is compatible with the economical use of their resources.

C.4.2   Duration of mutual agreement proceedings

4.52   Once discussions under the mutual agreement procedure have commenced, the proceedings may turn out to be lengthy. The complexity of transfer pricing cases may make it difficult for the tax administrations to reach a swift resolution. Distance may make it difficult for the tax administrations to meet frequently, and correspondence is often an unsatisfactory substitute for face-to-face discussions. Difficulties also arise from differences in language, procedures, and legal and accounting systems, and these may lengthen the duration of the process. The process also may be prolonged if the taxpayer delays in providing all the information the tax administrations require for a full understanding of the transfer pricing issue. However, delays do not always occur and, in practice, the consultations often result in a settlement of the problem in a relatively short time.

4.53   It may be possible to reduce the amount of time involved to conclude a mutual agreement procedure. Reducing the formalities required to operate the procedure may expedite the process. In this regard, personal contacts or conferences by telephone may be useful to establish more quickly whether an adjustment by one country may give rise to difficulty in another country. Such contacts are expensive but in the long run may prove to be more cost-effective than the time-consuming process of just a formal written communication. The OECD has developed an online Manual on Effective Mutual Agreement Procedures (MEMAP) which identifies a series of best practices that countries are encouraged to use to improve the effectiveness of their mutual agreement procedures.

4.54   More fundamentally, the introduction of an arbitration clause similar to the one at paragraph 5 of Article 25 to resolve issues after two years should considerably reduce the risk of lengthy mutual agreement procedures.

C.4.3   Taxpayer participation

4.55   Paragraph 1 of Article 25 of the OECD Model Tax Convention gives taxpayers the right to submit a request to initiate a mutual agreement procedure. Paragraph 34 of the Commentary on Article 25 provides that such requests should not be rejected without good reason. Circumstances in which a State may wish to deny a taxpayer access to the mutual agreement procedure and the appropriate ways to handle such circumstances are analysed at paragraphs 26-29 of the Commentary on Article 25.

4.56   However, although the taxpayer has the right to initiate the procedure, the taxpayer has no specific right to participate in the process. It has been argued that the taxpayer also should have a right to take part in the mutual agreement procedure, including the right at least to present its case to both competent authorities, and to be informed of the progress of the discussions. It should be noted in this respect that implementation of a mutual agreement in practice is subject to the taxpayer's acceptance. Some taxpayer representatives have suggested that the taxpayer also should have a right to be present at face-to-face discussions between the competent authorities. The purpose would be to ensure that there is no misunderstanding by the competent authorities of the facts and arguments that are relevant to the taxpayer's case.

4.57   The mutual agreement procedure envisaged in Article 25 of the OECD Model Tax Convention and adopted in many bilateral agreements is not a process of litigation. While input from the taxpayer in some cases can be helpful to the procedure, the taxpayer's ability to participate should be subject to the discretion of the competent authorities.

4.58   Outside the context of the actual discussions between the competent authorities, it is essential for the taxpayer to give the competent authorities all the information that is relevant to the issue in a timely manner. Tax administrations have limited resources and taxpayers should make every effort to facilitate the process. Further, because the mutual agreement procedure is fundamentally designed as a means of providing assistance to a taxpayer, the tax administrations should allow taxpayers every reasonable opportunity to present the relevant facts and arguments to them to ensure as far as possible that the matter is not subject to misunderstanding.

4.59   In practice, the tax administrations of many OECD member countries routinely give taxpayers such opportunities, keep them informed of the progress of the discussions, and often ask them during the course of the discussions whether they can accept the settlements contemplated by the competent authorities. These practices, already standard procedure in most countries, should be adopted as widely as possible. They are reflected in the OECD's MEMAP.

C.4.4   Publication of applicable procedures

4.60   It would be helpful to taxpayers if competent authorities were to develop and publicise their own domestic rules or procedures for utilising the mutual agreement procedure so that taxpayers may more readily understand the process. OECD member countries and a number of non-OECD economies have agreed to include references to their domestic rules or procedures in their regularly updated Dispute Resolution Country Profiles on the OECD website. The development and publication of such rules could also be helpful to tax administrations, especially if they are faced with the possibility of a large or growing number of cases in which mutual agreement with other tax administrations may be necessary or desirable, possibly saving them the need to answer a variety of enquiries or to develop procedures afresh in every case.

4.61   In publicising such rules and procedures it could be made clear, for example, how the taxpayer may bring a problem to the attention of the competent authority in order to start a discussion with the other country's competent authorities. The publication could indicate the official address to which the problem should be referred, the stage at which the competent authority would be prepared to take the matter up, the nature of the information necessary or helpful to the competent authority in handling the case, and so on. It could be helpful also to give guidance on the policy of the competent authorities regarding questions of transfer pricing and corresponding adjustments. This possibility could be explored unilaterally by competent authorities and, where appropriate, descriptions of their rules and procedures should be given suitable domestic publicity (respecting, however, taxpayer confidentiality).

4.62   There is no need for the competent authorities to agree to rules or guidelines governing the procedure, since the rules or guidelines would be limited in effect to the competent authority's domestic relationship with its own taxpayers. However, competent authorities should routinely communicate such unilateral rules or guidelines to the competent authorities of the other countries with which mutual agreement procedures are undertaken.

C.4.5 Problems concerning collection of tax deficiencies and accrual of interest

4.63   The process of obtaining relief from double taxation through a corresponding adjustment can be complicated by issues relating to the collection of tax deficiencies and the assessment of interest on those deficiencies or overpayment. A first problem is that the assessed deficiency may be collected before the corresponding adjustment proceeding is completed, because of a lack of domestic procedures allowing the collection to be suspended. This may cause the MNE group to pay the same tax twice until the issues can be resolved. This problem arises not only in the context of the mutual agreement procedure but also for internal appeals. Countries that do not have procedures to suspend collection during a mutual agreement procedure are encouraged to adopt them where permitted by domestic law, although subject to the right to seek security as protection against possible default by the taxpayer. See paragraphs 47-48 of the Commentary on Article 25.

4.64   Whether or not collection of the deficiency is suspended or partially suspended, other complications may arise. Because of the lengthy time period for processing many transfer pricing cases, the interest due on a deficiency or, if a corresponding adjustment is allowed, on the overpayment of tax in the other country can equal or exceed the amount of the tax itself. Tax administrations should be aware that inconsistent interest rules across the two jurisdictions may result in additional cost for the MNE group, or in other cases provide a benefit to the MNE group (*e.g.* where the interest paid in the country making the corresponding adjustment exceeds the interest imposed in the country making the primary adjustment) that would not have been available if the controlled transactions had been undertaken on an arm's length basis originally, and this should be taken into account in their mutual agreement proceedings.

4.65   The amount of interest (as distinct from the rate at which it is applied) may also have more to do with the year in which the jurisdiction making the corresponding adjustment attributes the corresponding adjustment. The jurisdiction making the corresponding adjustment may decide to make the adjustment in the year in which the primary adjustment is determined in which case relatively little interest is likely to be paid (regardless of the rate of interest paid) whereas the jurisdiction making the primary adjustment may seek to impose interest on the understated and uncollected tax liability from the year in which the controlled transactions took place (notwithstanding that a relatively low rate of interest may be imposed). The issue of in which year to make a corresponding adjustment is raised in paragraph 4.36. Therefore, it may be appropriate in certain cases for both competent authorities to agree not to assess interest from the taxpayer or pay interest to the taxpayer in connection with the adjustment at issue, but this may not be possible in the absence of a specific provision addressing this issue in the relevant bilateral treaty. This approach would also reduce administrative complexities. However, as the interest on the deficiency and the interest on the overpayment are attributable to different taxpayers in different jurisdictions, there would be no assurance under such an approach that a proper economic result would be achieved.

C.5   *Secondary adjustments*

4.66   Corresponding adjustments are not the only adjustments that may be triggered by a primary transfer pricing adjustment. Primary transfer pricing adjustments and their corresponding adjustments change the allocation of taxable profits of an MNE group for tax purposes but they do not alter the fact that the excess profits represented by the adjustment are not consistent with the result that would have arisen if the controlled transactions had been undertaken on an arm's length basis. To make the actual allocation of profits consistent with the primary transfer pricing adjustment, some countries having proposed a transfer pricing adjustment will assert under their domestic legislation a constructive transaction (a secondary transaction), whereby the excess profits resulting from a primary adjustment are treated as having been transferred in some other form and taxed accordingly. Ordinarily, the secondary transactions will take the form of constructive dividends, constructive equity contributions, or constructive loans. For example, a country making a primary adjustment to the income of a subsidiary of a foreign parent may treat the excess profits in the hands of the foreign parent as having been transferred as a dividend, in which case withholding tax may apply. It may be that the subsidiary paid an excessive transfer price to the foreign parent as a means of avoiding that withholding tax. Thus, secondary adjustments attempt to account for the difference between the re-determined taxable profits and the originally booked profits. The subjecting to tax of a secondary transaction gives rise to a secondary transfer pricing adjustment (a secondary adjustment). Thus, secondary adjustments may serve to prevent tax avoidance. The exact form that a secondary transaction takes and of the consequent secondary adjustment will depend on the facts of the case and on the tax laws of the country that asserts the secondary adjustment.

4.67   Another example of a tax administration seeking to assert a secondary transaction may be where the tax administration making a primary adjustment treats the excess profits as being a constructive loan from one associated enterprise to the other associated enterprise. In this case, an obligation to repay the loan would be deemed to arise. The tax administration making the primary adjustment may then seek to apply the arm's length principle to this secondary transaction to impute an arm's length rate of interest. The interest rate to be applied, the timing to be attached to the making of interest payments, if any, and whether interest is to be capitalised would generally need to be addressed. The constructive loan approach may have an effect not only for the year to which a primary adjustment relates but to subsequent years until such time as the constructive loan is considered by the tax administration asserting the secondary adjustment to have been repaid.

4.68   A secondary adjustment may result in double taxation unless a corresponding credit or some other form of relief is provided by the other country for the additional tax liability that may result from a secondary adjustment. Where a secondary adjustment takes the form of a constructive dividend any withholding tax which is then imposed may not be relievable because there may not be a deemed receipt under the domestic legislation of the other country.

4.69   The Commentary on paragraph 2 of Article 9 of the OECD Model Tax Convention notes that the Article does not deal with secondary adjustments, and thus it neither forbids nor requires tax administrations to make secondary adjustments. In a broad sense, the purpose of double tax agreements can be stated as being for the avoidance of double taxation and the prevention of fiscal evasion with respect to taxes on income and capital. Many countries do not make secondary adjustments either as a matter of practice or because their respective domestic provisions do not permit them to do so. Some countries might refuse to grant relief in respect of other countries' secondary adjustments and indeed they are not required to do so under Article 9.

4.70   Secondary adjustments are rejected by some countries because of the practical difficulties they present. For example, if a primary adjustment is made between brother-sister companies, the secondary adjustment may involve a hypothetical dividend from one of those companies up a chain to a common parent, followed by constructive equity contributions down another chain of ownership to reach the other company involved in the transaction. Many hypothetical transactions might be created, raising questions whether tax consequences should be triggered in other jurisdictions besides those involved in the transaction for which the primary adjustment was made. This might be avoided if the secondary transaction were a loan, but constructive loans are not used by most countries for this purpose and they carry their own complications because of issues relating to imputed interest. It would be inappropriate for minority shareholders that are not parties to the controlled transactions and that have accordingly not received excess cash to be considered recipients of a constructive dividend, even though a non-prorata dividend might be considered inconsistent with the requirements of applicable corporate law. In addition, as a result of the interaction with the foreign tax credit system, a secondary adjustment may excessively reduce the overall tax burden of the MNE group.

4.71   In light of the foregoing difficulties, tax administrations, when secondary adjustments are considered necessary, are encouraged to structure such adjustments in a way that the possibility of double taxation as a consequence thereof would be minimised, except where the taxpayer's behaviour suggests an intent to disguise a dividend for purposes of avoiding withholding tax. In addition, countries in the process of formulating or reviewing policy on this matter are recommended to take into consideration the above-mentioned difficulties.

4.72   Some countries that have adopted secondary adjustments also give the taxpayer receiving the primary adjustment another option that allows the taxpayer to avoid the secondary adjustment by having the taxpayer arrange for the MNE group of which it is a member to repatriate the excess profits to enable the taxpayer to conform its accounts to the primary adjustment. The repatriation could be effected either by setting up an account receivable or by reclassifying other transfers, such as dividend payments where the adjustment is between parent and subsidiary, as a payment of additional transfer price (where the original price was too low) or as a refund of transfer price (where the original price was too high).

4.73   Where a repatriation involves reclassifying a dividend payment, the amount of the dividend (up to the amount of the primary adjustment) would be excluded from the recipient's gross income (because it would already have been accounted for through the primary adjustment). The consequences would be that the recipient would lose any indirect tax credit (or benefit of a dividend exemption in an exemption system) and a credit for withholding tax that had been allowed on the dividend.

4.74   When the repatriation involves establishing an account receivable, the adjustments to actual cash flow will be made over time, although domestic law may limit the time within which the account can be satisfied. This approach is identical to using a constructive loan as a secondary transaction to account for excess profits in the hands of one of the parties to the controlled transaction. The accrual of interest on the account could have its own tax consequences, however, and this may complicate the process, depending upon when interest begins to accrue under domestic law (as discussed in paragraph 4.67). Some countries may be willing to waive the interest charge on these accounts as part of a competent authority agreement.

4.75   Where a repatriation is sought, a question arises about how such payments or arrangements should be recorded in the accounts of the taxpayer repatriating the payment to its associated enterprise so that both it and the tax administration of that country are aware that a repatriation has occurred or has been set up. The actual recording of the repatriation in the accounts of the enterprise from whom the repatriation is sought will ultimately depend on the form the repatriation takes. For example, where a dividend receipt is to be regarded by the tax administration making the primary adjustment and the taxpayer receiving the dividend as the repatriation, then this type of arrangement may not need to be specially recorded in the accounts of the associated enterprise paying the dividend, as such an arrangement may not affect the amount or characterisation of the dividend in its hands. On the other hand, where an account payable is set up, both the taxpayer recording the account payable and the tax administration of that country will need to be aware that the account payable relates to a repatriation so that any repayments from the account or of interest on the outstanding balance in the account are clearly able to be identified and treated according to the domestic laws of that country. In addition, issues may be presented in relation to currency exchange gains and losses.

4.76   As most OECD member countries at this time have not had much experience with the use of repatriation, it is recommended that agreements between taxpayers and tax administrations for a repatriation to take place be discussed in the mutual agreement proceeding where it has been initiated for the related primary adjustment.

D. Simultaneous tax examinations

D.1   Definition and background

4.77   A simultaneous tax examination is a form of mutual assistance, used in a wide range of international issues, that allows two or more countries to cooperate in tax investigations. Simultaneous tax examinations can be particularly useful where information based in a third country is a key to a tax investigation, since they generally lead to more timely and more effective exchanges of information. Historically, simultaneous tax examinations of transfer pricing issues have focused on cases where the true nature of transactions was obscured by the interposition of tax havens. However, in complex transfer pricing cases, it is suggested that simultaneous examinations could serve a broader role since they may improve the adequacy of data available to the participating tax administrations for transfer pricing analyses. It has also been suggested that simultaneous examinations could help reduce the possibilities for economic double taxation, reduce the compliance cost to taxpayers, and speed up the resolution of issues. In a simultaneous examination, if a reassessment is made, both countries involved should endeavour to reach a result that avoids double taxation for the MNE group.

4.78 Simultaneous tax examinations are defined in Part A of the OECD Model Agreement for the Undertaking of Simultaneous Tax Examinations ("OECD Model Agreement"). According to this agreement, a simultaneous tax examination means an "arrangement between two or more parties to examine simultaneously and independently, each on its own territory, the tax affairs of (a) taxpayer(s) in which they have a common or related interest with a view to exchanging any relevant information which they so obtain". This form of mutual assistance is not meant to be a substitute for the mutual agreement procedure. Any exchange of information as a result of the simultaneous tax examination continues to be exchanged via the competent authorities, with all the safeguards that are built into such exchanges. Practical information on simultaneous examinations can be found in the relevant module of the Manual on Information Exchange that was adopted by the Committee on Fiscal Affairs on 23 January 2006 (see http://www.oecd.org/ctp/eoi/manual).

4.79 While provisions that follow Article 26 of the OECD Model Tax Convention may provide the legal basis for conducting simultaneous examinations, competent authorities frequently conclude working arrangements that lay down the objectives of their simultaneous tax examination programs and practical procedures connected with the simultaneous tax examination and exchange of information. Once such an agreement has been reached on the general lines to be followed and specific cases have been selected, tax examiners and inspectors of each state will separately carry out their examination within their own jurisdiction and pursuant to their domestic law and administrative practice.

D.2 Legal basis for simultaneous tax examinations

4.80 Simultaneous tax examinations are within the scope of the exchange of information provision based on Article 26 of the OECD Model Tax Convention. Article 26 provides for cooperation between the competent authorities of the Contracting States in the form of exchanges of information necessary for carrying out the provisions of the Convention or of their domestic laws concerning taxes covered by the Convention. Article 26 and the Commentary do not restrict the possibilities of assistance to the three methods of exchanging information mentioned in the Commentary (exchange on request, spontaneous exchanges, and automatic exchanges).

4.81 Simultaneous tax examinations may be authorised outside the context of double tax treaties. For example, Article 12 of the Nordic Convention on Mutual Assistance in Tax Matters governs exchange of information and assistance in tax collection between the Nordic countries and provides for the possibility of simultaneous tax examinations. This convention gives common guidelines for the selection of cases and for carrying out such examinations. Article 8 of the joint Council of Europe and OECD Convention on Mutual Administrative Assistance in Tax Matters also provides expressly for the possibility of simultaneous tax examinations.

4.82   In all cases the information obtained by the tax administration of a state has to be treated as confidential under its domestic legislation and may be used only for certain tax purposes and disclosed only to certain persons and authorities involved in specifically defined tax matters covered by the tax treaty or mutual assistance agreement. The taxpayers affected are normally notified of the fact that they have been selected for a simultaneous examination and in some countries they may have the right to be informed when the tax administrations are considering a simultaneous tax examination or when information will be transmitted in conformity with Article 26. In such cases, the competent authority should inform its counterpart in the foreign state that such disclosure will occur.

D.3   *Simultaneous tax examinations and transfer pricing*

4.83   In selecting transfer pricing cases for simultaneous examinations, there may be major obstacles caused by the differences in time limits for conducting examinations or making assessments in different countries and the different tax periods open for examination. However, these problems may be mitigated by an early exchange of examination schedules between the relevant competent authorities to find out in which cases the tax examination periods coincide and to synchronise future examination periods. While at first glance an early exchange of examination schedules would seem beneficial, some countries have found that the chances of a treaty partner accepting a proposal are considerably better when one is able to present issues more comprehensively to justify a simultaneous examination.

4.84   Once a case is selected for a simultaneous examination it is customary for tax inspectors or examiners to meet, to plan, to coordinate and to follow closely the progress of the simultaneous tax examination. Especially in complex cases, meetings of the tax inspectors or examiners concerned may also be held with taxpayer participation to clarify factual issues. In those countries where the taxpayer has the right to be consulted before information is transferred to another tax administration, this procedure should also be followed in the context of a simultaneous examination. In this situation, that tax administration should inform in advance its treaty partners that it is subject to this requirement before the simultaneous examination is begun.

4.85   Simultaneous tax examinations may be a useful instrument to determine the correct tax liability of associated enterprises in cases where, for example, costs are shared or charged and profits are allocated between taxpayers in different taxing jurisdictions or more generally where transfer pricing issues are involved. Simultaneous tax examinations may facilitate an exchange of information on multinational business practices, complex transactions, cost contribution arrangements, and profit allocation methods in special fields such as global trading and innovative financial transactions. As a result, tax administrations may acquire a better understanding of and insight into the overall activities of an MNE and obtain extended possibilities of comparison and checking international transactions. Simultaneous tax examinations may also support the industry-wide exchange of information, which is aimed at developing knowledge of taxpayer behaviour, practices and trends within an industry, and other information that might be suitable beyond the specific cases examined.

4.86   One objective of simultaneous tax examinations is to promote compliance with transfer pricing regulations. Obtaining the necessary information and determining the facts and circumstances about such matters as the transfer pricing conditions of controlled transactions between associated enterprises in two or more tax jurisdictions may be difficult for a tax administration, especially in cases where the taxpayer in its jurisdiction does not cooperate or fails to provide the necessary information in due time. The simultaneous tax examination process can help tax administrations to establish these facts faster and more effectively and economically.

4.87   The process also might allow for the identification of potential transfer pricing disputes at an early stage, thereby minimising litigation with taxpayers. This could happen when, based upon the information obtained in the course of a simultaneous tax examination, the participating tax examiners or inspectors have the opportunity to discuss any differences in opinion with regard to the transfer pricing conditions which exist between the associated enterprises and are able to reconcile these contentions. When such a process is undertaken, the tax examiners or inspectors concerned should, as far as possible, arrive at concurring statements as to the determination and evaluation of the facts and circumstances of the controlled transactions between the associated enterprises, stating any disagreements about the evaluation of facts, and any differences with respect to the legal treatment of the transfer pricing conditions which exist between the associated enterprises. Such statements could then serve as a basis for subsequent mutual agreement procedures and perhaps obviate the problems caused by one country examining the affairs of a taxpayer long after the treaty partner country has finally settled the tax liability of the relevant associated enterprise. For example, such an approach could minimise mutual agreement procedure difficulties due to the lack of relevant information.

4.88   In some cases the simultaneous tax examination procedure may allow the participating tax administrations to reach an agreement on the transfer pricing conditions of a controlled transaction between the associated enterprises. Where an agreement is reached, corresponding adjustments may be made at an early stage, thus avoiding time-limit impediments and economic double taxation to the extent possible. In addition, if the agreement about the associated enterprises' transfer pricing is reached with the taxpayers' consent, time-consuming and expensive litigation may be avoided.

4.89   Even if no agreement between the tax administrations can be reached in the course of a simultaneous tax examination with respect to the associated enterprises' transfer pricing, the OECD Model Agreement envisions that either associated enterprise may be able to present a request for the opening of a mutual agreement procedure to avoid economic double taxation at an earlier stage than it would have if there were no simultaneous tax examination. If this is the case, then simultaneous tax examinations may significantly reduce the time span between a tax administration's adjustments made to a taxpayer's tax liability and the implementation of a mutual agreement procedure. Moreover, the OECD Model Agreement envisions that simultaneous tax examinations may facilitate mutual agreement procedures, because tax administrations will be able to build up more complete factual evidence for those tax adjustments for which a mutual agreement procedure may be requested by a taxpayer. Based upon the determination and evaluation of facts and the proposed tax treatment of the transfer pricing issues concerned as set forth in the tax administrations' statements described above, the practical operation of the mutual agreement procedure may be improved significantly, allowing the competent authorities to reach an agreement more easily.

4.90   The associated enterprises may also benefit from simultaneous tax examinations from the savings of time and resources due to the coordination of inquiries from the tax administrations involved and the avoidance of duplication. In addition, the simultaneous involvement of two or more tax administrations in the examination of transfer pricing between associated enterprises may provide the opportunity for an MNE to take a more active role in resolving its transfer pricing issues. By presenting the relevant facts and arguments to each of the participating tax administrations during the simultaneous tax examination the associated enterprises may help avoid misunderstandings and facilitate the tax administrations' concurring determination and evaluation of their transfer pricing conditions. Thus, the associated enterprises may obtain certainty with regard to their transfer pricing at an early stage. See paragraph 4.77.

D.4   Recommendation on the use of simultaneous tax examinations

4.91   As a result of the increased use of simultaneous tax examinations among OECD member countries, the Committee on Fiscal Affairs decided it would be useful to draft the OECD Model Agreement for those countries that are able and wish to engage in this type of cooperation. On 23 July 1992, the Council of the OECD made a recommendation to member countries to use this Model Agreement, which provides guidelines on the legal and practical aspects of this form of cooperation.

4.92   With the increasing internationalisation of trade and business and the complexity of transactions of MNEs, transfer pricing issues have become more and more important. Simultaneous tax examinations can alleviate the difficulties experienced by both taxpayers and tax administrations connected with the transfer pricing of MNEs. A greater use of simultaneous tax examinations is therefore recommended in the examination of transfer pricing cases and to facilitate exchange of information and the operation of mutual agreement procedures. In a simultaneous examination, if a reassessment is made, both countries involved should endeavour to reach a result that avoids double taxation for the MNE group.

E. Safe harbours

E.1   Introduction

4.93   Applying the arm's length principle can be a fact-intensive process and can require proper judgment. It may present uncertainty and may impose a heavy administrative burden on taxpayers and tax administrations that can be exacerbated by both legislative and compliance complexity. These facts have lead OECD member countries to consider whether safe harbour rules would be appropriate in the transfer pricing area.

E.2   Definition and concept of safe harbours

4.94   The difficulties in applying the arm's length principle may be ameliorated by providing circumstances in which taxpayers could follow a simple set of rules under which transfer prices would be automatically accepted by the national tax administration. Such provisions would be referred to as a "safe harbour" or "safe haven". Formally, in the context of taxation, a safe harbour is a statutory provision that applies to a given category of taxpayers and that relieves eligible taxpayers from certain obligations otherwise imposed by the tax code by substituting exceptional, usually simpler obligations. In the specific instance of transfer pricing, the administrative requirements of a safe harbour may vary from a total relief of targeted taxpayers from the obligation to conform with a country's transfer pricing legislation and regulations to the obligation to comply with various procedural rules as a condition for qualifying for the safe harbour. These rules could, for example, require taxpayers to establish transfer prices or results in a specific way, *e.g.* by applying a simplified transfer pricing method provided by the tax administration, or satisfy specific information reporting and record maintenance provisions with regard to controlled transactions. Such an approach requires a more substantial involvement from the tax administration, since the taxpayer's compliance with the procedural rules may need to be monitored.

4.95   A safe harbour may have two variants regarding the taxpayer's conditions of controlled transactions: certain transactions are excluded from the scope of application of transfer pricing provisions (in particular by setting thresholds), or the rules applying to them are simplified (for example by designating ranges within which prices or profits must fall). Both safe harbour targets may need to be revised and published periodically by the tax authorities. Safe harbours do not include procedures whereby a tax administration and a taxpayer agree on transfer pricing in advance of the controlled transactions (advance pricing arrangements), which are discussed in Section F of this chapter. The discussion in this section does not extend to tax provisions designed to prevent "excessive" debt in a foreign subsidiary ("thin capitalisation" rules), which will be the subject of subsequent work.

4.96   The provision of safe harbours raises significant questions about the degree of arbitrariness that would be created in determining transfer prices by eligible taxpayers, tax planning opportunities, and the potential for double taxation resulting from the possible incompatibility of the safe harbours with the arm's length principle.

E.3   *Factors supporting use of safe harbours*

4.97   The basic objectives of safe harbours are as follows: simplifying compliance for eligible taxpayers in determining arm's length conditions for controlled transactions; providing assurance to a category of taxpayers that the price charged or received on controlled transactions will be accepted by the tax administration without further review; and relieving the tax administration from the task of conducting further examination and audits of such taxpayers with respect to their transfer pricing.

E.3.1   Compliance relief

4.98   Application of the arm's length principle may require collection and analysis of data that may be difficult to obtain and/or evaluate. In certain cases, such complexity may be disproportionate to the size of the corporation or its level of controlled transactions.

4.99   Safe harbours could significantly ease compliance by exempting taxpayers from such provisions. Designed as a comfort mechanism, they allow greater flexibility especially in the areas where there are no matching or comparable arm's length prices. Under a safe harbour, taxpayers would know in advance the range of prices or profit rates within which the corporation must fall in order to qualify for the safe harbour. Meeting such conditions would merely require the application of a simplified method, predominantly a measure of profitability, which would spare the taxpayer the search for comparables, thus saving time and resources which would otherwise be devoted to determining transfer prices.

E.3.2   Certainty

4.100   Another advantage provided by a safe harbour would be the certainty that the taxpayer's transfer prices will be accepted by the tax administration. Qualifying taxpayers would have the assurance that they would not be subject to an audit or reassessment in connection with their transfer prices. The tax administration would accept without any further scrutiny any price or result exceeding a minimum threshold or falling within a predetermined range. For that purpose, taxpayers could be provided with relevant parameters which would provide a transfer price or a result deemed appropriate to the tax administration. This could be, for example, a series of sector-specific mark-ups or profit indicators.

E.3.3   Administrative simplicity

4.101   A safe harbour would result in a degree of administrative simplicity for the tax administration. Once the eligibility of certain taxpayers to the safe harbour has been established, those taxpayers would require minimal examination with respect to transfer prices or results of controlled transactions. Tax administrations could then allocate more resources to the examination of other transactions and taxpayers.

E.4   *Problems presented by use of safe harbours*

4.102   The availability of safe harbours for a given category of taxpayers would have a number of adverse consequences which must carefully be weighed by tax administrations against the expected benefits. These concerns stem from the facts that:

1.   The implementation of a safe harbour in a given country would not only affect tax calculations within that jurisdiction, but would also impinge on the tax calculations of associated enterprises in other jurisdictions; and

2.   It is difficult to establish satisfactory criteria for defining safe harbours, and accordingly they can potentially produce prices or results that may not be consistent with the arm's length principle.

The issue can be examined from several perspectives.

4.103   Under a safe harbour, taxpayers may not be required to follow a specific pricing method, or even have a pricing method for tax purposes. Where a safe harbour imposes a simplified transfer pricing method, it would be unlikely to correspond in all cases to the most appropriate method applicable to the facts and circumstances of the taxpayer under the regular transfer pricing provisions. For example, a safe harbour may impose a minimum profit percentage under a profit method when the taxpayer could have used the comparable uncontrolled price method or other transaction-based methods.

4.104   Such an occurrence could be considered as inconsistent with the arm's length principle, which requires the use of a pricing method that is consistent with the conditions that independent parties engaged in comparable transactions under comparable conditions would have agreed upon in the open market. Some sectors where goods, commodities or services are standard and market prices are widely publicised such as, for example, the oil and mining industries and the financial services sector could conceivably apply a safe harbour with a higher degree of precision and, thus, a lesser departure from the arm's length principle. But even these industry segments produce a wide range of results which a safe harbour would be unlikely to be able to accommodate to the satisfaction of the tax administrations. And the existence of published market prices would presumably also facilitate the use of transaction-based methods, in which case there may be no need for a safe harbour.

4.105   Even assuming that the pricing method imposed under a specific safe harbour is appropriate to the facts and circumstances of particular cases, the application of the safe harbour would nonetheless sacrifice accuracy in the reporting of transfer prices. This is inherent in safe harbours, under which transfer prices are predominantly established by reference to a standard target as opposed to the individual facts and circumstances of the transaction, as under the arm's length principle. It follows that the prices or results that produce compliance with the standard target may not be arm's length prices or results.

4.106   Safe harbours are likely to be arbitrary since they rarely fit exactly the varying facts and circumstances even of enterprises in the same trade or business. This arbitrariness could be minimised only with great difficulty by devoting a considerable amount of skilled labour to collecting, collating, and continuously revising a pool of information about prices and pricing developments. Obtaining relevant information for establishing and monitoring safe harbour parameters may therefore impose administrative burdens on tax administrations, because such information may not be readily available and may be accessible only through in-depth transfer pricing inquiries. Therefore, the extensive research necessary to set the safe harbour parameters accurately enough to satisfy the arm's length principle would jeopardise one of the purposes of a safe harbour, that of administrative simplicity.

E.4.1   Risk of double taxation and mutual agreement procedure difficulties

4.107   From a practical point of view, the most important concern raised by a safe harbour is its international impact. Safe harbours could affect the pricing strategy of corporations. The existence of safe harbour "targets" may induce taxpayers to modify the prices that they would otherwise have charged to controlled parties, in order to increase profits to meet the targets and thereby avoid transfer pricing scrutiny on audit. The concern of possible overstatement of taxable income in the country providing the safe harbour is greater where that country imposes significant penalties for understatement of tax or failure to meet documentation requirements, with the result that there may be added incentive to ensure that the transfer pricing is accepted without further review.

4.108   Taxpayers may value the certainty provided by the safe harbour to the point where they would raise the prices charged to associated enterprises for the purpose of qualifying for the safe harbour, notwithstanding the fact that those transfer prices would be above the relevant taxpayer's arm's length prices taking into account its specific circumstances. In that case, the safe harbour would work to the benefit of the tax administration providing the safe harbour, as more taxable income would be reported by such domestic taxpayers. On the other hand, the safe harbour would penalise both the foreign associated enterprises and their tax administrations, since less profits and taxable income would be reported in their respective jurisdictions. This would create an issue with respect to the proper sharing of tax revenue between tax jurisdictions.

4.109   Indeed, in such cases, the tax administration of the jurisdiction adversely affected may not be in a position to accept the prices charged to their taxpayers in connection with transactions with associated enterprises in the safe harbour country. The prices may differ from those obtained in these jurisdictions by the application of transfer pricing methods consistent with the arm's length principle. It would be expected that foreign tax administrations would challenge prices derived from the application of a safe harbour, with the result that the taxpayer would face the prospect of double taxation.

4.110   At the outset, one would argue that the possibility of double taxation would nullify the objectives of certainty and simplicity originally pursued by the taxpayer in electing the safe harbour. However, taxpayers may consider that a moderate level of double taxation is an acceptable price to be paid in order to obtain relief from the necessity of complying with complex transfer pricing rules.

4.111   It follows that double taxation may not, in itself, be a disqualifying factor against safe harbours. One may argue that the taxpayer alone should be required to make its own decision if the possibility of double taxation is acceptable in electing the safe harbour or not. However, in order to ensure that taxpayers make such a decision clearly on the basis of this trade-off, the country offering the safe harbour would need to make it explicit whether or not it would attempt to alleviate any eventual double taxation resulting from the use of the safe harbour. Since the safe harbour provides taxpayers with the privilege of avoiding any subsequent review or audit of their transfer prices resulting from the application of a safe harbour and given the nature of safe harbours, whose prices or results are, by design, only a proxy for those obtained under the arm's length principle, it is only appropriate that the taxpayer should equally be prepared, in electing the safe harbour, to bear any ensuing international double taxation resulting from the non-acceptance by a foreign tax administration of the transfer prices reported under the safe harbour. This would logically imply that taxpayers electing the safe harbour should generally be prohibited from bringing double taxation issues before the competent authorities should the use of the safe harbour result in international double taxation. Tax relief from double taxation attributable to a taxpayer's election of a safe harbour should be granted in the foreign country only if the taxpayer can prove that the results of meeting the safe harbour are consistent with the arm's length principle.

4.112   However, transfer pricing adjustments of foreign tax administrations will be complicated when the MNE has chosen a safe harbour in another country, because the taxpayer is likely to dispute the adjustment to prevent double taxation. The prospect that mutual agreement procedures are generally not available to adjust prices or results downwards that have been set under a safe harbour regime may therefore have a detrimental effect on the tax administration in the foreign countries.

4.113   The adoption of safe harbour regimes in one country may require that the other countries' tax administrations examine the transfer pricing policy of all companies associated with enterprises that have elected a safe harbour in order to identify all cases of potential inconsistency with the arm's length principle. Failure to do so could amount to a transfer of tax revenue from those countries to the country providing the safe harbour. Consequently, any administrative simplicity gained by the tax administration of the safe harbour country would be obtained at the expense of other countries, which, in order to protect their own tax base, would have to determine systematically whether the prices or results permitted under the safe harbour are consistent with what would be obtained by the application of their own transfer pricing rules. The administrative burden saved by the country offering the safe harbour would therefore be shifted to the foreign jurisdictions.

4.114   Double taxation possibilities would exist not only where a single country adopts a safe harbour. Adoption of a safe harbour by more than one country would not avoid double taxation if each taxing jurisdiction were to adopt conflicting approaches and methods. The parameters of two countries' safe harbours for specific industry segments are likely to deviate since both countries would want to safeguard their revenues. In theory, international coordination could achieve the degree of harmonisation among national systems that would be required to prevent double taxation. However, in practice, it is most unlikely that two jurisdictions could harmonise conflicting safe harbours that would eliminate double taxation.

E.4.2   Possibility of opening avenues for tax planning

4.115   Safe harbours would also provide taxpayers with tax planning opportunities. Enterprises may have an incentive to modify their transfer prices in order to shift taxable income to other jurisdictions. This may also possibly induce tax avoidance, to the extent that artificial arrangements are entered into for the purpose of exploiting the safe harbour provisions.

4.116   If a safe harbour were based on an industry average, tax planning opportunities might exist for taxpayers with better than average profitability. For example, a cost-efficient company selling at the arm's length price may be earning a mark-up of 15 percent on controlled sales. This corporation would have an incentive to elect a safe harbour providing for a 10 percent mark up. The company would, under the safe harbour, be taxed on a scaled-down profits figure, notwithstanding the fact that the underlying transfer prices on controlled transactions would be significantly below the arm's length prices. Consequently, taxable income would be shifted out of the country. When applied on a large scale, this could mean significant revenue lost for the country offering the safe harbour. By design, the tax administration would have no recourse to counter such instances of profit shifting.

4.117   Safe harbours may potentially result in the international under-taxation of income, to the extent that they result in prices or profits not approximating the arm's length principle and allow taxable income to be shifted to low tax countries or tax havens.

4.118   Whether a country is prepared possibly to suffer some erosion of its own tax base in implementing a safe harbour is for that country to decide. The basic trade-off in making such a policy decision is between the scope and attractiveness of the safe harbour for taxpayers on the one hand, and tax revenue erosion on the other. The more attractive a safe harbour is for a taxpayer, the more taxpayers will elect to use it, thereby reducing the taxation authority's administrative burden. On the other hand, the more attractive the safe harbour is, the more tax revenue is likely to be lost due to under-reporting of income. However, the magnitude of the respective costs and benefits of such a trade-off is irrelevant if the tax administration is not prepared, as a matter of principle, to surrender any discretionary power with respect to the assessment of a taxpayer's liability.

E.4.3   Equity and uniformity issues

4.119   Finally, safe harbours raise equity and uniformity issues. By implementing a safe harbour, one would create two distinct sets of rules in the transfer pricing area, one requiring conformity of prices with the arm's length principle and another requiring conformity with a different and simplified set of conditions. Since criteria would necessarily be required to differentiate those taxpayers eligible for the safe harbour, similar and possibly competing taxpayers could, in some circumstances, find themselves on opposite sides of the safe harbour threshold, thus resulting in similar taxpayers enjoying different tax treatment: one meeting the safe harbour rules and thus being relieved from regular compliance provisions and the other being obliged to do business exclusively in conformity with the arm's length principle (either because the enterprise in fact deals at arm's length or because it is subject to transfer pricing legislation that is based on the arm's length principle). Preferential tax treatment under safe harbour regimes for a specific category of taxpayers could entail discrimination and competitive distortions.

E.5   *Recommendations on use of safe harbours*

4.120   The foregoing analysis suggests that while safe harbours could accomplish a number of objectives relating to the compliance with and administration of transfer pricing provisions, they raise fundamental problems. They could potentially have perverse effects on the pricing decisions of enterprises engaged in controlled transactions. They may also have a negative impact on the tax revenues of the country implementing the safe harbour as well as on the countries whose associated enterprises engage in controlled transactions with taxpayers electing a safe harbour. More importantly, safe harbours are generally not compatible with the enforcement of transfer prices consistent with the arm's length principle. These drawbacks must be measured against the expected benefits of safe harbours, certainty, and compliance simplicity on the taxpayer's side and relief from administrative burden on the tax administration's side.

4.121   Under the normal administration of tax laws, certainty cannot be guaranteed for the taxpayer, because administrations must retain the ability to review any aspect of a taxpayer's income tax assessment, including the area of transfer pricing. Fundamentally, the introduction of a safe harbour means that the tax administration surrenders a portion of its discretionary power in favour of automatic rules. Tax administrations may not be prepared to go that far, and may consider it essential to retain the ability to verify the accuracy of a taxpayer's self-assessed tax liability and its basis. Compliance simplicity may also often be subordinated to other tax policy objectives such as reasonable and adequate documentation and reporting and the prevention of tax avoidance.

4.122   On the other hand, tax administrations have considerable flexibility in administering tax law. They can choose to concentrate more resources on cases involving large taxpayers or an important proportion of controlled transactions and show more tolerance towards smaller taxpayers. While more flexible administrative practices towards smaller taxpayers are not a substitute for a formal safe harbour, they may achieve, to a lesser extent, the same objectives pursued by safe harbours. In view of the above considerations, special statutory derogations for categories of taxpayers in the determination of transfer pricing are not generally considered advisable, and consequently the use of safe harbours is not recommended.

F. Advance pricing arrangements[1]

F.1   Definition and concept of advance pricing arrangements

4.123   An advance pricing arrangement ("APA") is an arrangement that determines, in advance of controlled transactions, an appropriate set of criteria (*e.g.* method, comparables and appropriate adjustments thereto, critical assumptions as to future events) for the determination of the transfer pricing for those transactions over a fixed period of time. An APA is formally initiated by a taxpayer and requires negotiations between the taxpayer, one or more associated enterprises, and one or more tax administrations. APAs are intended to supplement the traditional administrative, judicial, and treaty mechanisms for resolving transfer pricing issues. They may be most useful when traditional mechanisms fail or are difficult to apply. Detailed guidelines for conducting advance pricing arrangements under the mutual agreement procedure ("MAP APAs") were adopted in October 1999 and are found as an annex to this chapter.

4.124   One key issue in the concept of APAs is how specific they can be in prescribing a taxpayer's transfer pricing over a period of years, for example whether only the transfer pricing methodology or more particular results can be fixed in a particular case. In general, great care must be taken if the APA goes beyond the methodology, the way it will be applied, and the critical assumptions, because more specific conclusions rely on predictions about future events.

4.125   The reliability of any prediction used in an APA depends both on the nature of the prediction and the critical assumptions on which the prediction is based. For example, it would not be reasonable to assert that the arm's length short-term borrowing rate for a certain corporation on intra-group borrowings will remain at six percent during the entire coming three years. It would be more plausible to predict that the rate will be LIBOR plus a fixed percentage. The prediction would become even more reliable if an appropriate critical assumption were added regarding the company's credit rating (*e.g.* the addition to LIBOR will change if the credit rating changes).

4.126   As another example, it would not be appropriate to specify a profit split formula between associated enterprises if it is expected that the allocation of functions between the enterprises will be unstable. It would, however, be possible to prescribe a profit split formula if the role of each

---

[1]   Additional guidance for conducting Advance Pricing Arrangements under the Mutual Agreement Procedure is found in the Annex to Chapter IV.

enterprise were articulated in critical assumptions. In certain cases, it might even be possible to make a reasonable prediction on the appropriateness of an actual profit split ratio if enough assumptions were provided.

4.127   In deciding how specific an APA can be in a particular case, tax administrations should recognise that predictions of absolute future profit experience seems least plausible. It may be possible to use profit ratios of independent enterprises as comparables, but these also are often volatile and hard to predict. Use of appropriate critical assumptions and use of ranges may enhance the reliability of predictions. Historical data in the industry in question can also be a guide.

4.128   In sum, the reliability of a prediction depends on the facts and circumstances of each actual case. Taxpayers and tax administrations need to pay close attention to the reliability of a prediction when considering the scope of an APA. Unreliable predictions should not be included in APAs. The appropriateness of a method and its application can usually be predicted, and the relevant critical assumptions made, with more reliability than future results (price or profit level).

4.129   Some countries allow for unilateral arrangements where the tax administration and the taxpayer in its jurisdiction establish an arrangement without the involvement of other interested tax administrations. However, a unilateral APA may affect the tax liability of associated enterprises in other tax jurisdictions. Where unilateral APAs are permitted, the competent authorities of other interested jurisdictions should be informed about the procedure as early as possible to determine whether they are willing and able to consider a bilateral arrangement under the mutual agreement procedure. In any event, countries should not include in any unilateral APA they may conclude with a taxpayer a requirement that the taxpayer waive access to the mutual agreement procedure if a transfer pricing dispute arises, and if another country raises a transfer pricing adjustment with respect to a transaction or issue covered by the unilateral APA, the first country is encouraged to consider the appropriateness of a corresponding adjustment and not to view the unilateral APA as an irreversible settlement.

4.130   Because of concerns over double taxation, most countries prefer bilateral or multilateral APAs (*i.e.* an arrangement in which two or more countries concur), and indeed some countries will not grant a unilateral APA (*i.e.* an arrangement between the taxpayer and one tax administration) to taxpayers in their jurisdiction. The bilateral (or multilateral) approach is far more likely to ensure that the arrangements will reduce the risk of double taxation, will be equitable to all tax administrations and taxpayers involved, and will provide greater certainty to the taxpayers concerned. It is also the case in some countries that domestic provisions do not permit the tax administrations to enter into binding agreements directly with the taxpayers, so that APAs can be concluded with the competent authority of a treaty partner only under the mutual agreement procedure. For purposes of the discussion in this section, an APA is not intended to include a unilateral arrangement except where specific reference to a unilateral APA is made.

4.131   Tax administrations may find APAs particularly useful in profit allocation or income attribution issues arising in the context of global securities and commodity trading operations, and also in handling multilateral cost contribution arrangements. The concept of APAs also may be useful in resolving issues raised under Article 7 of the OECD Model Tax Convention relating to allocation problems, permanent establishments, and branch operations.

4.132   APAs, including unilateral ones, differ in some ways from more traditional private rulings that some tax administrations issue to taxpayers. An APA generally deals with factual issues, whereas more traditional private rulings tend to be limited to addressing questions of a legal nature based on facts presented by a taxpayer. The facts underlying a private ruling request may not be questioned by the tax administration, whereas in an APA the facts are likely to be thoroughly analysed and investigated. In addition, an APA usually covers several transactions, several types of transactions on a continuing basis, or all of a taxpayer's international transactions for a given period of time. In contrast, a private ruling request usually is binding only for a particular transaction.

4.133   The cooperation of the associated enterprises is vital to a successful APA negotiation. For example, the associated enterprises ordinarily would be expected to provide the tax administrations with the methodology that they consider most reasonable under the particular facts and circumstances. The associated enterprises also should submit documentation supporting the reasonableness of their proposal, which would include, for example, data relating to the industry, markets, and countries to be covered by the agreement. In addition, the associated enterprises may identify uncontrolled businesses that are comparable or similar to the associated enterprises' businesses in terms of the economic activities performed and the transfer pricing conditions, e.g. economic costs and risks incurred, and perform a functional analysis as described in Chapter I of these Guidelines.

4.134   Typically, associated enterprises are allowed to participate in the process of obtaining an APA, by presenting the case to and negotiating with the tax administrations concerned, providing necessary information, and reaching agreement on the transfer pricing issues. From the associated enterprises' perspective, this ability to participate may be seen as an advantage over the conventional mutual agreement procedure.

4.135   At the conclusion of an APA process, the tax administrations should provide confirmation to the associated enterprises in their jurisdiction that no transfer pricing adjustment will be made as long as the taxpayer follows the terms of the arrangements. There should also be a provision in an APA (perhaps by reference to a range) that provides for possible revision or cancellation of the arrangement for future years when business operations change significantly, or when uncontrolled economic circumstances (*e.g.* significant changes in currency exchange rates) critically affect the reliability of the methodology in a manner that independent enterprises would consider significant for purposes of their transfer pricing.

4.136   An APA may cover all of the transfer pricing issues of a taxpayer (as is preferred by some countries) or may provide a flexibility to the taxpayer to limit the APA request to specified affiliates and intercompany transactions. An APA would apply to prospective years and transactions and the actual term would depend on the industry, products or transactions involved. The associated enterprises may limit their request to specified prospective tax years. An APA can provide an opportunity to apply the agreed transfer pricing methodology to resolve similar transfer pricing issues in open prior years. However, this application would require the agreement of the tax administration, the taxpayer, and, where appropriate, the treaty partner.

4.137   Each tax administration involved in the APA will naturally wish to monitor compliance with the APA by the taxpayers in its jurisdiction, and this is generally done in two ways. First, it may require a taxpayer that has entered into an APA to file annual reports demonstrating the extent of its compliance with the terms and conditions of the APA and that critical assumptions remain relevant. Second, the tax administration may continue to examine the taxpayer as part of the regular audit cycle but without re-evaluating the methodology. Instead, the tax administration may limit the examination of the transfer pricing to verifying the initial data relevant to the APA proposal and determining whether or not the taxpayer has complied with the terms and conditions of the APA. With regard to transfer pricing, a tax administration may also examine the reliability and accuracy of the representations in the APA and annual reports and the accuracy and consistency of how the particular methodology has been applied. All other issues not associated with the APA fall under regular audit jurisdiction.

4.138   An APA should be subject to cancellation, even retroactively, in the case of fraud or misrepresentation of information during an APA negotiation, or when a taxpayer fails to comply with the terms and conditions of an APA. Where an APA is proposed to be cancelled or revoked, the tax administration proposing the action should notify the other tax administrations of its intention and of the reasons for such action.

F.2   *Possible approaches for legal and administrative rules governing advance pricing arrangements*

4.139   APAs involving the competent authority of a treaty partner should be considered within the scope of the mutual agreement procedure under Article 25 of the OECD Model Tax Convention, even though such arrangements are not expressly mentioned there. Paragraph 3 of that Article provides that the competent authorities shall endeavour to resolve by mutual agreement any difficulties or doubts arising as to the interpretation or application of the Convention. Although paragraph 50 of the Commentary indicates that the matters covered by this paragraph are difficulties of a general nature concerning a category of taxpayers, it specifically acknowledges that the issues may arise in connection with an individual case. In a number of cases, APAs arise from cases where the application of transfer pricing to a particular category of taxpayer gives rise to doubts and difficulties. Paragraph 3 of Article 25 also indicates that the competent authorities may consult together for the elimination of double taxation in cases not provided for in the Convention. Bilateral APAs should fall within this provision because they have as one of their objectives the avoidance of double taxation. Even though the Convention provides for transfer pricing adjustments, it specifies no particular methodologies or procedures other than the arm's length principle as set out in Article 9. Thus, it could be considered that APAs are authorised by paragraph 3 of Article 25 because the specific transfer pricing cases subject to an APA are not otherwise provided for in the Convention. The exchange of information provision in Article 26 also could facilitate APAs, as it provides for cooperation between competent authorities in the form of exchanges of information.

4.140   Tax administrations might additionally rely on general domestic authority to administer taxes as the authority for entering into APAs. In some countries tax administrations may be able to issue specific administrative or procedural guidelines to taxpayers describing the appropriate tax treatment of transactions and the appropriate pricing methodology. As mentioned above, the tax codes of some OECD member countries include provisions that allow taxpayers to obtain specific rulings for different purposes. Even though these rulings were not designed specifically to cover APAs, they may be broad enough to be used to include APAs.

4.141   Some countries lack the basis in their domestic law to enter into APAs. However, when a tax convention contains a clause regarding the mutual agreement procedure similar to Article 25 of the OECD Model Tax Convention, the competent authorities generally should be allowed to conclude an APA, if transfer pricing issues were otherwise likely to result in double taxation, or would raise difficulties or doubts as to the interpretation or application of the Convention. Such an arrangement would be legally binding for both States and would create rights for the taxpayers involved. Inasmuch as double tax treaties take precedence over domestic law, the lack of a basis in domestic law to enter into APAs would not prevent application of APAs on the basis of a mutual agreement procedure.

F.3   Advantages of advance pricing arrangements

4.142   An APA programme can assist taxpayers by eliminating uncertainty through enhancing the predictability of tax treatment in international transactions. Provided the critical assumptions are met, an APA can provide the taxpayers involved with certainty in the tax treatment of the transfer pricing issues covered by the APA for a specified period of time. In some cases, an APA may also provide an option to extend the period of time to which it applies. When the term of an APA expires, the opportunity may also exist for the relevant tax administrations and taxpayers to renegotiate the APA. Because of the certainty provided by an APA, a taxpayer may be in a better position to predict its tax liabilities, thereby providing a tax environment that is favourable for investment.

4.143   APAs can provide an opportunity for both tax administrations and taxpayers to consult and cooperate in a non-adversarial spirit and environment. The opportunity to discuss complex tax issues in a less confrontational atmosphere than in a transfer pricing examination can stimulate a free flow of information among all parties involved for the purpose of coming to a legally correct and practicably workable result. The non-adversarial environment may also result in a more objective review of the submitted data and information than may occur in a more adversarial context (*e.g.* litigation). The close consultation and cooperation required between the tax administrations in an APA program also leads to closer relations with treaty partners on transfer pricing issues.

4.144   An APA may prevent costly and time-consuming examinations and litigation of major transfer pricing issues for taxpayers and tax administrations. Once an APA has been agreed, less resources may be needed for subsequent examination of the taxpayer's return, because more information is known about the taxpayer. It may still be difficult, however, to monitor the application of the arrangement. The APA process itself may also present time savings for both taxpayers and tax administrations over the time that would be spent in a conventional examination, although in the aggregate there may be no net time savings, for example, in jurisdictions that do not have an audit procedure and where the existence of an APA may not directly affect the amount of resources devoted to compliance.

4.145 Bilateral and multilateral APAs substantially reduce or eliminate the possibility of juridical or economic double or non taxation since all the relevant countries participate. By contrast, unilateral APAs do not provide certainty in the reduction of double taxation because tax administrations affected by the transactions covered by the APA may consider that the methodology adopted does not give a result consistent with the arm's length principle. In addition, bilateral and multilateral APAs can enhance the mutual agreement procedure by significantly reducing the time needed to reach an agreement since competent authorities are dealing with current data as opposed to prior year data that may be difficult and time-consuming to produce.

4.146 The disclosure and information aspects of an APA programme as well as the cooperative attitude under which an APA can be negotiated may assist tax administrations in gaining insight into complex international transactions undertaken by MNEs. An APA programme can improve knowledge and understanding of highly technical and factual circumstances in areas such as global trading and the tax issues involved. The development of specialist skills that focus on particular industries or specific types of transactions will enable tax administrations to give better service to other taxpayers in similar circumstances. Through an APA programme tax administrations have access to useful industry data and analysis of pricing methodologies in a cooperative environment.

F.4   *Disadvantages relating to advance pricing arrangements*

4.147 Unilateral APAs may present significant problems for tax administrations and taxpayers alike. From the point of view of other tax administrations, problems arise because they may disagree with the APA's conclusions. From the point of view of the associated enterprises involved, one problem is the possible effect on the behaviour of the associated enterprises. Unlike bilateral or multilateral APAs, the use of unilateral APAs may not lead to an increased level of certainty for the taxpayer involved and a reduction in economic or juridical double taxation for the MNE group. If the taxpayer accepts an arrangement that over-allocates income to the country making the APA in order to avoid lengthy and expensive transfer pricing enquiries or excessive penalties, the administrative burden shifts from the country providing the APA to other tax jurisdictions. Taxpayers should not feel compelled to enter into APAs for these reasons.

4.148   Another problem with a unilateral APA is the issue of corresponding adjustments. The flexibility of an APA may lead the taxpayer and the associated party to accommodate their pricing to the range of permissible pricing in the APA. In a unilateral APA, it is critical that this flexibility preserve the arm's length principle since a foreign competent authority is not likely to allow a corresponding adjustment arising out of an APA that is inconsistent, in its view, with the arm's length principle.

4.149   Another possible disadvantage would arise if an APA involved an unreliable prediction on changing market conditions without adequate critical assumptions, as discussed above. To avoid the risk of double taxation, it is necessary for an APA program to remain flexible, because a static APA may not satisfactorily reflect arm's length conditions.

4.150   An APA program may initially place a strain on transfer pricing audit resources, as tax administrations will generally have to divert resources earmarked for other purposes (*e.g.* examination, advising, litigation, etc.) to the APA programme. Demands may be made on the resources of a tax administration by taxpayers seeking the earliest possible conclusion to an APA request, keeping in mind their business objectives and time scales, and the APA programme as a whole will tend to be led by the demands of the business community. These demands may not coincide with the resource planning of the tax administrations, thereby making it difficult to process efficiently both the APAs and other equally important work. Renewing an APA, however, is likely to be less time-consuming than the process of initiating an APA. The renewal process may focus on updating and adjusting facts, business and economic criteria, and computations. In the case of bilateral arrangements, the agreement of the competent authorities of both Contracting States is to be obtained on the renewal of an APA to avoid double taxation (or non-taxation).

4.151   Another potential disadvantage could occur where one tax administration has undertaken a number of bilateral APAs which involve only certain of the associated enterprises within an MNE group. A tendency may exist to harmonise the basis for concluding later APAs in a way similar to those previously concluded without sufficient regard being had to the conditions operating in other markets. Care should therefore be taken with interpreting the results of previously concluded APAs as being representative across all markets.

4.152   Concerns have also been expressed that, because of the nature of the APA procedure, it will interest taxpayers with a good voluntary compliance history. Experience in some countries has shown that, most often, taxpayers which would be interested in APAs are very large corporations which would be audited on a regular basis, with their pricing methodology then being examined in any event. The difference in the examination conducted of their transfer pricing would be one of timing rather than extent. As well, it has not been demonstrated that APAs will be of interest solely or principally to such taxpayers. Indeed, there are some early indications that taxpayers, having experienced difficulty with tax administrations on transfer pricing issues and not wishing these difficulties to continue, are often interested in applying for an APA. There is then a serious danger of audit resources and expertise being diverted to these taxpayers and away from the investigation of less compliant taxpayers, where these resources could be better deployed in reducing the risk of losing tax revenue. The balance of compliance resources may be particularly difficult to achieve since an APA programme tends to require highly experienced and often specialised staff. Requests for APAs may be concentrated in particular areas or sectors, *e.g.* global trading, and this can overstretch the specialist resources already allocated to those areas by the authorities. Tax administrations require time to train experts in specialist fields in order to meet unforeseeable demands from taxpayers for APAs in those areas.

4.153   In addition to the foregoing concerns, there are a number of possible pitfalls as described below that could arise if an APA program were improperly administered, and tax administrations who use APAs should make strong efforts to eliminate the occurrence of these problems as APA practice evolves.

4.154   For example, an APA might seek more detailed industry and taxpayer specific information than would be requested in a transfer pricing examination. In principle, this should not be the case and the documentation required for an APA should not be more onerous than for an examination, except for the fact that in an APA the tax administration will need to have details of predictions and the basis for those predictions, which may not be central issues in a transfer pricing examination that focuses on completed transactions. In fact, an APA should seek to limit the documentation, as discussed above, and focus the documentation more closely on the issues in light of the taxpayer's business practices. Tax administrations need to recognise that:

a)   Publicly available information on competitors and comparables is limited;

b)   Not all taxpayers have the capacity to undertake in-depth market analyses; and,

c) Only parent companies may be knowledgeable about group pricing policies.

5.155 Another possible concern is that an APA may allow the tax administration to make a closer study of the transactions at issue than would occur in the context of a transfer pricing examination, depending on the facts and circumstances. The taxpayer must provide detailed information relating to its transfer pricing and satisfy any other requirements imposed for the verification of compliance with the terms and conditions of the APA. At the same time, the taxpayer is not sheltered from normal and routine examinations by the tax administration on other issues. An APA also does not shelter a taxpayer from examination of its transfer pricing activities. The taxpayer may still have to establish that it has complied in good faith with the terms and conditions of the APA, that the material representations in the APA remain valid, that the supporting data used in applying the methodology were correct, that the critical assumptions underlying the APA are still valid and are applied consistently, and that the methodology is applied consistently. Tax administrations should, therefore, seek to ensure that APA procedures are not unnecessarily cumbersome and that they do not make more demand of taxpayers than are strictly required by the scope of the APA application.

4.156 Problems could also develop if tax administrations misuse information obtained in an APA in their examination practices. If the taxpayer withdraws from its APA request or if the taxpayer's application is rejected after consideration of all of the facts, any nonfactual information provided by the taxpayer in connection with the APA request, such as settlement offers, reasoning, opinions, and judgments, cannot be treated as relevant in any respect to the examination. In addition, the fact that a taxpayer has applied unsuccessfully for an APA should not be taken into account by the tax administration in determining whether to commence an examination of that taxpayer.

4.157 Tax administrations also should ensure the confidentiality of trade secrets and other sensitive information and documentation submitted to them in the course of an APA proceeding. Therefore, domestic rules against disclosure should be applied. In a bilateral APA the confidentiality requirements on treaty partners would apply, thereby preventing public disclosure of confidential data.

4.158 An APA program cannot be used by all taxpayers because the procedure can be expensive and time-consuming and small taxpayers generally may not be able to afford it. This is especially true if independent experts are involved. APAs may therefore only assist in resolving mainly large transfer pricing cases. In addition, the resource implications of an APA program may limit the number of requests a tax administration can entertain. In evaluating APAs, tax administrations can alleviate these potential problems by ensuring that the level of inquiry is adjusted to the size of the international transactions involved.

F.5   Recommendations

F.5.1   In general

4.159   Since the Guidelines were published in their original version in 1995, a significant number of OECD member countries have acquired experience with APAs. Those countries which do have some experience seem to be satisfied so far, so that it can be expected that under the appropriate circumstances the experience with APAs will continue to expand. The success of APA programs will depend on the care taken in determining the proper degree of specificity for the arrangement based on critical assumptions, the proper administration of the program, and the presence of adequate safeguards to avoid the pitfalls described above, in addition to the flexibility and openness with which all parties approach the process.

4.160   There are some continuing issues regarding the form and scope of APAs that require greater experience for full resolution and agreement among member countries, such as the question of unilateral APAs. The Committee on Fiscal Affairs intends to monitor carefully any expanded use of APAs and to promote greater consistency in practice among those countries that choose to use them.

F.5.2   Coverage of an arrangement

4.161   When considering the scope of an APA, taxpayers and tax administrations need to pay close attention to the reliability of any predictions so as to exclude unreliable predictions. In general, great care must be taken if the APA goes beyond the methodology, its application, and critical assumptions. See paragraphs 4.123-4.128.

F.5.3   Unilateral versus bilateral (multilateral) arrangements

4.162   Wherever possible, an APA should be concluded on a bilateral or multilateral basis between competent authorities through the mutual agreement procedure of the relevant treaty. A bilateral APA carries less risk of taxpayers feeling compelled to enter into an APA or to accept a non-arm's-length agreement in order to avoid expensive and prolonged enquiries and possible penalties. A bilateral APA also significantly reduces the chance of any profits either escaping tax altogether or being doubly taxed, Moreover, concluding an APA through the mutual agreement procedure may be the only form that can be adopted by a tax administration which lacks domestic legislation to conclude binding agreements directly with the taxpayer.

F.5.4   Equitable access to APAs for all taxpayers

4.163   As discussed above, the nature of APA proceedings may *de facto* limit their accessibility to large taxpayers. The restriction of APAs to large taxpayers may raise questions of equality and uniformity, since taxpayers in identical situations should not be treated differently. A flexible allocation of examination resources may alleviate these concerns. Tax administrations also may need to consider the possibility of adopting a streamlined access for small taxpayers. Tax administrations should take care to adapt their levels of inquiry, in evaluating APAs, to the size of the international transactions involved.

F.5.5   Developing working agreements between competent authorities and improved procedures

4.164   Between those countries that use APAs, greater uniformity in APA practices could be beneficial to both tax administrations and taxpayers. Accordingly, the tax administrations of such countries may wish to consider working agreements with the competent authorities for the undertaking of APAs. These agreements may set forth general guidelines and understandings for the reaching of mutual agreement in cases where a taxpayer has requested an APA involving transfer pricing issues.

4.165   In addition, bilateral APAs with treaty partners should conform to certain requirements. For example, the same necessary and pertinent information should be made available to each tax administration at the same time, and the agreed upon methodology should be in accordance with the arm's length principle.

G. Arbitration

4.166   As trade and investment have taken on an increasingly international character, the tax disputes that, on occasion, arise from such activities have likewise become increasingly international. And more particularly, the disputes no longer involve simply controversy between a taxpayer and its tax administration but also concern disagreements between tax administrations themselves. In many of these situations, the MNE group is primarily a stakeholder and the real parties in interest are the governments involved. Although traditionally problems of double taxation have been resolved through the mutual agreement procedure, relief is not guaranteed if the tax administrations, after consultation, cannot reach an agreement on their own and if there is no mechanism, such as an arbitration clause similar to the one of paragraph 5 of Article 25, to provide the possibility of a resolution. However, where a particular tax treaty contains an arbitration clause similar to the one of paragraph 5 of Article 25, this extension of the mutual agreement procedure makes a resolution of the case still possible by submitting one or more issues on which the competent authorities cannot reach an agreement to arbitration.

4.167   In the 2008 update to the OECD Model Tax Convention, Article 25 was supplemented with a new paragraph 5 which provides that, in the cases where the competent authorities are unable to reach an agreement within two years, the unresolved issues will, at the request of the person who presented the case, be solved through an arbitration process. This extension of the mutual agreement procedure ensures that where the competent authorities cannot reach an agreement on one or more issues that prevent the resolution of a case, a resolution of the case will still be possible by submitting those issues to arbitration. Arbitration under paragraph 5 of Article 25 is an integral part of the mutual agreement procedure and does not constitute an alternative route to solving tax treaty disputes between States. Paragraphs 63-85 of the Commentary on Article 25 provide guidance on the arbitration phase of the mutual agreement procedure.

4.168   The existence of an arbitration clause similar to paragraph 5 of Article 25 in a particular bilateral treaty should make the mutual agreement procedure itself more effective even in cases where resort to arbitration is not necessary. The very existence of this possibility should encourage greater use of the mutual agreement procedure since both governments and taxpayers will know at the outset that the time and effort put into the mutual agreement procedure will be likely to produce a satisfactory result. Further, governments will have an incentive to ensure that the mutual agreement procedure is conducted efficiently in order to avoid the necessity of subsequent supplemental procedures.

Chapter V

Documentation

A. Introduction

5.1   This chapter provides general guidance for tax administrations to take into account in developing rules and/or procedures on documentation to be obtained from taxpayers in connection with a transfer pricing inquiry. It also provides guidance to assist taxpayers in identifying documentation that would be most helpful in showing that their controlled transactions satisfy the arm's length principle and hence in resolving transfer pricing issues and facilitating tax examinations.

5.2   Documentation obligations may be affected by rules governing burden of proof in the relevant jurisdiction. In most jurisdictions, the tax administration bears the burden of proof. Thus, the taxpayer need not prove the correctness of its transfer pricing in such cases unless the tax administration makes a *prima facie* case showing that the pricing is inconsistent with the arm's length principle. The discussion of documentation in this chapter is not intended to impose a greater burden on taxpayers than is required by domestic rules. However, it should be noted that even where the burden of proof is on the tax administration, the tax administration might still reasonably oblige the taxpayer to produce documentation about its transfer pricing, because without adequate information the tax administration would not be able to examine the case properly. In fact, where the taxpayer does not provide adequate documentation, there may be a shifting of burden of proof in some jurisdictions in the manner of a rebuttable presumption in favour of the adjustment proposed by the tax administration. Perhaps more importantly, both the tax administration and the taxpayer should endeavour to make a good faith showing that their determinations of transfer pricing are consistent with the arm's length principle regardless of where the burden of proof lies. In examination practices the behaviour of the tax administration should not be affected by the knowledge that the taxpayer bears the burden of proof where this is the case. The burden of proof should never be used by either tax administrations or taxpayers as a justification for making groundless or unverifiable assertions about transfer pricing.

B. Guidance on documentation rules and procedures

5.3   Each taxpayer should endeavour to determine transfer pricing for tax purposes in accordance with the arm's length principle, based upon information reasonably available at the time of the determination. Thus, a taxpayer ordinarily should give consideration to whether its transfer pricing is appropriate for tax purposes before the pricing is established. For example, it would be reasonable for a taxpayer to have made a determination regarding whether comparable data from uncontrolled transactions are available. The taxpayer also could be expected to examine, based on information reasonably available, whether the conditions used to establish transfer pricing in prior years have changed, if those conditions are to be used to determine transfer pricing for the current year.

5.4   The taxpayer's process of considering whether transfer pricing is appropriate for tax purposes should be determined in accordance with the same prudent business management principles that would govern the process of evaluating a business decision of a similar level of complexity and importance. It would be expected that the application of these principles will require the taxpayer to prepare or refer to written materials that could serve as documentation of the efforts undertaken to comply with the arm's length principle, including the information on which the transfer pricing was based, the factors taken into account, and the method selected. It would be reasonable for tax administrations to expect taxpayers when establishing their transfer pricing for a particular business activity to prepare or to obtain such materials regarding the nature of the activity and the transfer pricing, and to retain such material for production if necessary in the course of a tax examination. Such actions should assist taxpayers in filing correct tax returns. Note, however, that there should be no contemporaneous obligation at the time the pricing is determined or the tax return is filed to produce these types of documents or to prepare them for review by a tax administration. The documents that it would be appropriate to request with the tax return are described in paragraph 5.15.

5.5   Because the tax administration's ultimate interest would be satisfied if the necessary documents were submitted in a timely manner when requested by the tax administration in the course of an examination, the document storage process should be subject to the taxpayer's discretion. For instance, the taxpayer may choose to store relevant documents in the form of unprocessed originals or in a well-compiled book, and in whichever language it might prefer, prior to the time the documents must be provided to the tax administration. The taxpayer should, however, comply with reasonable requests for translation of documents that are made available to the tax administration.

5.6   In considering whether transfer pricing is appropriate for tax purposes, it may be necessary in applying principles of prudent business management for the taxpayer to prepare or refer to written materials that would not otherwise be prepared or referred to in the absence of tax considerations, including documents from foreign associated enterprises. When requesting submission of these types of documents, the tax administration should take great care to balance its need for the documents against the cost and administrative burden to the taxpayer of creating or obtaining them. For example, the taxpayer should not be expected to incur disproportionately high costs and burdens to obtain documents from foreign associated enterprises or to engage in an exhaustive search for comparable data from uncontrolled transactions if the taxpayer reasonably believes, having regard to the principles of these Guidelines, either that no comparable data exists or that the cost of locating the comparable data would be disproportionately high relative to the amounts at issue. Tax administrations should also recognise that they can avail themselves of the exchange of information articles in bilateral double tax conventions to obtain such information, where it can be expected to be produced in a timely and efficient manner.

5.7   Thus, while some of the documents that might reasonably be used or relied upon in determining arm's length transfer pricing for tax purposes may be of the type that would not have been prepared or obtained other than for tax purposes, the taxpayer should be expected to have prepared or obtained such documents only if they are indispensable for a reasonable assessment of whether the transfer pricing satisfies the arm's length principle and can be obtained or prepared by the taxpayer without a disproportionately high cost being incurred. The taxpayer should not be expected to have prepared or obtained documents beyond the minimum needed to make a reasonable assessment of whether it has complied with the arm's length principle.

5.8   Consistent with the above guidance, taxpayers should not be obligated to retain documents that were prepared or referred to in connection with transactions occurring in years for which adjustment is time-barred beyond a reasonable period of retention consistent with the body of general domestic law for similar types of documents. In addition, tax administrations ordinarily should not request documents relating to such years, even where the documentation has been retained. However, at times such documents may be relevant to a transfer pricing inquiry for a subsequent year that is not time barred, for example where taxpayers are voluntarily keeping such records in relation to long-term contracts, or to determine whether comparability standards relating to the application of a transfer pricing method in that subsequent year are satisfied. Tax administrations should bear in mind the difficulties in locating documents for prior years and should restrict such requests to instances where they have good reason in connection with the transaction under examination for reviewing the documents in question.

5.9   Tax administrations also should limit requests for documents that became available only after the transaction in question occurred to those that are reasonably likely to contain relevant information as determined under principles governing the use of multiple year data in Chapter III or information about the facts that existed at the time the transfer pricing was determined. In considering whether documentation is adequate, a tax administration should have regard to the extent to which that information reasonably could have been available to the taxpayer at the time transfer pricing was established.

5.10   Tax administrations further should not require taxpayers to produce documents that are not in the actual possession or control of the taxpayer or otherwise reasonably available, *e.g.* information that cannot be legally obtained, or that is not actually available to the taxpayer because it is confidential to the taxpayer's competitor or because it is unpublished and cannot be obtained by normal enquiry or market data.

5.11   In many cases, information about foreign associated enterprises is essential to transfer pricing examinations. However, gathering such information may present a taxpayer with difficulties that it does not encounter in producing its own documents. When the taxpayer is a subsidiary of a foreign associated enterprise or is only a minority shareholder, information may be difficult to obtain because the taxpayer does not have control of the associated enterprise. In any case, accounting standards and legal documentation requirements (including time limits for preparation and submission) differ from country to country. The documents requested by the taxpayer may not be of the type that prudent business management principles would suggest the foreign associated enterprise would maintain, and substantial time and cost may be involved in translating and producing documents. These considerations should be taken into account in determining the taxpayer's enforceable documentation obligation.

5.12   It might not be necessary to extend the information required to all associated enterprises involved in the controlled transactions under review. For example, in establishing a transfer price for a distributor with limited functions performed, it might be adequate to obtain information about those functions without extending the information requested to other members of the MNE group.

5.13   Tax administrations should take care to ensure that there is no public disclosure of trade secrets, scientific secrets, or other confidential data. Tax administrations therefore should use discretion in requesting this type of information and should do so only if they can undertake that the information will remain confidential from outside parties, except to the extent disclosure is required in public court proceedings or judicial decisions. Every endeavour should be made to ensure that confidentiality is maintained to the extent possible in such proceedings and decisions.

5.14   Taxpayers should recognise that notwithstanding limitations on documentation requirements, a tax administration will have to make a determination of arm's length transfer pricing even if the information available is incomplete. As a result, the taxpayer must take into consideration that adequate record-keeping practices and the voluntary production of documents can improve the persuasiveness of its approach to transfer pricing. This will be true whether the case is relatively straightforward or complex, but the greater the complexity and unusualness of the case, the more significance will attach to documentation.

5.15   Tax administrations should limit the amount of information that is requested at the stage of filing the tax return. At that time, no particular transaction has been identified for transfer pricing review. It would be quite burdensome if detailed documentation were required at this stage on all cross-border transactions between associated enterprises, and on all enterprises engaging in such transactions. Therefore, it would be unreasonable to require the taxpayer to submit documents with the tax return specifically demonstrating the appropriateness of all transfer price determinations. The result could be to impede international trade and foreign investment. Any documentation requirement at the tax return filing stage should be limited to requiring the taxpayer to provide information sufficient to allow the tax administration to determine approximately which taxpayers need further examination.

C. Useful information for determining transfer pricing

5.16   The information relevant to an individual transfer pricing enquiry depends on the facts and circumstances of the case. For that reason it is not possible to define in any generalised way the precise extent and nature of information that would be reasonable for the tax administration to require and for the taxpayer to produce at the time of examination. However, there are certain features common to any transfer pricing enquiry that depend on information in respect of the taxpayer, the associated enterprises, the nature of the transaction, and the basis on which the transaction is priced. The following section outlines the information that could be relevant, depending on the individual circumstances. It is intended to demonstrate the kind of information that would facilitate the enquiry in the generality of cases, but it should be underscored that the information described below should not be viewed as a minimum compliance requirement. Similarly, it is not intended to set forth an exhaustive list of the information that a tax administration may be entitled to request.

5.17   An analysis under the arm's length principle generally requires information about the associated enterprises involved in the controlled transactions, the transactions at issue, the functions performed, information derived from independent enterprises engaged in similar transactions or businesses, and other factors discussed elsewhere in these Guidelines, taking into account as well the guidance in paragraph 5.4. Some additional information about the controlled transaction in question could be relevant. This could include the nature and terms of the transaction, economic conditions and property involved in the transactions, how the product or service that is the subject of the controlled transaction in question flows among the associated enterprises, and changes in trading conditions or renegotiations of existing arrangements. It also could include a description of the circumstances of any known transactions between the taxpayer and an independent party that are similar to the transaction with a foreign associated enterprise and any information that might bear upon whether independent enterprises dealing at arm's length under comparable circumstances would have entered into a similarly structured transaction. Other useful information may include a list of any known comparable companies having transactions similar to the controlled transactions.

5.18   In particular transfer pricing cases it may be useful to refer to information relating to each associated enterprise involved in the controlled transactions under review, such as:

a)   an outline of the business;

b)   the structure of the organisation;

c)   ownership linkages within the MNE group;

d)   the amount of sales and operating results from the last few years preceding the transaction;

e)   the level of the taxpayer's transactions with foreign associated enterprises, for example the amount of sales of inventory assets, the rendering of services, the rent of tangible assets, the use and transfer of intangible property, and interest on loans.

5.19   Information on pricing, including business strategies and special circumstances at issue, may also be useful. This could include factors that influenced the setting of prices or the establishment of any pricing policies for the taxpayer and the whole MNE group. For example, these policies might be to add a mark up to manufacturing cost, to deduct related costs from sales prices to end users in the market where the foreign associated enterprises are conducting a wholesale business, or to employ an integrated pricing or cost contribution policy on a whole group basis. Information on the factors that lead to the development of any such policies may well help an MNE to convince tax administrations that its transfer pricing policies are consistent with the transactional conditions in the open market. It could also be useful to have an explanation of the selection, application, and consistency with the arm's length principle of the transfer pricing method used to establish the transfer pricing. It should be noted in this respect that the information most useful to establishing arm's length pricing may vary depending upon the method being used.

5.20   Special circumstances would include details concerning any set-off transactions that have an effect on determining the arm's length price. In such a case, documents are useful to help describe the relevant facts, the qualitative connection between the transactions, and the quantification of the set-off. Contemporaneous documentation helps minimise the use of hindsight. As discussed in Chapter III, a set-off transaction may occur, for example, where the seller supplies goods at a lower price, because the buyer provides services to the seller free of charge; where a higher royalty is established to compensate for an intentionally lower price of goods; and where a royalty-free cross-licence agreement is concluded concerning the use of industrial property or technical know-how.

5.21   Other special circumstances could involve management strategy or the type of business. Examples are circumstances under which the taxpayer's business is conducted in order to enter a new market, to increase share in an existing market, to introduce new products into a market, or to fend off increasing competition.

5.22   General commercial and industry conditions affecting the taxpayer also may be relevant. Relevant information could include information explaining the current business environment and its forecasted changes; and how forecasted incidents influence the taxpayer's industry, market scale, competitive conditions, regulatory framework, technological progress, and foreign exchange market.

5.23   Information about functions performed (taking into account assets used and risks assumed) may be useful for the functional analysis that ordinarily would be undertaken to apply the arm's length principle. The functions include manufacturing, assemblage, management of purchase and materials, marketing, wholesale, stock control, warranty administration, advertising and marketing activities, carriage and warehousing activities, lending and payment terms, training, and personnel.

5.24   The possible risks assumed that are taken into account in the functional analysis may include risks of change in cost, price, or stock, risks relating to success or failure of research and development, financial risks including change in the foreign exchange and interest rates, risks of lending and payment terms, risks for manufacturing liability, business risk related to ownership of assets, or facilities.

5.25   Financial information may also be useful if there is a need to compare profit and loss between the associated enterprises with which the taxpayer has transactions subject to the transfer pricing rules. This information might include documents that explain the profit and loss to the extent necessary to evaluate the appropriateness of the transfer pricing policy within an MNE group. It also could include documents concerning expenses borne by foreign associated enterprises, such as sales promotion expenses or advertising expenses.

5.26   Some relevant financial information might also be in the possession of the foreign associated enterprise. This information could include reports on manufacturing costs, costs of research and development, and/or general and administrative expenses.

5.27   Documents also may be helpful for showing the process of negotiations for determining or revising prices in controlled transactions. When taxpayers negotiate to establish or to revise a price with associated enterprises, documents may be helpful that forecast profit and administrative and selling expenses to be incurred by foreign subsidiaries such as personnel, depreciation, marketing, distribution, or transportation expenses, and that explain how transfer prices are determined; for example, by deducting gross margins for subsidiaries from the estimated sales prices to end-users.

D. Summary of recommendations on documentation

5.28   Taxpayers should make reasonable efforts at the time transfer pricing is established to determine whether the transfer pricing is appropriate for tax purposes in accordance with the arm's length principle. Tax administrations should have the right to obtain the documentation prepared or referred to in this process as a means of verifying compliance with the arm's length principle. However, the extensiveness of this process should be determined in accordance with the same prudent business management principles that would govern the process of evaluating a business decision of a similar level of complexity and importance. Moreover, the need for the documents should be balanced by the costs and administrative burdens, particularly where this process suggests the creation of documents that would not otherwise be prepared or referred to in the absence of tax considerations. Documentation requirements should not impose on taxpayers costs and burdens disproportionate to the circumstances. Taxpayers should nonetheless recognise that adequate record-keeping practices and voluntary production of documents facilitate examinations and the resolution of transfer pricing issues that arise.

5.29   Tax administrations and taxpayers alike should commit themselves to a greater level of cooperation in addressing documentation issues, in order to avoid excessive documentation requirements while at the same time providing for adequate information to apply the arm's length principle reliably. Taxpayers should be forthcoming with relevant information in their possession, and tax administrations should recognise that they can avail themselves of exchange of information articles in certain cases so that less need be asked of the taxpayer in the context of an examination. The Committee on Fiscal Affairs intends to study the issue of documentation further to develop additional guidance that might be given to assist taxpayers and tax administrations in this area.

Chapter VI

Special Considerations for Intangible Property

A. Introduction

6.1   This chapter discusses special considerations that arise in seeking to establish whether the conditions made or imposed in transactions between associated enterprises involving intangible property reflect arm's length transactions. Particular attention to intangible property transactions is appropriate because the transactions are often difficult to evaluate for tax purposes. The chapter discusses the application of appropriate methods under the arm's length principle for establishing transfer pricing for transactions involving intangible property used in commercial activities, including marketing activities. It also discusses specific difficulties that arise when the enterprises conducting marketing activities are not the legal owners of marketing intangibles such as trademarks and trade names. Cost contribution arrangements among associated enterprises for research and development expenditures that may result in intangible property are discussed in Chapter VIII.

6.2   For the purposes of this chapter, the term "intangible property" includes rights to use industrial assets such as patents, trademarks, trade names, designs or models. It also includes literary and artistic property rights, and intellectual property such as know-how and trade secrets. This chapter concentrates on business rights, that is intangible property associated with commercial activities, including marketing activities. These intangibles are assets that may have considerable value even though they may have no book value in the company's balance sheet. There also may be considerable risks associated with them (*e.g.* contract or product liability and environmental damages).

B. Commercial intangibles

B.1   In general

6.3   Commercial intangibles include patents, know-how, designs, and models that are used for the production of a good or the provision of a service, as well as intangible rights that are themselves business assets transferred to customers or used in the operation of business (*e.g.* computer software). Marketing intangibles are a special type of commercial intangible with a somewhat different nature, as discussed below. For purposes of clarity, commercial intangibles other than marketing intangibles are referred to as trade intangibles. Trade intangibles often are created through risky and costly research and development (R&D) activities, and the developer generally tries to recover the expenditures on these activities and obtain a return thereon through product sales, service contracts, or licence agreements. The developer may perform the research activity in its own name, *i.e.* with the intention of having legal and economic ownership of any resulting trade intangible, on behalf of one or more other group members under an arrangement of contract research where the beneficiary or beneficiaries have legal and economic ownership of the intangible, or on behalf of itself and one or more other group members under an arrangement in which the members involved are engaged in a joint activity and have economic ownership of the intangible (also discussed in Chapter VIII on cost contribution arrangements). Reciprocal licensing (cross-licensing) is not uncommon, and there may be other more complicated arrangements as well.

6.4   Marketing intangibles include trademarks and trade names that aid in the commercial exploitation of a product or service, customer lists, distribution channels, and unique names, symbols, or pictures that have an important promotional value for the product concerned. Some marketing intangibles (*e.g.* trademarks) may be protected by the law of the country concerned and used only with the owner's permission for the relevant product or services. The value of marketing intangibles depends upon many factors, including the reputation and credibility of the trade name or the trademark fostered by the quality of the goods and services provided under the name or the mark in the past, the degree of quality control and ongoing R&D, distribution and availability of the goods or services being marketed, the extent and success of the promotional expenditures incurred in order to familiarise potential customers with the goods or services (in particular advertising and marketing expenditures incurred in order to develop a network of supporting relationships with distributors, agents, or other facilitating agencies), the value of the market to which the marketing intangibles will provide access, and the nature of any right created in the intangible under the law.

6.5   Intellectual property such as know-how and trade secrets can be trade intangibles or marketing intangibles. Know-how and trade secrets are proprietary information or knowledge that assists or improves a commercial activity, but that is not registered for protection in the manner of a patent or trademark. The term know-how is perhaps a less precise concept. Paragraph 11 of the Commentary on Article 12 of the OECD Model Tax Convention gives the following definition: "[Know-how] generally corresponds to undivulged information of an industrial, commercial or scientific nature arising from previous experience, which has practical application in the operation of an enterprise and from the disclosure of which an economic benefit can be derived". Know-how thus may include secret processes or formulae or other secret information concerning industrial, commercial or scientific experience that is not covered by patent. Any disclosure of know-how or a trade secret could substantially reduce the value of the property. Know-how and trade secrets frequently play a significant role in the commercial activities of MNE groups.

6.6   Care should be taken in determining whether or when a trade or marketing intangible exists. For example, not all research and development expenditures produce a valuable trade intangible, and not all marketing activities result in the creation of a marketing intangible. It can be difficult to evaluate the degree to which any particular expenditure has successfully resulted in a business asset and to calculate the economic effect of that asset for a given year.

6.7   For example, marketing activities may encompass a wide range of business activities, such as market research, designing or planning products suitable to market needs, sales strategies, public relations, sales, service, and quality control. Some of these activities may not have an impact beyond the year in which they are performed, and so would properly be treated as current expenses rather than as capitalisable expenditures. Other activities may have both short-term and long-term effect. The treatment of such activities is likely to be important in a functional analysis carried out in order to establish comparability for the purposes of transfer pricing. In some cases, the costs of marketing activities and, with respect to trade activities, R&D expenditures, may be sought to be recovered through the charging for associated goods and services, whereas in other cases there may have been created intangible property on which a royalty is separately charged, or a combination of the two.

B.2 Examples: patents and trademarks

6.8   The differences between trade and marketing intangibles can be seen in a comparison of patents and trademarks. Patents are basically concerned with the production of goods (which may be sold or used in connection with the provision of services) while trademarks are used in promoting the sale of goods or services. A patent gives an exclusive right to its owner to use a given invention for a limited period of time. A trademark may continue indefinitely; its protection will disappear only under special circumstances (voluntary renunciation, no renewal in due time, cancellation or annulment following a judicial decision, etc.). A trademark is a unique name, symbol or picture that the owner or licensee may use to identify special products or services of a particular manufacturer or dealer and, as a corollary, to prohibit their use by other parties for similar purposes under the protection of domestic and international law. Trademarks may confer a valuable market status on the goods or services to which they are attached, whether or not those goods or services are otherwise unique. Patents may create a monopoly in certain products or services whereas trademarks alone do not, because competitors may be able to sell the same or similar products so long as they use different distinctive signs.

6.9   Patents are usually the result of risky and costly research and development and the developer will try to recover its costs (and earn a return) through the sale of products covered by the patent, licensing others to use the invention (often a product or process), or through the outright sale of the patent. The legal creation of a new trademark (or one newly introduced to a given market) is usually not an expensive matter. In contrast, it will very often be an expensive business to make it valuable and to ensure that the value is maintained (or increased). Intensive and costly advertising campaigns and other marketing activities will ordinarily be necessary as will expenditure on the control of the quality of the trademarked product. The value and any changes will depend to an extent on how effectively the trademark is promoted in the markets in which it is used. Value will also depend on the reputation of the owner for quality in production and rendering of services and on how well this reputation is maintained. In certain cases, the value for the licensor may increase as the result of efforts and expenditure by the licensee. In some cases patents, because of their outstanding quality, may also have a very strong marketing effect similar to that of a pure trademark and payments for the right to use such patents may have to be looked at in much the same light as payments for the right to use a trademark.

6.10   Trademarks may be established for goods, either for specific products or for a line of products. They are perhaps most familiar at the consumer market level, but they are likely to be encountered at all market levels. Trademarks may also be acquired for services. The ownership of a trademark would normally be vested in one person, for example, a legally independent company. A tradename (often the name of an enterprise) may have the same force of penetration as a trademark and may indeed be registered in some specific form as a trademark. The names of certain MNEs in pharmaceutical or electronic industries, for example, have an excellent sales promotion value, and they may be used for the marketing of a variety of goods or services. The names of well-known persons, designers, sports figures, actors, people working in show business, etc., may also be associated with tradenames and trademarks, and they have often been very successful marketing instruments.

6.11   A trademark may be sold, licensed, or otherwise transferred by one person to another. Various kinds of licence contracts are concluded in practice. A distributor could be allowed to use a trademark without a licence agreement in selling products manufactured by the owner of the trademark, but trademark licensing also has become a common practice, particularly in international trade. Thus, the owner of a trademark may grant a licence to the trademark to another enterprise to use for goods that it produces itself or buys from other sources (or from the licensor, *e.g.* where goods or components are purchased generically in a separate transaction without a trademark). The terms and conditions of licence agreements may vary to a considerable extent.

6.12   It is sometimes difficult to make a clear-cut distinction between income from trade and marketing intangibles. For instance, in research-oriented industries, the trademark and trade name are vital components in securing sufficient income to reward past research and undertake new projects, particularly as patents are time-limited. Building up brand confidence and trademark recognition is therefore vitally important to ensure that the product continues to be commercially viable after the patent expires or even in cases where no patent was developed. See Section D describing arm's length arrangements involving marketing intangibles.

C. Applying the arm's length principle

C.1   *In general*

6.13   The general guidance set out in Chapters I, II, and III for applying the arm's length principle pertains equally to the determination of transfer pricing between associated enterprises for intangible property. This principle can, however, be difficult to apply to controlled transactions involving intangible property because such property may have a special character complicating the search for comparables and in some cases making value difficult to determine at the time of the transaction. Further, for wholly legitimate business reasons due to the relationship between them, associated enterprises might sometimes structure a transfer in a manner that independent enterprises would not contemplate (see paragraphs 1.11 and 1.64).

6.14   Arm's length pricing for intangible property must take into account for the purposes of comparability the perspective of both the transferor of the property and the transferee. From the perspective of the transferor, the arm's length principle would examine the pricing at which a comparable independent enterprise would be willing to transfer the property. From the perspective of the transferee, a comparable independent enterprise may or may not be prepared to pay such a price, depending on the value and usefulness of the intangible property to the transferee in its business. The transferee will generally be prepared to pay this licence fee if the benefit it reasonably expects to secure from the use of the intangibles is satisfactory having regard to other options realistically available. Given that the licensee will have to undertake investments or otherwise incur expenditures to use the licence it has to be determined whether an independent enterprise would be prepared to pay a licence fee of the given amount considering the expected benefits from the additional investments and other expenditures likely to be incurred.

6.15   This analysis is important to ensure that an associated enterprise is not required to pay an amount for the purchase or use of intangible property that is based on the highest or most productive use when the property is of more limited usefulness to the associated enterprise given its business operations and other relevant circumstances. In such a case, the usefulness of the property should be taken into account when determining comparability. This discussion highlights the importance of taking all the facts and circumstances into consideration when determining comparability of transactions.

C.2   *Identifying arrangements made for the transfer of intangible property*

6.16   The conditions for transferring intangible property may be those of an outright sale of the intangible or, more commonly, a royalty under a licensing arrangement for rights in respect of the intangible property. A royalty would ordinarily be a recurrent payment based on the user's output, sales, or in some rare circumstances, profits. When the royalty is based on the licensee's output or sales, the rate may vary according to the turnover of the licensee. There are also instances where changed facts and circumstances (*e.g.* new designs, increased advertising of the trademark by the owner) could lead to a revision of the conditions of remuneration.

6.17   The compensation for the use of intangible property may be included in the price charged for the sale of goods when, for example, one enterprise sells unfinished products to another and, at the same time, makes available its experience for further processing of these products. Whether it could be assumed that the transfer price for the goods includes a licence charge and that, consequently, any additional payment for royalties would ordinarily have to be disallowed by the country of the buyer, would depend very much upon the circumstances of each deal and there would appear to be no general principle which can be applied except that there should be no double deduction for the provision of technology. The transfer price may be a package price, *i.e.* for the goods and for the intangible property, in which case, depending on the facts and circumstances, an additional payment for royalties may not need to be paid by the purchaser for being supplied with technical expertise. This type of package pricing may need to be disaggregated to calculate a separate arm's length royalty in countries that impose royalty withholding taxes.

6.18   In some cases, intangible property will be bundled in a package contract including rights to patents, trademarks, trade secrets, and know-how. For example, an enterprise may grant a licence in respect of all the industrial and intellectual properties it owns. The parts of the package may need to be considered separately to verify the arm's length character of the transfer (see paragraph 3.11). It also is important to take into account the value of services such as technical assistance and training of employees that the developer may render in connection with the transfer. Similarly, benefits provided by the licensee to the licensor by way of improvements to products or processes may need to be taken into account. These services should be evaluated by applying the arm's length principle, taking into account the special considerations for services described in Chapter VII. It may be important in this respect to distinguish between the various means of making know-how available. Guidance on these issues is provided by paragraph 11-11.6 of the Commentary on Article 12 of the OECD Model Tax Convention.

6.19   A know-how contract and a service contract may be dealt with differently in a particular country according to its internal tax legislation or to the tax treaties it has concluded with other countries. This issue is one which will be given further attention from the Working Party No. 1 on Double Taxation and Related Questions. For example, whether or not a withholding tax is levied on payments made to non-residents may depend on the way the contract is viewed. If the payment is seen as service fees, it is usually not taxed in the country of origin unless the receiving enterprise carries on business in that country through a permanent establishment situated therein and the fee is attributable to the permanent establishment. On the other hand, royalties paid for the use of intangible property are subject to a withholding tax in some countries.

C.3   Calculation of an arm's length consideration

6.20   In applying the arm's length principle to controlled transactions involving intangible property, some special factors relevant to comparability between the controlled and uncontrolled transactions should be considered. These factors include the expected benefits from the intangible property (possibly determined through a net present value calculation). Other factors include: any limitations on the geographic area in which rights may be exercised; export restrictions on goods produced by virtue of any rights transferred; the exclusive or non-exclusive character of any rights transferred; the capital investment (to construct new plants or to buy special machines), the start-up expenses and the development work required in the market; the possibility of sub-licensing, the licensee's distribution network, and whether the licensee has the right to participate in further developments of the property by the licensor.

6.21   When the intangible property involved is a patent, the analysis of comparability should also take into account the nature of the patent (*e.g.* product or process patent) and the degree and duration of protection afforded under the patent laws of the relevant countries, bearing in mind that new patents may be developed speedily on the basis of old ones, so that the effective protection of the intangible property may be prolonged considerably. Not only the duration of the legal protection but also the length of the period during which patents are likely to maintain their economic value is important. An entirely new and distinctive "breakthrough" patent may make existing patents rapidly obsolete and will command a higher price than one either designed to improve a process already governed by an existing patent or one for which substitutes are readily available.

6.22   Other factors for patents include the process of production for which the property is used, and the value that the process contributes to the final product. For example, where a patented invention covers only one component of a device, it could be inappropriate to calculate the royalty for the invention by reference to the selling price for the complete product. In such a case, a royalty based on a proportion of the selling price would have to take into account the relative value of the component to the other components of the product. Also, in analysing functions performed (including assets used and risks assumed) for transactions involving intangible property, the risks considered should include product and environmental liability, which have become increasingly important.

6.23   In establishing arm's length pricing in the case of a sale or license of intangible property, it is possible to use the CUP method where the same owner has transferred or licensed comparable intangible property under comparable circumstances to independent enterprises. The amount of consideration charged in comparable transactions between independent enterprises in the same industry can also be a guide, where this information is available, and a range of pricing may be appropriate. Offers to independent parties or genuine bids of competing licensees also may be taken into account. If the associated enterprise sub-licenses the property to independent parties, it may also be possible to use some form of the resale price method to analyse the terms of the controlled transaction.

6.24   In the sale of goods incorporating intangible property, it may also be possible to use the CUP or resale price method following the principles in Chapter II. When marketing intangibles (*e.g.* a trademark) are involved, the analysis of comparability should consider the value added by the trademark, taking into account consumer acceptability, geographical significance, market shares, sales volume, and other relevant factors. When trade intangibles are involved, the analysis of comparability should moreover consider the value attributable to such intangibles (patent protected or otherwise exclusive intangibles) and the importance of the ongoing R&D functions.

6.25   For example, it may be the case that a branded athletic shoe transferred in a controlled transaction is comparable to an athletic shoe transferred under a different brand name in an uncontrolled transaction both in terms of the quality and specification of the shoe itself and also in terms of the consumer acceptability and other characteristics of the brand name in that market. Where such a comparison is not possible, some help also may be found, if adequate evidence is available, by comparing the volume of sales and the prices chargeable and profits realised for trademarked goods with those for similar goods that do not carry the trademark. It therefore may be possible to use sales of unbranded products as comparable transactions to sales of branded products that are otherwise comparables, but only to the extent that adjustments can be made to account for any value added by the trademark. For example, branded athletic shoe "A" may be comparable to an unbranded shoe in all respects (after adjustments) except for the brand name itself. In such a case, the premium attributable to the brand might be determined by comparing an unbranded shoe with different features, transferred in an uncontrolled transaction, to its branded equivalent, also transferred in an uncontrolled transaction. Then it may be possible to use this information as an aid in determining the price of branded shoe "A", although adjustments may be necessary for the effect of the difference in features on the value of the brand. However, adjustments may be particularly difficult where a trademarked product has a dominant market position such that the generic product is in essence trading in a different market, particularly where sophisticated products are involved.

6.26   In cases involving highly valuable intangible property, it may be difficult to find comparable uncontrolled transactions. It therefore may be difficult to apply the traditional transaction methods and the transactional net margin method, particularly where both parties to the transaction own valuable intangible property or unique assets used in the transaction that distinguish the transaction from those of potential competitors. In such cases the profit split method may be relevant although there may be practical problems in its application.

6.27   In assessing whether the conditions of a transaction involving intangible property reflect arm's length transactions, the amount, nature, and incidence of the costs incurred in developing or maintaining the intangible property might be examined as an aid to determining comparability or possibly relative value of the contributions of each party, particularly where a profit split method is used. However, there is no necessary link between costs and value. In particular, the actual fair market value of intangible property is frequently not measurable in relation to the costs involved in developing and maintaining the property. One reason is that intangible property, such as patents and know-how, may be the result of long-lasting and expensive R&D. The actual size of R&D budgets depends on a variety of factors, including the policy of competitors or potential competitors, the expected profitability of the research activity, and the trend of profits; or considerations based on some relation to turnover, or an assessment of the yield from R&D activity in the past as a basis for fixing future expenditure levels. R&D budgets may be sought to be covered by product sales even though the products in question may not be a direct or even perhaps an indirect result of the R&D. Another reason is that intangible property may require ongoing R&D and quality control that may benefit a range of products.

C.4 Arm's length pricing when valuation is highly uncertain at the time of the transaction[1]

6.28   As stated at the outset of this section, intangible property may have a special character complicating the search for comparables and in some cases making value difficult to determine at the time of a controlled transaction involving the property. When valuation of intangible property at the time of the transaction is highly uncertain, the question is raised how arm's length pricing should be determined. The question should be resolved, both by taxpayers and tax administrations, by reference to what independent enterprises would have done in comparable circumstances to take account of the valuation uncertainty in the pricing of the transaction.

6.29   Depending on the facts and circumstances, there are a variety of steps that independent enterprises might undertake to deal with high uncertainty in valuation when pricing a transaction. One possibility is to use anticipated benefits (taking into account all relevant economic factors) as a means for establishing the pricing at the outset of the transaction. In determining the anticipated benefits, independent enterprises would take into account the extent to which subsequent developments are foreseeable and predictable. In some cases, independent enterprises might find that the projections of anticipated benefits are sufficiently reliable to fix the pricing for the transaction at the outset on the basis of those projections, without reserving the right to make future adjustments.

6.30   In other cases, independent enterprises might not find that pricing based on anticipated benefits alone provides an adequate protection against the risks posed by the high uncertainty in valuing the intangible property. In such cases, independent enterprises might adopt shorter-term agreements or include price adjustment clauses in the terms of the agreement, to protect against subsequent developments that might not be predictable. For example, a royalty rate could be set to increase as the sales of the licensee increase.

6.31   Also, independent enterprises may determine to bear the risk of unpredictable subsequent developments to a certain degree, however with the joint understanding that major unforeseen developments changing the fundamental assumptions upon which the pricing was determined would lead to the renegotiation of the pricing arrangements by mutual agreement of the parties. For example, such renegotiation might occur at arm's length if a

---

[1]   An example illustrating the application of the arm's length principle to intangible property with highly uncertain valuation is found in the Annex to Chapter VI.

royalty rate based on sales for a patented drug turned out to be vastly excessive due to an unexpected development of an alternative low-cost treatment. The excessive royalty might remove the incentive of the licensee to manufacture the drug at all, in which case the agreement might be renegotiated (although whether this in fact would happen would depend upon all the facts and circumstances).

6.32   When tax administrations evaluate the pricing of a controlled transaction involving intangible property where valuation is highly uncertain at the outset, the arrangements that would have been made in comparable circumstances by independent enterprises should be followed. Thus, if independent enterprises would have fixed the pricing based upon a particular projection, the same approach should be used by the tax administration in evaluating the pricing. In such a case, the tax administration could, for example, inquire into whether the associated enterprises made adequate projections, taking into account all the developments that were reasonably foreseeable, without using hindsight.

6.33   It is recognised that a tax administration may find it difficult, particularly in the case of an uncooperative taxpayer, to establish what profits were reasonably foreseeable at the time that the transaction was entered into. For example, such a taxpayer, at an early stage, may transfer intangibles to an affiliate, set a royalty that does not reflect the subsequently demonstrated value of the intangible for tax or other purposes, and later take the position that it was not possible at the time of the transfer to predict the subsequent success of the product. In such a case, the subsequent developments might prompt a tax administration to inquire what independent enterprises would have done on the basis of information reasonably available at the time of the transaction. In particular, consideration should be paid to whether the associated enterprises intended to and did make projections that independent enterprises would have considered adequate, taking into account the reasonably foreseeable developments and in light of the risk of unforeseeable developments, and whether independent enterprises would have insisted on some additional protections against the risk of high uncertainty in valuation.

6.34   If independent enterprises would have insisted on a price adjustment clause in comparable circumstances, the tax administration should be permitted to determine the pricing on the basis of such a clause. Similarly, if independent enterprises would have considered unforeseeable subsequent developments so fundamental that their occurrence would have led to a prospective renegotiation of the pricing of a transaction, such developments should also lead to a modification of the pricing of a comparable controlled transaction between associated enterprises.

6.35   It is recognised that tax administrations may not be able to conduct an audit of a taxpayer's return until several years after it has been filed. In such a case, a tax administration would be entitled to adjust the amount of consideration with respect to all open years up to the time when the audit takes place, on the basis of the information that independent enterprises would have used in comparable circumstances to set the pricing.

D. Marketing activities undertaken by enterprises not owning trademarks or trade names

6.36   Difficult transfer pricing problems can arise when marketing activities are undertaken by enterprises that do not own the trademarks or tradenames that they are promoting (such as a distributor of branded goods). In such a case, it is necessary to determine how the marketer should be compensated for those activities. The issue is whether the marketer should be compensated as a service provider, *i.e.* for providing promotional services, or whether there are any cases in which the marketer should share in any additional return attributable to the marketing intangibles. A related question is how the return attributable to the marketing intangibles can be identified.

6.37   As regards the first issue – whether the marketer is entitled to a return on the marketing intangibles above a normal return on marketing activities – the analysis requires an assessment of the obligations and rights implied by the agreement between the parties. It will often be the case that the return on marketing activities will be sufficient and appropriate. One relatively clear case is where a distributor acts merely as an agent, being reimbursed for its promotional expenditures by the owner of the marketing intangible. In that case, the distributor would be entitled to compensation appropriate to its agency activities alone and would not be entitled to share in any return attributable to the marketing intangible.

6.38   Where the distributor actually bears the cost of its marketing activities (*i.e.* there is no arrangement for the owner to reimburse the expenditures), the issue is the extent to which the distributor is able to share in the potential benefits from those activities. In general, in arm's length transactions the ability of a party that is not the legal owner of a marketing intangible to obtain the future benefits of marketing activities that increase the value of that intangible will depend principally on the substance of the rights of that party. For example, a distributor may have the ability to obtain benefits from its investments in developing the value of a trademark from its turnover and market share where it has a long-term contract of sole distribution rights for the trademarked product. In such cases, the distributor's share of benefits should be determined based on what an independent distributor would obtain in comparable circumstances. In some cases, a distributor may bear extraordinary marketing expenditures beyond what an independent distributor with similar rights might incur for the benefit of its own distribution activities. An independent distributor in such a case might obtain an additional return from the owner of the trademark, perhaps through a decrease in the purchase price of the product or a reduction in royalty rate.

6.39   The other question is how the return attributable to marketing activities can be identified. A marketing intangible may obtain value as a consequence of advertising and other promotional expenditures, which can be important to maintain the value of the trademark. However, it can be difficult to determine what these expenditures have contributed to the success of a product. For instance, it can be difficult to determine what advertising and marketing expenditures have contributed to the production or revenue, and to what degree. It is also possible that a new trademark or one newly introduced into a particular market may have no value or little value in that market and its value may change over the years as it makes an impression on the market (or perhaps loses its impact). A dominant market share may to some extent be attributable to marketing efforts of a distributor. The value and any changes will depend to an extent on how effectively the trademark is promoted in the particular market. More fundamentally, in many cases higher returns derived from the sale of trademarked products may be due as much to the unique characteristics of the product or its high quality as to the success of advertising and other promotional expenditures. The actual conduct of the parties over a period of years should be given significant weight in evaluating the return attributable to marketing activities. See paragraphs 3.75-3.79 (multiple year data).

Chapter VII

Special Considerations for Intra-Group Services

A. Introduction

7.1   This chapter discusses issues that arise in determining for transfer pricing purposes whether services have been provided by one member of an MNE group to other members of that group and, if so, in establishing arm's length pricing for those intra-group services. The chapter does not address except incidentally whether services have been provided in a cost contribution arrangement, and if so the appropriate arm's length pricing, *i.e.* where members of an MNE group jointly acquire, produce or provide goods, services, and/or intangible property, allocating the costs for such activity amongst the members participating in the arrangement. Cost contribution arrangements are the subject of Chapter VIII.

7.2   Nearly every MNE group must arrange for a wide scope of services to be available to its members, in particular administrative, technical, financial and commercial services. Such services may include management, coordination and control functions for the whole group. The cost of providing such services may be borne initially by the parent, by a specially designated group member ("a group service centre"), or by another group member. An independent enterprise in need of a service may acquire the services from a service provider who specialises in that type of service or may perform the service for itself (*i.e.* in house). In a similar way, a member of an MNE group in need of a service may acquire it directly or indirectly from independent enterprises, or from one or more associated enterprises in the same MNE group (*i.e.* intra-group), or may perform the service for itself. Intra-group services often include those that are typically available externally from independent enterprises (such as legal and accounting services), in addition to those that are ordinarily performed internally (*e.g.* by an enterprise for itself, such as central auditing, financing advice, or training of personnel).

7.3   Intra-group arrangements for rendering services are sometimes linked to arrangements for transferring goods or intangible property (or the licensing thereof). In some cases, such as know-how contracts containing a service element, it may be very difficult to determine where the exact border lies between the transfer or licensing of property and the transfer of services. Ancillary services are frequently associated with the transfer of technology. It may therefore be necessary to consider the principles for aggregation and segregation of transactions in Chapter III where a mixed transfer of services and property is involved.

7.4   Intra-group service activities may vary considerably among MNE groups, as does the extent to which those activities provide a benefit, or expected benefit, to one or more group members. Each case is dependent upon its own facts and circumstances and the arrangements within the group. For example, in a decentralised group, the parent may limit its intra-group activity to monitoring its investments in its subsidiaries in its capacity as a shareholder. In contrast, in a centralised or integrated group, the board of directors and senior management of the parent company may make all important decisions concerning the affairs of its subsidiaries and the parent company may carry out all marketing, training and treasury functions.

B. Main issues

7.5   There are two issues in the analysis of transfer pricing for intra-group services. One issue is whether intra-group services have in fact been provided. The other issue is what the intra-group charge for such services for tax purposes should be in accordance with the arm's length principle. Each of these issues is discussed below.

B.1   Determining whether intra-group services have been rendered

7.6   Under the arm's length principle, the question whether an intra-group service has been rendered when an activity is performed for one or more group members by another group member should depend on whether the activity provides a respective group member with economic or commercial value to enhance its commercial position. This can be determined by considering whether an independent enterprise in comparable circumstances would have been willing to pay for the activity if performed for it by an independent enterprise or would have performed the activity in-house for itself. If the activity is not one for which the independent enterprise would have been willing to pay or perform for itself, the activity ordinarily should not be considered as an intra-group service under the arm's length principle.

7.7   The analysis described above quite clearly depends on the actual facts and circumstances, and it is not possible in the abstract to set forth categorically the activities that do or do not constitute the rendering of intra-group services. However, some guidance may be given to elucidate how the analysis would be applied for some common types of activities undertaken in MNE groups.

7.8   Some intra-group services are performed by one member of an MNE group to meet an identified need of one or more specific members of the group. In such a case, it is relatively straightforward to determine whether a service has been provided. Ordinarily an independent enterprise in comparable circumstances would have satisfied the identified need either by performing the activity in-house or by having the activity performed by a third party. Thus, in such a case, an intra-group service ordinarily would be found to exist. For example, an intra-group service would normally be found where an associated enterprise repairs equipment used in manufacturing by another member of the MNE group.

7.9   A more complex analysis is necessary where an associated enterprise undertakes activities that relate to more than one member of the group or to the group as a whole. In a narrow range of such cases, an intra-group activity may be performed relating to group members even though those group members do not need the activity (and would not be willing to pay for it were they independent enterprises). Such an activity would be one that a group member (usually the parent company or a regional holding company) performs solely because of its ownership interest in one or more other group members, *i.e.* in its capacity as shareholder. This type of activity would not justify a charge to the recipient companies. It may be referred to as a "shareholder activity", distinguishable from the broader term "stewardship activity" used in the 1979 Report. Stewardship activities covered a range of activities by a shareholder that may include the provision of services to other group members, for example services that would be provided by a coordinating centre. These latter types of non-shareholder activities could include detailed planning services for particular operations, emergency management or technical advice (trouble shooting), or in some cases assistance in day-to-day management.

7.10   The following examples (which were described in the 1984 Report) will constitute shareholder activities, under the standard set forth in paragraph 7.6:

a)   Costs of activities relating to the juridical structure of the parent company itself, such as meetings of shareholders of the parent, issuing of shares in the parent company and costs of the supervisory board;

b)   Costs relating to reporting requirements of the parent company including the consolidation of reports;

c)   Costs of raising funds for the acquisition of its participations.

In contrast, if for example a parent company raises funds on behalf of another group member which uses them to acquire a new company, the parent company would generally be regarded as providing a service to the group member. The 1984 Report also mentioned "costs of managerial and control (monitoring) activities related to the management and protection of the investment as such in participations". Whether these activities fall within the definition of shareholder activities as defined in these Guidelines would be determined according to whether under comparable facts and circumstances the activity is one that an independent enterprise would have been willing to pay for or to perform for itself.

7.11   In general, no intra-group service should be found for activities undertaken by one group member that merely duplicate a service that another group member is performing for itself, or that is being performed for such other group member by a third party. An exception may be where the duplication of services is only temporary, for example, where an MNE group is reorganising to centralise its management functions. Another exception would be where the duplication is undertaken to reduce the risk of a wrong business decision (*e.g.* by getting a second legal opinion on a subject).

7.12   There are some cases where an intra-group service performed by a group member such as a shareholder or coordinating centre relates only to some group members but incidentally provides benefits to other group members. Examples could be analysing the question whether to reorganise the group, to acquire new members, or to terminate a division. These activities could constitute intra-group services to the particular group members involved, for example those members who will make the acquisition or terminate one of their divisions, but they may also produce economic benefits for other group members not involved in the object of the decision by increasing efficiencies, economies of scale, or other synergies. The incidental benefits ordinarily would not cause these other group members to be treated as receiving an intra-group service because the activities producing the benefits would not be ones for which an independent enterprise ordinarily would be willing to pay.

7.13   Similarly, an associated enterprise should not be considered to receive an intra-group service when it obtains incidental benefits attributable solely to its being part of a larger concern, and not to any specific activity being performed. For example, no service would be received where an associated enterprise by reason of its affiliation alone has a credit-rating higher than it would if it were unaffiliated, but an intra-group service would usually exist where the higher credit rating were due to a guarantee by another group member, or where the enterprise benefitted from the group's reputation deriving from global marketing and public relations campaigns. In this respect, passive association should be distinguished from active promotion of the MNE group's attributes that positively enhances the profit-making potential of particular members of the group. Each case must be determined according to its own facts and circumstances.

7.14   Other activities that may relate to the group as a whole are those centralised in the parent company or a group service centre (such as a regional headquarters company) and made available to the group (or multiple members thereof). The activities that are centralised depend on the kind of business and on the organisational structure of the group, but in general they may include administrative services such as planning, coordination, budgetary control, financial advice, accounting, auditing, legal, factoring, computer services; financial services such as supervision of cash flows and solvency, capital increases, loan contracts, management of interest and exchange rate risks, and refinancing; assistance in the fields of production, buying, distribution and marketing; and services in staff matters such as recruitment and training. Group service centres also often carry out research and development or administer and protect intangible property for all or part of the MNE group. These type of activities ordinarily will be considered intra-group services because they are the type of activities that independent enterprises would have been willing to pay for or to perform for themselves.

7.15   In considering whether a charge for the provision of services would be made between independent enterprises, it would also be relevant to consider the form that an arm's length consideration would take had the transaction occurred between independent enterprises dealing at arm's length. For example, in respect of financial services such as loans, foreign exchange and hedging, remuneration would generally be built into the spread and it would not be appropriate to expect a further service fee to be charged if such were the case.

7.16   Another issue arises with respect to services provided "on call". The question is whether the availability of such services is itself a separate service for which an arm's length charge (in addition to any charge for services actually rendered) should be determined. A parent company or a group service centre may be on hand to provide services such as financial, managerial, technical, legal or tax advice and assistance to members of the group at any time. In that case, a service may be rendered to associated enterprises by having staff, equipment, etc., available. An intra-group service would exist to the extent that it would be reasonable to expect an independent enterprise in comparable circumstances to incur "standby" charges to ensure the availability of the services when the need for them arises. It is not unknown, for example, for an independent enterprise to pay an annual "retainer" fee to a firm of lawyers to ensure entitlement to legal advice and representation if litigation is brought. Another example is a service contract for priority computer network repair in the event of a breakdown.

7.17   These services may be available on call and they may vary in amount and importance from year to year. It is unlikely that an independent enterprise would incur stand-by charges where the potential need for the service was remote, where the advantage of having services on-call was negligible, or where the on-call services could be obtained promptly and readily from other sources without the need for stand-by arrangements. Thus, the benefit conferred on a group company by the on-call arrangements should be considered, perhaps by looking at the extent to which the services have been used over a period of several years rather than solely for the year in which a charge is to be made, before determining that an intra-group service is being provided.

7.18   The fact that a payment was made to an associated enterprise for purported services can be useful in determining whether services were in fact provided, but the mere description of a payment as, for example, "management fees" should not be expected to be treated as *prima facie* evidence that such services have been rendered. At the same time, the absence of payments or contractual agreements does not automatically lead to the conclusion that no intra-group services have been rendered.

B.2   Determining an arm's length charge

B.2.1   In general

7.19   Once it is determined that an intra-group service has been rendered, it is necessary, as for other types of intra-group transfers, to determine whether the amount of the charge, if any, is in accordance with the arm's length principle. This means that the charge for intra-group services should be that which would have been made and accepted between independent enterprises in comparable circumstances. Consequently, such transactions should not be treated differently for tax purposes from comparable transactions between independent enterprises, simply because the transactions are between enterprises that happen to be associated.

B.2.2 Identifying actual arrangements for charging for intra-group services

7.20   To identify the amount, if any, that has actually been charged for services, a tax administration will need to identify what arrangements, if any, have actually been put in place between the associated enterprises to facilitate charges being made for the provision of services between them. In certain cases, the arrangements made for charging for intra-group services can be readily identified. These cases are where the MNE group uses a direct-charge method, *i.e.* where the associated enterprises are charged for specific services. In general, the direct-charge method is of great practical convenience to tax administrations because it allows the service performed and the basis for the payment to be clearly identified. Thus, the direct-charge method facilitates the determination of whether the charge is consistent with the arm's length principle.

7.21   An MNE group should often be able to adopt direct charging arrangements, particularly where services similar to those rendered to associated enterprises are also rendered to independent parties. If specific services are provided not only to associated enterprises but also to independent enterprises in a comparable manner and as a significant part of its business, it could be presumed that the MNE has the ability to demonstrate a separate basis for the charge (*e.g.* by recording the work done and costs expended in fulfilling its third party contracts). As a result, MNEs in such a case are encouraged to adopt the direct-charge method in relation to their transactions with associated enterprises. It is accepted, however, that this approach may not always be appropriate if, for example, the services to independent parties are merely occasional or marginal.

7.22   A direct-charge method for charging for intra-group services is so difficult to apply in practice in many cases for MNE groups that such groups have developed other methods for charging for services provided by parent companies or group service centres. In these cases, the practice of MNE groups for charging for intra-group services is often to make arrangements that are either a) readily identifiable but not based on a direct-charge method; or b) not readily identifiable and either incorporated into the charge for other transfers, allocated amongst group members on some basis, or in some cases not allocated amongst group members at all.

7.23   In such cases, MNE groups may find they have few alternatives but to use cost allocation and apportionment methods which often necessitate some degree of estimation or approximation, as a basis for calculating an arm's length charge following the principles in Section B.2.3 below. Such methods are generally referred to as indirect-charge methods and should be allowable provided sufficient regard has been given to the value of the services to recipients and the extent to which comparable services are provided between independent enterprises. These methods of calculating charges would generally not be acceptable where specific services that form a main business activity of the enterprise are provided not only to associated enterprises but also to independent parties. While every attempt should be made to charge fairly for the service provided, any charging has to be supported by an identifiable and reasonably foreseeable benefit. Any indirect-charge method should be sensitive to the commercial features of the individual case (*e.g.* the allocation key makes sense under the circumstances), contain safeguards against manipulation and follow sound accounting principles, and be capable of producing charges or allocations of costs that are commensurate with the actual or reasonably expected benefits to the recipient of the service.

7.24   In some cases, an indirect charge method may be necessary due to the nature of the service being provided. One example is where the proportion of the value of the services rendered to the various relevant entities cannot be quantified except on an approximate or estimated basis. This problem may occur, for example, where sales promotion activities carried on centrally (*e.g.* at international fairs, in the international press, or through other centralised advertising campaigns) may affect the quantity of goods manufactured or sold by a number of affiliates. Another case is where a separate recording and analysis of the relevant service activities for each beneficiary would involve a burden of administrative work that would be disproportionately heavy in relation to the activities themselves. In such cases, the charge could be determined by reference to an allocation among all potential beneficiaries of the costs that cannot be allocated directly, *i.e.* costs that cannot be specifically assigned to the actual beneficiaries of the various services. To satisfy the arm's length principle, the allocation method chosen must lead to a result that is consistent with what comparable independent enterprises would have been prepared to accept. See Section B.2.3 below.

7.25   The allocation might be based on turnover, or staff employed, or some other basis. Whether the allocation method is appropriate may depend on the nature and usage of the service. For example, the usage or provision of payroll services may be more related to the number of staff than to turnover, while the allocation of the stand-by costs of priority computer back-up could be allocated in proportion to relative expenditure on computer equipment by the group members.

7.26   The compensation for services rendered to an associated enterprise may be included in the price for other transfers. For instance, the price for licensing a patent or know-how may include a payment for technical assistance services or centralised services performed for the licensee or for managerial advice on the marketing of the goods produced under the licence. In such cases, the tax administration and the taxpayers would have to check that there is no additional service fee charged and that there is no double deduction.

7.27   When an indirect charge method is used, the relationship between the charge and the services provided may be obscured and it may become difficult to evaluate the benefit provided. Indeed, it may mean that the enterprise being charged for a service itself has not related the charge to the service. Consequently, there is an increased risk of double taxation because it may be more difficult to determine a deduction for costs incurred on behalf of group members if compensation cannot be readily identified, or for the recipient of the service to establish a deduction for any amount paid if it is unable to demonstrate that services have been provided.

7.28   In identifying arrangements for charging any retainer for the provision of "on call" services (as discussed in paragraphs 7.16 and 7.17), it may be necessary to examine the terms for the actual use of the services since these may include provisions that no charge is made for actual use until the level of usage exceeds a predetermined level.

B.2.3   Calculating the arm's length consideration

7.29   In trying to determine the arm's length price in relation to intra-group services, the matter should be considered both from the perspective of the service provider and from the perspective of the recipient of the service. In this respect, relevant considerations include the value of the service to the recipient and how much a comparable independent enterprise would be prepared to pay for that service in comparable circumstances, as well as the costs to the service provider.

7.30   For example, from the perspective of an independent enterprise seeking a service, the service providers in that market may or may not be willing or able to supply the service at a price that the independent enterprise is prepared to pay. If the service providers can supply the wanted service within a range of prices that the independent enterprise would be prepared to pay, then a deal will be struck. From the point of view of the service provider, a price below which it would not supply the service and the cost to it are relevant considerations to address, but they are not necessarily determinative of the outcome in every case.

7.31   The method to be used to determine arm's length transfer pricing for intra-group services should be determined according to the guidelines in Chapters I, II, and III. Often, the application of these guidelines will lead to use of the CUP or cost plus method for pricing intra-group services. A CUP method is likely to be the most appropriate method where there is a comparable service provided between independent enterprises in the recipient's market, or by the associated enterprise providing the services to an independent enterprise in comparable circumstances. For example, this might be the case where accounting, auditing, legal, or computer services are being provided subject to the controlled and uncontrolled transactions being comparable. A cost plus method would likely be the most appropriate method in the absence of a CUP where the nature of the activities involved, assets used, and risks assumed are comparable to those undertaken by independent enterprises. As indicated in Chapter II, Part II, in applying the cost plus method, there should be a consistency between the controlled and uncontrolled transactions in the categories of cost that are included. Transactional profit methods may be used where they are the most appropriate to the circumstances of the case (see paragraphs 2.1-2.11). In exceptional cases, for example where it may be difficult to apply the CUP method or the cost-plus method, it may be helpful to take account of more than one method (see paragraph 2.11) in reaching a satisfactory determination of arm's length pricing.

7.32   It may be helpful to perform a functional analysis of the various members of the group to establish the relationship between the relevant services and the members' activities and performance. In addition, it may be necessary to consider not only the immediate impact of a service, but also its long-term effect, bearing in mind that some costs will never actually produce the benefits that were reasonably expected when they were incurred. For example, expenditure on preparations for a marketing operation might *prima facie* be too heavy to be borne by a member in the light of its current resources; the determination whether the charge in such a case is arm's length should consider expected benefits from the operation and the possibility that the amount and timing of the charge in some arm's length arrangements might depend on the results of the operation. The taxpayer should be prepared to demonstrate the reasonableness of its charges to associated enterprises in such cases.

7.33   Depending on the method being used to establish an arm's length charge for intra-group services, the issue may arise whether it is necessary that the charge be such that it results in a profit for the service provider. In an arm's length transaction, an independent enterprise normally would seek to charge for services in such a way as to generate profit, rather than providing the services merely at cost. The economic alternatives available to the recipient of the service also need to be taken into account in determining the arm's length charge. However, there are circumstances (*e.g.* as outlined in the discussion on business strategies in Chapter I) in which an independent enterprise may not realise a profit from the performance of service activities alone, for example where a supplier's costs (anticipated or actual) exceed market price but the supplier agrees to provide the service to increase its profitability, perhaps by complementing its range of activities. Therefore, it need not always be the case that an arm's length price will result in a profit for an associated enterprise that is performing an intra--group service.

7.34   For example, it may be the case that the market value of intra-group services is not greater than the costs incurred by the service provider. This could occur where, for example, the service is not an ordinary or recurrent activity of the service provider but is offered incidentally as a convenience to the MNE group. In determining whether the intra-group services represent the same value for money as could be obtained from an independent enterprise, a comparison of functions and expected benefits would be relevant to assessing comparability of the transactions. An MNE group may still determine to provide the service intra-group rather than using a third party for a variety of reasons, perhaps because of other intra-group benefits (for which arm's length compensation may be appropriate). It would not be appropriate in such a case to increase the price for the service above what would be established by the CUP method just to make sure the associated enterprise makes a profit. Such a result would be contrary to the arm's length principle. However, it is important to ensure that all benefits to the recipient are properly taken into account.

7.35   Where the cost plus method is determined to be the most appropriate method to the circumstances of the case, the analysis would require examining whether the costs incurred by the group service provider need some adjustment to make the comparison of the controlled and uncontrolled transactions reliable. For example, if the controlled transaction has a higher proportion of overhead costs to direct costs than the otherwise comparable transaction, it may be inappropriate to apply the mark-up achieved in that transaction without adjusting the cost base of the associated enterprise to make a valid comparison. In some cases, the costs that would be incurred by the recipient were it to perform the service for itself may be instructive of the type of arrangement an recipient would be prepared to accept for the service in dealing at arm's length.

7.36   When an associated enterprise is acting only as an agent or intermediary in the provision of services, it is important in applying the cost-plus method that the return or mark-up is appropriate for the performance of an agency function rather than for the performance of the services themselves. In such a case, it may not be appropriate to determine arm's length pricing as a mark-up on the cost of the services but rather on the costs of the agency function itself, or alternatively, depending on the type of comparable data being used, the mark-up on the cost of services should be lower than would be appropriate for the performance of the services themselves. For example, an associated enterprise may incur the costs of renting advertising space on behalf of group members, costs that the group members would have incurred directly had they been independent. In such a case, it may well be appropriate to pass on these costs to the group recipients without a mark-up, and to apply a mark-up only to the costs incurred by the intermediary in performing its agency function.

7.37   While as a matter of principle tax administrations and taxpayers should try to establish the proper arm's length pricing, it should not be overlooked that there may be practical reasons why a tax administration in its discretion exceptionally might be willing to forgo computing and taxing an arm's length price from the performance of services in some cases, as distinct from allowing a taxpayer in appropriate circumstances to merely allocate the costs of providing those services. For instance, a cost-benefit analysis might indicate the additional tax revenue that would be collected does not justify the costs and administrative burdens of determining what an appropriate arm's length price might be in some cases. In such cases, charging all relevant costs rather than an arm's length price may provide a satisfactory result for MNEs and tax administrations. This concession is unlikely to be made by tax administrations where the provision of a service is a principal activity of the associated enterprise, where the profit element is relatively significant, or where direct charging is possible as a basis from which to determine the arm's length price.

C. Some examples of intra-group services

7.38   This section sets forth several examples of transfer pricing issues in the provision of intra-group services. The examples are provided for illustrative purposes only. When dealing with individual cases, it is necessary to explore the actual facts and circumstances to judge the applicability of any transfer pricing method.

7.39   One example involves debt-factoring activities, where an MNE group decides to centralise the activities for economic reasons. For example, it may be prudent to centralise the debt-factoring activities to limit currency and debt risks and to minimise administrative burdens. A debt-factoring centre that takes on this responsibility is performing intra-group services for which an arm's length charge should be made. A CUP method could be appropriate in such a case.

7.40   Contract manufacturing is another example of an activity that may involve intra-group services. In such cases the producer may get extensive instruction about what to produce, in what quantity and of what quality. The production company bears low risks and may be assured that its entire output will be purchased, assuming quality requirements are met. In such a case the production company could be considered as performing a service, and the cost plus method could be appropriate, subject to the principles in Chapter II.

7.41   Contract research is an example of an intra-group service involving highly skilled personnel that is often crucial to the success of the group. The actual arrangements can take a variety of forms from the undertaking of detailed programmes laid down by the principal party, extending to agreements where the research company has discretion to work within broadly defined categories. In the latter instance, generally involving frontier research, the additional functions of identifying commercially valuable areas and assessing the risk of unsuccessful research can be a critical factor in the performance of the group as a whole. However, the research company itself is often insulated from financial risk since it is normally arranged that all expenses will be reimbursed whether the research was successful or not. In addition, intangible property deriving from research activities is generally owned by the principal company and so risks relating to the commercial exploitation of that property are not assumed by the research company itself. In such a case a cost plus method may be appropriate, subject to the principles in Chapter II.

7.42   Another example of intra-group services is the administration of licences. The administration and enforcement of intangible property rights should be distinguished from the exploitation of those rights for this purpose. The control of a licence might be handled by a group service centre responsible for monitoring possible licence infringements and for enforcing licence rights.

Chapter VIII

Cost Contribution Arrangements

A. Introduction

8.1   This chapter discusses cost contribution arrangements (CCAs) between two or more associated enterprises (possibly along with independent enterprises). There are many types of CCAs and this chapter does not intend to discuss or describe the tax consequences of every variation. Rather, the purpose of the chapter is to provide some general guidance for determining whether the conditions established by associated enterprises for a CCA are consistent with the arm's length principle. The tax consequences of a CCA will depend upon whether the arrangement is structured in accordance with the arm's length principle according to the provisions of this chapter and is adequately documented. This chapter does not resolve all significant issues regarding the administration and tax consequences of CCAs. For example, further guidance may be needed on measuring the value of contributions to CCAs, in particular regarding when cost or market prices are appropriate, and the effect of government subsidies or tax incentives (see paragraphs 8.15 and 8.17). Further development might also be useful regarding the tax characterisation of contributions, balancing payments and buy-in/buy-out payments (see paragraphs 8.23, 8.25, 8.33 and 8.35). Additional work will be undertaken as necessary to update and elaborate this chapter as more experience is gained in the actual operation of CCAs.

8.2   Section B provides a general definition and overview of the concept of CCAs. Section C describes the standard for determining whether a CCA satisfies the arm's length principle. The discussion includes guidance on how to measure contributions for this purpose, guidance on whether balancing payments are needed (*i.e.* payments between participants to adjust their proportionate shares of contributions), and guidance on how contributions and balancing payments should be treated for tax purposes. Section C also addresses the determining of participants and the treatment of special purpose companies. Section D discusses the adjustments to be made in the event that the conditions of a CCA are found to be inconsistent with the arm's length principle, including adjustments of the proportionate shares of contributions under the arrangement. Section E addresses issues relating to entry into or withdrawal from a CCA after the arrangement has already commenced. Section F discusses suggestions for structuring and documenting CCAs.

B. Concept of a CCA

B.1   In general

8.3   A CCA is a framework agreed among business enterprises to share the costs and risks of developing, producing or obtaining assets, services, or rights, and to determine the nature and extent of the interests of each participant in those assets, services, or rights. A CCA is a contractual arrangement rather than necessarily a distinct juridical entity or permanent establishment of all the participants. In a CCA, each participant's proportionate share of the overall contributions to the arrangement will be consistent with the participant's proportionate share of the overall expected benefits to be received under the arrangement, bearing in mind that transfer pricing is not an exact science. Further, each participant in a CCA would be entitled to exploit its interest in the CCA separately as an effective owner thereof and not as a licensee, and so without paying a royalty or other consideration to any party for that interest. Conversely, any other party would be required to provide a participant proper consideration (*e.g.* a royalty), for exploiting some or all of that participant's interest.

8.4   Some benefits of the CCA activity will be known in advance, whereas other benefits, for example, the outcome of research and development activities, will be uncertain. Some types of CCA activities will produce benefits in the short term, while others have a longer time frame or may not be successful. Nevertheless, in a CCA there is always an expected benefit that each participant seeks from its contribution, including the attendant rights to have the CCA properly administered. Each participant's interest in the results of the CCA activity should be established from the outset, even where the interest is inter-linked with that of other participants, *e.g.* because legal ownership of developed intangible property is vested in only one of them but all of them have effective ownership interests.

B.2 Relationship to other chapters

8.5   Chapter VI and Chapter VII provide guidance on how to determine an arm's length consideration for an intra-group transfer of, respectively, intangible property and services. This chapter's goal is to provide supplementary guidance where resources and skills are pooled and the consideration received is, in part or whole, the reasonable expectation of mutual benefits. Thus, the provisions of Chapters VI and VII, and indeed all the other chapters of these Guidelines, will continue to apply to the extent relevant, for instance in measuring the amount of a contribution to a CCA as part of the process of determining the proportionate shares of contributions. MNEs are encouraged to observe the guidance of this chapter in order to ensure that their CCAs are in accordance with the arm's length principle.

B.3 Types of CCAs

8.6   Perhaps the most frequently encountered type of CCA is an arrangement for the joint development of intangible property, where each participant receives a share of rights in the developed property. In such a CCA, each participant is accorded separate rights to exploit the intangible property, for example in specific geographic areas or applications. Stated more generally, a participant uses the intangible property for its own purposes rather than in a joint activity with other participants. The separate rights obtained may constitute actual legal ownership; alternatively, it may be that only one of the participants is the legal owner of the property, but economically all the participants are co-owners. In cases where a participant has an effective ownership interest in any property developed by the CCA and the contributions are in the appropriate proportions, there is no need for a royalty payment or other consideration for use of the developed property consistent with the interest that the participant has acquired.

8.7   While CCAs for research and development of intangible property are perhaps most common, CCAs need not be limited to this activity. CCAs could exist for any joint funding or sharing of costs and risks, for developing or acquiring property or for obtaining services. For example, business enterprises may decide to pool resources for acquiring centralised management services, or for the development of advertising campaigns common to the participants' markets.

C. Applying the arm's length principle

C.1   In general

8.8   For the conditions of a CCA to satisfy the arm's length principle, a participant's contributions must be consistent with what an independent enterprise would have agreed to contribute under comparable circumstances given the benefits it reasonably expects to derive from the arrangement. What distinguishes contributions to a CCA from an ordinary intra-group transfer of property or services is that part or all of the compensation intended by the participants is the expected benefits to each from the pooling of resources and skills. Independent enterprises do enter into arrangements to share costs and risks when there is a common need from which the enterprises can mutually benefit. For instance, independent parties at arm's length might want to share risks (*e.g.* of high technology research) to minimise the loss potential from an activity, or they might engage in a sharing of costs or in joint development in order to achieve savings, perhaps from economies of scale, or to improve efficiency and productivity, perhaps from the combination of different individual strengths and spheres of expertise. More generally, such arrangements are found when a group of companies with a common need for particular activities decides to centralise or undertake jointly the activities in a way that minimises costs and risks to the benefit of each participant.

8.9   The expectation of mutual benefit is fundamental to the acceptance by independent enterprises of an arrangement for pooling resources and skills without separate compensation. Independent enterprises would require that each participant's proportionate share of the actual overall contributions to the arrangement is consistent with the participant's proportionate share of the overall expected benefits to be received under the arrangement. To apply the arm's length principle to a CCA, it is therefore necessary to determine that all the parties to the arrangement have the expectation of benefits, then to calculate each participant's relative contribution to the joint activity (whether in cash or in kind), and finally to determine whether the allocation of CCA contributions (as adjusted for any balancing payments made among participants) is proper. It should be recognised that these determinations may bear a degree of uncertainty. The potential exists for contributions to be allocated among CCA participants so as to result in an overstatement of taxable profits in some countries and the understatement of taxable profits in others, measured against the arm's length principle. For that reason, taxpayers should be prepared to substantiate the basis of their claim with respect to the CCA (see Section F).

C.2   Determining participants

8.10   Because the concept of mutual benefit is fundamental to a CCA, it follows that a party may not be considered a participant if the party does not have a reasonable expectation that it will benefit from the CCA activity itself (and not just from performing part or all of that activity). A participant therefore must be assigned a beneficial interest in the property or services that are the subject of the CCA, and have a reasonable expectation of being able directly or indirectly (*e.g.* through licensing arrangements or sales, whether to associated or independent enterprises) to exploit or use the interest that has been assigned.

8.11   The requirement of an expected benefit does not impose a condition that the subject activity in fact be successful. For example, research and development may fail to produce commercially valuable intangible property. However, if the activity continues to fail to produce any actual benefit over a period in which the activity would normally be expected to produce benefits, tax administrations may question whether the parties would continue their participation had they been independent enterprises (see the sections in Chapter I on business strategies (particularly 1.63), and losses (1.70-1.72).

8.12   In some cases, the participants in a CCA may decide that all or part of the subject activity will be carried out by a separate company that is not a participant under the standard of paragraph 8.10 above. In such a case of contract research and/or manufacturing, an arm's length charge would be appropriate to compensate the company for services being rendered to the CCA participants. This would be the case even where, for example, the company is an affiliate of one or more of the CCA participants and has been incorporated in order to secure limited liability exposure in case of a high-risk research and development CCA activity. The arm's length charge for the company would be determined under the general principles of Chapter I, including inter alia consideration of functions performed, assets used, and risks assumed, as well as the special considerations affecting an arm's length charge for services as described in Chapter VII, particularly paragraphs 7.29-7.37.

C.3   The amount of each participant's contribution

8.13   For the purpose of determining whether a CCA satisfies the arm's length principle – *i.e.* whether each participant's proportionate share of the overall contributions to the CCA is consistent with the participant's proportionate share of the overall expected benefits – it is necessary to measure the value or amount of each participant's contributions to the arrangement.

8.14   Under the arm's length principle, the value of each participant's contribution should be consistent with the value that independent enterprises would have assigned to that contribution in comparable circumstances. Therefore, in determining the value of contributions to a CCA the guidance in Chapters I through VII of these Guidelines should be followed. For example, as indicated in Chapter I of these Guidelines, the application of the arm's length principle would take into account, *inter alia,* the contractual terms and economic circumstances particular to the CCA, *e.g.* the sharing of risks and costs.

8.15   No specific result can be provided for all situations, but rather the questions must be resolved on a case-by-case basis, consistent with the general operation of the arm's length principle. Countries have experience both with the use of costs and with the use of market prices for the purposes of measuring the value of contributions to arm's length CCAs. It is unlikely to be a straightforward matter to determine the relative value of each participant's contribution except where all contributions are made wholly in cash, for example, where the activity is being carried on by an external service provider and the costs are jointly funded by all participants.

8.16   It is important that the evaluation process recognises all contributions made by participants to the arrangement, including property or services that are used partly in the CCA activity and also partly in the participant's separate business activities. It can be difficult to measure contributions that involve shared property or services, for example where a participant contributes the partial use of capital assets such as buildings and machines or performs supervisory, clerical, and administrative functions for the CCA and for its own business. It will be necessary to determine the proportion of the assets used or services that relate to the CCA activity in a commercially justifiable way with regard to recognised accounting principles and the actual facts, and adjustments, if material, may be necessary to achieve consistency when different jurisdictions are involved. Once the proportion is determined, the contribution can be measured in accordance with the principles in the rest of the chapter.

8.17   In measuring a participant's contribution, there is an issue regarding any savings arising from subsidies or tax incentives (including credits on investments) that may be granted by a government. Whether and if so to what extent these savings should be taken into account in measuring the value of a participant's contribution depends upon whether independent enterprises would have done so in comparable circumstances.

8.18   Balancing payments may be required to adjust participants' proportionate shares of contributions. A balancing payment increases the value of the contributions of the payer and decreases the value of the contributions of the payee by the amount of the payment. Balancing payments should maintain the arm's length condition that each participant's proportionate share of the overall contributions be consistent with its proportionate share of the overall expected benefits to be received under the arrangement. For the tax treatment of balancing payments, see paragraph 8.25 below.

C.4   Determining whether the allocation is appropriate

8.19   There is no rule that could be universally applied to determine whether each participant's proportionate share of the overall contributions to a CCA activity is consistent with the participant's proportionate share of the overall benefits expected to be received under the arrangement. The goal is to estimate the shares of benefits expected to be obtained by each participant and to allocate contributions in the same proportions. The shares of expected benefits might be estimated based on the anticipated additional income generated or costs saved by each participant as a result of the arrangement. Other techniques to estimate expected benefits (*e.g.* using the price charged in sales of comparable assets and services) may be helpful in some cases. Another approach that is frequently used in practice would be to reflect the participants' proportionate shares of expected benefits by using an allocation key. The possibilities for allocation keys include sales, units used, produced, or sold, gross or operating profit, the number of employees, capital invested, and so forth. Whether any particular allocation key is appropriate depends on the nature of the CCA activity and the relationship between the allocation key and the expected benefits.

8.20   To the extent that a material part or all of the benefits of a CCA activity are expected to be realised in the future and not currently, the allocation of contributions will take account of projections about the participants' shares of those benefits. Use of projections may raise problems for tax administrations in verifying that such projections have been made in good faith and in dealing with cases where the projections vary markedly from the actual results. The problems may be exacerbated where the CCA activity ends several years before expected benefits actually materialise. It may be appropriate, particularly where benefits are expected to be realised in the future, for a CCA to provide for possible adjustments of proportionate shares of contributions over the term of the CCA on a prospective basis to reflect changes in relevant circumstances resulting in changes in shares of benefits. In situations where actual results differ markedly from projections, tax administrations might be prompted to inquire whether the projections made would have been considered acceptable by independent enterprises in comparable circumstances, taking into account all the developments that were reasonably foreseeable by the participants, without using hindsight.

8.21   In estimating the relative expected benefits accruing from R&D directed towards the development of a new product line or process, one measure sometimes used by businesses is the projected sales of the new product line or projected stream of royalties to be received from licensing the new process. This example is for illustration only and it is not intended to suggest a preference for the use of sales data for any particular case. Whatever the indicator, if benefits are expected to be realised in the future, care must be taken to ensure that any current data used are a reliable indicator of the future pattern of shares of benefits.

8.22   Whatever the allocation method, adjustments to the measure used may be necessary to account for differences in the expected benefits to be received by the participants, *e.g.* in the timing of their expected benefits, whether their rights are exclusive, the different risks associated with their receipt of benefits, etc. The allocation key most relevant to any particular CCA may change over time. If an arrangement covers multiple activities, it will be important to take this into account in choosing an allocation method, so that the contributions being allocated are properly related to the benefits expected by the participants. One approach (though not the only one) is to use more than one allocation key. For example, if there are five participants in a CCA, one of which cannot benefit from certain research activities undertaken within the CCA, then in the absence of some form of set-off or reduction in contribution the costs associated with those activities might be allocated only to the other four participants. In this case, two allocation keys might be used to allocate the costs. Also, exchange of information between treaty partners, the mutual agreement procedure, and bilateral or multilateral advance pricing arrangements may help establish the acceptability of the method of allocation.

C.5   *The tax treatment of contributions and balancing payments*

8.23   Contributions by a participant to a CCA should be treated for tax purposes in the same manner as would apply under the general rules of the tax system(s) applicable to that participant if the contributions were made outside a CCA to carry on the activity that is the subject of the CCA (*e.g.* to perform research and development, to obtain a beneficial interest in property needed to carry out the CCA activity). The character of the contribution, *e.g.* as a research and development expense, will depend on the nature of the activity being undertaken by the CCA and will determine how it is recognised for tax purposes. Frequently, the contributions would be treated as deductible expenses by reference to these criteria. No part of a contribution in respect of a CCA would constitute a royalty for the use of intangible property, except to the extent that the contribution entitles the contributor to obtain only a right to use intangible property belonging to a participant (or a third party) and the contributor does not also obtain a beneficial interest in the intangible property itself.

8.24   Because a participant's proper contribution to a CCA is to be rewarded by the expected benefits to be derived from the arrangement and these expected benefits may not accrue until a later period, there is generally no immediate recognition of income to the contributor at the time the contribution is made. The return to the contributor on its contribution will be recognised either in the form of cost savings (in which case there may not be any income generated directly by the CCA activity), or obtained as the results of the activity generate income (or loss) for the participant, for instance, in the case of R&D. Of course, in some cases such as the provision of services the benefits arising from the arrangement may flow in the same period in which the contribution is made and would therefore be recognised in that period.

8.25   A balancing payment should be treated as an addition to the costs of the payer and as a reimbursement (and therefore a reduction) of costs to the recipient. A balancing payment would not constitute a royalty for the use of intangible property, except to the extent that the payment entitles the payer to obtain only a right to use intangible property belonging to a participant (or a third party) and the payer does not also obtain a beneficial interest in the intangible property itself. In some cases a balancing payment might exceed the recipient's allowable expenditures or costs for tax purposes determined under the domestic tax system, in which case the excess could be treated as taxable profit.

D. Tax consequences if a CCA is not arm's length

8.26   A CCA will be considered consistent with the arm's length principle where each participant's proportionate share of the overall contributions to the arrangement, adjusted for any balancing payments, is consistent with the participant's proportionate share of the overall expected benefits to be received under the arrangement. Where this is not the case, the consideration received by at least one of the participants for its contributions will be inadequate, and the consideration received by at least one other participant for its contribution will be excessive, relative to what independent enterprises would have received. In such a case, the arm's length principle would require that an adjustment be made. The nature of the adjustment will depend upon the facts and circumstances, but most often will be an adjustment of the net contribution through making or imputing a balancing payment. Where the commercial reality of an arrangement differs from the terms purportedly agreed by the participants, it may be appropriate to disregard part or all of the terms of the CCA. These situations are discussed below.

D.1   Adjustment of contributions

8.27   Where a participant's proportionate share of the overall contributions to a CCA, adjusted for any balancing payments, is not consistent with the participant's proportionate share of the overall expected benefits to be received under the arrangement, a tax administration is entitled to adjust the participant's contribution (although bearing in mind that tax administrations should hesitate from making minor or marginal adjustments). See paragraph 2.10. Such a situation may arise where the measurement of a participant's proportionate contributions of property or services has been incorrectly determined, or where the participants' proportionate expected benefits have been incorrectly assessed, *e.g.* where the allocation key when fixed or adjusted for changed circumstances was not adequately reflective of proportionate expected benefits. See paragraph 8.19. Normally the adjustment would be made by a balancing payment from one or more participants to another being made or imputed.

8.28   If a CCA is otherwise acceptable and carried out faithfully, having regard to the recommendations of Section F, tax administrations should generally refrain from making an adjustment based on a single fiscal year. Consideration should be given to whether each participant's proportionate share of the overall contributions is consistent with the participant's proportionate share of the overall expected benefits from the arrangement over a period of years (see paragraphs 3.75-3.79).

D.2   Disregarding part or all of the terms of a CCA

8.29   In some cases, the facts and circumstances may indicate that the reality of an arrangement differs from the terms purportedly agreed by the participants. For example, one or more of the claimed participants may not have any reasonable expectation of benefit from the CCA activity. Although in principle the smallness of a participant's share of expected benefits is no bar to eligibility, if a participant that is performing all of the subject activity is expected to have only a small fraction of the overall expected benefits, it may be questioned whether the reality of the arrangements for that party is to share in mutual benefits or whether the appearance of sharing in mutual benefits has been constructed to obtain more favourable tax results. In such cases, the tax administration may determine the tax consequences as if the terms of the arrangements had been consistent with those that might reasonably have been expected had the arrangements involved independent enterprises, in accordance with the guidance in paragraphs1.64-1.69.

8.30   A tax administration may also disregard part or all of the purported terms of a CCA where over time there has been a substantial discrepancy between a participant's proportionate share of contributions (adjusted for any balancing payments) and its proportionate share of expected benefits, and the commercial reality is that the participant bearing a disproportionately high share of the contributions should be entitled to a greater beneficial interest in the subject of the CCA. In such a case, that participant might be entitled to an arm's length compensation for the use of that interest by the other participants. In circumstances that indicate an attempt to abuse the rules governing CCAs, it may be appropriate for a tax administration to disregard the CCA in its entirety.

E. CCA entry, withdrawal, or termination

8.31   An entity that becomes a participant in an already active CCA might obtain an interest in any results of prior CCA activity, such as intangible property developed through the CCA, work in-progress and the knowledge obtained from past CCA activities. In such a case, the previous participants effectively transfer part of their respective interests in the results of prior CCA activity. Under the arm's length principle, any transfer of pre-existing rights from participants to a new entrant must be compensated based upon an arm's length value for the transferred interest. This compensation is called a "buy-in" payment. The relevant terminology varies across jurisdictions, and so sometimes any contribution (or balancing payment) made in recognition of the transfer of pre-existing property or rights is called a buy-in payment, whether or not it is made by a new entrant to the CCA. For purposes of this chapter, however, the term "buy-in payment" is limited to payments made by new entrants to an already active CCA for obtaining an interest in any results of prior CCA activity. Other contributions, including balancing payments, are addressed separately in this chapter.

8.32   The amount of a buy-in payment should be determined based upon the arm's length value of the rights the new entrant is obtaining, taking into account the entrant's proportionate share of overall expected benefits to be received under the CCA. It is possible that the results of prior CCA activity may have no value, in which case there would be no buy-in payment. There may also be cases where a new participant brings already existing intangible property to the CCA, and that balancing payments would be appropriate from the other participants in recognition of this contribution. In such cases, the balancing payments and the buy-in payment could be netted, although appropriate records must be kept of the full amounts of the separate payments for tax administration purposes.

8.33   A buy-in payment should be treated for tax purposes in the same manner as would apply under the general rules of the tax system(s) (including conventions for the avoidance of double taxation) applicable to the respective participants as if the payment were made outside a CCA for acquiring the interest being obtained, *e.g.* an interest in intangible property already developed by the CCA, work in progress and the knowledge obtained from past CCA activities. No part of a buy-in payment in respect of a CCA would constitute a royalty for the use of intangible property, except to the extent that the payment entitles the payer to obtain only a right to use intangible property belonging to a participant (or a third party) and the payer does not also obtain a beneficial interest in such intangible property itself.

8.34   Issues similar to those relating to a buy-in could arise when a participant leaves a CCA. In particular, a participant who leaves a CCA may dispose of its interest in the results of past CCA activity (including work in progress) to the other participants. If there is an effective transfer of property rights at the time of a participant's withdrawal, the transfer should be compensated according to the arm's length principle. This compensation is called a "buy-out" payment.

8.35   In some cases, the results of prior CCA activity may have no value, in which case there would be no buy-out payment. In addition, the amount of the buy-out payment under the arm's length principle should consider the perspective of the remaining participants. For example, in some cases a participant's withdrawal results in an identifiable and quantifiable reduction in the value of the continuing CCA activity. Where, however, the value of a remaining participant's interest in the results of past CCA activity has not increased as a result of the withdrawal, a buy-out payment from that participant would not be appropriate. A buy-out payment should be treated for tax purposes in the same manner as would apply under the general rules of the tax system(s) (including conventions for the avoidance of double taxation) applicable to the respective participants as if the payment were made outside a CCA as consideration for the disposal of the pre-existing rights (*e.g.* an interest in intangible property already developed by the CCA, work-in-progress and the knowledge obtained from past activities undertaken within the CCA). No part of a buy-out payment in respect of a CCA would constitute a royalty for the use of intangible property, except to the extent that the payment entitles the payer to obtain only a right to use intangible property belonging to the departing participant and the payer does not also obtain a beneficial interest in the intangible property itself.

8.36   There may be instances in which the absence of buy-in and buy-out payments is not a problem. For example, such provisions would not be required where the arrangement is solely for the provision of services that participants jointly acquire and pay for on a current basis and the services do not result in the creation of any property or right.

8.37   When a member enters or withdraws from a CCA, it may also be necessary to adjust the proportionate shares of contributions (based on changes in proportionate shares of expected benefits) for the increased or reduced number of participants who remain after the entry or withdrawal.

8.38   There may be cases where, even though the CCA does not contain terms addressing the consequences of participants entering or withdrawing, the participants make appropriate buy-in and buy-out payments and adjust proportionate shares of contributions (reflecting changes in proportionate shares of expected benefits) when changes in membership have occurred. The absence of express terms should not prevent a conclusion that a CCA exists in respect of past activities, provided the intention and conduct of the parties involved is otherwise consistent with the guidelines contained in this chapter. However, ideally such arrangements should be amended to address future changes in membership expressly.

8.39   When a CCA terminates, the arm's length principle would require that each participant receive a beneficial interest in the results of the CCA activity consistent with the participant's proportionate share of contributions to the CCA throughout its term (adjusted by balancing payments actually made including those made incident to the termination). Alternatively, a participant could be properly compensated according to the arm's length principle by one or more other participants for surrendering its interest in the results of the CCA activity.

F. Recommendations for structuring and documenting CCAs

8.40   A CCA should be structured in a manner that conforms to the arm's length principle. A CCA at arm's length normally would meet the following conditions:

a)   The participants would include only enterprises expected to derive mutual benefits from the CCA activity itself, either directly or indirectly (and not just from performing part or all of that activity). See paragraph 8.10;

b)   The arrangement would specify the nature and extent of each participant's beneficial interest in the results of the CCA activity;

c) No payment other than the CCA contributions, appropriate balancing payments and buy-in payments would be made for the beneficial interest in property, services, or rights obtained through the CCA;

d) The proportionate shares of contributions would be determined in a proper manner using an allocation method reflecting the sharing of expected benefits from the arrangement;

e) The arrangement would allow for balancing payments or for the allocation of contributions to be changed prospectively after a reasonable period of time to reflect changes in proportionate shares of expected benefits among the participants; and

f) Adjustments would be made as necessary (including the possibility of buy-in and buy-out payments) upon the entrance or withdrawal of a participant and upon termination of the CCA.

8.41 As indicated in Chapter V on Documentation, it would be expected that application of prudent business management principles would lead the participants to a CCA to prepare or to obtain materials about the nature of the subject activity, the terms of the arrangement, and its consistency with the arm's length principle. Implicit in this is that each participant should have full access to the details of the activities to be conducted under the CCA, projections on which the contributions are to be made and expected benefits determined, and budgeted and actual expenditures for the CCA activity. All this information could be relevant and useful to tax administrations in the context of a CCA and taxpayers should be prepared to provide it upon request. The information relevant to any particular CCA will depend on the facts and circumstances. It should be emphasised that the information described in this list is neither a minimum compliance standard nor an exhaustive list of the information that a tax administration may be entitled to request.

8.42 The following information would be relevant and useful concerning the initial terms of the CCA:

a) A list of participants;

b) A list of any other associated enterprises that will be involved with the CCA activity or that are expected to exploit or use the results of the subject activity;

c) The scope of the activities and specific projects covered by the CCA;

d)   The duration of the arrangement;

e)   The manner in which participants' proportionate shares of expected benefits are measured, and any projections used in this determination;

f)   The form and value of each participant's initial contributions, and a detailed description of how the value of initial and ongoing contributions is determined and how accounting principles are applied consistently to all participants in determining expenditures and the value of contributions;

g)   The anticipated allocation of responsibilities and tasks associated with the CCA activity between participants and other enterprises;

h)   The procedures for and consequences of a participant entering or withdrawing from the CCA and the termination of the CCA; and

i)   Any provisions for balancing payments or for adjusting the terms of the arrangement to reflect changes in economic circumstances.

8.43   Over the duration of the CCA term, the following information could be useful:

a)   Any change to the arrangement (*e.g.* in terms, participants, subject activity), and the consequences of such change;

b)   A comparison between projections used to determine expected benefits from the CCA activity with the actual results (however, regard should be had to paragraph 3.74); and

c)   The annual expenditure incurred in conducting the CCA activity, the form and value of each participant's contributions made during the CCA's term, and a detailed description of how the value of contributions is determined and how accounting principles are applied consistently to all participants in determining expenditures and the value of contributions.

Chapter IX

Transfer Pricing Aspects of Business Restructurings

Introduction

A. Scope

A.1   Business restructurings that are within the scope of this chapter

9.1   There is no legal or universally accepted definition of business restructuring. In the context of this chapter, business restructuring is defined as the cross-border redeployment by a multinational enterprise of functions, assets and/or risks. A business restructuring may involve cross-border transfers of valuable intangibles, although this is not always the case. It may also or alternatively involve the termination or substantial renegotiation of existing arrangements. Business restructurings that are within the scope of this chapter primarily consist of internal reallocation of functions, assets and risks within an MNE, although relationships with third parties (*e.g.* suppliers, sub-contractors, customers) may also be a reason for the restructuring and/or be affected by it.

9.2   Since the mid-90's, business restructurings have often involved the centralisation of intangible assets and of risks with the profit potential attached to them. They have typically consisted of:

- Conversion of full-fledged distributors into limited-risk distributors or commissionnaires for a foreign associated enterprise that may operate as a principal,

- Conversion of full-fledged manufacturers into contract-manufacturers or toll-manufacturers for a foreign associated enterprise that may operate as a principal,

- Transfers of intangible property rights to a central entity (*e.g.* a so-called "IP company") within the group.

9.3   There are also business restructurings whereby more intangibles and/or risks are allocated to operational entities (*e.g.* to manufacturers or distributors). Business restructurings can also consist of the rationalisation, specialisation or de-specialisation of operations (manufacturing sites and / or processes, research and development activities, sales, services), including the downsizing or closing of operations. The arm's length principle and guidance in this chapter apply in the same way to all types of business restructuring transactions that fall within the definition given at paragraph 9.1, irrespective of whether they lead to a more centralised or less centralised business model.

9.4   Business representatives who participated in the OECD consultation process in 2005-2009 explained that among the business reasons for restructuring are the wish to maximise synergies and economies of scale, to streamline the management of business lines and to improve the efficiency of the supply chain, taking advantage of the development of Internet-based technologies that has facilitated the emergence of global organisations. They also indicated that business restructurings may be needed to preserve profitability or limit losses in a downturn economy, *e.g.* in the event of an over-capacity situation.

A.2   *Issues that are within the scope of this chapter*

9.5   This chapter contains a discussion of the transfer pricing aspects of business restructurings, *i.e.* of the application of Article 9 (Associated enterprises) of the OECD Model Tax Convention and of these Guidelines to business restructurings.

9.6   Business restructurings are typically accompanied by a reallocation of profits among the members of the MNE group, either immediately after the restructuring or over a few years. One major objective of this chapter in relation to Article 9 is to discuss the extent to which such a reallocation of profits is consistent with the arm's length principle and more generally how the arm's length principle applies to business restructurings. The implementation of integrated business models and the development of global organisations, where they are done for bona fide commercial reasons, highlight the difficulty of reasoning in the arm's length theoretical environment which treats members of an MNE group as if they were independent parties. This conceptual difficulty with applying the arm's length principle in practice is acknowledged in these Guidelines (see paragraphs 1.10-1.11). Notwithstanding this problem, these Guidelines reflect the OECD Member countries' strong support for the arm's length principle and for efforts to describe its application and refine its operation in practice (see paragraphs 1.14-1.15). When discussing the issues that arise in the context of business restructuring, the OECD has kept this conceptual difficulty in mind in an attempt to develop approaches that are realistic and reasonably pragmatic.

9.7   This chapter only covers transactions between associated enterprises in the context of Article 9 of the OECD Model Tax Convention and does not address the attribution of profits within a single enterprise on the basis of Article 7 of the OECD Model Tax Convention, as this is the subject of WP6's report on the Attribution of Profits to Permanent Establishments.[1] The guidance that is provided under Article 9 has been developed independently from the Authorised OECD Approach ("AOA") that was developed for Article 7.

9.8   Domestic anti-abuse rules and CFC legislation are not within the scope of this chapter. The domestic tax treatment of an arm's length payment, including rules regarding the deductibility of such a payment and how domestic capital gains tax provisions may apply to an arm's length capital payment, are also not within the scope of this chapter. Moreover, while they raise important issues in the context of business restructurings, VAT and indirect taxes are not covered in this chapter.

B. Applying Article 9 of the OECD Model Tax Convention and these Guidelines to business restructurings: theoretical framework

9.9   This chapter starts from the premise that the arm's length principle and these Guidelines do not and should not apply differently to restructurings or post-restructuring transactions than to transactions that were structured as such from the beginning. The relevant question under Article 9 of the OECD Model Tax Convention and the arm's length principle is whether there are conditions made or imposed in a business restructuring that differ from the conditions that would be made between independent enterprises. This is the theoretical framework in which all the

---

[1]   See Report on the Attribution of Profits to Permanent Establishments, approved by the Committee on Fiscal Affairs on 24 June 2008 and by the Council for publication on 17 July 2008 and the 2010 Sanitised version of the Report on the Attribution of Profits to Permanent Establishments, approved by the Committee on Fiscal Affairs on 22 June 2010 and by the Council for publication on 22 July 2010.

guidance in this chapter should be read. This chapter is composed of four parts which should be read together.

Part I: Special considerations for risks

A. Introduction

9.10   Risks are of critical importance in the context of business restructurings. An examination of the allocation of risks between associated enterprises is an essential part of the functional analysis. Usually, in the open market, the assumption of increased risk would also be compensated by an increase in the expected return, although the actual return may or may not increase depending on the degree to which the risks are actually realised (see paragraph 1.45). Business restructurings often result in local operations being converted into low risk operations (*e.g.* "low risk distributors", or "low risk contract manufacturers") and being allocated relatively low (but generally stable) returns on the grounds that the entrepreneurial risks are borne by another party to which the residual profit is allocated. It is therefore important for tax administrations to assess the reallocation of the significant risks of the business that is restructured and the consequences of that reallocation on the application of the arm's length principle to the restructuring itself and to the post-restructuring transactions. This part covers the allocation of risks between associated enterprises in an Article 9 context and in particular the interpretation and application of paragraphs 1.47 to 1.53. It is intended to provide general guidance on risks which will be of relevance to specific issues addressed elsewhere in this chapter, including Part II's analysis of the arm's length compensation for the restructuring itself, Part III's analysis of the remuneration of the post-restructuring controlled transactions, and Part IV's analysis of the recognition or non-recognition of transactions presented by a taxpayer.

B. Contractual terms

9.11   Unlike in the AOA that was developed for Article 7, the examination of risks in an Article 9 context starts from an examination of the contractual terms between the parties, as those generally define how risks are to be divided between the parties. Contractual arrangements are the starting point for determining which party to a transaction bears the risk associated with it. Accordingly, it would be a good practice for associated enterprises to document in writing their decisions to allocate or transfer significant risks before the transactions with respect to which the risks will be borne or transferred occur, and to document the evaluation of the consequences on profit potential of significant risk reallocations. As noted at paragraph 1.52, the terms of a transaction may be found in written contracts or in correspondence and/or other communications between the parties. Where no written terms exist, the contractual relationships of the parties must be deduced from their conduct and the economic principles that generally govern relationships between independent enterprises.

9.12   However, as noted at paragraphs 1.47 to 1.53, a tax administration is entitled to challenge the purported contractual allocation of risk between associated enterprises if it is not consistent with the economic substance of the transaction. Therefore, in examining the risk allocation between associated enterprises and its transfer pricing consequences, it is important to review not only the contractual terms but also the following additional questions:

- Whether the conduct of the associated enterprises conforms to the contractual allocation of risks (see Section B.1 below),

- Whether the allocation of risks in the controlled transaction is arm's length (see Section B.2 below), and

- What the consequences of the risk allocation are (see Section B.3 below).

B.1   *Whether the conduct of the associated enterprises conforms to the contractual allocation of risks*

9.13   In transactions between independent enterprises, the divergence of interests between the parties ensures that they will ordinarily seek to hold each other to the terms of the contract, and that contractual terms will be ignored or modified after the fact generally only if it is in the interests of both parties. The same divergence of interests may not exist in the case of associated enterprises, and it is therefore important to examine whether the conduct of the parties conforms to the terms of the contract or whether the parties' conduct indicates that the contractual terms have not been followed or are a sham. In such cases, further analysis is required to determine the true terms of the transaction.

9.14   The parties' conduct should generally be taken as the best evidence concerning the true allocation of risk. Paragraph 1.48 provides an example in which a manufacturer sells property to an associated distributor in another country and the distributor is claimed to assume all exchange rate risks, but the transfer price appears in fact to be adjusted so as to insulate the distributor from the effects of exchange rate movements. In such a case, the tax administrations may wish to challenge the purported allocation of exchange rate risk.

9.15   Another example that is relevant to business restructurings is where a foreign associated enterprise assumes all the inventory risks by contract. When examining such a risk allocation, it may be relevant to examine for instance where the inventory write-downs are taken (*i.e.* whether the domestic taxpayer is in fact claiming the write-downs as deductions) and evidence may be sought to confirm that the parties' conduct supports the allocation of these risks as per the contract.

9.16   A third example relates to the determination of which party bears credit risk in a distribution arrangement. In full-fledged distribution agreements, the bad debt risk is generally borne by the distributor who books the sales revenue (notwithstanding any risk mitigation or risk transfer mechanism that may be put in place). This risk would generally be reflected in the balance sheet at year end. However, the extent of the risk borne by the distributor at arm's length may be different if the distributor receives indemnification from another party (*e.g.* from the supplier) for irrecoverable claims, and/or if its purchase price is determined on a resale price or commission basis that is proportionate to the cash (rather than invoiced) revenue. The examination of the actual conditions of the transactions between the parties, including the pricing of the transactions and the extent, if any, to which it is affected by credit risk, can provide evidence of whether in actual fact it is the supplier or the distributor (or both) who bear(s) the bad debt risk.

B.2   Determining whether the allocation of risks in the controlled transaction is arm's length

9.17   Relevant guidance on the examination of risks in the context of the functional analysis is found at paragraphs 1.47-1.51.

B.2.1   Role of comparables

9.18   Where data evidence a similar allocation of risk in comparable uncontrolled transactions, then the contractual risk allocation between the associated enterprises is regarded as arm's length. In this respect, comparables data may be found either in a transaction between one party to the controlled transaction and an independent party ("internal comparable") or in a transaction between two independent enterprises, neither of which is a party to the controlled transaction ("external comparable"). Generally, the search for comparables to assess the consistency with the arm's length principle of a risk allocation will not be done in isolation from the general comparability analysis of the transactions with which the risk is associated.

The comparables data will be used to assess the consistency with the arm's length principle of the controlled transaction, including the allocation of significant risks in said transaction.

B.2.2 Cases where comparables are not found

9.19   Of greater difficulty and contentiousness is the situation where no comparable is found to evidence the consistency with the arm's length principle of the risk allocation in a controlled transaction. Just because an arrangement between associated enterprises is one not seen between independent parties should not of itself mean the arrangement is non-arm's length. However, where no comparables are found to support a contractual allocation of risk between associated enterprises, it becomes necessary to determine whether that allocation of risk is one that might be expected to have been agreed between independent parties in similar circumstances.

9.20   This determination is by nature subjective, and it is desirable to provide some guidance on how to make such a determination in order to limit to the extent possible the uncertainties and risks of double taxation it can create. One relevant, although not determinative factor that can assist in this determination is the examination of which party(ies) has (have) relatively more control over the risk, as discussed in paragraphs 9.22-9.28 below. In arm's length transactions, another factor that may influence an independent party's willingness to take on a risk is its financial capacity to assume that risk, as discussed in paragraphs 9.29-9.32. Beyond the identification of these two relevant factors, it is not possible to provide prescriptive criteria that would provide certainty in all situations. The determination that the risk allocation in a controlled transaction is not one that would have been agreed between independent parties should therefore be made with great caution considering the facts and circumstances of each case.

9.21   The reference to the notions of "control over risk" and of "financial capacity to assume the risk" is not intended to set a standard under Article 9 of the OECD Model Tax Convention whereby risks would always follow capital or people functions. The analytical framework under Article 9 is different from the AOA that was developed under Article 7 of the OECD Model Tax Convention.

B.2.2.1   Risk allocation and control

Relevance of the notion of "control"

9.22   The question of the relationship between risk allocation and control as a factor relevant to economic substance is addressed at paragraph

1.49. The statement in that paragraph is based on experience. In the absence of comparables evidencing the consistency with the arm's length principle of the risk allocation in a controlled transaction, the examination of which party has greater control over the risk can be a relevant factor to assist in the determination of whether a similar risk allocation would have been agreed between independent parties in comparable circumstances. In such situations, if risks are allocated to the party to the controlled transaction that has relatively less control over them, the tax administration may decide to challenge the arm's length nature of such risk allocation.

Meaning of "control" in this context

9.23   In the context of paragraph 1.49, "control" should be understood as the capacity to make decisions to take on the risk (decision to put the capital at risk) and decisions on whether and how to manage the risk, internally or using an external provider. This would require the company to have people – employees or directors – who have the authority to, and effectively do, perform these control functions. Thus, when one party bears a risk, the fact that it hires another party to administer and monitor the risk on a day-to-day basis is not sufficient to transfer the risk to that other party.

9.24   While it is not necessary to perform the day-to-day monitoring and administration functions in order to control a risk (as it is possible to outsource these functions), in order to control a risk one has to be able to assess the outcome of the day-to-day monitoring and administration functions by the service provider (the level of control needed and the type of performance assessment would depend on the nature of the risk). This can be illustrated as follows.

9.25   Assume that an investor hires a fund manager to invest funds on its account. Depending on the agreement between the investor and the fund manager, the latter may be given the authority to make all the investment decisions on behalf of the investor on a day-to-day basis, although the risk of loss in value of the investment would be borne by the investor. In such an example, the investor is controlling its risks through three relevant decisions: the decision to hire (or terminate the contract with) that particular fund manager, the decision of the extent of the authority it gives to the fund manager and objectives it assigns to the latter, and the decision of the amount of the investment that it asks this fund manager to manage. Moreover, the fund manager would generally be required to report back to the investor on a regular basis as the investor would want to assess the outcome of the fund manager's activities. In such a case, the fund manager is providing a service and managing his business risk from his own perspective (*e.g.* to protect his credibility). The fund manager's operational risk, including the possibility of losing a client, is distinct from his client's investment risk. This illustrates the fact that an investor who gives to another person the authority to make all the day-to-day investment decisions does not necessarily transfer the investment risk to the person making these day-to-day decisions.

9.26   As another example, assume that a principal hires a contract researcher to perform research on its behalf. Assume the arrangement between the parties is that the principal bears the risk of failure of the research and will be the owner of the outcome of the research in case of success, while the contract researcher is allocated a guaranteed remuneration irrespective of whether the research is a success or a failure, and no right to ownership on the outcome of the research. Although the day-to-day research would be carried on by the scientific personnel of the contract researcher, the principal would be expected to make a number of relevant decisions in order to control its risk, such as: the decision to hire (or terminate the contract with) that particular contract researcher, the decision of the type of research that should be carried out and objectives assigned to it, and the decision of the budget allocated to the contract researcher. Moreover, the contract researcher would generally be required to report back to the principal on a regular basis, *e.g.* at predetermined milestones. The principal would be expected to be able to assess the outcome of the research activities. The contract researcher's own operational risk, *e.g.* the risk of losing a client or of suffering a penalty in case of negligence, is distinct from the failure risk borne by the principal.

9.27   As a third example, suppose now that a principal hires a contract manufacturer to manufacture products on its behalf, using technology that belongs to the principal. Assume that the arrangement between the parties is that the principal guarantees to the contract manufacturer that it will purchase 100% of the products that the latter will manufacture according to technical specifications and designs provided by the principal and following a production plan that sets the volumes and timing of product delivery, while the contract manufacturer is allocated a guaranteed remuneration irrespective of whether and if so at what price the principal is able to re-sell the products on the market. Although the day-to-day manufacturing would be carried on by the personnel of the contract manufacturer, the principal would be expected to make a number of relevant decisions in order to control its market and inventory risk, such as: the decision to hire (or terminate the contract with) that particular contract manufacturer, the decision of the type of products that should be manufactured, including their technical specifications, and the decision of the volumes to be manufactured by the contract manufacturer and of the timing of delivery. The principal would be expected to be able to assess the outcome of the manufacturing activities, including quality control of the manufacturing process and of the manufactured products. The contract manufacturer's own operational risk, *e.g.* the risk of losing a client or of suffering a penalty in case of negligence or failure to comply with the quality and other requirements set by the principal, is distinct from the market and inventory risks borne by the principal.

9.28   It should be borne in mind that there are also, as acknowledged at paragraph 1.49, risks over which neither party has significant control. There are risks which are typically beyond the scope of either party to influence (*e.g.* economic conditions, money and stock market conditions, political environment, social patterns and trends, competition and availability of raw materials and labour), although the parties can make a decision whether or not to expose themselves to those risks and whether and if so how to mitigate those risks. As far as risks over which neither party has significant control are concerned, control would not be a helpful factor in the determination of whether their allocation between the parties is arm's length.

B.2.2.2   Financial capacity to assume the risk

9.29   Another relevant, although not determinative factor that can assist in the determination of whether a risk allocation in a controlled transaction is one which would have been agreed between independent parties in comparable circumstances is whether the risk-bearer has, at the time when risk is allocated to it, the financial capacity to assume (*i.e.* to take on) the risk.

9.30   Where risk is contractually assigned to a party (hereafter "the transferee") that does not have, at the time when the contract is entered into, the financial capacity to assume it, *e.g.* because it is anticipated that it will not have the capacity to bear the consequences of the risk should it materialise and that it also does not put in place a mechanism to cover it, doubts may arise as to whether the risk would be assigned to this party at arm's length. In effect, in such a situation, the risk may have to be effectively borne by the transferor, the parent company, creditors, or another party, depending on the facts and circumstances of the case, irrespective of the contractual terms that purportedly assigned it to the transferee.

9.31   This can be illustrated as follows. Assume that Company A bears product liability towards customers and enters into a contract with Company B according to which the latter will reimburse A for any claim that A may suffer in relation to such liability. The risk is contractually transferred from A to B. Assume now that, at the time when the contract is entered into, Company B does not have the financial capacity to assume the risk, *i.e.* it is anticipated that B will not have the capacity to reimburse A, should a claim arise, and also does not put in place a mechanism to cover the risk in case it materialises. Depending on the facts and circumstances of the case, this may cause A to effectively bear the costs of the product liability risk materialising, in which case the transfer of risk from A to B would not be effective. Alternatively, it may be that the parent company of B or another party will cover the claim that A has on B, in which case the transfer of risk away from A would be effective (although the claim would not be reimbursed by B).

9.32   The financial capacity to assume the risk is not necessarily the financial capacity to bear the full consequences of the risk materialising, as it can be the capacity for the risk-bearer to protect itself from the consequences of the risk materialising. Furthermore, a high level of capitalisation by itself does not mean that the highly capitalised party carries risk.

B.2.2.3   Illustration

9.33   The overall process of determining whether the allocation of risks in a controlled transaction is arm's length can be illustrated as shown in the diagram below.

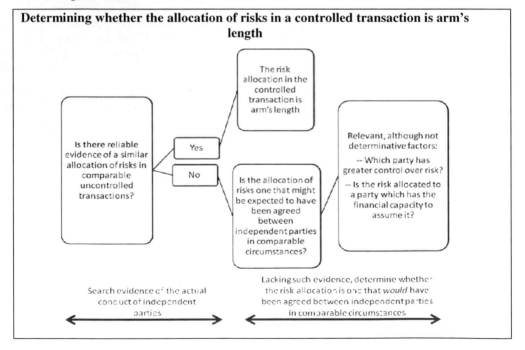

B.2.3 Difference between making a comparability adjustment and not recognising the risk allocation in the controlled transaction[2]

9.34   The difference between making a comparability adjustment and not recognising the risk allocation in a controlled transaction can be illustrated with the following example which is consistent with the example at paragraph 1.69. Suppose a manufacturer in Country A has associated distributors in Country B. Suppose that the tax administration of Country A is examining the manufacturer's controlled transactions and in particular the allocation of excess inventory risk between the manufacturer and its associated distributors in Country B. It is assumed that in the particular case, the excess inventory risk is significant and warrants a detailed transfer pricing analysis. As a starting point, the tax administration would examine the contractual terms between the parties and whether they have economic substance, determined by reference to the conduct of the parties, and are arm's length. Assume that in the particular case there is no doubt that the actual conduct of the parties is consistent with the contractual terms, *i.e.* that the manufacturer actually bears the excess inventory risk in its controlled transactions with associated distributors.

9.35   In determining whether the contractual risk allocation is arm's length, the tax administration would examine whether there is evidence from comparable uncontrolled transactions supporting the risk allocation in the manufacturer's controlled transactions. If such evidence exists, whether from internal or external comparables, there would be no reason to challenge the risk allocation in the taxpayer's controlled transactions.

9.36   Assume now that there is no evidence from internal or external comparable uncontrolled transactions supporting the risk allocation in the manufacturer's controlled transactions. As noted at paragraph 1.69, the fact that independent enterprises do not allocate risks in the same way as the taxpayer in its controlled transactions is not sufficient for not recognising the risk allocation in the controlled transactions, but it might be a reason to examine the economic logic of the controlled distribution arrangement more closely. In that case, it would be necessary to determine whether the contractual risk allocation in the controlled transactions would have been agreed at arm's length. One factor that can assist in this determination is an examination of which party(ies) has(ve) greater control over the excess inventory risk (see paragraphs 1.49 and 9.22-9.28 above). As noted at paragraph 9.20, in arm's length transactions, another factor that may

---

2   This section addresses the relationship between the guidance at paragraph 1.49 and paragraphs 1.64-1.69.

influence the allocation of risk to an independent party is its financial capacity, at the time of the risk allocation, to assume that risk.

9.37   It may be the case that, despite the lack of comparable uncontrolled transactions supporting the same risk allocation as the one in the taxpayer's controlled transaction, such risk allocation is found to have economic substance and to be commercially rational, *e.g.* because the manufacturer has relatively more control over the excess inventory risk as it makes the decisions on the quantities of products purchased by the distributors. In such a case, the risk allocation would be respected and a comparability adjustment might be needed in order to eliminate the effects of any material difference between the controlled and uncontrolled transactions being compared.

9.38   Assume now that the tax administration finds that the taxpayer's arrangements made in relation to its controlled transactions, and in particular the allocation of excess inventory risk to the manufacturer, differ from those which would have been adopted by independent enterprises behaving in a commercially rational manner and that in comparable circumstances, a manufacturer would not agree at arm's length to take on substantial excess inventory risk by, for example, agreeing to repurchase from the distributors at full price any unsold inventory. In such a case, the tax administration would seek to arrive at a reasonable solution through a pricing adjustment. In the exceptional circumstances however where a reasonable solution cannot be arrived at through a pricing adjustment, the tax administration may re-assign the consequences from the risk allocation to the associated distributors following the guidance at paragraphs 1.47-1.50 (*e.g.* by challenging the manufacturer's obligation to repurchase unsold inventory at full price) if the allocation of that risk is one of the comparability factors affecting the controlled transaction under examination.

B.3   What the consequences of the risk allocation are

B.3.1   Effects of a risk allocation that is recognised for tax purposes

9.39   In general, the consequence for one party of being allocated the risk associated with a controlled transaction, where such a risk allocation is found to be consistent with the arm's length principle, is that such party should:

a)   Bear the costs, if any, of managing (whether internally or by using associated or independent service providers) or mitigating the risk (*e.g.* costs of hedging, or insurance premium),

b) Bear the costs that may arise from the realisation of the risk. This also includes, where relevant, the anticipated effects on asset valuation (*e.g.* inventory valuation) and / or the booking of provisions, subject to the application of the relevant domestic accounting and tax rules; and

c) Generally be compensated by an increase in the expected return (see paragraph 1.45).

9.40   The reallocation of risks amongst associated enterprises can lead to both positive and negative effects for the transferor and for the transferee: on the one hand, potential losses and possible liabilities may, as a result of the transfer, shift to the transferee; on the other hand, the expected return attached to the risk transferred may be realised by the transferee rather than the transferor.

9.41   One important issue is to assess whether a risk is economically significant, *i.e.* it carries significant profit potential, and, as a consequence, whether the reallocation of that risk may explain a significant reallocation of profit potential.   The significance of a risk will depend on its size, the likelihood of its realisation and its predictability, as well as on the possibility to mitigate it. If a risk is assessed to be economically insignificant, then the bearing or reallocation of that risk would not ordinarily explain a substantial amount of or decrease in the entity's profit potential. At arm's length a party would not be expected to transfer a risk that is perceived as economically insignificant in exchange for a substantial decrease in its profit potential.

9.42   For instance, where a buy-sell distributor which is converted into a commissionnaire transfers the ownership of inventory to an overseas principal and where this transfer leads to a transfer of inventory risk, the tax administration would want to assess whether the inventory risk that is transferred is economically significant. It may want to ask:

- What the level of investment in inventory is,

- What the history of stock obsolescence is,

- What the cost of insuring it is, and

- What the history of loss in transit (if uninsured) is.

9.43   Accounting statements may provide useful information on the probability and quantum of certain risks (e.g. bad debt risks, inventory risks), but there are also economically significant risks that may not be recorded as such in the financial accounts (e.g. market risks).

B.3.2 Can the use of a transfer pricing method create a low risk environment?

9.44   The question of the relationship between the choice of a particular transfer pricing method and the level of risk left with the entity that is remunerated using that method is an important one in the context of business restructuring. It is quite commonly argued that because an arrangement is remunerated using a cost plus or TNMM that guarantees a certain level of gross or net profit to one of the parties, that party operates in a low risk environment. In this regard, one should distinguish between, on the one hand, the pricing arrangement according to which prices and other financial conditions of a transaction are contractually set and, on the other hand, the transfer pricing method that is used to test whether the price, margin or profits from a transaction are arm's length.

9.45   With respect to the former, the terms on which a party to a transaction is compensated cannot be ignored in evaluating the risk borne by that party. In effect, the pricing arrangement can directly affect the allocation of certain risks between the parties and can in some cases create a low risk environment. For instance, a manufacturer may be protected from the risk of price fluctuation of raw material as a consequence of its being remunerated on a cost plus basis that takes account of its actual costs. On the other hand, there can also be some risks the allocation of which does not derive from the pricing arrangement. For instance, remunerating a manufacturing activity on a cost plus basis may not as such affect the allocation of the risk of termination of the manufacturing agreement between the parties.

9.46   Concerning the transfer pricing method used to test the prices, margins or profits from the transaction, it should be the most appropriate transfer pricing method to the circumstances of the case (see paragraph 2.2). In particular, it should be consistent with the allocation of risk between the parties (provided such allocation of risk is arm's length), as the risk allocation is an important part of the functional analysis of the transaction. Thus, it is the low (or high) risk nature of a business that will dictate the selection of the most appropriate transfer pricing method, and not the contrary. See Part III of this chapter for a discussion of the arm's length remuneration of the post-restructuring arrangements.

C. Compliance issues

9.47   It is a good practice for taxpayers to set up a process to establish, monitor and review their transfer prices, taking into account the size of the transactions, their complexity, the level of risk involved, and whether they are performed in a stable or changing environment (see paragraphs 3.80-3.83). The process of assessing the consistency with the arm's length principle of a taxpayer's risk allocations can be burdensome and costly. It would be reasonable to expect that the extent and depth of the analysis will depend:

- On the materiality of the risk and in particular on whether it has a significant profit potential attached to it, and

- On whether significant changes in the risk allocation have occurred, *e.g.* following a significant change of risk profile as a result of a restructuring.

Part II: Arm's length compensation for the restructuring itself

A. Introduction

9.48   A business restructuring may involve cross-border transfers of something of value, *e.g.* of valuable intangibles, although this is not always the case. It may also or alternatively involve the termination or substantial renegotiation of existing arrangements, *e.g.* manufacturing arrangements, distribution arrangements, licenses, service agreements, etc. The transfer pricing consequences of the transfer of something of value are discussed at Section D of this part and the transfer pricing consequences of the termination or substantial renegotiation of existing arrangements are discussed at Section E.

9.49   Under Article 9 of the OECD Model Tax Convention, where the conditions made or imposed in a transfer of functions, assets and/or risks, and/or in the termination or renegotiation of a contractual relationship between two associated enterprises located in two different countries differ from those that would be made or imposed between independent enterprises, then any profits which would, but for those conditions, have accrued to one of the enterprises, but, by reason of those conditions, have not so accrued, may be included in the profits of that enterprise and taxed accordingly.

B. Understanding the restructuring itself

9.50   The determination of whether the conditions made or imposed in a business restructuring transaction are arm's length will generally be informed by a comparability analysis, and in particular by an examination of the functions performed, assets used and risks assumed by the parties, as well as of the contractual terms, economic circumstances and business strategies.

9.51   Where uncontrolled transactions that are potentially comparable to the restructuring transactions are identified, the comparability analysis will also aim at assessing the reliability of the comparison and, where needed and possible, at determining reasonably accurate comparability adjustments to eliminate the material effects of differences that may exist between the situations being compared.

9.52   It may be that comparable uncontrolled transactions for a restructuring transaction between associated enterprises are not found. This does not of itself mean that the restructuring is not arm's length, but it is still necessary to establish whether it satisfies the arm's length principle.[3] In such cases, determining whether independent parties might be expected to have agreed to the same conditions in comparable circumstances may be usefully informed by a review of:

- The restructuring transactions and the functions, assets and risks before and after the restructuring (see Section B.1);

- The business reasons for and the expected benefits from the restructuring, including the role of synergies (see Section B.2);

- The options realistically available to the parties (see Section B.3).

B.1   *Identifying the restructuring transactions: functions, assets and risks before and after the restructuring*

9.53   Restructurings can take a variety of different forms and may involve only two or more than two members of an MNE group. For example, a simple pre-restructuring arrangement could involve a full-fledged manufacturer producing goods and selling them to an associated full-fledged distributor for on-sale into the market. The restructuring could involve a modification to that two-party arrangement, whereby the distributor is converted to a limited risk distributor or commissionnaire, with risks previously borne by the full-fledged distributor being assumed by the manufacturer (see discussion of risks in Part I of this chapter). Frequently, the restructuring will be more complicated, with functions performed, assets used and/or risks assumed by either or both parties to a pre-restructuring arrangement shifting to one or more additional members of the group.

9.54   In order to determine the arm's length compensation payable upon a restructuring to any restructured entity within an MNE group, as well as the member of the group that should bear such compensation, it is important to identify the transaction or transactions occurring between the restructured entity and one or more other members of the group. This analysis will typically include an identification of the functions, assets and risks before and after the restructuring. It may be important to perform an evaluation of the rights and obligations of the restructured entity under the pre-restructuring arrangement (including in relevant circumstances those existing under contract and commercial law) and of the manner and extent to which those rights and obligations change as a result of the restructuring.

---

[3]   See paragraph 1.11.

9.55   Obviously, any evaluation of the rights and obligations of the restructured entity must be based upon the requirement that those rights and obligations reflect the economic principles that generally govern relationships between independent enterprises (see paragraphs 1.52 and 1.53). For example, a restructured entity may legally be under a short term or "at will" contractual arrangement at the time of the restructuring. However, the actual conduct of the entity in the years or decades prior to the restructuring may be indicative of a longer-term arrangement, and hence greater rights than those indicated by the legal contractual arrangement.

9.56   In the absence of evidence of rights and obligations in a comparable situation, it may be necessary to determine what rights and obligations would have been put in place had the two parties transacted with each other at arm's length. In making such an evaluation, care must be taken to avoid the use of hindsight (see paragraph 3.74).

B.2   *Understanding the business reasons for and the expected benefits from the restructuring, including the role of synergies*

9.57   Business representatives who participated in the OECD consultation process explained that multinational businesses, regardless of their products or sectors, increasingly needed to reorganize their structures to provide more centralized control and management of manufacturing, research and distribution functions. The pressure of competition in a globalised economy, savings from economies of scale, the need for specialization and the need to increase efficiency and lower costs were all described as important in driving business restructuring. Where anticipated synergies are put forward by a taxpayer as an important business reason for the restructuring, it would be a good practice for the taxpayer to document, at the time the restructuring is decided upon or implemented, what these anticipated synergies are and on what assumptions they are anticipated. This is a type of documentation that is likely to be produced at the group level for non-tax purposes, to support the decision-making process of the restructuring. For Article 9 purposes, it would be a good practice for the taxpayer to document how these anticipated synergies impact at the entity level in applying the arm's length principle. Furthermore, while anticipated synergies may be relevant to the understanding of a business restructuring, care must be taken to avoid the use of hindsight in *ex post* analyses (see paragraph 3.74).

9.58   The fact that a business restructuring may be motivated by anticipated synergies does not necessarily mean that the profits of the MNE group will effectively increase after the restructuring. It may be the case that enhanced synergies make it possible for the MNE group to derive additional profits compared to what the situation would have been in the future if the restructuring had not taken place, but there may not necessarily be additional profits compared to the pre-restructuring situation, for instance if the restructuring is needed to maintain competitiveness rather than to increase it. In addition, expected synergies do not always materialise – there can be cases where the implementation of a global business model designed to derive more group synergies in fact leads to additional costs and less efficiency.

B.3   Other options realistically available to the parties

9.59   The application of the arm's length principle is based on the notion that independent enterprises, when evaluating the terms of a potential transaction, will compare the transaction to the other options realistically available to them, and they will only enter into the transaction if they see no alternative that is clearly more attractive. In other words, independent enterprises would only enter into a transaction if it does not make them worse off than their next best option. Consideration of the other options realistically available may be relevant to comparability analysis, to understand the respective positions of the parties.

9.60   Thus, in applying the arm's length principle, a tax administration evaluates each transaction as structured by the taxpayer, unless such transaction is not recognised in accordance with the guidance at paragraph 1.65. However, alternative structures realistically available are considered in evaluating whether the terms of the controlled transaction (particularly pricing) would be acceptable to an uncontrolled taxpayer faced with the same alternatives and operating under comparable circumstances. If a more profitable structure could have been adopted, but the economic substance of the taxpayer's structure does not differ from its form and the structure is not commercially irrational such that it would practically impede a tax administration from determining an appropriate transfer price, the transaction is not disregarded. However, the consideration in the controlled transaction may be adjusted by reference to the profits that could have been obtained in the alternative structure, since independent enterprises will only enter into a transaction if they see no alternative that is clearly more attractive.

9.61   At arm's length, there are situations where an entity would have had one or more options realistically available to it that would be clearly more attractive than to accept the conditions of the restructuring (taking into account all the relevant conditions, including the commercial and market conditions going forward, the profit potential of the various options and any compensation or indemnification for the restructuring), including possibly the option not to enter into the restructuring transaction. In such cases, an independent party may not have agreed to the conditions of the restructuring.

9.62   At arm's length, there are also situations where the restructured entity would have had no clearly more attractive option realistically available to it than to accept the conditions of the restructuring, *e.g.* a contract termination – with or without indemnification as discussed at Section E below. In longer-term contracts, this may occur by invoking an exit clause that allows for one party to prematurely exit the contract with just cause. In contracts that allow either party to opt out of the contract, the party terminating the arrangement may choose to do so because it has determined, subject to the terms of the termination clause, that it is more favourable to stop using the function, or to internalise it, or to engage a cheaper or more efficient provider (recipient) or to seek more lucrative opportunities (provider). In case the restructured entity transfers rights or other assets or an ongoing concern to another party, it might however be compensated for such a transfer as discussed in Section D below.

9.63   The arm's length principle requires an evaluation of the conditions made or imposed between associated enterprises, at the level of each of them. The fact that the cross-border redeployment of functions, assets and/or risks may be motivated by sound commercial reasons at the level of the MNE group, *e.g.* in order to try to derive synergies at a group level, does not answer the question whether it is arm's length from the perspectives of each of the restructured entities.

9.64   The reference to the notion of options realistically available is not intended to create a requirement for taxpayers to document all possible hypothetical options realistically available. As noted at paragraph 3.81, when undertaking a comparability analysis, there is no requirement for an exhaustive search of all possible relevant sources of information. Rather, the intention is to provide an indication that, if there is a realistically available option that is clearly more attractive, it should be considered in the analysis of the conditions of the restructuring.

C. Reallocation of profit potential as a result of a business restructuring

C.1   *Profit potential*

9.65   An independent enterprise does not necessarily receive compensation when a change in its business arrangements results in a reduction in its profit potential or expected future profits. The arm's length principle does not require compensation for a mere decrease in the expectation of an entity's future profits. When applying the arm's length principle to business restructurings, the question is whether there is a transfer of something of value (rights or other assets) or a termination or substantial renegotiation of existing arrangements and that transfer, termination or substantial renegotiation would be compensated between independent parties in comparable circumstances. These two situations are discussed in Sections D and E below.

9.66   In these Guidelines, "profit potential" means "expected future profits". In some cases it may encompass losses. The notion of "profit potential" is often used for valuation purposes, in the determination of an arm's length compensation for a transfer of intangibles or of an ongoing concern, or in the determination of an arm's length indemnification for the termination or substantial renegotiation of existing arrangements, once it is found that such compensation or indemnification would have taken place between independent parties in comparable circumstances.

9.67   In the context of business restructurings, profit potential should not be interpreted as simply the profits/losses that would occur if the pre-restructuring arrangement were to continue indefinitely. On the one hand, if an entity has no discernable rights and/or other assets at the time of the restructuring, then it has no compensable profit potential. On the other hand, an entity with considerable rights and/or other assets at the time of the restructuring may have considerable profit potential, which must ultimately be appropriately remunerated in order to justify the sacrifice of such profit potential.

9.68   In order to determine whether at arm's length the restructuring itself would give rise to a form of compensation, it is essential to understand the restructuring, including the changes that have taken place, how they have affected the functional analysis of the parties, what the business reasons for and the anticipated benefits from the restructuring were, and what options would have been realistically available to the parties, as discussed in Section B.

C.2   Reallocation of risks and profit potential

9.69   Business restructurings often involve changes in the respective risk profiles of the associated enterprises. Risk reallocations can follow from a transfer of something of value as discussed in Section D below, and/or from a termination or substantial renegotiation of existing arrangements, as discussed in Section E. General guidance on the transfer pricing aspects of risks is found in Part I of this chapter.

9.70   Take the example of a conversion of a full-fledged manufacturer into a contract manufacturer. In such a case, while a cost plus reward might be an arm's length remuneration for undertaking the post-restructuring contract manufacturing operations, a different question is whether there should be indemnification at arm's length for the change in the existing arrangements which results in the surrender of the riskier profit potential by the manufacturer, taking into account its rights and other assets.

9.71   As another example, assume a distributor is operating at its own risk under a long term contractual arrangement for a given type of transaction. Assume that, based on its rights under the long term contract with respect to these transactions, it has the option realistically available to it to accept or refuse being converted into a low risk distributor operating for a foreign associated enterprise, and that an arm's length remuneration for such a low risk distribution activity is estimated to be a stable profit of +2% per year while the excess profit potential associated with the risks would now be attributed to the foreign associated enterprise. Assume for the purpose of this example that such a restructuring would be implemented solely via a renegotiation of the existing contractual arrangements, with no transfer of assets taking place. From the perspective of the distributor, the question arises as to whether the new arrangement (taking into account both the remuneration for the post-restructuring transactions and any compensation for the restructuring itself) would make it as well off as or better off than its realistic – albeit riskier – alternatives. If not, this would imply that the post-restructuring arrangement is mis-priced or that additional compensation would be needed to appropriately remunerate the distributor for the restructuring. From the perspective of the foreign associated enterprise, the question arises whether and if so to what extent it would be willing to accept the risk at arm's length in situations where the distributor continues to perform the same activity in a new capacity.

9.72   At arm's length, the response is likely to depend on the rights and other assets of the parties, on the profit potential of the distributor and of its associated enterprise in relation to both business models (full-fledged and low risk distributor) as well as the expected duration of the new arrangement. The perspective of the distributor can be illustrated with the following example.

Note: This example is for illustration only. It is not intended to say anything about the choice of the most appropriate transfer pricing method, about aggregation of transactions, or about arm's length remuneration rates for distribution activities. It is assumed in this example that the change in the allocation of risk to the distributor derives from the renegotiation of the existing distribution arrangement which reallocates risk between the parties. This example is intended to illustrate the perspective of the distributor. It does not take account of the perspective of the foreign associated enterprise (principal), although both perspectives should be taken into account in the transfer pricing analysis.

Distributor's pre-conversion profits: historical data from the last five years (full risk activity) (net profit margin / sales)	Distributor's future profit expectations for the next three years (if had remained full-risk, assuming it had the option realistically available to do so) (net profit margin / sales)	Distributor's post-conversion profits (low risk activity) (net profit margin / sales)
Case no. 1: Year 1: (-2%) Year 2: + 4% Year 3: + 2% Year 4: 0 Year 5: + 6%	[-2% to + 6%] with significant uncertainties within that range	guaranteed, stable profit of +2% per year
Case no. 2: Year 1: + 5% Year 2: + 10% Year 3: + 5% Year 4: + 5% Year 5: + 10%	[+5% to + 10%] with significant uncertainties within that range	guaranteed, stable profit of +2% per year
Case no. 3: Year 1: + 5% Year 2: + 7% Year 3: + 10% Year 4: + 8% Year 5: + 6%	[0% to + 4%] with significant uncertainties within that range (*e.g.* due to new competitive pressures)	guaranteed, stable profit of +2% per year

9.73   In case no. 1, the distributor is surrendering a profit potential with significant uncertainties for a relatively low but stable profit. Whether an independent party would be willing to do so would depend on its anticipated return under both scenarios, on its level of risk tolerance, on its options realistically available and on possible compensation for the restructuring itself. In case no. 2, it is unlikely that independent parties in the distributor's situation would agree to relocate the risks and associated profit potential for no additional compensation if they had the option to do otherwise. Case no. 3 illustrates the fact that the analysis should take account of the profit potential going forward and that, where there is a significant change in the commercial or economic environment, relying on historical data alone will not be sufficient.

D. Transfer of something of value (*e.g.* an asset or an ongoing concern)

9.74   Sections D.1 to D.3 below contain a discussion of some typical transfers that can arise in business restructurings: transfers of tangible assets, of intangible assets and of activities (ongoing concern).

D.1   Tangible assets

9.75   Business restructurings can involve the transfer of tangible assets (*e.g.* equipment) by a restructured entity to a foreign associated enterprise. Although it is generally considered that transfers of tangible assets do not raise any significant transfer pricing difficulty, one common issue relates to the valuation of inventories that are transferred upon the conversion by a restructured manufacturer or distributor to a foreign associated enterprise (*e.g.* a principal), where the latter takes title to the inventories as from the implementation of the new business model and supply chain arrangements.

Illustration

Note: The following example is solely intended to illustrate the issue around valuation of inventory transfers. It is not intended to say anything about whether or not a particular restructuring should be recognised by tax authorities or whether or not it is consistent with the arm's length principle, nor is it intended to suggest that a particular transfer pricing method is always acceptable for restructured operations.

9.76   Assume a taxpayer, which is a member of an MNE group, used to operate as a "fully-fledged" manufacturer and distributor. According to the pre-restructuring business model, the taxpayer purchased raw materials, manufactured finished products using tangible and intangible property that belonged to it or was rented/licensed to it, performed marketing and distribution functions and sold the finished products to third party customers. In doing so, the taxpayer was bearing a series of risks such as inventory risks, bad debt risks and market risks.

9.77   Assume the arrangement is restructured and the taxpayer now operates as a so-called "toll-manufacturer" and "stripped distributor". As part of the restructuring, a foreign associated enterprise is established that acquires various trade and marketing intangibles from various affiliates including the taxpayer. Further to the restructuring, raw materials are to be acquired by the foreign associated enterprise, put in consignment in the premises of the taxpayer for manufacturing in exchange for a manufacturing fee. The stock of finished products will belong to the foreign associated enterprise and be acquired by the taxpayer for immediate re-sale to third party customers (*i.e.* the taxpayer will only purchase the finished products once it has concluded a sale with a customer). Under this new business model, the foreign associated enterprise will bear the inventory risks that were previously borne by the taxpayer.

9.78   Assume that in order to migrate from the pre-existing arrangement to the restructured one, the raw materials and finished products that are on the balance sheet of the taxpayer at the time the new arrangement is put in place are transferred to the foreign associated enterprise. The question arises how to determine the arm's length transfer price for the inventories upon the conversion. This is an issue that can typically be encountered where there is a transition from one business model to another. The arm's length principle applies to transfers of inventory among associated enterprises situated in different tax jurisdictions. The choice of the appropriate transfer pricing method depends upon the comparability (including functional) analysis of the parties. The functional analysis may have to cover a transition period over which the transfer is being implemented. For instance, in the above example:

- One possibility could be to determine the arm's length price for the raw material and finished products by reference to comparable uncontrolled prices, to the extent the comparability factors can be met by such comparable uncontrolled prices, *i.e.* that the conditions of the uncontrolled transaction are comparable to the conditions of the transfer that takes place in the context of the restructuring.

- Another possibility could be to determine the transfer price for the finished products as the resale price to customers minus an arm's length remuneration for the marketing and distribution functions that still remain to be performed.

- A further possibility would be to start from the manufacturing costs and add an arm's length mark-up to remunerate the manufacturer for the functions it performed, assets it used and risks it assumed with respect to these inventories. There are however cases where the market value of the inventories is too low for a profit element to be added on costs at arm's length.

9.79   The choice of the appropriate transfer pricing method depends in part on which part of the transaction is the less complex and can be evaluated with the greater certainty (the functions performed, assets used and risks assumed by the manufacturer, or the marketing and sales functions that remain to be performed taking account of the assets to be used and risks to be assumed to perform these functions). See paragraphs 3.18–3.19 on the choice of the tested party.

D.2   *Intangible assets*

9.80   Transfers of intangible assets raise difficult questions both as to the identification of the assets transferred and as to their valuation. Identification can be difficult because not all valuable intangible assets are legally protected and registered and not all valuable intangible assets are recorded in the accounts. Relevant intangible assets might potentially include rights to use industrial assets such as patents, trademarks, trade names, designs or models, as well as copyrights of literary, artistic or scientific work (including software) and intellectual property such as know-how and trade secrets. They may also include customer lists, distribution channels, unique names, symbols or pictures. An essential part of the analysis of a business restructuring is to identify the significant intangible assets that were transferred (if any), whether independent parties would have remunerated their transfer, and what their arm's length value is.

9.81   The determination of the arm's length price for a transfer of intangible property right should take account of both the perspective of the transferor and of the transferee (see paragraph 6.14). It will be affected by a number of factors among which are the amount, duration and riskiness of the expected benefits from the exploitation of the intangible property, the nature of the property right and the restrictions that may be attached to it (restrictions in the way it can be used or exploited, geographical restrictions, time limitations), the extent and remaining duration of its legal protection (if any), and any exclusivity clause that might be attached to the right. Valuation of intangibles can be complex and uncertain. The general guidance on intangibles and on cost contribution arrangements that is found in Chapters VI and VIII can be applicable in the context of business restructurings.

D.2.1 Disposal of intangible rights by a local operation to a central location (foreign associated enterprise)

9.82 Business restructurings sometimes involve the transfer of intangible assets that were previously owned and managed by one or more local operation(s) to a central location situated in another tax jurisdiction (*e.g.* a foreign associated enterprise that operates as a principal or as a so-called "IP company"). The intangible assets transferred may or may not be valuable for the transferor and/or for the MNE group as a whole. In some cases the transferor continues to use the intangible transferred, but does so in another legal capacity (*e.g.* as a licensee of the transferee, or through a contract that includes limited rights to the intangible such as a contract manufacturing arrangement using patents that were transferred; or a "stripped" distribution arrangement using a trademark that was transferred); in some other cases it does not.

9.83 MNE groups may have sound business reasons to centralize ownership and management of intangible property. An example in the context of business restructuring is a transfer of intangibles that accompanies the specialisation of manufacturing sites within an MNE group. In a pre-restructuring environment, each manufacturing entity may be the owner and manager of a series of patents – for instance if the manufacturing sites were historically acquired from third parties with their intangible property. In a global business model, each manufacturing site can be specialised by type of manufacturing process or by geographical area rather than by patent. As a consequence of such a restructuring the MNE group might proceed with the transfer of all the locally owned and managed patents to a central location which will in turn give contractual rights (through licences or manufacturing agreements) to all the group's manufacturing sites to manufacture the products falling in their new areas of competence, using patents that were initially owned either by the same or by another entity within the group.

9.84 The arm's length principle requires an evaluation of the conditions made or imposed between associated enterprises, at the level of each of them. The fact that centralisation of intangible property rights may be motivated by sound commercial reasons at the level of the MNE group does not answer the question whether the disposal is arm's length from the perspectives of both the transferor and the transferee.

9.85   Also in the case where a local operation disposes of its intangible property rights to a foreign associated enterprise and continues to use the intangibles further to the disposal, but does so in a different legal capacity (*e.g.* as a licensee), the conditions of the transfer should be assessed from both the transferor's and the transferee's perspectives, in particular by examining the pricing at which comparable independent enterprises would be willing to transfer and acquire the property. See paragraph 9.81. The determination of an arm's length remuneration for the subsequent ownership, use and exploitation of the transferred asset should take account of the extent of the functions performed, assets used and risks assumed by the parties in relation to the intangible transferred. This is particularly relevant to business restructurings as several countries have expressed a concern that relevant information on the functions, assets and risks of foreign associated enterprises is often not made available to them.

9.86   Where the business restructuring provides for a transfer of an intangible asset followed by a new arrangement whereby the transferor will continue to use the intangible transferred, the entirety of the commercial arrangement between the parties should be examined in order to assess whether the transactions are at arm's length. If an independent party were to transfer an asset that it intends to continue exploiting, it would be prudent for it to negotiate the conditions of such a future use (*e.g.* in a license agreement) concomitantly with the conditions of the transfer. In effect, there will generally be a relationship between the determination of an arm's length compensation for the transfer, the determination of an arm's length compensation for the post-restructuring transactions in relation to the transferred intangible, such as future license fees that may be payable by the transferor to be able to continue using the asset, and the expected future profitability of the transferor from its future use of the asset. For instance, an arrangement whereby a patent is transferred for a price of 100 in Year N and a license agreement is concomitantly concluded according to which the transferor will continue to use the patent transferred in exchange for a royalty of 100 per year over a 10-year period is unlikely to be consistent with the arm's length principle.

D.2.2   Intangible transferred at a point in time when it does not have an established value

9.87   Difficulties can arise in the context of business restructuring where an intangible is disposed of at a point in time when it does not yet have an established value (*e.g.* pre-exploitation), especially where there is a significant gap between the level of expected future profits that was taken into account in the valuation made at the time of the sale transaction and the actual profits derived by the transferee from the exploitation of the intangibles thus acquired. When valuation of intangible property at the time of the transaction is highly uncertain, the question is raised how arm's length pricing should be determined. The question should be resolved, both by taxpayers and tax administrations, by reference to what independent enterprises would have done in comparable circumstances to take account of the valuation uncertainty in the pricing of the transaction. See paragraphs 6.28-6.35 and examples in the Annex to Chapter VI "Examples to illustrate the Transfer Pricing Guidelines on intangible property and highly uncertain valuation."

9.88   Following that guidance, the main question is to determine whether the valuation was sufficiently uncertain at the outset that the parties at arm's length would have required a price adjustment mechanism, or whether the change in value was so fundamental a development that it would have led to a renegotiation of the transaction. Where this is the case, the tax administration would be justified in determining the arm's length price for the transfer of the intangible on the basis of the adjustment clause or re-negotiation that would be provided at arm's length in a comparable uncontrolled transaction. In other circumstances, where there is no reason to consider that the valuation was sufficiently uncertain at the outset that the parties would have required a price adjustment clause or would have renegotiated the terms of the agreement, there is no reason for tax administrations to make such an adjustment as it would represent an inappropriate use of hindsight. The mere existence of uncertainty at the time of the transaction should not require an *ex-post* adjustment without a consideration of what third parties would have done or agreed between them.

D.2.3   Local intangibles

9.89   Where a local full-fledged operation is converted into a "limited risk, limited intangibles, low remuneration" operation, the questions arise of whether this conversion entails the transfer by the restructured local entity to a foreign associated enterprise of valuable intangible assets such as customer lists and whether there are local intangible assets that remain with the local operation.

9.90   In particular, in the case of the conversion of a full-fledged distributor into a limited risk distributor or commissionnaire, it may be important to examine whether the distributor has developed local marketing intangibles over the years prior to it being restructured and if so, what the nature and the value of these intangibles are, and whether they were transferred to an associated enterprise. Where such local intangibles are found to be in existence and to be transferred to a foreign associated enterprise, the arm's length principle should apply to determine whether and if so how to compensate such a transfer, based on what would be agreed between independent parties in comparable circumstances. On the other hand, where such local intangibles are found to be in existence and to remain in the restructured entity, they should be taken into account in the functional analysis of the post-restructuring activities. They may accordingly influence the selection and application of the most appropriate transfer pricing method for the post-restructuring controlled transactions, and/or be remunerated separately, *e.g.* via royalty payments made by the foreign associated enterprise which will exploit them as from the restructuring to the restructured entity over the life-span of the intangibles.[4]

D.2.4   Contractual rights

9.91   Contractual rights can be valuable intangible assets. Where valuable contractual rights are transferred (or surrendered) between associated enterprises, they should be remunerated at arm's length, taking account of the value of the rights transferred from the perspectives of both the transferor and the transferee.

9.92   Tax administrations have expressed concerns about cases they have observed in practice where an entity voluntarily terminates a contract that provided benefits to it, in order to allow a foreign associated enterprise to enter into a similar contract and benefit from the profit potential attached to it. For instance, assume that company A has valuable long-term contracts with independent customers that carry significant profit potential for A. Assume that at a certain point in time, A voluntarily terminates its contracts with its customers under circumstances where the latter are legally or commercially obligated to enter into similar arrangements with company B, a foreign entity that belongs to the same MNE group as A. As a consequence, the contractual rights and attached profit potential that used to lie with A now lie with B. If the factual situation is that B could only enter into the contracts with the customers subject to A's surrendering its own contractual rights to its benefit, and that A only terminated its contracts with its customers knowing that the latter were legally or commercially obligated to conclude similar arrangements with B, this in substance would consist in a tri-partite transaction and it may amount to a transfer of valuable contractual rights from A to B that may have to be remunerated at arm's

---

[4]   See Part III of this chapter for a discussion of the remuneration of the post-restructuring arrangements.

length, depending on the value of the rights surrendered by A from the perspectives of both A and B.

D.3   Transfer of activity (ongoing concern)

D.3.1   Valuing a transfer of activity

9.93   Business restructurings sometimes involve the transfer of an ongoing concern, *i.e.* a functioning, economically integrated business unit. The transfer of an ongoing concern in this context means the transfer of assets, bundled with the ability to perform certain functions and bear certain risks. Such functions, assets and risks may include, among other things: tangible and intangible property; liabilities associated with holding certain assets and performing certain functions, such as R&D and manufacturing; the capacity to carry on the activities that the transferor carried on before the transfer; and any resource, capabilities, and rights. The valuation of a transfer of an ongoing concern should reflect all the valuable elements that would be remunerated between independent parties in comparable circumstances. For example, in the case of a business restructuring that involves the transfer of a business unit that includes, among other things, research facilities staffed with an experienced research team, the valuation of such ongoing concern should reflect, among other things, the value of the facility and the value (if any) of the workforce in place that would be agreed upon at arm's length.

9.94   The determination of the arm's length compensation for a transfer of an ongoing concern does not necessarily amount to the sum of the separate valuations of each separate element that comprises the aggregate transfer. In particular, if the transfer on an ongoing concern comprises multiple contemporaneous transfers of interrelated assets, risks, or functions, valuation of those transfers on an aggregate basis may be necessary to achieve the most reliable measure of the arm's length price for the ongoing concern. Valuation methods that are used, in acquisition deals, between independent parties may prove useful to valuing the transfer of an ongoing concern between associated enterprises.

9.95   An example is the case where a manufacturing activity that used to be performed by M1, one entity of the MNE group, is re-located to another entity, M2 (*e.g.* to benefit from location savings). Assume M1 transfers to M2 its machinery and equipment, inventories, patents, manufacturing processes and know-how, and key contracts with suppliers and clients. Assume that several employees of M1 are relocated to M2 in order to assist M2 in the start of the manufacturing activity so relocated.

Assume such a transfer would be regarded as a transfer of an ongoing concern, should it take place between independent parties. In order to determine the arm's length remuneration, if any, of such a transfer between associated enterprises, it should be compared with a transfer of an ongoing concern between independent parties rather than with a transfer of isolated assets.

D.3.2   Loss-making activities

9.96   Not every case where a restructured entity loses functions, assets and / or risks involves an actual loss of expected future profits. In some restructuring situations, the circumstances may be such that, rather than losing a "profit-making opportunity", the restructured entity is actually being saved from the likelihood of a "loss-making opportunity". An entity may agree to a restructuring and a loss of functions, assets and / or risks as a better option than going out of business altogether. If the restructured entity is forecasting future losses absent the restructuring (*e.g.* it operates a manufacturing plant that is uneconomic due to increasing competition from low-cost imports), then there may be in fact no loss of any profit-making opportunity from restructuring rather than continuing to operate its existing business. In such circumstances, the restructuring might deliver a benefit to the restructured entity from reducing or eliminating future losses if such losses exceed the restructuring costs.

9.97   The question was raised of whether the transferee should in fact be compensated by the transferor for taking over a loss-making activity. The response depends on whether an independent party in comparable circumstances would have been willing to pay for getting rid of the loss-making activity, or whether it would have considered other options such as closing down the activity; and on whether a third party would have been willing to acquire the loss-making activity (*e.g.* because of possible synergies with its own activities) and if so under what conditions, *e.g.* subject to compensation. There can be circumstances where an independent party would be willing to pay, *e.g.* if the financial costs and social risks of closing down the activity would be such that the transferor finds it more advantageous to pay a transferee who will attempt to reconvert the activity and will be responsible for any redundancy plan that may be needed.

9.98   The situation might however be different where the loss-making activity provided other benefits such as synergies with other activities performed by the same taxpayer. There can also be circumstances where a loss-making activity is maintained because it produces some benefits to the group as a whole. In such a case, the question arises whether at arm's length the entity that maintains the loss-making activity should be compensated by those who benefit from it being maintained.

D.4   Outsourcing

9.99   In outsourcing cases, it may happen that a party voluntarily decides to undergo a restructuring and to bear the associated restructuring costs in exchange for anticipated savings. For instance, assume a taxpayer that is manufacturing and selling products in a high-cost jurisdiction decides to outsource the manufacturing activity to an associated enterprise situated in a low-cost jurisdiction. Further to the restructuring, the taxpayer will purchase from its associated enterprise the products manufactured and will continue to sell them to third party customers. The restructuring may entail restructuring costs for the taxpayer while at the same time making it possible for it to benefit from cost savings on future procurements compared to its own manufacturing costs. Independent parties implement this type of outsourcing arrangement and do not necessarily require explicit compensation from the transferee if the anticipated cost savings for the transferor are greater than its restructuring costs.[5]

E. Indemnification of the restructured entity for the termination or substantial renegotiation of existing arrangements

9.100   Where an existing contractual relationship is terminated or substantially renegotiated in the context of a business restructuring, the restructured entity might suffer detriments such as restructuring costs (*e.g.* write-off of assets, termination of employment contracts), re-conversion costs (*e.g.* in order to adapt its existing operation to other customer needs), and/or a loss of profit potential. In business restructurings, existing arrangements are often renegotiated in such a way that the respective risk profiles of the parties are changed, with consequences on the allocation of profit potential among them. For instance, a full-fledged distribution arrangement is converted into a low-risk distribution or commissionnaire arrangement; a full-fledged manufacturing arrangement is converted into a contract-manufacturing or toll-manufacturing arrangement. In these situations, the question arises of whether independent parties in similar circumstances would have agreed for an indemnification to be paid to the restructured entity (and if so how to determine such an indemnification).

---

[5]   A further issue discussed in paragraphs 9.148-9.153 is whether and if so how location savings should be allocated between the parties at arm's length.

9.101   The renegotiation of existing arrangements is sometimes accompanied by a transfer of rights or other assets. For instance, the termination of a distribution contract is sometimes accompanied by a transfer of intangibles. In such cases, the guidance at Sections D and E of this part should be read together.

9.102   For the purpose of this chapter, indemnification means any type of compensation that may be paid for detriments suffered by the restructured entity, whether in the form of an up-front payment, of a sharing in restructuring costs, of lower (or higher) purchase (or sale) prices in the context of the post-restructuring operations, or of any other form.

9.103   There should be no presumption that all contract terminations or substantial renegotiations should give a right to indemnification at arm's length. In order to assess whether an indemnification would be warranted at arm's length, it is important to examine the circumstances at the time of the restructuring, particularly the rights and other assets of the parties as well as, where relevant, the options realistically available to the parties. For this purpose, the following four conditions may be important:

- Whether the arrangement that is terminated, non-renewed or substantially re-negotiated is formalised in writing and provides for an indemnification clause (see Section E.1 below);

- Whether the terms of the arrangement and the existence or non-existence of an indemnification clause or other type of guarantee (as well as the terms of such a clause where it exists) are arm's length (see Section E.2 below);

- Whether indemnification rights are provided for by commercial legislation or case law (see Section E.3 below); and

- Whether at arm's length another party would have been willing to indemnify the one that suffers from the termination or re-negotiation of the agreement (see Section E.4 below).

E.1 Whether the arrangement that is terminated, non-renewed or substantially renegotiated is formalised in writing and provides for an indemnification clause

9.104 Where the terminated, non-renewed or re-negotiated arrangement is formalised in writing,[6] the starting point of the analysis should be a review of whether the conditions for termination, non-renewal or renegotiation of the contract were respected (*e.g.* with regard to any required notice period) and of whether an indemnification clause or other kind of guarantee for termination, non-renewal or renegotiation is provided for. As noted at paragraph 1.53, in transactions between independent enterprises, the divergence of interests between the parties ensures that they will ordinarily seek to hold each other to the terms of the contract, and that contractual terms will be ignored or modified after the fact generally only if it is in the interests of both parties.

9.105 However, the examination of the terms of the contract between the associated enterprises may not suffice from a transfer pricing perspective as the mere fact that a given terminated, non-renewed or renegotiated contract did not provide an indemnification or guarantee clause does not necessarily mean that this is arm's length, as discussed below.

E.2 Whether the terms of the arrangement and the existence or non-existence of an indemnification clause or other type of guarantee (as well as the terms of such a clause where it exists) are arm's length

9.106 Between independent parties, there are cases of contracts that are terminated, non-renewed or substantially renegotiated with no indemnification. However, because the same divergence of interests that exists between independent parties may not exist in the case of associated enterprises, the question can arise whether the terms of a contract between associated enterprises are arm's length, *i.e.* whether independent parties in comparable conditions would have concluded such a contract (for instance a contract that contains no indemnification clause or guarantee of any kind in case of termination, non-renewal or renegotiation). Where comparables data evidence a similar indemnification clause (or absence thereof) in

---

6 As noted at paragraph 1.52, the terms of a transaction may also be found in correspondence/communications between the parties other than a written contract. Where no written terms exist, the contractual relationships of the parties must be deduced from their conduct and the economic principles that generally govern relationships between independent enterprises.

comparable circumstances, the indemnification clause (or absence thereof) in a controlled transaction will be regarded as arm's length. In those cases however where such comparables data are not found, the determination of whether independent parties would have agreed to such an indemnification clause (or absence thereof) should take into account the rights and other assets of the parties, at the time of entering into the arrangement and of its termination or renegotiation, and might be assisted by an examination of the options realistically available to the parties. [7]

9.107   When examining whether the conditions of an arrangement are arm's length, it may be necessary to examine both the remuneration of the transactions that are the object of the arrangement and the financial conditions of the termination thereof, as both can be inter-related. In effect, the terms of a termination clause (or the absence thereof) may be a significant element of the functional analysis of the transactions and specifically of the analysis of the risks of the parties, and may accordingly need to be taken into account in the determination of an arm's length remuneration for the transactions. Similarly, the remuneration of the transactions will affect the determination of whether the conditions of the termination of the arrangement are at arm's length.

9.108   In some situations, it may be the case that, in comparable circumstances, an independent party would not have had any option realistically available that would be clearly more attractive to it than to accept the conditions of the termination or substantial renegotiation of the contract. In some other cases, it may be that, on the basis of an examination of the substance of the arrangement and of the actual conduct of the associated enterprises, an implicit longer term contract should be implied whereby the terminated party would have been entitled to some indemnification in case of early termination.

9.109   One circumstance that deserves particular attention, because it could have influenced the terms of the contract had it been concluded between independent parties, is the situation where the now-terminated contract required one party to make a significant investment for which an arm's length return might only be reasonably expected if the contract was maintained for an extended period of time. This created a financial risk for the party making the investment in case the contract was terminated before the end of such period of time. The degree of the risk would depend on whether the investment was highly specialised or could be used (possibly subject to some adaptations) for other clients. Where the risk was material, it

---

[7]   See paragraphs 9.59-9.64 for a discussion of options realistically available.

would have been reasonable for independent parties in comparable circumstances to take it into account when negotiating the contract.

9.110   An example would be where a manufacturing contract between associated enterprises requires the manufacturer to invest in a new manufacturing unit. Assume an arm's length return on the investment can reasonably be anticipated by the manufacturer at the time the contract is concluded, subject to the manufacturing contract lasting for at least five years, for the manufacturing activity to produce at least x units per year, and for the remuneration of the manufacturing activity to be calculated on a basis (*e.g.* y\$/unit) that is expected to generate an arm's length return on the total investment in the new manufacturing unit. Assume that after three years, the associated enterprise terminates the contract in accordance with its terms in the context of a group-wide restructuring of the manufacturing operations. Assume the manufacturing unit is highly specialised and the manufacturer further to the termination has no other choice than to write off the assets. The question arises of whether in comparable circumstances, an independent manufacturer in the first place would have sought to mitigate the financial risk linked to the investment in case of termination of its manufacturing contract before the end of the five-year period it needed to obtain an arm's length return on its investment.

9.111   The general guidance in Part I of this chapter on how to determine whether a risk allocation is arm's length would be relevant in such a case. In case comparable uncontrolled transactions are found that evidence a similar allocation of risks in uncontrolled transactions (taking account in particular the conditions of the investment, the remuneration of the manufacturing activity and the conditions of the termination), then the risk allocation between the associated enterprises would be regarded as arm's length.

9.112   In case such evidence is not found, the question would be whether independent parties would have agreed to a similar allocation of risk. This will depend on the facts and circumstances of the transaction and in particular on the rights and other assets of the parties.

- At arm's length the party making the investment might not be willing to assume with no guarantee a risk (termination risk) that is controlled by the other (see paragraphs 1.49 and 9.17-9.33). There can be a variety of ways in which such a risk might have been taken into account in contract negotiations, for instance by providing for an appropriate indemnification clause in case of early termination, or for an option for the party making the investment to transfer it at a given price to the other party in case the investment becomes useless to the former due to the early termination of the contract by the latter.

- Another possible approach would have been to factor the risk linked with the possible termination of the contract into the determination of the remuneration of the activities covered by the contract (*e.g.* by factoring the risk into the determination of the remuneration of the manufacturing activities and using third party comparables that bear comparable risks). In such a case the party making the investment consciously accepts the risk and is rewarded for it; no separate indemnification for the termination of the contract seems necessary.

- Finally, in some cases, the risks might be shared between the parties, *e.g.* the party terminating the contract might bear part of the termination costs incurred by the terminated one.

9.113   A similar issue may arise in the case where a party has undertaken development efforts resulting in losses or low returns in the early period and above-normal returns are expected in periods following the termination of the contract.

9.114   In the case where the conditions made or imposed between associated enterprises with respect to the termination, non-renewal or substantial renegotiation of their existing arrangements differ from the conditions that would be made between independent enterprises, then any profits that would, but for those conditions, have accrued to one of the enterprises, but, by reason of those conditions, have not so accrued, may be included in the profits of that enterprise and taxed accordingly.

E.3   *Whether indemnification rights are provided for by commercial legislation or case law*

9.115   In the assessment of whether the conditions of the termination or non-renewal of an existing arrangement are arm's length, the possible recourse that may be offered by the applicable commercial law might provide some helpful insights. The applicable commercial legislation or case law may provide useful information on indemnification rights and terms and conditions that could be expected in case of termination of specific types of agreements, *e.g.* of a distributorship agreement. Under such rules, it may be that the terminated party has the right to claim before the courts an indemnification irrespective of whether or not it was provided for in the contract. Where the parties belong to the same MNE group, however, the terminated party is unlikely in practice to litigate against its associated enterprise in order to seek such an indemnification, and the conditions of the termination may therefore differ from the conditions that would be made between independent enterprises in similar circumstances.

E.4 Whether at arm's length another party would have been willing to indemnify the one that suffers from the termination or re-negotiation of the agreement

9.116   The transfer pricing analysis of the conditions of the termination or substantial renegotiation of an agreement should take account of both the perspectives of the transferor and of the transferee. Taking account of the transferee's perspective is important both to value the amount of an arm's length indemnification, if any, and to determine what party should bear it. It is not possible to derive a single answer for all cases and the response should be based on an examination of the facts and circumstances of the case, and in particular of the rights and other assets of the parties, of the economic rationale for the termination, of the determination of what party(ies) is (are) expected to benefit from it, and of the options realistically available to the parties. This can be illustrated as follows.

9.117   Assume a manufacturing contract between two associated enterprises, entity A and entity B, is terminated by A (B being the manufacturer). Assume A decides to use another associated manufacturer, entity C, to continue the manufacturing that was previously performed by B. As noted at paragraph 9.103, there should be no presumption that all contract terminations or substantial renegotiations should give a right to indemnification at arm's length. Assume that it is determined, following the guidance at Sections E.1 to E.3 above, that in the circumstances of the case, should the transaction take place between independent parties, B would be in a position to claim an indemnification for the detriment suffered from the termination. The question arises of whether such an indemnification should be borne by A (*i.e.* the party terminating the contract), C (*i.e.* the party taking over the manufacturing activity previously performed by B), their parent company P, or any other party.

9.118   As indicated in Section E.1, the starting point in the analysis would be a review of the contractual terms between A and B. In some cases, contractual terms involving C, P and/or another party might also be relevant. The response depends on whether at arm's length these entities would be willing to pay such a termination indemnification.

9.119   There can be situations where A would be willing to bear the indemnification costs at arm's length, for instance because it expects that the termination of its agreement with B will make it possible for it to derive costs savings through its new manufacturing agreement with C, and that the present value of these expected costs savings is greater than the amount of the indemnification.

9.120   There can be situations where C would be willing to pay such an amount as an entrance fee to obtain the manufacturing contract from A, *e.g.* if the present value of the expected profits to be derived from its new manufacturing contract makes it worth the investment for C.   In such situations, the payment by C might be organised in a variety of ways, for instance it might be that C would be paying B, or that C would be paying A, or that C would be constructively paying A by meeting A's indemnification obligation to B.

9.121   There can be cases where at arm's length A and C would be willing to share the indemnification costs.

9.122   There can also be cases where neither A nor C would be willing to bear the indemnification costs at arm's length because neither of them expects to derive sufficient benefits from the change. It can be the case that such termination is part of a group-wide restructuring decided by the parent company P in order to derive group-wide synergies, and that the indemnification of B should be borne by P at arm's length (unless, for example, B, notwithstanding that its contract has been terminated or renegotiated, derives benefits from group-wide synergies that outweigh the cost to it of termination or renegotiation).

Part III: Remuneration of post-restructuring controlled transactions

A. Business restructurings versus "structuring"

A.1   General principle: no different application of the arm's length principle

9.123   The arm's length principle and these Guidelines do not and should not apply differently to post-restructuring transactions as opposed to transactions that were structured as such from the beginning. Doing otherwise would create a competitive distortion between existing players who restructure their activities and new entrants who implement the same business model without having to restructure their business.

9.124   Comparable situations must be treated in the same way. The selection and practical application of an appropriate transfer pricing method must be determined by the comparability analysis, including the functional analysis of the parties and a review of the contractual arrangements. The same comparability standard and the same guidance on the selection and application of transfer pricing methods apply irrespective of whether or not an arrangement came into existence as a result of a restructuring of a previously existing structure.

9.125   However, business restructuring situations involve change, and the arm's length principle must be applied not only to the post-restructuring transactions, but also to additional transactions that take place upon the restructuring and consist in the redeployment of functions, assets and/or risks. The application of the arm's length principle to those additional transactions is discussed in Part II of this chapter.

9.126   In addition, the comparability analysis of an arrangement that results from a business restructuring might reveal some factual differences compared to the one of an arrangement that was structured as such from the beginning, as discussed below. These factual differences do not affect the arm's length principle or the way the guidance in these Guidelines should be interpreted and applied, but they may affect the comparability analysis and therefore the outcome of this application. See Section D on comparing the pre- and post-restructuring situations.

A.2   *Possible factual differences between situations that result from a restructuring and situations that were structured as such from the beginning*

9.127   Where an arrangement between associated enterprises replaces an existing arrangement (restructuring), there may be factual differences in the starting position of the restructured entity compared to the position of a newly set up operation. Such differences can arise for example from the fact that the post-restructuring arrangement is negotiated between parties that have had prior contractual and commercial relationships. In such a situation, depending on the facts and circumstances of the case and in particular on the rights and obligations derived by the parties from these prior arrangements, this may affect the options realistically available to the parties in negotiating the terms of the new arrangement and therefore the conditions of the restructuring and / or of the post-restructuring arrangements.[8] For instance, assume a party has proved in the past to be able to perform well as a "full-fledged distributor" performing a whole range of marketing and selling functions, employing and developing valuable marketing intangible assets and assuming a range of risks associated with its activity such as inventory risks, bad debt risks and market risks. Assume that its distribution contract is re-negotiated and converted into a "limited risk distribution" contract whereby it will perform limited marketing activities under the supervision of a foreign associated enterprise, employ limited marketing intangibles and bear limited risks in its relationship with the foreign associated enterprise and customers. The restructured distributor may be able to negotiate an arrangement that does not contain a trial period or other similar unfavourable conditions, while such a trial period or conditions may be common for new distributors.

9.128   Where there is an ongoing business relationship between the parties before and after the restructuring, there may also be an inter-relationship between on the one hand the conditions of the pre-restructuring activities and/or of the restructuring itself, and on the other hand the conditions for the post-restructuring arrangements, as discussed in Section C below.

9.129   Some differences in the starting position of the restructured entity compared to the position of a newly set up operation can relate to the established presence of the operation. For instance, if one compares a situation where a long-established "full-fledged distributor" is converted

---

[8]   See paragraphs 9.59-9.64 for a discussion of options realistically available in the context of determining the arm's length compensation for the restructuring itself.

into a "limited risk distributor" with a situation where a "limited risk distributor" is established in a market where the group did not have any previous commercial presence, market penetration efforts might be needed for the new entrant which are not needed for the converted entity. This may affect the comparability analysis and the determination of the arm's length remuneration in both situations.

9.130   When one compares a situation where a long-established "full-fledged distributor" is converted into a "limited risk distributor" with a situation where a "limited risk distributor" has been in existence in the market for the same duration, there might also be differences because the "full-fledged distributor" may have performed some functions, borne some expenses (*e.g.* marketing expenses), assumed some risks and contributed to the development of some intangibles before its conversion that the long-existing "limited risk distributor" may not have performed, borne, assumed or contributed to. The question arises whether at arm's length such additional functions, assets and risks should only affect the remuneration of the distributor before its being converted, whether they should be taken into account to determine a remuneration of the transfers that take place upon the conversion (and if so how), whether they should affect the remuneration of the restructured "limited risk distributor" (and if so how), or a combination of these three possibilities. For instance, if it is found that the pre-restructuring activities led the "full-fledged distributor" to own some intangibles while the long-established "limited risk distributor" does not, the arm's length principle may require these intangibles either to be remunerated upon the restructuring if they are transferred by the "full-fledged distributor" to a foreign associated enterprise, or to be taken into account in the determination of the arm's length remuneration of the post-restructuring activities if they are not transferred.[9]

9.131   Where a restructuring involves a transfer to a foreign associated enterprise of risks that were previously assumed by a taxpayer, it may be important to examine whether the transfer of risks only concerns the future risks that will arise from the post-restructuring activities or also the risks existing at the time of the restructuring as a result of pre-conversion activities, *i.e.* there is a cut-off issue. For instance, assume that a distributor was bearing bad debt risks which it will no longer bear after its being restructured as a "limited risk distributor", and that it is being compared with a long-established "limited risk distributor" that never bore bad debt risk. It may be important when comparing both situations to examine whether the "limited risk distributor" that results from a conversion still

---

[9]   See paragraphs 9.80-9.92 for a discussion of the application of the arm's length principle to transfers of intangibles.

bears the risks associated with bad debts that arose before the restructuring at the time it was full-fledged, or whether all the bad debt risks including those that existed at the time of the conversion were transferred.

9.132   The same remarks and questions apply for other types of restructurings, including other types of restructuring of sales activities as well as restructurings of manufacturing activities, research and development activities, or other services activities.

B. Application to business restructuring situations: selection and application of a transfer pricing method for the post-restructuring controlled transactions

9.133   The selection and application of a transfer pricing method to post-restructuring controlled transactions must derive from the comparability analysis of the transaction. It is essential to understand what the functions, assets and risks involved in the post-restructuring transactions are, and what party performs, uses or assumes them. This requires information to be available on the functions, assets and risks of both parties to a transaction, *e.g.* the restructured entity and the foreign associated enterprise with which it transacts. The analysis should go beyond the label assigned to the restructured entity, as an entity that is labelled as a "commissionnaire" or "limited distributor" can sometimes be found to own valuable local intangibles and to continue to assume significant market risks, and an entity that is labelled as a "contract manufacturer" can sometimes be found to pursue significant development activities or to own and use unique intangibles. In post-restructuring situations, particular attention should be paid to the identification of the valuable intangible assets and the significant risks that effectively remain with the restructured entity (including, where applicable, local non-protected intangibles), and to whether such an allocation of intangibles and risks satisfies the arm's length principle. Issues regarding risks and intangibles are discussed in Parts I and II of this chapter. See in particular paragraphs 9.44-9.46 for a discussion of the relationship between the selection of a transfer pricing method and the risk profile of the party.

9.134   Post-restructuring arrangements may pose certain challenges with respect to the identification of potential comparables in cases where the restructuring implements a business model that is hardly found between independent enterprises.

9.135   There are cases where comparables (including internal comparables) are available, subject to possible comparability adjustments being performed. One example of a possible application of the CUP method would be the case where an enterprise that used to transact independently with the MNE group is acquired, and the acquisition is followed by a restructuring of the now controlled transactions. Subject to a review of the five comparability factors and of the possible effect of the controlled and uncontrolled transactions taking place at different times, it might be the case that the conditions of the pre-acquisition uncontrolled transactions provide a CUP for the post-acquisition controlled transactions. Even where the conditions of the transactions are restructured, it might still be possible, depending on the facts and circumstances of the case, to adjust for the transfer of functions, assets and/or risks that occurred upon the restructuring. For instance, a comparability adjustment might be performed to account for a difference in what party bears bad debt risk.

9.136   Another example of a possible application of the CUP method would be the case where independent parties provide manufacturing, selling or service activities comparable to the ones provided by the restructured affiliate. Given the recent development of outsourcing activities, it may be possible in some cases to find independent outsourcing transactions that provide a basis for using the CUP method in order to determine the arm's length remuneration of post-restructuring controlled transactions. This of course is subject to the condition that the outsourcing transactions qualify as uncontrolled transactions and that the review of the five comparability factors provides sufficient comfort that either no material difference exists between the conditions of the uncontrolled outsourcing transactions and the conditions of the post-restructuring controlled transactions, or that reliable enough adjustments can be made (and are effectively made) to eliminate such differences.

9.137   Whenever a comparable is proposed, it is important to ensure that a comparability analysis is performed in order to identify material differences, if any, between the controlled and uncontrolled transactions and, where necessary and possible, to adjust for such differences. In particular, the comparability analysis might reveal that the restructured entity continues to perform valuable and significant functions and/or the presence of local intangibles and/or of significant risks that remain in the "stripped" entity after the restructuring but are not found in the proposed comparables. See Section A on the possible differences between restructured activities and start-up situations.

9.138   The identification of potential comparables has to be made with the objective of finding the most reliable comparables data in the circumstances of the case, keeping in mind the limitations that may exist in availability of information and the compliance costs involved (see paragraphs 3.2 and 3.80). It is recognised that the data will not always be perfect. There are also cases where comparables data are not found. This does not necessarily mean that the controlled transaction is not arm's length. In such cases, it may be necessary to determine whether the conditions of the controlled transaction would have been agreed, had the parties transacted with each other at arm's length. Notwithstanding the difficulties that can arise in the process of searching comparables, it is necessary to find a reasonable solution to all transfer pricing cases. Following the guidance at paragraph 2.2, even in cases where comparables data are scarce and imperfect, the choice of the most appropriate transfer pricing method to the circumstances of the case should be consistent with the nature of the controlled transaction, determined in particular through a functional analysis.

C. Relationship between compensation for the restructuring and post-restructuring remuneration

9.139   There may in some circumstances be an important inter-relationship between the compensation for the restructuring and an arm's length reward for operating the business post-restructuring. This can be the case where a taxpayer disposes of business operations to an associated enterprise with which it must then transact business as part of those operations. One example of such a relationship is found in paragraph 9.99 on outsourcing.[10]

9.140   Another example would be where a taxpayer that operates a manufacturing and distribution activity restructures by disposing of its distribution activity to a foreign associated enterprise to which the taxpayer will in the future sell the goods it manufactures. The foreign associated enterprise would expect to be able to earn an arm's length reward for its investment in acquiring and operating the business. In this situation, the taxpayer might agree with the foreign associated enterprise to forgo receipt of part or all of the up-front compensation for the business that may be payable at arm's length, and instead obtain comparable financial benefit over time through selling its goods to the foreign associated enterprise at prices that are higher than the latter would otherwise agree to if the up-front compensation had been paid. Alternatively, the parties might agree to set an up-front compensation payment for the restructuring that is partly offset through future lower transfer prices for the manufactured products than would have been set otherwise. See Part II of this chapter for a discussion of situations where compensation would be payable at arm's length for the restructuring itself.

---

[10]   See also paragraphs 9.82-9.86.

9.141   In other words, in this situation where the taxpayer will have an ongoing business relationship as supplier to the foreign associated enterprise that carries on an activity previously carried on by the taxpayer, the taxpayer and the foreign associated enterprise have the opportunity to obtain economic and commercial benefits through that relationship (*e.g.* the sale price of goods) which may explain for instance why compensation through an up-front capital payment for transfer of the business was foregone, or why the future transfer price for the products might be different from the prices that would have been agreed absent a restructuring operation.   In practice, however, it might be difficult to structure and monitor such an arrangement. While taxpayers are free to choose the form of compensation payments, whether up-front or over time, tax administrations when reviewing such arrangements would want to know how the compensation for the post-restructuring activity was possibly affected to take account of the foregone compensation, if any, for the restructuring itself. Specifically, in such a case, the tax administration would want to look at the entirety of the arrangements, while being provided with a separate evaluation of the arm's length compensation for the restructuring and for the post-restructuring transactions.

D. Comparing the pre- and post-restructuring situations

9.142   A relevant question is the role if any of comparisons that can be made of the profits actually earned by a party to a controlled transaction prior to and after the restructuring. In particular, it can be asked whether it would be appropriate to determine a restructured entity's post-restructuring profits by reference to its pre-restructuring profits, adjusted to reflect the transfer or relinquishment of particular functions, assets and risks.[11]

9.143   One important issue with such before-and-after comparisons is that a comparison of the profits from the post-restructuring controlled transactions with the profits made in controlled transactions prior to the restructuring would not suffice given Article 9 of the OECD Model Tax Convention provides for a comparison to be made with uncontrolled transactions. Comparisons of a taxpayer's controlled transactions with other controlled transactions are irrelevant to the application of the arm's length principle and therefore should not be used by a tax administration as the basis for a transfer pricing adjustment or by a taxpayer to support its transfer pricing policy.

---

[11]   This is a different question from the one of profit potential that is discussed in Part II of this chapter.

9.144   Another issue with before-and-after comparisons is the likely difficulty of valuing the basket of functions, assets and risks that were lost by the restructured entity, keeping in mind that it is not always the case that these functions, assets and risks are transferred to another party.

9.145   That being said, in business restructurings, before-and-after comparisons could play a role in understanding the restructuring itself and could be part of a before-and-after comparability (including functional) analysis to understand the changes that accounted for the changes in the allocation of profit / loss amongst the parties. In effect, information on the arrangements that existed prior to the restructuring and on the conditions of the restructuring itself could be essential to understand the context in which the post-restructuring arrangements were put in place and to assess whether such arrangements are arm's length. It can also shed light on the options realistically available to the restructured entity. [12]

9.146   A comparability (including functional) analysis of the business before and after the restructuring may reveal that while some functions, assets and risks were transferred, other functions may still be carried out by the "stripped" entity under contract for the foreign associated enterprise. A careful review of the respective roles of the foreign associated enterprise and of the "stripped" entity will determine what the most appropriate transfer pricing method to the circumstances of the case is, for instance whether or not it is appropriate to allocate the whole residual profit to the foreign associated enterprise in view of the actual risks and intangibles of the "stripped" entity and of the foreign associated enterprise.

9.147   There will also be cases where before-and-after comparisons can be made because the transactions prior to the restructuring were not controlled, for instance where the restructuring follows an acquisition, and where adjustments can reliably be made to account for the differences between the pre-restructuring uncontrolled transactions and the post-restructuring controlled transactions. See example at paragraph 9.135. Whether such uncontrolled transactions provide reliable comparables would have to be evaluated in light of the guidance at paragraph 3.2.

---

[12]   See paragraphs 9.59-9.64 for a discussion of options realistically available; see also paragraphs 9.127-9.132 for a discussion of possible factual differences between situations that result from a restructuring and situations that were structured as such from the beginning and of how such differences may affect the options realistically available to the parties in negotiating the terms of the new arrangement and therefore the conditions of the restructuring and/or of the post-restructuring arrangements.

E. Location savings

9.148   Location savings can be derived by an MNE group that relocates some of its activities to a place where costs (such as labour costs, real estate costs, etc.) are lower than in the location where the activities were initially performed, account being taken of the possible costs involved in the relocation (such as termination costs for the existing operation, possibly higher infrastructure costs in the new location, possibly higher transportation costs if the new operation is more distant from the market, training costs of local employees, etc.). Where a business strategy aimed at deriving location savings is put forward as a business reason for restructuring, the discussion at paragraphs 1.59-1.63 is relevant.

9.149   Where significant location savings are derived further to a business restructuring, the question arises of whether and if so how the location savings should be shared among the parties. The response should obviously depend on what independent parties would have agreed in similar circumstances. The conditions that would be agreed between independent parties would normally depend on the functions, assets and risks of each party and on their respective bargaining powers.

9.150   Take the example of an enterprise that designs, manufactures and sells brand name clothes. Assume that the manufacturing process is basic and that the brand name is famous and represents a highly valuable intangible. Assume that the enterprise is established in Country A where the labour costs are high and that it decides to close down its manufacturing activities in Country A and to relocate them in an affiliate company in Country B where labour costs are significantly lower. The enterprise in Country A retains the rights on the brand name and continues designing the clothes. Further to this restructuring, the clothes will be manufactured by the affiliate in Country B under a contract manufacturing arrangement. The arrangement does not involve the use of any significant intangible owned by or licensed to the affiliate or the assumption of any significant risks by the affiliate in Country B. Once manufactured by the affiliate in Country B, the clothes will be sold to the enterprise in Country A which will on-sell them to third party customers. Assume that this restructuring makes it possible for the group formed by the enterprise in Country A and its affiliate in Country B to derive significant location savings. The question arises whether the location savings should be attributed to the enterprise in Country A, or its affiliate in Country B, or both (and if so in what proportions).

9.151   In such an example, given that the relocated activity is a highly competitive one, it is likely that the enterprise in Country A has the option realistically available to it to use either the affiliate in Country B or a third party manufacturer. As a consequence, it should be possible to find comparables data to determine the conditions in which a third party would be willing at arm's length to manufacture the clothes for the enterprise. In such a situation, a contract manufacturer at arm's length would generally be attributed very little, if any, part of the location savings. Doing otherwise would put the associated manufacturer in a situation different from the situation of an independent manufacturer, and would be contrary to the arm's length principle.

9.152   As another example, assume now that an enterprise in Country X provides highly specialised engineering services to independent clients. The enterprise is very well known for its high quality standard. It charges a fee to its independent clients based on a fixed hourly rate that compares with the hourly rate charged by competitors for similar services in the same market. Suppose that the wages for qualified engineers in Country X are high. The enterprise subsequently opens a subsidiary in Country Y where it hires equally qualified engineers for substantially lower wages, and subcontracts a large part of its engineering work to its subsidiary in Country Y, thus deriving significant location savings for the group formed by the enterprise and its subsidiary. Clients continue to deal directly with the enterprise in Country X and are not necessarily aware of the sub-contracting arrangement. For some period of time, the well known enterprise in Country X can continue to charge its services at the original hourly rate despite the significantly reduced engineer costs. After a certain period of time, however, it is forced due to competitive pressures to decrease its hourly rate and pass on part of the location savings to its clients. In this case also, the question arises of which party(ies) within the MNE group should be attributed the location savings at arm's length: the subsidiary in Country Y, the enterprise in Country X, or both (and if so in what proportions).

9.153   In this example, it might be that there is a high demand for the type of engineering services in question and the subsidiary in Country Y is the only one able to provide them with the required quality standard, so that the enterprise in Country X does not have many other options available to it than to use this service provider. It might be that the subsidiary in Country Y has developed a valuable intangible corresponding to its technical know-how. Such an intangible would need to be taken into account in the determination of the arm's length remuneration for the sub-contracted services. In appropriate circumstances (*e.g.* if there are significant unique contributions such as intangibles used by both the enterprise in Country X and its subsidiary in Country Y), the use of a transactional profit split method may be considered.

F. Example: implementation of a central purchasing function

9.154   This section illustrates the application of the arm's length principle in the case of the implementation of a central purchasing function. It reflects the central importance of comparability analyses and in particular of the functional analysis in order to understand the role played by each of the parties in the creation of synergies, costs savings, or other integration effects. The list below is not intended to cover all the possible situations but only the most frequent ones. Which transfer pricing method is the most appropriate will depend on the facts and circumstances of the case. In particular, a determination of which party(ies) should be allocated the cost savings or inefficiencies created by the centralisation of the purchasing function will depend on the particular circumstances of each case.

9.155   Assume an MNE group puts in place a central purchasing entity that will negotiate with third party suppliers the purchases of raw materials used by all the manufacturing plants of the group in their manufacturing processes. Depending in particular on the respective functional analyses of the manufacturing plants and of the central purchasing entity and on the contractual terms they have agreed upon, a variety of remuneration schemes and transfer pricing methods could be considered.

9.156   First, there will be cases where the CUP method will be applicable. Assume the central purchasing entity purchases the raw materials from third party suppliers and sells them to the manufacturing plants. The CUP method might be applicable if the raw materials are traded on a commodity market (see paragraph 2.18). It may also be the case that the price that was paid by the manufacturing plants before the interposition of the central purchasing entity or the price paid by independent parties for comparable raw materials may, subject to a review of the facts and circumstances and of the effects of the controlled and uncontrolled transactions taking place at different times, be used as a comparable uncontrolled price to determine the price at which the manufacturing plants should acquire the raw materials from the central purchasing entity. However, such a CUP, if unadjusted, may well mean that all the costs savings would be attributed to the central purchasing entity. As noted at paragraph 9.154, a determination of whether or not this would be an arm's length condition has to be made on a case by case basis. Should it be determined that in the circumstances of the case, a portion of the cost savings should be attributed to the manufacturing entities, then the question would arise whether the CUP should and could be adjusted accordingly.

9.157   Where the CUP method cannot be used, *e.g.* because the price of the raw materials fluctuates and the price paid by the manufacturing entities before the setting up of the central purchasing entity cannot serve as a reference, the cost plus method might be considered. For instance, the central purchasing entity might purchase the raw materials from third party suppliers and re-sell them to the manufacturing plants at cost plus, *i.e.* the new purchase price of the raw material by the central purchasing entity plus an arm's length mark-up. In such a case, the mark-up rate attributed to the central purchasing entity should be comparable to the mark-up rate earned in comparable uncontrolled trading activities.

9.158   In some cases, the central purchasing entity acts as an agent either for the suppliers or for the purchasers (or both) and is remunerated by a commission fee paid either by the suppliers or by the purchasers (or both). This might be the case where the central purchasing entity negotiates with the third party suppliers but does not take title to the inventories, *i.e.* the manufacturing plants continue to acquire the raw materials directly from the suppliers but at a discounted price obtained thanks to the activity of the central purchasing entity and to the participation of the group of manufacturing plants in the arrangement. The commission fee might be proportional to the supplies (especially if paid by the supplier) or to the discounts obtained (especially if paid by the manufacturing plants). It should be comparable to the commission fee that would be charged by independent parties for comparable agency functions in similar circumstances.

9.159   It may happen that what would be *prima facie* regarded as an arm's length mark-up on costs or commission fee from the perspective of the central purchasing entity in effect leads to determining purchase prices for the manufacturing entities that are higher than the prices they could obtain by themselves. If the incremental costs that are created for the manufacturers are material (*e.g.* they materially affect, on a recurrent basis, the basket of products channelled through the central purchasing entity), the question arises whether independent manufacturers would have agreed to pay such higher prices and what the economic rationale would be, or whether at arm's length the central purchasing entity should bear part or all of the inefficiencies through a reduction of its sales prices to the manufacturers. The response will depend on the facts and circumstances of the case. Key to the analysis will be the determination of the benefits that could reasonably be expected by the parties (manufacturing entities and central purchasing entity) from the implementation of the central purchasing function, and of the options realistically available to them, including in appropriate cases the option not to participate in the central purchasing in case the expected benefits were not as attractive as under other options. Where benefits could reasonably have been expected by the parties, it will be key to analyse the reasons for the central purchasing entity's apparent inefficiency, the contractual terms under which the central purchasing entity operates and the functional analysis of the manufacturers and of the central purchasing entity, in particular their respective roles and responsibilities in the decisions that led to the inefficiencies. This analysis should make it possible to determine what party(ies) should be allocated the inefficiency costs and to what extent. Where this analysis indicates that inefficiencies should be allocated to the central purchasing entity, one way of doing so would be to price the sale transactions to the manufacturing entities by reference to CUP *i.e.* based on prices that the manufacturing entities could obtain on the free market for comparable supplies in comparable circumstances. No inference should be drawn however that any inefficiencies should be allocated by default to the central purchasing function, or that the positive effects of synergies should always be shared amongst the members of the group.

9.160   Finally, there might be some cases where the costs savings (or costs) generated by the centralisation of the purchasing function would be shared amongst the central purchasing entity and the manufacturing plants through a form of profit split.

Part IV: Recognition of the actual transactions undertaken

A. Introduction

9.161   An important starting point for any transfer pricing analysis is to properly identify and characterise the controlled transaction under review. Paragraphs 1.64-1.69 deal with the relevance of the actual transactions undertaken by associated enterprises and discusses the exceptional circumstances in which it may be legitimate and appropriate for a tax administration not to recognise, for transfer pricing purposes, a transaction that is presented by a taxpayer.

9.162   Paragraphs 1.64-1.69 are limited to the non-recognition of transactions for the purposes of making transfer pricing adjustments covered by Article 9 of the OECD Model Tax Convention (*i.e.* adjustments in accordance with the arm's length principle). They do not provide any guidance as to a country's ability to characterise transactions differently under other aspects of its domestic law. A discussion of the relationship between domestic anti-abuse rules and treaties is found in the Commentary on Article 1 of the OECD Model Tax Convention (see in particular paragraphs 9.5, 22 and 22.1 of the Commentary).

9.163   MNEs are free to organise their business operations as they see fit. Tax administrations do not have the right to dictate to an MNE how to design its structure or where to locate its business operations. MNE groups cannot be forced to have or maintain any particular level of business presence in a country. They are free to act in their own best commercial and economic interests in this regard. In making this decision, tax considerations may be a factor. Tax administrations, however, have the right to determine the tax consequences of the structure put in place by an MNE, subject to the application of treaties and in particular of Article 9 of the OECD Model Tax Convention. This means that tax administrations may perform where appropriate transfer pricing adjustments in accordance with Article 9 of the OECD Model Tax Convention and/or other types of adjustments allowed by their domestic law (*e.g.* under general or specific anti-abuse rules), to the extent that such adjustments are compatible with their treaty obligations.

B. Transactions actually undertaken. Role of contractual terms. Relationship between paragraphs 1.64-1.69 and other parts of these Guidelines

9.164   In the Article 9 context, an examination of the application of the arm's length principle to controlled transactions should start from the transactions actually undertaken by the associated enterprises, and the terms of contracts play a major role (see paragraph 1.64). As acknowledged in paragraphs 1.47-1.51 and 1.64-1.69, however, such a review of the contractual terms is not sufficient.

9.165   According to Article 9 of the OECD Model Tax Convention, a tax administration may adjust the profits of a taxpayer where the conditions of a controlled transaction differ from the conditions that would be agreed between independent enterprises. In practice transfer pricing adjustments consist in adjustments of the profits of an enterprise attributable to adjustments to the price and / or other conditions of a controlled transaction (*e.g.* payment terms or allocation of risks). This does not mean that all transfer pricing adjustments, whether involving an adjustment only to the price or also (or alternatively) to other conditions of a controlled transaction, or as a result of evaluating separately transactions which are presented as a package in accordance to the guidance at paragraphs 3.11 and 6.18, should be viewed as consisting in the non-recognition of a controlled transaction under paragraphs 1.64-1.69. In effect, such adjustments may result from the examination of comparability, see in particular paragraph 1.33. Paragraphs 1.48-1.54 provide guidance on the possibility for a tax administration to challenge contractual terms where they are not consistent with the economic substance of the transaction or where they do not conform with the conduct of the parties.

9.166   A discussion of how to determine whether the allocation of risks in a transaction between associated enterprises is arm's length is found in Part I of this chapter. As discussed at paragraph 9.11, the examination of risks in an Article 9 context starts from an examination of the contractual terms between the parties, as those generally define how risks are to be divided between the parties. However, as noted at paragraphs 1.48-1.54, a purported allocation of risk between associated enterprises is respected only to the extent that it is consistent with the economic substance of the transaction. Therefore, in examining the risk allocation between associated enterprises and its transfer pricing consequences, it is important to review not only the contractual terms but also whether the associated enterprises conform to the contractual allocation of risks and whether the contractual terms provide for an arm's length allocation of risks. In evaluating the latter, two important factors that come into play are whether there is evidence from comparable uncontrolled transactions of a comparable allocation of risks and, in the absence of such evidence, whether the risk allocation makes commercial sense (and in particular whether the risk is allocated to the party that has greater control over it). Paragraphs 9.34-9.38 contain an explanation of the difference between making a comparability adjustment and not recognising the risk allocation in the controlled transaction and a discussion of the relationship between the guidance at paragraph 1.49 and paragraphs 1.64-1.69.

9.167   A similar reasoning is developed in Part II of this chapter with respect to indemnification rights for the termination or substantial renegotiation of an existing arrangement. Paragraph 9.103 indicates that, in addition to examining whether the arrangement that is terminated, non-renewed or substantially renegotiated is formalised in writing and provides for an indemnification clause, it may be important to assess whether the terms of the arrangement and the possible existence or non-existence of an indemnification clause or other type of guarantee (as well as the terms of such a clause where it exists) are arm's length.

C. Application of paragraphs 1.64-1.69 of these Guidelines to business restructuring situations

C.1   *Non-recognition only in exceptional cases*

9.168   Paragraphs 1.64-1.69 explicitly limit the non-recognition of the actual transaction or arrangement to exceptional cases. This indicates that the non-recognition of a transaction is not the norm but an exception to the general principle that a tax administration's examination of a controlled transaction ordinarily should be based on the transaction actually undertaken by the associated enterprises as it has been structured by them.[13] The word "exceptional" in this context is similar in meaning to "rare" or "unusual". It reflects that in most cases it is expected that the arm's length principle under Article 9 can be satisfied by determining arm's length pricing for the arrangement as actually undertaken and structured.

---

[13]   As noted at paragraph 1.53, it is important to examine whether the conduct of the parties conforms to the terms of the contract or whether the parties' conduct indicates that the contractual terms have not been followed or are a sham. In such cases, further analysis is required to determine the true terms of the transaction and a pricing adjustment might not be the solution.

9.169   In accordance with paragraphs 1.64-1.69, it may exceptionally be appropriate for a tax administration not to recognise the parties' characterisation or structuring of a transaction or arrangement where, having regard to all of the facts and circumstances, it concludes that:

- The economic substance of the transaction or arrangement differs from its form (Section C.2); or

- Independent enterprises in comparable circumstances would not have characterised or structured the transaction or arrangement as the associated enterprises have, and arm's length pricing cannot reliably be determined for that transaction or arrangement (Sections C.3 and C.4).

Both of these situations are instances where the parties' characterisation or structuring of the transaction or arrangement is regarded as the result of conditions that would not have existed between independent enterprises (see paragraph 1.66).

C.2   Determining the economic substance of a transaction or arrangement

9.170   The economic substance of a transaction or arrangement is determined by examining all of the facts and circumstances, such as the economic and commercial context of the transaction or arrangement, its object and effect from a practical and business point of view, and the conduct of the parties, including the functions performed, assets used and risks assumed by them.

C.3   Determining whether arrangements would have been adopted by independent enterprises

9.171   The second circumstance in paragraph 1.65 explicitly refers to the situation where the arrangements adopted by the associated enterprises "differ from those which would have been adopted by independent enterprises behaving in a commercially rational manner…" Consistent with paragraph 9.163, tax administrations should not ordinarily interfere with the business decisions of a taxpayer as to how to structure its business arrangements. A determination that a controlled transaction is not commercially rational must therefore be made with great caution, and only in exceptional circumstances lead to the non-recognition of the associated enterprise arrangements.

9.172   Where reliable data show that comparable uncontrolled transactions exist, it cannot be argued that such transactions between associated enterprises would lack commercial rationality. The existence of comparables data evidencing arm's length pricing for an associated enterprise arrangement demonstrates that it is commercially rational for independent enterprises in comparable circumstances. On the other hand, however, the mere fact that an associated enterprise arrangement is not seen between independent enterprises does not in itself mean that it is not arm's length nor commercially rational (see paragraph 1.11).

9.173   Business restructurings often lead MNE groups to implement global business models that are hardly if ever found between independent enterprises, taking advantage of the very fact that they are MNE groups and that they can work in an integrated fashion. For instance, MNE groups may implement global supply chains or centralised functions that are not found between independent enterprises. It is therefore often difficult to assess whether such business models are of the kind that independent enterprises behaving in a commercially rational manner would have implemented. This lack of comparables does not mean of course that the implementation of such global business models should automatically be regarded as not commercially rational.

9.174   What is being tested is whether the outcome (the arrangement adopted) accords with what would result from normal commercial behaviour of independent enterprises; it is not a behaviour test in the sense of requiring the associated enterprises to actually behave as would independent enterprises in negotiating and agreeing to the terms of the arrangement. Thus, whether the associated enterprises actually engaged in real bargaining or simply acted in the best interests of the MNE group as a whole in agreeing to a restructuring does not determine whether the arrangement would have been adopted by independent enterprises behaving in a commercially rational manner or whether arm's length pricing has been reached.

9.175   The application of the arm's length principle is based on the notion that independent enterprises will not enter into a transaction if they see an alternative that is clearly more attractive. See paragraphs 9.59-9.64. As discussed there, a consideration of the options realistically available can be relevant to determining arm's length pricing for an arrangement. It can also be relevant to the question of whether arrangements adopted by associated enterprises differ from those which would have been adopted by independent enterprises behaving in a commercially rational manner. There may be exceptional cases in which arm's length pricing cannot reliably be determined for the arrangement actually adopted, and it is concluded that the arrangement would not have been adopted in comparable circumstances by independent enterprises behaving in a commercially rational manner (see Section C.4).

9.176   An independent enterprise would not enter into a restructuring transaction if it sees an alternative option that is realistically available and clearly more attractive, including the option not to enter into the restructuring. In evaluating whether a party would at arm's length have had other options realistically available to it that were clearly more attractive, due regard should be given to all the relevant conditions of the restructuring, to the rights and other assets of the parties, to any compensation or indemnification for the restructuring itself and to the remuneration for the post-restructuring arrangements (as discussed in Parts II and III of this chapter) as well as to the commercial circumstances arising from participation in an MNE group (see paragraph 1.11).

9.177   In assessing the commercial rationality of a restructuring, the question may arise whether to look at one transaction in isolation or whether to examine it in a broader context, taking account of other transactions that are economically inter-related. It will generally be appropriate to look at the commercial rationality of a restructuring as a whole. For instance, where examining a sale of an intangible that is part of a broader restructuring involving changes to the arrangements relating to the development and use of the intangible, then the commercial rationality of the intangible sale should not be examined in isolation of these changes. On the other hand, where a restructuring involves changes to more than one element or aspect of a business that are not economically inter-related, the commercial rationality of particular changes may need to be separately considered. For example, a restructuring may involve centralising a group's purchasing function and centralising the ownership of valuable intangible property unrelated to the purchasing function. In such a case, the commercial rationality of centralising the purchasing function and of centralising the ownership of valuable intangible property may need to be evaluated separately from one another.

9.178   There can be group-level business reasons for an MNE group to restructure. However, it is worth re-emphasising that the arm's length principle treats the members of an MNE group as separate entities rather than as inseparable parts of a single unified business (see paragraph 1.6). As a consequence, it is not sufficient from a transfer pricing perspective that a restructuring arrangement makes commercial sense for the group as a whole: the arrangement must be arm's length at the level of each individual taxpayer, taking account of its rights and other assets, expected benefits from the arrangement (*i.e.* consideration of the post-restructuring arrangement plus any compensation payments for the restructuring itself), and realistically available options.

9.179   Where a restructuring is commercially rational for the MNE group as a whole, it is expected that an appropriate transfer price (that is, compensation for the post-restructuring arrangement plus any compensation payments for the restructuring itself) would generally be available to make it arm's length for each individual group member participating in it. See Part II of this chapter, Section B.

C.4 *Determining whether a transaction or arrangement has an arm's length pricing solution*

9.180 Under the second circumstance discussed at paragraph 1.65, a second cumulative criterion is that "the actual structure practically impedes the tax administration from determining an appropriate transfer price." If an appropriate transfer price (*i.e.* an arm's length price that takes into account the comparability – including functional – analysis of both parties to the transaction or arrangement) can be arrived at in the circumstances of the case, irrespective of the fact that the transaction or arrangement may not be found between independent enterprises and that the tax administration might have doubts as to the commercial rationality of the taxpayer entering into the transaction or arrangement, the transaction or arrangement would not be disregarded under the second circumstance in paragraph 1.65. Otherwise, the tax administration may decide that this is a case for not recognising the transaction or arrangement under the second circumstance in paragraph 1.65.

C.5 *Relevance of tax purpose*

9.181 Under Article 9 of the OECD Model Tax Convention, the fact that a business restructuring arrangement is motivated by a purpose of obtaining tax benefits does not of itself warrant a conclusion that it is a non-arm's length arrangement.[14] The presence of a tax motive or purpose does not of itself justify non-recognition of the parties' characterisation or structuring of the arrangement under paragraphs 1.64 to 1.69.

9.182 Provided functions, assets and/or risks are actually transferred, it can be commercially rational from an Article 9 perspective for an MNE group to restructure in order to obtain tax savings. However, this is not relevant to whether the arm's length principle is satisfied at the entity level for a taxpayer affected by the restructuring (see paragraph 9.178).

---

[14] As indicated at paragraph 9.8, domestic anti-abuse rules are not within the scope of this chapter.

C.6 Consequences of non-recognition under paragraphs 1.64 to 1.69

9.183   Under the first circumstance of paragraph 1.65, where the economic substance of a transaction differs from its form, the tax administration may disregard the parties' characterisation of the transaction and re-characterise it in accordance with its substance.

9.184   With respect to the second circumstance, paragraph 1.65 contains an example of non-recognition of a sale and note that while it may be proper to respect the transaction as a transfer of commercial property, it would nevertheless be appropriate for a tax administration to conform the terms of that transfer in their entirety (and not simply by reference to pricing) to those that might reasonably have been expected had the transfer of property been the subject of a transaction involving independent enterprises. In such a case, the tax administration would seek to adjust the conditions of the agreement in a commercially rational manner.

9.185   In both circumstances, Article 9 would allow an adjustment of conditions to reflect those which the parties would have attained had the transaction been structured in accordance with the economic and commercial reality of parties dealing at arm's length (see paragraph 1.66). In doing so, tax administrations would have to determine what is the underlying reality behind a contractual arrangement in applying the arm's length principle (see paragraph 1.67).

9.186   Paragraph 1.68 provides some guidance on the case where a tax administration may find it useful to refer to alternatively structured transactions between independent enterprises to determine whether the controlled transaction as structured satisfies the arm's length principle. Whether evidence from a particular alternative can be considered will depend on the facts and circumstances of the particular case, including the number and accuracy of the adjustments necessary to account for differences between the controlled transaction and the alternative as well as the quality of any other evidence that may be available.

9.187   That guidance indicates that the tax administration would seek to substitute for the non-recognised transaction an alternative characterisation or structure that comports as closely as possible with the facts of the case, *i.e.* one that is consistent with the functional changes to the taxpayer's business resulting from the restructuring, comports as closely as possible with the economic substance of the case, and reflects the results that would have derived had the transaction been structured in accordance with the commercial reality of independent parties. For example, where one element of a restructuring arrangement involves the closing down of a factory, any recharacterisation of the restructuring cannot ignore the reality that the factory no longer operates. Similarly, where one element of a restructuring involves the actual relocation of substantive business functions, any recharacterisation of the restructuring cannot ignore the fact that those functions were actually relocated. As another example, where a restructuring arrangement involves a transfer of property between two parties, any non-recognition of the restructuring arrangement would need to reflect that a transfer of such property occurred between the two parties, although it may be appropriate to replace the character of the transfer with an alternative characterisation that comports as closely as possible with the facts of the case (*e.g.* a purported transfer of all rights in the property might be recharacterised as a mere lease or licence of the property, or vice versa).

D. Examples

D.1   Example (A): Conversion of a full-fledged distributor into a "risk-less" distributor

9.188   Company Z is a well known distributor of luxury products. It owns a valuable trade name, valuable retail points, and valuable long term contracts with suppliers. It is acquired by an MNE Group which operates under a global business model whereby all the trade names and other valuable intangibles are owned by Company V in Country V, all the key supplier contracts are held by Company W in Country W which is responsible for the management of group-wide supplier contracts, and all the retail points are owned by a real estate company in Country X. Immediately after the acquisition, the Group decides to restructure Company Z by transferring its trade name to Company V, its valuable supplier contracts to Company W and its retail points to Company X, all in exchange for lump sum payments. As a consequence of the transfer, Company Z is now operating as a commissionnaire for Company W. Its post-restructuring profit potential is dramatically less than its pre-restructuring one. Representatives from the MNE Group explain that the business reason for the restructuring is to align the operating model of Company Z with the operating model of the rest of the MNE Group, and that this prospect was one key factor in the acquisition deal. The management of Company Z has had no other choice than to accept the restructuring given the acquisition that has taken place. It indicates that the transfer of its trade name, contracts and retail points was priced at arm's length, and that the remuneration for its post-restructuring activities will also be priced at arm's length.

9.189   Assuming that in this case the actual conduct of the parties is consistent with the form of the restructuring, the economic substance of the arrangement would not differ from how it is characterised and structured by the parties. It is expected that the determination of arm's length pricing for the restructuring itself and for the post-restructuring activities would result in an arm's length outcome for each of the parties, in which case the restructuring transactions would be recognised.

D.2   Example (B): Transfer of valuable intangibles to a shell company

9.190   An MNE manufactures and distributes products the value of which is not determined by the technical features of the products, but rather by the brand name and exposure. The MNE wants to differentiate itself from its competitors through the development of brand names with great value, by implementing a carefully developed and expensive marketing strategy. The brand names are owned by Company A in Country A. The development, maintenance and execution of a worldwide marketing strategy are the main value driver of the MNE, performed by 125 employees at Company A's head office. The value of the brand names results in a high consumer price for the products. Company A's head office also provides central services for the group affiliates (*e.g.* human resource management, legal, tax). The products are manufactured by affiliates under contract manufacturing arrangements with Company A. They are distributed by affiliates who purchase them from Company A. The profits derived by Company A after having allocated an arm's length remuneration to the contract manufacturers and distributors are considered to be the remuneration for the intangibles, marketing activities and central services of Company A.

9.191   Then a restructuring takes place. The brand names are transferred by Company A to a newly set up affiliate, Company Z in Country Z in exchange for a lump sum payment. After the restructuring, Company A is remunerated on a cost plus basis for the services it performs for Company Z and the rest of the group. The remuneration of the affiliated contract manufacturers and distributors remains the same. The excess profits after remuneration of the contract manufacturers, distributors, and Company A head office services are paid to Company Z. From the comparability analysis the following conclusions can be drawn:

- There is no reliable evidence from uncontrolled comparable transactions of the ownership of brand names and attached risks being attributed between independent enterprises in the same manner as in the controlled transaction between Company A and Company Z;

- Company Z is managed by a local trust company. It does not have people (employees or directors) who have the authority to and effectively do perform control functions in relation to the risks associated with the strategic development of the brand names. It also does not have the financial capacity to assume these risks.

- High ranking officials from Company A's head office fly to Country Z once a year to formally validate the strategic decisions necessary to operate the company. These decisions are prepared by Company A's head office in Country A before the meetings take place in Country Z. The MNE considers that these activities are service activities performed by Company A's head office for Z. These strategic decision-making activities are remunerated at cost plus in the same way as the central services are remunerated (*e.g.* human resource management, legal, tax).

- The development, maintenance and execution of the worldwide marketing strategy are still performed by the same employees of Company A's head office and remunerated on a cost plus basis. Company A does not have a contractual incentive to maximise the value of the brand names or the market share because it is remunerated on a cost plus basis.

9.192   A full consideration of all of the facts and circumstances warrants a conclusion that the economic substance of the arrangement differs from its form. In particular, the facts indicate that Company Z has no real capability to assume the risks it is allocated under the arrangement as characterised and structured by the parties. Furthermore, there is no evidence of any business reasons for the arrangement. In such a case paragraph 1.65 allows a tax administration to not recognise the structure adopted by the parties.[15]

D.3   Example (C): Transfer of intangible that is recognised

9.193   The fact pattern is the same as in example (B), except that part of Company A's head office is effectively relocated to Country Z: 30 of the 125 head office employees are dismissed, another 30 are transferred to the new Company Z in Country Z, and 15 new employees are directly hired by Company Z in Country Z to take over functions performed by the dismissed employees. The employees of Company Z have the skills and competences to do the strategic development of the brand name and to execute the worldwide marketing strategy. Furthermore, it is assumed in this example that Company Z has the financial capacity to assume the risks associated

---

[15]   This is notwithstanding any possible application of general anti-avoidance rules and notwithstanding the question about Company Z's place of effective management.

with the strategic development of the brand names. Company Z, which is now the legal owner of the brand names actively carries on the development, maintenance and execution of a worldwide marketing strategy. The employees of Company Z have the authority to and actually perform control functions in relation to the risks associated with the strategic development of the brand names. The services provided by the remainder of Company A's head office in Country A are central services (*e.g.* human resources management, legal and tax) as well as support marketing functions that are closely monitored by the personnel of Company Z. The main reason for the group entering into this restructuring is to benefit from a favourable tax regime in Country Z compared to the tax regime in Country A.

9.194   The changes in fact pattern from Example (B) support a conclusion that the economic substance of the arrangement does not differ from its form, and that independent enterprises in comparable circumstances acting in a commercially rational manner would have characterised or structured the arrangement as the associated enterprises have. Given this, a tax administration should seek to achieve an arm's length outcome in this situation by determining arm's length pricing for the restructuring itself and the parties' post-restructuring activities based upon recognising the arrangement actually undertaken.[16]

---

[16]   This does not say anything about the possible application of domestic anti-abuse rules.

List of Annexes

- Annex to the OECD Transfer Pricing Guidelines: Guidelines for monitoring procedures on the OECD Transfer Pricing Guidelines and the involvement of the business community

- Annex I to Chapter II: Sensitivity of gross and net profit indicators.

- Annex II to Chapter II: Example to illustrate the application of the residual profit split method.

- Annex III to Chapter II: Illustration of different measures of profits when applying a transactional profit split method.

- Annex to Chapter III: Example of a working capital adjustment.

- Annex to Chapter IV: Guidelines for conducting Advance Pricing Arrangements under the Mutual Agreement Procedure ("MAP APAs").

- Annex to Chapter VI: Examples to illustrate the guidance on intangible property and highly uncertain valuation.

Annex to the OECD Transfer Pricing Guidelines

Guidelines for Monitoring Procedures on the OECD Transfer Pricing Guidelines and the Involvement of the Business Community

A. Background

1.   In July 1995, the OECD Council approved for publication the *Transfer Pricing Guidelines for Multinational Enterprises and Tax Administrations* ("the Guidelines"), submitted by the Committee on Fiscal Affairs ("the Committee"). At the same time, the OECD Council endorsed the Committee's recommendation that the Guidelines be reviewed and up-dated periodically as appropriate based upon the experience of member countries and the business community with the application of the principles and methods set forth in the Guidelines. For this purpose, and to facilitate on-going clarifications and improvements, the OECD Council instructed the Committee to undertake a period of monitoring international transfer pricing experience. The monitoring role is seen as an integrated part of the agreement reached in July 1995 and its successful implementation is a key feature to getting a consistent application of the Guidelines. The Council Recommendation "instructs the Committee on Fiscal Affairs to monitor the implementation of the 1995 Report in cooperation with the tax authorities of member countries and with the participation of the business community and to recommend to the Council to amend and update, if necessary, the 1995 Report in the light of this monitoring".

2.   To summarise, the main purpose of the monitoring is to examine how far member countries' legislation, regulations and administrative practices are consistent with the Guidelines and to identify areas where the Guidelines may require amendments or additions. The monitoring should not only lead to identification of problematic issues, but also to the identification of practices followed by one or more member countries in

applying the Guidelines which could be usefully extended to other countries. The monitoring is not intended to arbitrate on particular cases.

3.   The monitoring is expected to be an on-going process and to cover all aspects of the Guidelines but with particular emphasis on the use of transactional profit methods. The purpose of this note is to set forth some procedures for carrying out the monitoring, thereby implementing the instruction of the OECD Council. These procedures will be implemented gradually. Further revisions may be necessary once the procedures have been put into practice.

4.   In line with the Council's Recommendation, there will be a role for the business community in the monitoring and this role is set out in Section C.

B. Process

5.   The monitoring process will be carried out through four related projects: 1. peer reviews of member country practices; 2. identification and analysis of difficult case paradigms; 3. review of changes in legislation, regulations, and administrative practices; and 4. development of examples. Each of these is discussed below.

B.1   Peer reviews

6.   The Working Party No. 6 on Taxation of Multinational Enterprises ("the Working Party") has been undertaking peer reviews of the transfer pricing practices of member countries over the course of the last few years. The peer reviews aim to gain detailed information on legislation, practices and experiences of transfer pricing in member countries. The Delegates of the Working Party jointly decide which country should be reviewed and which countries would conduct the review. The reviews follow guidelines approved by the Committee.

7.   The peer review guidelines call for a report to be submitted to the Working Party for each reviewed country. The report covers the legal basis for dealing with transfer pricing issues, any country guidelines to direct enforcement practices, approaches commonly used to address a complex transfer pricing problem, administrative arrangements for handling transfer pricing cases, case law principles, and experience with data gathering and taxpayer documentation. The report also is to describe experiences with administrative approaches to avoiding and resolving transfer pricing disputes (*e.g.* mutual agreement procedure, advance pricing arrangements and safe harbours).

8.   Peer reviews will continue to be carried out but at three different levels:

1. The first level would be an *"issue review"*, which would look at the approach taken by all member countries to a particular issue of widespread significance. Ideally, the review should link up with other aspects of the monitoring process. For example, the best way to solve any problems emerging from such a review may be to analyse the issue in more detail by developing difficult case paradigms (see Section B.2 of this annex) or to develop practical examples for insertion in the Guidelines (see Section B.4 of this annex).

2. The second level would be a *"limited review"* in that it would only look at the approach of a particular country or countries in relation to a specific and relatively narrow issue. The review would be carried out by two reviewers for each country and the level of input necessary would depend on the nature of the issue

3. The third level would be a *"full review"* of a particular country which would be carried out according to the existing peer review guidelines referred to in paragraph 7 of this annex. A "full review" would therefore address directly the interpretation and application of the Guidelines in the particular member country.

Selection Criteria

9.   To improve the effectiveness of the peer review process it is essential that the reviews are undertaken selectively and concentrate on the areas of greatest difficulty in applying the Guidelines. The final decision to undertake any of the three types of review will be made by the full Working Party having regard both to the overall usefulness of any review to the work of the Working Party in monitoring the application of the Guidelines and to whether there are sufficient resources available to undertake the proposed review. It is important that any review, once undertaken, is completed to a high standard so that worthwhile conclusions can be drawn from it.

B.2   Identification and analysis of difficult case paradigms

10.   A key aspect of monitoring will be to identify and then to analyse difficult fact patterns and problem areas which may be illustrated by practical examples and which present obstacles to an internationally consistent application of the transfer pricing methods set out in the Guidelines. Monitoring will also include areas where the Guidelines appear

to offer no or inadequate guidance to tax authorities or taxpayers. All member countries will be actively involved in this process and recognise that resources will be required to ensure its success. The business community will also be involved in the monitoring (see Section C of this annex).

11.   The first issue is the procedure to be used and the responsibility assigned for identifying the difficult case paradigms, focusing on issues and situations where the Guidelines may provide no or inadequate guidance or where member countries might be interpreting the Guidelines differently and therefore presenting obstacles to an internationally consistent application of the Guidelines. Member countries can identify areas where, in their view, the Guidelines might not address or adequately address a particular issue.

12.   In the context of the regular meetings of tax inspectors organised by the Committee on Fiscal Affairs, the Working Party will arrange biennial meetings of tax examiners to discuss difficult case paradigms and to provide an input to any appropriate updates to the Guidelines. OECD will consider the difficult case paradigms only from the perspective of monitoring the application of the Guidelines.

13.   Individual countries would take responsibility at meetings of Working Party No. 6 for leading discussions of the difficult case paradigms and of problematic areas that can be illustrated with practical examples.

14.   The outcomes envisaged by the Working Party from the identification and analysis of difficult case paradigms could include the development of examples illustrating the application of the Guidelines in cases (identified for discussion) where the principles already contained within the Guidelines can be applied. It could also include identification of areas where the Guidelines could be amended to provide clearer guidance or where new material could be inserted into the Guidelines.

B.3   Updates of legislation and practice

15.   The Secretariat will solicit from member countries reports on developments in their domestic transfer pricing legislation, regulations, and administrative practices, consistent with the invitation of the Council.

B.4   Development of examples

16.   The foregoing monitoring procedures will parallel the development of additional hypothetical examples to be added to the Guidelines. The examples are not intended to develop new principles or to

cover new issues but rather to assist in interpreting principles and in addressing difficult issues already discussed in the Guidelines. To ensure that they are of practical value and avoid being overly prescriptive the examples will be short, based on stated facts and relatively straightforward so that their scope is not so confined that the guidance they provide is of narrow and limited application. The examples will fall into two broad categories. The first will consist of illustrations of the application of the methods and approaches described in the Guidelines. The second set of examples will be designed to aid in the selection of a suitable transfer pricing method or methods. Although hypothetical, the examples will draw on the practical experiences of tax administrations and taxpayers in applying the arm's length principle under the Guidelines, and will contribute to the establishing of good practices.

C. Involvement of the business community

17.   It is not intended that the OECD should intervene in the resolution of transfer pricing disputes between a taxpayer and a tax administration. The monitoring process is not intended to be a form of arbitration and so taxpayers will not be able to present individual cases for resolution by the Working Party. Nevertheless, as foreseen in the Guidelines and the Council Recommendation, the business community will be encouraged to identify problematic issues (preferably illustrated with practical but hypothetical examples) which raise questions about the internationally consistent application of the Guidelines.

18.   The Business Industry Advisory Committee ("BIAC") will be invited to present practical difficulties in monitoring the application of the Guidelines to the Working Party for its consideration of the adequacy of the guidance provided in the Guidelines in relation to such areas, respecting confidentiality of the information.

19.   In contributing to the OECD role of monitoring the implementation of the Guidelines, the business community would be encouraged to take particular note of the guidance given at paragraph 17 of this annex. It should therefore focus on issues that give rise to either theoretical or practical difficulties and not on specific and unresolved transfer pricing cases. However, it may be useful to illustrate a particular issue by reference to a hypothetical example. In constructing such an example, which could draw upon features taken from a number of real cases, care should be taken to ensure it remains hypothetical and does not resemble a current case, and that the features described should be restricted to the problematic issues concerned in order to avoid an impression of setting any general precedent for the resolution of an individual case.

C.1   Peer reviews

20.   It is felt that one of the strengths of the peer review process is that the review is conducted solely by peers *i.e.* in this case the other member countries. That way the process is conducted in a positive and constructive manner so that best practice can be passed on and worse practice improved. However, the general guidance to the business community encourages them to identify problematic issues which may be suitable for further analysis and the Working Party will be able to take account of this input when making its final selection of issues for the revised peer review.

21.   It is also envisaged that once an issue or a country has been selected by the Working Party for further review, the BIAC will be notified of the decision so that they have the opportunity to comment. If the issue is one originally identified by the BIAC – particularly in the context of issue reviews – they would be kept informed of the Working Party's discussion on these issues and asked, if necessary, to provide additional clarification. However, a further role for the BIAC in the peer review process beyond that already described is not contemplated at the moment.

C.2   Identification and analysis of difficult case paradigms and the development of examples

22.   The difficult case paradigms are intended to illustrate issues and situations where the Guidelines provide no or inadequate guidance. Practical examples when complete will be inserted into the Guidelines to provide illustrations of particular principles. There is a clear role for the business community in assisting in the development of paradigms or examples by contributing the practical experience of their members. The Working Party will ask for comments on both the difficult case paradigms and the practical examples at regular stages in their development. BIAC may also initiate paradigms or examples, provided the caveats in paragraph 17 of this annex are followed so that there can be no question of the process being used to resolve a particular transfer pricing case.

C.3   Updates of legislation and practice

23.   The aim of this element in the monitoring process is to keep the member countries informed about developments in each others' countries. There are usually well established ways at the national level by which the business community can make an input into any developments in the transfer pricing legislation, regulations and administrative practices of a member country. At the level of the OECD, the BIAC will have an opportunity to bring to the attention of the Working Party changes in

legislation or practices in both member and non-member countries, which it considered were inconsistent with the Guidelines or which it felt could give rise to practical problems in terms of implementation without, of course, referring to individual cases.

24.   The input from the BIAC will be discussed at the regular joint meetings between the BIAC and the Working Party.

Annex I to Chapter II

Sensitivity of Gross and Net Profit Indicators

See Chapter II, Part III, Section B of these Guidelines for general guidance on the application of the transactional net margin method.

The assumptions about arm's length arrangements in the following examples are intended for illustrative purposes only and should not be taken as prescribing adjustments and arm's length arrangements in actual cases of particular industries. While they seek to demonstrate the principles of the sections of the Guidelines to which they refer, those principles must be applied in each case according to the specific facts and circumstances of that case.

Furthermore, the comments below relate to the application of a transactional net margin method in the situations where, given the facts and circumstances of the case and in particular the comparability (including functional) analysis of the transaction and the review of the information available on uncontrolled comparables, such a method is found to be the most appropriate method to be used.

1.   It is recognised that the transactional net margin method can be less sensitive to some differences in the characteristics of products than the comparable uncontrolled price or resale price methods. In practice when applying the transactional net margin method a greater emphasis is generally placed on functional comparability than on the characteristics of products. The transactional net margin method can however be less sensitive to some differences in functions which are reflected in variations in operating expenses as illustrated below.

Illustration 1:

Effect of a difference in the extent and complexity of the marketing function performed by a distributor

The example below is for illustration only. It is not intended to provide any guidance on the selection of the transfer pricing method or of comparables, on the efficiency of distributors or on arm's length rates of return, but only to illustrate the effects of differences between the extent and complexity of the marketing function of a distributor and of comparables.

	Case 1 The distributor performs a limited marketing function	Case 2 The distributor performs a more significant marketing function
Sales of product **(For illustration purposes, assume both sell the same volume of the same product on the same market at the same price)**	1,000	1,000
Purchase price from manufacturer taking account of the significance of the marketing function in accordance to the functional analysis	600	480 (*)
Gross margin	400 (40%)	520 (52%)
Marketing expenses	50	150
Other expenses (overheads)	300	300
Net profit margin	50 (5%)	70 (7%)

(*) Assume that in this case the difference of 120 in transaction price corresponds to the difference in the extent and complexity of the marketing function performed by the distributor (additional expense of 100 plus remuneration of the function of the distributor)

2.　　　Under Illustration 1, if a taxpayer is operating with an associated manufacturer as in case 2 while the third party "comparables" are operating as in case 1, and assuming that the difference in the extent and complexity of the marketing function is not identified because of for instance insufficiently detailed information on the third party "comparables", then the risk of error when applying a gross margin method could amount to 120 (12% x 1,000), while it would amount to 20 (2% x 1,000) if a net margin method was applied. This illustrates the fact that, depending on the circumstances of the case and in particular of the effect of the functional differences on the cost structure and on the revenue of the "comparables", net profit margins can be less sensitive than gross margins to differences in the extent and complexity of functions.

Illustration 2:

Effect of a difference in the level of risk assumed by a distributor

The example below is for illustration only. It is not intended to provide any guidance on the selection of the transfer pricing method or of comparables, on the efficiency of distributors or on arm's length rates of return, but only to illustrate the effects of differences between the level of risk assumed by a distributor and by comparables.

	Case 1 The distributor does not assume the risk of obsolescence of products because it benefits from a "buy-back" clause whereby all unsold inventory is purchased back by the manufacturer.	Case 2 The distributor assumes the risk of obsolescence of products. It does not benefit from a "buy-back" clause in its contractual relationship with the manufacturer.
Sales of product (For illustration purposes, assume both sell the same volume of the same product on the same market at the same price)	1,000	1,000
Purchase price from manufacturer taking account of the obsolescence risk in accordance with the functional analysis	700	640 (*)
Gross margin	300 (30%)	360 (36%)
Loss on obsolete inventory	0	50
Other expenses (overheads)	250	250
Net profit margin	50 (5%)	60 (6%)

(*) Assume that in this case the difference of 60 in transaction price corresponds to the difference in the allocation of the obsolescence risk between the manufacturer and the distributor (additional loss estimated 50 plus remuneration of the risk of the distributor), *i.e.* it is the price for the contractual "buy-back" clause.

3.   Under Illustration 2, if a controlled transaction is performed as in case 1 while the third party "comparables" are operating as in case 2, and assuming that the difference in the level of risks is not identified due to insufficiently detailed information on the third party "comparables", then the risk of error when applying a gross margin method could amount to 60 (6% x 1,000) instead of 10 (1% x 1,000) if a net margin method is applied. This illustrates the fact that, depending on the circumstances of the case and in particular of the effect of the differences in the level of risks on the cost structure and on the revenue of the "comparables", net profit margins can be less sensitive than gross margins to differences in the level of risks (assuming the contractual allocation of risks is arm's length).

4.   Consequently, enterprises performing different functions may have a wide range of gross profit margins while still earning broadly similar levels of net profits. For instance, business commentators note that the transactional net margin method would be less sensitive to differences in volume, extent and complexity of functions and operating expenses. On the other hand, the transactional net margin method may be more sensitive than the cost plus or resale price methods to differences in capacity utilisation, because differences in the levels of absorption of indirect fixed costs (*e.g.* fixed manufacturing costs or fixed distribution costs) would affect the net profit but may not affect the gross margin or gross mark-up on costs if not reflected in price differences, as illustrated below.

Illustration 3:

Effect of a difference in manufacturers' capacity utilization

The example below is for illustration only and is not intended to provide any guidance on the selection of the transfer pricing method or of comparables, or on arm's length rates of return, but only to illustrate the effects of differences between the capacity utilisation of a manufacturer and of comparables.

In monetary units (m.u.)	Case 1 The manufacturer operates in full capacity: 1,000 units per year	Case 2 The manufacturer operates in excess capacity *i.e.* only manufactures 80% of what it could manufacture in full capacity: 800 units per year
Sales of manufactured products (For illustration purposes, assume both manufacturers have the same total capacity, and that they both manufacture and sell the same product on the same market which have the same price of 1 m.u. per manufactured product) (*).	1,000	800
Cost of goods sold: direct costs plus standard allocation of indirect manufacturing costs. (For illustration purposes, assume both manufacturers have the same variable cost of goods sold per manufactured unit, *i.e.* 0.75 m.u. per manufactured product, and fixed personnel costs of 50).	Variable: 750 Fixed: 50 Total: 800	Variable: 600 Fixed: 50 Total: 650
Gross mark-up on cost of goods sold	200 (25%)	150 (23%)
Indirect costs (For illustration purposes, assume both manufacturers have the same indirect costs)	150	150
Net profit margin	50 (5%)	Breakeven

(*) This assumes that the arm's length price of the manufactured products is not affected by the manufacturer's capacity utilisation.

5.   Under Illustration 3, if a controlled transaction is performed as in case 1 while the third party "comparables" are operating as in case 2, and assuming that the difference in the capacity utilisation is not identified due to insufficiently detailed information on the third party "comparables", then the risk of error when applying a gross margin method could amount to 16 (2% x 800) instead of 50 (5% x 1000) if a net margin method is applied. This illustrates the fact that net profit indicators can be more sensitive than gross mark-ups or gross margins to differences in the capacity utilisation, depending on the facts and circumstances of the case and in particular on the proportion of fixed and variable costs and on whether it is the taxpayer or the "comparable" which is in an over-capacity situation.

Annex II to Chapter II

Example to Illustrate the Application of the Residual Profit Split Method

See Chapter II, Part III, Section C of these Guidelines for general guidance on the application of the profit split method.

The adjustments and assumptions about arm's length arrangements in the examples that follow are intended for illustrative purposes only and should not be taken as prescribing adjustments and arm's length arrangements in actual cases or particular industries. While they seek to demonstrate the principles of the Sections of the Guidelines to which they refer, those principles must be applied in each case according to the specific facts and circumstances of that case.

1.   The success of an electronics product is linked to the innovative technological design both of its electronic processes and of its major component. That component is designed and manufactured by associated company A, is transferred to associated company B which designs and manufactures the rest of the product, and is distributed by associated company C. Information exists to verify by means of a resale price method that the distribution functions and risks of Company C are being appropriately rewarded by the transfer price of the finished product from B to C.

2.   The most appropriate method to price the component transferred from A to B may be a CUP, if a sufficiently similar comparable could be found. See paragraph 2.14 of the Guidelines. However, since the component transferred from A to B reflects the innovative technological advance enjoyed by company A in this market, in this example it proves impossible (after the appropriate functional and comparability analyses have been carried out) to find a reliable CUP to estimate the correct price that A could command at arm's length for its product. Calculating a return on A's manufacturing costs could however provide an estimate of the profit element

which would reward A's manufacturing functions, ignoring the profit element attributable to the intangible used therein. A similar calculation could be performed on company B's manufacturing costs, to give an estimate of B's profit derived from its manufacturing functions, ignoring the profit element attributable to its intangible. Since B's selling price to C is known and is accepted as an arm's length price, the amount of the residual profit accrued by A and B together from the exploitation of their respective intangible property can be determined. See paragraphs 2.108 and 2.121 of the Guidelines. At this stage the proportion of this residual profit properly attributable to each enterprise remains undetermined.

3.   The residual profit may be split based on an analysis of the facts and circumstances that might indicate how the additional reward would have been allocated at arm's length. Paragraph 2.121 of the Guidelines. The R&D activity of each company is directed towards technological design relating to the same class of item, and it is established for the purposes of this example that the relative amounts of R&D expenditure reliably measure the relative value of the companies' contributions. See paragraph 2.120 of the Guidelines. This means that each company's contribution to the product's technological innovation may reliably be measured by their relative expenditure on research and development, so that, if A's R&D expenditure is 15 and B's 10, the residual could be split 3/5 for A and 2/5 for B.

4.   Some figures may assist in following the example:

a)   **Profit & Loss of A and B**

		A		B
Sales		50		100
Less:				
Purchases		(10)		(50)
Manufacturing costs		(15)		(20)
Gross profits		25		30
Less:				
R&D	15		10	
Operating expenses	10	(25)	10	(20)
Net profit		**0**		**10**

b)   **Determine routine profit on manufacturing by A and B, and calculate total residual profit**

5.   It is established, for both jurisdictions, that third-party comparable manufacturers without innovative intangible property earn a return on manufacturing costs (excluding purchases) of 10% (ratio of net profit to the direct and indirect costs of manufacturing).[1] See paragraph 2.121 of the Guidelines. A's manufacturing costs are 15, and so the return on costs would attribute to A a manufacturing profit of 1.5. B's equivalent costs are 20, and so the return on costs would attribute to B a manufacturing profit of 2.0. The residual profit is therefore 6.5, arrived at by deducting from the combined net profit of 10 the combined manufacturing profit of 3.5.

c)   **Allocate residual profit**

6.   The initial allocation of profit (1.5 to A and 2.0 to B) rewards the manufacturing functions of A and B, but does not recognise the value of their respective R&D that has resulted in a technologically advanced product. That residual can, therefore, be split between A and B based on their share of total R&D costs, since, for the purposes of this example[2], it can reliably be assumed that the companies' relative expenditure on R&D accurately reflects their relative contributions to the value of the product's technological innovation. A's R&D expenditure is 15 and B's 10, giving combined R&D expenditure of 25. The residual is 6.5 which may be allocated 15/25 to A and 10/25 to B, resulting in a share of 3.9 and 2.6 respectively, as below:

A's share 6.5 x 15/25= 3.9
B's share 6.5 x 10/25= 2.6.

---

[1] This 10% return does not technically correspond to a cost plus mark-up in its strictest sense because it yields net profit rather than gross profit. But neither does the 10% return correspond to a TNMM margin in its strictest sense, since the cost base does not include operating expenses. The net return on manufacturing costs is being used as a convenient and practical first stage of the profit split method, because it simplifies the determination of the amount of residual net profit attributable to intangible property.

[2] But see paragraph 6.27 of the Guidelines.

d)   **Recalculate Profits**

7.   A's net profits would thus become $1.5 + 3.9 = 5.4$.

B's net profits would thus become $2.0 + 2.6 = 4.6$.

The revised P & L for tax purposes would appear as:

		A		B
Sales		55.4		100
Less:				
Purchases		(10)		(55.4)
Manufacturing costs		(15)		(20)
Gross profit		30.4		24.6
Less:				
R & D	15		10	
Operating expenses	10	(25)	10	(20)
Net profit		**5.4**		**4.6**

Note

8.   The example is intended to exemplify in a simple manner the mechanisms of a residual profit split and should not be interpreted as providing general guidance as to how the arm's length principle should apply in identifying arm's length comparables and determining an appropriate split. It is important that the principles that it seeks to illustrate are applied in each case taking into account the specific facts and circumstances of the case. In particular, it should be noted that the allocation of the residual split may need considerable refinement in practice in order to identify and quantify the appropriate basis for the allocation. Where R&D expenditure is used, differences in the types of R&D conducted may need to be taken into account, *e.g.* because different types of R&D may have different levels of risk associated with them, which would lead to different levels of expected returns at arm's length. Relative levels of current R&D expenditure also may not adequately reflect the contribution to the earning of current profits that is attributable to intangible property developed or acquired in the past.

Annex III to Chapter II

Illustration of Different Measures of Profits When Applying a Transactional Profit Split Method

See Chapter II, Part III, Section C of these Guidelines for general guidance on the application of the transactional profit split method.

The assumptions about arm's length arrangements in the following examples are intended for illustrative purposes only and should not be taken as prescribing adjustments and arm's length arrangements in actual cases of particular industries. While they seek to demonstrate the principles of the sections of the Guidelines to which they refer, those principles must be applied in each case according to the specific facts and circumstances of that case.

Furthermore, the comments below relate to the application of a transactional profit split method in the situations where, given the facts and circumstances of the case and in particular the comparability (including functional) analysis of the transaction and the review of the information available on uncontrolled comparables, such a method is found to be the most appropriate method to be used.

1.   Below are some illustrations of the effect of choosing a measure of profits to determine the combined profits to be split when applying a transactional profit split method.

2.   Assume A and B are two associated enterprises situated in two different tax jurisdictions. Both manufacture the same widgets and incur expenditure that results in the creation of an intangible asset which they can mutually use. For the purpose of this example, it is assumed that the nature of this particular asset is such that the value of the asset contribution attributable to each of A and B in the year in question is proportional to A and B's relative expenditure on the asset in that year. (It should be noted that this assumption will not always be true in practice. This is because there may be cases where the relative values of asset contributions attributable to each party would be based on accumulated expenditure from the prior, as well as current years.) Assume A and B exclusively sell products to third

parties. Assume that it is determined that the most appropriate method to be used is a residual profit split method, that the manufacturing activities of A and B are simple, non-unique transactions that should be allocated an initial return of 10% of the Cost of Goods Sold and that the residual profit should be split in proportion to A's and B's intangible asset expenditure. The following figures are for illustration only:

	A	B	Combined A + B
Sales	100	300	400
Cost Of Goods Sold	60	170	230
Gross Profit	40	130	170
Overhead expenses	3	6	9
Other operating expenses	2	4	6
Intangible asset expenditure	30	40	70
Operating Profit	5	80	85

3.   **Step one: determining the initial return for the non-unique manufacturing transactions (Cost of Goods Sold + 10% in this example)**

A	60 + (60 * 10 %) = 66	→ Initial return for the manufacturing transactions of A =	6
B	170 + (170 * 10 %) = 187	→ Initial return for the manufacturing transactions of B =	17
		Total profit allocated through initial returns (6+17) =	23

4.   **Step two: determining the residual profit to be split**

a)   *In case it is determined as the operating profit:*

Combined Operating Profit	85
Profit already allocated (initial returns for manufacturing transactions)	23
Residual profit to be split in proportion to A's and B's intangible asset expenditure	62

Residual profit allocated to A:	62 * 30/70	26.57
Residual profit allocated to B:	62 * 40/70	35.43
Total profits allocated to A:	6 (initial return) + 26.57 (residual)	32.57
Total profits allocated to B:	17 (initial return) + 35.43 (residual)	52.43
Total		85

b)   *In case it is determined as the operating profit before overhead expenses (assuming it is determined that the overhead expenses of A and B do not relate to the transaction examined and should be excluded from the determination of the combined profits to be split):*

	A	B	Combined A + B
Sales	100	300	400
Cost Of Goods Sold	60	170	230
Gross Profit	40	130	170
Other operating expenses	2	4	6
Intangible asset expenditure	30	40	70
Operating Profit before overhead expenses	8	86	94
Overhead expenses	3	6	9
Operating Profit	5	80	85

Combined Operating Profit before overhead expenses	94
Profit already allocated (initial returns for manufacturing transactions)	23
Residual profit before overhead expenses to be split in proportion to A's and B's intangible asset expenditure	71

Residual profit allocated to A:	71 * 30/70	30.43
Residual profit allocated to B:	71 * 40/70	40.57

Total profits allocated to A:	6 (initial return) + 30.43 (residual) – 3 (overhead expenses)	33.43
Total profits allocated to B:	17 (initial return) + 40.57 (residual) – 6 (overhead expenses)	51.57
Total		85

5.   As shown in the above example, excluding some specific items from the determination of the combined profits to be split implies that each party remains responsible for its own expenses in relation to it. As a consequence, the decision whether or not to exclude some specific items must be consistent with the comparability (including functional) analysis of the transaction.

6.   As another example, in some cases it may be appropriate to back out a category of expenses to the extent that the allocation key used in the residual profit split analysis relies on those expenses. For example, in cases where relative expenditure contributing to the development of an intangible

asset is determined to be the most appropriate profit split factor, residual profits can be based on operating profits *before* that expenditure. After determining the split of residual profits, each associated enterprise then subtracts its own expenditure. This can be illustrated as follows. Assume the facts are the same as in the example at paragraph 2 above and assume the overhead expenses are not excluded from the determination of the residual profit to be split.

7.   *Step one: determining the basic return for the manufacturing activities (Cost of Goods Sold + 10% in this example)*

Same as at paragraph 3.

8.   *Step two: determining the residual profit to be split*

a)   *In case it is determined as the operating profit after intangible asset expenditure:*

Same as at paragraph 4, case a)

b)   *In case it is determined as the operating profit before* intangible asset expenditure:

	A	B	Combined A + B
Sales	100	300	400
Cost Of Goods Sold	60	170	230
Gross Profit	40	130	170
Overhead expenses	3	6	9
Other operating expenses	2	4	6
Operating profit intangible asset expenditure	35	120	155
Intangible asset expenditure	30	40	70
Operating Profit	5	80	85

Combined Operating Profit before intangible asset expenditure	155
Profit already allocated (initial returns for manufacturing transactions)	23
Residual profit before intangible asset expenditure to be split in proportion to A's and B's intangible asset expenditure	132
Residual profit allocated to A:	132 * 30/70	56.57
Residual profit allocated to B:	132 * 40/70	75.43

Total profits allocated to A:	6 (initial return) + 56.57 (residual) – 30 (intangible asset expenditure)	32.57
Total profits allocated to B:	17 (initial return) + 75.43 (residual) – 40 (intangible asset expenditure)	52.43
Total		85

i.e. A and B are allocated the same profits as in the case where the profit to be split is determined as the operating profit after intangible asset expenditure, see case a) above.

9.   This example illustrates the fact that, when the allocation key used to split the residual profit relies on a category of expenses incurred during the period, it is indifferent whether the residual profit to be split is determined before said expenses and the expenses are deducted by each party, or whether the residual profit to be split is determined after said expenses. The outcome can however be different in the case where the split factor is based on the accumulated expenditure of the prior as well as current years (see paragraph 2 above).

Annex to Chapter III

Example of a Working Capital Adjustment

See Chapter III, Section A.6 of these Guidelines for general guidance on comparability adjustments.

The assumptions about arm's length arrangements in the following examples are intended for illustrative purposes only and should not be taken as prescribing adjustments and arm's length arrangements in actual cases of particular industries. While they seek to demonstrate the principles of the sections of the Guidelines to which they refer, those principles must be applied in each case according to the specific facts and circumstances of that case.

This example is provided for illustration purposes as it represents one way, but not necessarily the only way, in which such an adjustment can be calculated.

Furthermore, the comments below relate to the application of a transactional net margin method in the situations where, given the facts and circumstances of the case and in particular the comparability (including functional) analysis of the transaction and the review of the information available on uncontrolled comparables, such a method is found to be the most appropriate method to be used.

Introduction

1.   This simple example shows how to make an adjustment in recognition of differences in levels of working capital between a tested party (TestCo) and a comparable (CompCo). See paragraphs 3.47-3.54 of these Guidelines for general guidance on comparability adjustments. Working capital adjustments may be warranted when applying the transactional net margin method. In practice they are usually found when applying a transactional net margin method, although they might also be applicable in cost plus or resale price methods. Working capital adjustments should only

be considered when the reliability of the comparables will be improved and reasonably accurate adjustments can be made. They should not be automatically made and would not be automatically accepted by tax administrations.

Why make a working capital adjustment?

2.   In a competitive environment, money has a time value. If a company provided, say, 60 days trade terms for payment of accounts, the price of the goods should equate to the price for immediate payment plus 60 days of interest on the immediate payment price. By carrying high accounts receivable a company is allowing its customers a relatively long period to pay their accounts. It would need to borrow money to fund the credit terms and/or suffer a reduction in the amount of cash surplus which it would otherwise have available to invest. In a competitive environment, the price should therefore include an element to reflect these payment terms and compensate for the timing effect.

3.   The opposite applies to higher levels of accounts payable. By carrying high accounts payable, a company is benefitting from a relatively long period to pay its suppliers. It would need to borrow less money to fund its purchases and/or benefit from an increase in the amount of cash surplus available to invest. In a competitive environment, the cost of goods sold should include an element to reflect these payment terms and compensate for the timing effect.

4.   A company with high levels of inventory would similarly need to either borrow to fund the purchase or reduce the amount of cash surplus which the company is able to invest. Note that the interest rate might be affected by the funding structure (*e.g.* where the purchase of inventory is partly funded by equity) or by the risk associated with holding specific types of inventory.

5.   Making a working capital adjustment is an attempt to adjust for the differences in time value of money between the tested party and potential comparables with an assumption that the difference should be reflected in profits. The underlying reasoning is that:

- A company will need funding to cover the time gap between the time it invests money (*i.e.* pays money to supplier) and the time it collects the investment (*i.e.* collects money from customers)

- This time gap is calculated as: the period needed to sell inventories to customers + (plus) the period needed to collect money from customers – (less) the period granted to pay debts to suppliers.

6.   **The process of calculating working capital adjustments:**

a)   Identify differences in the levels of working capital. Generally trade receivables, inventory and trade payables are the three accounts considered. The transactional net margin method is applied relative to an appropriate base, for example costs, sales or assets (see paragraph 2.58 of the Guidelines). If the appropriate base is sales, for example, then any differences in working capital levels should be measured relative to sales.

b)   Calculate a value for differences in levels of working capital between the tested party and the comparable relative to the appropriate base and reflecting the time value of money by use of an appropriate interest rate.

c)   Adjust the result to reflect differences in levels of working capital. The following example adjusts the comparable's result to reflect the tested party's levels of working capital. Alternative calculations are to adjust the tested party's results to reflect the comparables levels of working capital or to adjust both the tested party and the comparable's results to reflect "zero" working capital.

A practical example of calculating working capital adjustments:

7.   The following calculation is hypothetical. It is only to demonstrate how a working capital adjustment can be calculated.

TestCo	Year 1	Year 2	Year 3	Year 4	Year 5
Sales	$179.5m	$182.5m	$187m	$195m	$198m
Earnings Before Interest & Tax (EBIT)	$1.5m	$1.83m	$2.43m	$2.54m	$1.78m
EBIT/Sales (%)	0.8%	1%	1.3%	1.3%	0.9%
Working Capital (at end of year)[1]					
Trade Receivables (R)	$30m	$32m	$33m	$35m	$37m
Inventories (I)	$36m	$36m	$38m	$40m	$45m
Trade Payables (P)	$20m	$21m	$26m	$23m	$24m
Receivables (R) + Inventory (I) – Payables (P)	$46m	$47m	$45m	$52m	$58m
(R + I – P) / Sales	25.6%	25.8%	24.1%	26.7%	29.3%

CompCo	Year 1	Year 2	Year 3	Year 4	Year 5
	$120.4m	$121.2m	$121.8m	$126.3m	$130.2m
Earnings Before Interest & Tax (EBIT)	$1.59m	$3.59m	$3.15m	$4.18m	$6.44m
EBIT/Sales (%)	1.32%	2.96%	2.59%	3.31%	4.95%
Working Capital (at end of year)[1]					
Trade Receivables (R)	$17m	$18m	$20m	$22m	$23m
Inventory (I)	$18m	$20m	$26m	$24m	$25m
Trade Payables (P)	$11m	$13m	$11m	$15m	$16m
Receivables (R) + Inventory (I) – Payables (P)	$24m	$25m	$35m	$31m	$32m
(R + I – P) / Sales	19.9%	20.6%	28.7%	24.5%	24.6%

---

[1] See comment at paragraph 8.

Working Capital Adjustment	Year 1	Year 2	Year 3	Year 4	Year 5
TestCo's (R + I – P) / Sales	25.6%	25.8%	24.1%	26.7%	29.3%
CompCo's (R + I – P) / Sales	19.9%	20.6%	28.7%	24.5%	24.6%
Difference (D)	5.7%	5.1%	-4.7%	2.1%	4.7%
Interest Rate (i)	4.8%	5.4%	5.0%	5.5%	4.5%
Adjustment (D*i)	0.27%	0.28%	-0.23%	0.12%	0.21%
CompCo's EBIT/Sales (%)	1.32%	2.96%	2.59%	3.31%	4.95%
Working Capital Adjusted EBIT / Sales for CompCo	1.59%	3.24%	2.35%	3.43%	5.16%

8.   Some observations:

- An issue in making working capital adjustments is what point in time are the Receivables, Inventory and Payables compared between the tested party and the comparables. The above example compares their levels on the last day of the financial year. This may not, however, be appropriate if this timing does not give a representative level of working capital over the year. In such cases, averages might be used if they better reflect the level of working capital over the year.

- A major issue in making working capital adjustments involves the selection of the appropriate interest rate (or rates) to use. The rate (or rates) should generally be determined by reference to the rate(s) of interest applicable to a commercial enterprise operating in the same market as the tested party. In most cases a commercial loan rate will be appropriate. In cases where the tested party's working capital balance is negative (that is Payables > Receivables + Inventory), a different rate may be appropriate. The rate used in the above example reflects the rate at which TestCo is able to borrow funds in its local market. This example also assumes that the same interest rate is appropriate for payables, receivables and inventory, but that may or may not be the case in practice. Where different rates of interest are found to be appropriately applicable to individual classes of assets or liabilities, the calculation may be considerably more complex than shown above.

- The purpose of working capital adjustments is to improve the reliability of the comparables. There is a question whether working capital adjustments should be made when the results of some comparables can be reliably adjusted while the results of some others cannot.

Annex to Chapter IV:

Guidelines for Conducting Advance Pricing Arrangements under the Mutual Agreement Procedure ("MAP APAs")

A. Background

A.1   Introduction

1.   Advance Pricing Arrangements ("APAs") are the subject of extensive discussion in the *Transfer Pricing Guidelines for Multinational Enterprises and Tax Administrations* at Chapter IV, Section F. The development of working arrangements between competent authorities is considered at paragraph 4.164:

> Between those countries that use APAs, greater uniformity in APA practices could be beneficial to both tax administrations and taxpayers. Accordingly, the tax administrations of such countries may wish to consider working agreements with the competent authorities for the undertaking of APAs. These agreements may set forth general guidelines and understandings for the reaching of mutual agreement in cases where a taxpayer has requested an APA involving transfer pricing issues.

It should be noted that the use of the term "agreement" in the above quotation is not intended to give any status to such procedural arrangements above that provided for by the Mutual Agreement Article of the OECD Model Tax Convention. Additionally, the Committee on Fiscal Affairs stated at paragraph 4.160 of the Guidelines that it intended "to monitor carefully any expanded use of APAs and to promote greater consistency in practice amongst those countries that choose to use them."

2.   This annex follows up on the above recommendations. The objective is to improve the consistency of application of APAs by providing guidance to tax administrations on how to conduct mutual agreement procedures involving APAs. Although the focus of the annex is on the role of tax administrations, the opportunity is taken to discuss how best the taxpayer can contribute to the process. This guidance is intended for use by those countries – both OECD members and non-members – that wish to use APAs.

A.2   *Definition of an APA*

3.   Many jurisdictions have had, for some time, procedures (*e.g.* rulings) enabling the taxpayer to obtain some degree of certainty regarding how the law will be applied in a given set of circumstances. The legal consequences of the proposed action are determined in advance, based on assumptions about the factual basis. The validity of this determination is dependent upon the assumptions being supported by the facts when the actual transactions take place. The term APA refers to a procedural arrangement between a taxpayer or taxpayers and a tax administration intended to resolve potential transfer pricing disputes in advance. The APA differs from the classic ruling procedure, in that it requires the detailed review and to the extent appropriate, verification of the factual assumptions on which the determination of legal consequences is based, before any such determination can be made. Further, the APA provides for a continual monitoring of whether the factual assumptions remain valid throughout the course of the APA period.

4.   An APA is defined in the first sentence of paragraph 4.123 of the Guidelines as "an arrangement that determines, in advance (emphasis added) of controlled transactions, an appropriate set of criteria (*e.g.* method, comparables and appropriate adjustments thereto, critical assumptions as to future events) for the determination of the transfer pricing for those transactions over a fixed period of time." It is also stated in paragraph 4.131 that "The concept of APAs also may be useful in resolving issues raised under Article 7 of the OECD Model Tax Convention relating to allocation problems, permanent establishments, and branch operations."

5.   In the Guidelines (see paragraph 4.129) the arrangements solely between a taxpayer or taxpayers and a tax administration are referred to as "unilateral APAs". The Guidelines encourage bilateral APAs and recommend at paragraph 4.162 that "Wherever possible, an APA should be concluded on a bilateral or multilateral basis between competent authorities through the mutual agreement procedure of the relevant treaty." A bilateral APA is based on a single mutual agreement between the competent

authorities of two tax administrations under the relevant treaty. A multilateral APA is a term used to describe a situation where there is more than one bilateral mutual agreement.

6.   Although, commonly an APA will cover cross-border transactions involving more than one taxpayer and legal enterprise, *i.e.* between members of a MNE group, it is also possible for an APA to apply to only one taxpayer and legal enterprise. For example, consider an enterprise in Country A that trades through branches in Countries B, C and D. In order to have certainty that double taxation will not occur, countries A, B, C and D will need to share a common understanding of the measure of profits to be attributed to each jurisdiction in respect of that trading activity under Article 7 of the OECD Model Tax Convention. This certainty could be achieved by the negotiation of a series of separate, but mutually consistent, bilateral mutual agreements, *i.e.* between A and B, A and C and A and D. The existence of multiple bilateral mutual agreements raises a number of special issues and these are discussed further in Section B, paragraphs 21-27 of this annex.

7.   It is important to distinguish the different types of APAs and so the bilateral or multilateral APAs, which are the main subject of this annex, are hereafter referred to as "MAP APAs". The APAs that do not involve a mutual agreement negotiation are referred to as "unilateral APAs". The generic term "APA" is used where the feature to be discussed applies to both types of APA. It should be noted that, in the vast majority of cases a bilateral APA will be concluded under the mutual agreement procedure of a double tax convention. However, in some cases where a bilateral APA has been sought and the treaty is not appropriate, or where a treaty is not applicable, the competent authorities of some countries may nevertheless conclude an arrangement using the executive power conferred on the heads of tax authorities. The term MAP APA should be interpreted, with the necessary adaptations, as including such exceptional agreements.

8.   The focus of this annex is on providing guidance to enable tax authorities to resolve disputes through the mutual agreement procedure, thereby helping to eliminate the risk of potential double taxation and providing the taxpayer with reasonable certainty of tax treatment. However, it should be noted that there are other mechanisms for achieving the same goals which are not discussed in this annex.

A.3   *Objectives of the APA process*

9.   It has been the experience of a number of countries that the resolution of transfer pricing disputes by traditional audit or examination techniques has often proved very difficult and also costly for taxpayers and

tax authorities both in terms of time and resources. Such techniques inevitably examine transfer prices (and the surrounding conditions) some time after they were set and there can be genuine difficulties in obtaining sufficient information to evaluate properly whether arm's length prices were used at the time they were set. These difficulties led in part to the development of the APA process as an alternative way of solving transfer pricing issues in some cases in order to avoid some of the problems described above. The objectives of an APA process are to facilitate principled, practical and co-operative negotiations, to resolve transfer pricing issues expeditiously and prospectively, to use the resources of the taxpayer and the tax administration more efficiently, and to provide a measure of predictability for the taxpayer.

10.   To be successful, the process should be administered in a non-adversarial, efficient and practical fashion and requires the co-operation of all the participating parties. It is intended to supplement, rather than replace, the traditional administrative, judicial, and treaty mechanisms for resolving transfer pricing issues. Consideration of an APA may be most appropriate when the methodology for applying the arm's length principle gives rise to significant questions of reliability and accuracy, or when the specific circumstances of the transfer pricing issues being considered are unusually complex.

11.   One of the key objectives of the MAP APA process is the elimination of potential double taxation. Unilateral APAs give rise to considerable concerns in this area, which is why "most countries prefer bilateral or multilateral APAs" (paragraph 4.130 of the Guidelines). However, some kind of confirmation or agreement between the taxpayer and the tax administration is necessary in order to give effect to the MAP APA in each of the participating jurisdictions. The exact form of such confirmation or agreement depends on the domestic procedures in each jurisdiction (discussed in more detail at paragraphs 65-66 of this annex). Such a confirmation or agreement also provides a mechanism to ensure that the taxpayer complies with the terms and conditions of the MAP APA on which this confirmation or agreement is based.

12.   Further, in order to meet the objectives described in this section, the MAP APA process needs to be conducted in a neutral manner. In particular, the process should be neutral as regards the residence of the taxpayer, the jurisdiction in which the request for the MAP APA was initiated, the audit or examination status of the taxpayer and the selection of taxpayers in general for audit or examination. The guidance at paragraph 4.156 of the Guidelines on possible misuse by tax administrations in their examination practices of information obtained in the APA process should

also be borne in mind. The guidance given in this annex is intended to assist in attaining the objectives described in this section.

B. Eligibility for a MAP APA

B.1   Treaty issues

13.   The first question that arises is whether it is possible for there to be an APA. The eligibility of a taxpayer to apply for a unilateral APA will be determined by the specific domestic requirements of the relevant tax administration. MAP APAs are governed by the mutual agreement procedure of the applicable double tax agreement, Article 25 of the OECD Model Tax Convention, and are administered at the discretion of the relevant tax administrations.

14.   In some cases the taxpayer will only request a unilateral APA. The reasons for the taxpayer not requesting a MAP APA should be explored. Following the guidance given by the Guidelines at paragraph 4.162 that "wherever possible, an APA should be concluded on a bilateral or multilateral basis", the tax authorities should encourage the taxpayer to request a MAP APA if the circumstances so warrant. Some countries if they determine that another tax administration should be involved may refuse to enter into unilateral negotiations with the taxpayer, even though the taxpayer still insists on a unilateral approach.

15.   The negotiation of a MAP APA requires the consent of the relevant competent authorities. In some cases, the taxpayer will take the initiative by making simultaneous requests to the affected competent authorities. In other cases the taxpayer may file a request with one jurisdiction under the relevant domestic procedure and ask it to contact the other affected jurisdiction(s) to see if a MAP APA is possible. Consequently, as soon as is administratively practicable, the competent authority in that jurisdiction should notify the relevant tax treaty partner(s) to determine whether they want to participate. The other tax administration should respond to the invitation as quickly as practicable, bearing in mind the need to have sufficient time to evaluate whether their participation is possible or feasible.

16.   However, Article 25 does not oblige the competent authorities to enter into MAP APAs at the request of the taxpayer. The willingness to enter into MAP APAs will depend on the particular policy of a country and how it interprets the mutual agreement article of its bilateral treaties. Some competent authorities will only consider such an agreement for cases that

require the resolution of "difficulties or doubts arising as to the interpretation or application of the Convention". The desire of the taxpayer for certainty of treatment is therefore not, in isolation, sufficient to pass the above threshold. Other competent authorities apply a less restrictive threshold for entering into MAP APAs, based on their view that the MAP APA process should be encouraged. Additionally, the taxpayer must qualify for the benefit of a particular treaty (*e.g.* by qualifying as a resident of one of the Contracting States) and must satisfy any other criteria contained in the mutual agreement article.

B.2   *Other factors*

17.   The fact that a taxpayer may be under audit or examination should not prevent the taxpayer from requesting a MAP APA in respect of prospective transactions. The audit or examination and the mutual agreement procedure are separate processes and generally can be resolved separately. Audit or examination activities would not normally be suspended by a tax administration whilst the MAP APA is being considered, unless it is agreed by all parties that the audit or examination should be held in abeyance because the obtaining of the MAP APA would assist with the completion of the audit or examination. Nevertheless, the treatment of the transactions being audited or examined may be informed by the methodology agreed to be applied prospectively under the MAP APA, provided that the facts and circumstances surrounding the transaction under audit or examination are comparable with those relating to the prospective transactions. This issue is discussed further in paragraph 69 below.

18.   The ability to conclude a MAP APA is predicated on full co-operation by the taxpayer. The taxpayer and any associated enterprises should: a) provide their full co-operation in assisting the tax administrations with the evaluation of their proposal; and b) provide, upon request, any additional information necessary for that evaluation, for example, details of their transfer pricing transactions, business arrangements, forecasts and business plans, and financial performance. It is desirable that this commitment from the taxpayer be sought before commencing the MAP APA process.

19.   In some cases the freedom of one or both competent authorities to agree to a MAP APA may be limited, for example by a legally binding decision affecting issues subject to the APA proposals. In such circumstances, as the MAP APA process is by definition consensual, it is within the discretion of the affected competent authorities (subject to the domestic laws and policies of each jurisdiction) whether to engage in MAP APA discussions. For example, a competent authority may decline to enter

into discussions if it determines that such a limitation on the position of the other competent authority unacceptably reduces the likelihood of mutual agreement. However, it is likely that in many cases MAP APA discussions would be viewed as desirable even though the flexibility of one or both competent authorities is restricted. This is a matter for the competent authorities to determine on a case by case basis.

20.   When deciding whether a MAP APA is appropriate, a key consideration is the extent of the advantage to be gained by agreeing a method for avoiding the risk of double taxation in advance. This requires the exercise of judgement and the need to balance the efficient use of limited resources, both financial and human, with the desire to reduce the likelihood of double taxation. Tax administrations might consider the following items as relevant:

a)   Does the methodology and the other terms and conditions of the proposal respect the guidance given by the Guidelines? If not, it will be desirable to get the taxpayer to revise the proposal accordingly, in order to increase the chances of reaching a mutual agreement. As paragraph 17 of the preface to the Guidelines states "these guidelines are also intended primarily to govern the resolution of transfer pricing cases in mutual agreement proceedings".

b)   Are any "difficulties or doubts as to the interpretation or application of the Convention" likely to significantly increase the risk of double taxation and so justify the use of resources to settle any problems in advance of the proposed transactions?

c)   Would the transactions covered by the proposal be ongoing in nature and is there a significant part of any limited life project left?

d)   Are the transactions in question seriously contemplated and not of a purely hypothetical nature? The process should not be used to find out the likely views of the tax administration on a general point of principle - there are other established methods for doing this in many countries.

e)   Is a transfer pricing audit already in progress in relation to past years where the fact pattern was substantially similar? If so, the outcome of the audit may be expedited by participating in a MAP APA, the terms of which could then be applied to inform or resolve the audit and any unresolved mutual agreement for earlier years.

B.3 Multilateral MAP APAs

21. The desire for certainty has resulted in an emerging trend for taxpayers to seek multilateral MAP APAs covering their global operations. The taxpayer approaches each of the affected jurisdictions with an overall proposal and suggests that it would be desirable if the negotiations be conducted on a multilateral basis involving all the affected jurisdictions, rather than by a series of separate negotiations with each tax authority. It should be noted that there is no multilateral method of implementing any agreement that may be reached, except by concluding a series of separate bilateral MAP APAs. The successful negotiation of a series of bilateral MAP APAs in this way would provide greater certainty and lower costs to the MNE group than if separate MAP APAs were undertaken bilaterally and in isolation of each other.

22. Although, as described above, there are potential benefits to having multilateral MAP APAs, a number of issues need to be considered. First, it is unlikely to be appropriate for a single transfer pricing methodology to be applied to the wide variety of facts and circumstances, transactions and countries likely to be the subject of a multilateral MAP APA, unless the methodology can be appropriately adapted to reflect the particular facts and circumstances found in each country. Therefore, care would need to be taken by all the participating jurisdictions to ensure that the methodology, even after such adaptation, represented a proper application of the arm's length principle in the conditions found in their country.

23. Second, issues also arise because under a multilateral MAP APA several competent authorities are effectively involved in a process that was designed for a bilateral process. One issue is the extent to which it may be necessary to exchange information between all the affected jurisdictions. This could be problematic in cases where there are no transaction flows or common transactions between two or more of the affected treaty partners, so creating doubts as to whether the information is relevant to the particular bilateral MAP APA being discussed. However, in cases where similar transactions are conducted by different parts of the MNE or in which the area considered relates to trading on an integrated basis, there may be a need to have information about flows between other parties in order to be able to understand and evaluate the flows that are the subject of the particular bilateral MAP APA. Another problem is that it may be difficult to judge whether such information is indeed relevant prior to obtaining it.

24. Further, even if the information is relevant to the particular bilateral MAP APA, there may still be potential problems of confidentiality preventing the exchange of that information, either under the terms of the

exchange of information article(s) of the relevant treaty or under the domestic law of one of the participating tax administrations. Given the wide range of possible circumstances likely to be found in multilateral MAP APAs, no general solution to these problems can be prescribed. Rather such issues need to be addressed specifically in each of the separate bilateral MAP APAs.

25.   In cases where information about flows between other parties is found to be relevant, some exchange of information problems could possibly be overcome by not relying on treaty information exchange provisions, but instead asking the taxpayer to assume responsibility for providing information to all the affected tax administrations (though procedures would still be needed to verify that the same information is in fact provided to all tax administrations). Finally, in some cases the mutual agreement articles of the relevant treaties may not provide an adequate basis for such multilateral consideration and discussion, although the mutual agreement article of the OECD Model Tax Convention is designed to assist in the elimination of double taxation in a wide variety of circumstances, and therefore would, if applicable, appear to provide adequate authority in most situations.

26.   In summary, as discussed in Section A, the desire by the taxpayer for certainty is not by itself sufficient to oblige a tax administration to enter into a MAP APA where this might be inappropriate. An invitation to participate in a multilateral MAP APA would therefore be evaluated in accordance with the usual criteria for determining whether a bilateral MAP APA could be pursued and each proposed bilateral APA would also be separately evaluated. A decision would then be taken whether the completion of the negotiations for the bilateral MAP APAs that the administration has decided to pursue, would best be served by its participation in multilateral negotiations. This evaluation will be made on a case-by-case basis.

27.   The development of multilateral MAP APAs is at a relatively early stage, except perhaps in the global trading field. Indeed, where global trading is conducted on a fully integrated basis (*i.e.* the trading and risk management of a book of financial products takes place in a number of different locations, usually at least three), a multilateral, as opposed to a bilateral, APA has become the norm[1]. It is intended to monitor closely further developments in the area of multilateral MAP APAs.

---

[1]   For more details see OECD (1998), *The Taxation of Global Trading of Financial Instruments*, OECD, Paris.

C. Request for MAP APAs

C.1   Introduction

28.   Although a MAP APA by its nature involves an agreement between tax administrations, the process needs considerable involvement by the taxpayer or taxpayers in order to be successful. This section looks at the first stages in this process, namely the request for the MAP APA which is normally initiated by the taxpayer(s). (N.B. Some tax administrations consider that they should take the initiative and actively encourage taxpayers to make requests in appropriate cases, for example following completion of an audit or risk assessment analysis.) Once it has been decided that a MAP APA is indeed appropriate, the primary responsibility for providing the participating tax administrations with sufficient information for them to be able to conduct mutual agreement negotiations will inevitably rest with the taxpayer(s). Consequently, the taxpayer should submit a detailed proposal for review by the relevant tax administration and be prepared to provide further information as requested by the tax administration.

C.2   Preliminary discussions

29.   A feature of many domestic procedures for the obtaining of a unilateral APA is the ability to have a preliminary meeting (or meetings) before a formal request is made. Such a meeting (or meetings) provides a taxpayer with an opportunity to discuss with the tax administration the suitability of an APA, the type and extent of information which may be required and the scope of any analyses required for the completion of a successful APA. (For example, the extent of any functional analysis of affiliated enterprises; identification, selection and adjustment of comparables; and the need for, and the scope of, market, industry and geographic analyses.) The process also provides the taxpayer with an opportunity to discuss any concerns regarding disclosure and confidentiality of data, the term of the APA and the like. Experience has generally shown that the ability to have such preliminary discussions expedites the processing of any subsequent formal MAP APA proposal.

30.   In the context of a MAP APA, the ability of the relevant competent authorities to have preliminary discussions with the taxpayer(s) may also be useful. In addition to the matters mentioned above, the discussions could usefully explore whether the circumstances were suitable for a MAP APA, for example whether there were sufficient "difficulties or doubts as to the interpretation or application of the Convention".

31.   The preliminary meeting may also have a useful role in clarifying the expectations and objectives of the taxpayer(s) and the tax administration. It also provides an opportunity to explain the process, the policy of the tax administration on MAP APAs and to give details of any procedures for giving effect in domestic law to the agreement when completed. At the same time, the tax administration could provide guidance as to the content of the proposal, and the time frame for evaluating and concluding the mutual agreement. Tax administrations should publish general guidance on the MAP APA process in accordance with the recommendation for other types of mutual agreements at paragraphs 4.60-4.61 of the Guidelines.

32.   The preliminary meeting process may be conducted on either an anonymous or a named basis, depending on domestic custom and practice. If on an anonymous basis, however, sufficient information about the operations will be required in order to make any discussion meaningful. The form of any meetings should be agreed between the parties and a preliminary meeting may range from an informal discussion to a formal presentation. Typically, it is in the taxpayer's interest to provide the tax administration with a memorandum outlining the topics for discussion. More than one preliminary meeting may be required in order to achieve the objective of having an informal discussion of the potential suitability of a MAP APA request, its likely scope, the appropriateness of a methodology or the type and extent of information to be provided by the taxpayer.

33.   As well as informal discussions with its taxpayer(s), it may be useful for the respective competent authorities to have an early exchange of views on whether a MAP APA would be appropriate. This could avoid unnecessary work if it is unlikely that one of the competent authorities will participate. These discussions may be of an informal nature and do not necessarily require a formal face to face meeting. Also there may be opportunities to have such exchanges during the course of regular competent authority meetings and negotiations.

C.3   MAP APA Proposals

C.3.1   Introduction

34.   If the taxpayer wishes to pursue a MAP APA request, it will need to make a detailed proposal to the relevant tax administration, pursuant to any domestic procedural requirements, *e.g.* a requirement to file the request with a designated part of the domestic tax administration. For a MAP APA, the purpose of the taxpayer's proposal is to give the relevant competent authorities all the information needed to evaluate the proposal and to

undertake mutual agreement discussions. Countries have a number of ways of ensuring the competent authorities get the necessary information. One way is for the taxpayer to be able to make the proposal directly to the competent authority. Another way of achieving this goal is for the taxpayer to make available a copy of any domestic APA proposal to the other participating jurisdictions. Ideally, the exact form and content of the proposal will have been established at any preliminary meetings.

C.3.2. Activities usually covered in a MAP APA process

35. The scope of the MAP APA would depend on the wishes of the participating jurisdictions, as well as those of the taxpayer. It can apply to resolve issues covered by Articles 7 and 9 of the OECD Model Convention and would determine to what extents profits would arise in the tax jurisdictions involved.

36. The MAP APA may cover all of the transfer pricing issues of a taxpayer (or of the members of a MNE group) or may be more limited, for example to a particular transaction, sets of transactions, product lines or to only some members of a MNE group. Some countries, whilst recognising the need for flexibility in the process, have concerns over the appropriateness of specific issue APAs. It may be difficult to evaluate some issues in isolation, for example where the transactions covered by the proposal are highly interrelated with transactions not covered by the proposal, or where there is a need to analyse transfer pricing issues in a wider context because intentional set offs are involved (see paragraphs 3.13-3.17 of the Guidelines).

37. A MAP APA may also cover issues other than the transfer pricing methodology, provided that these other issues are sufficiently clearly connected to the underlying transfer pricing issues so as to make it worthwhile attempting to resolve them in advance and provided that the other issues come within the terms of the mutual agreement article in the relevant treaty. That will be something to be decided between the affected parties for each individual case.

C.3.3 Content of a MAP APA proposal

38. The content of the proposal and the extent of the necessary supporting information and documentation will depend on the facts and circumstances of each case and the requirements of the individual participating tax administrations. It is therefore not considered practicable to list or define exactly what should be provided. The guiding principle, however, should be to provide the information and documentation necessary

to explain the facts relevant to the proposed methodology and to demonstrate its application in accordance with the appropriate Article of the relevant treaty. The proposal should therefore be consistent with any general guidance given by the Commentary of the OECD Model Tax Convention on the corresponding Articles, together with the guidance on the application of the arm's length principle of Article 9 given by the Guidelines in cases involving transfer pricing between associated enterprises.

39.   In terms of the supporting information and documentation to be included, the guidance in Chapter IV (paragraphs 4.154-4.157) and Chapter V of the Guidelines on documentation requirements should be borne in mind. However, because of the prospective nature of the agreement sought, different types of information may need to be supplied than in mutual agreement cases, which only relate to transactions already undertaken. As a guide, the following information may be of general relevance for MAP APAs, although it should be stressed that the list below is not intended to be exhaustive or prescriptive in nature:

a)   The transactions, products, businesses or arrangements that will be covered by the proposal; (including, if applicable, a brief explanation of why not all of the transactions, products, businesses or arrangements of the taxpayer(s) involved in the request have been included);

b)   The enterprises and permanent establishments involved in these transactions or arrangements;

c)   The other country or countries which have been requested to participate;

d)   Information regarding the world-wide organisational structure, history, financial statement data, products, functions and assets (tangible and intangible) of any associated enterprises involved;

e)   A description of the proposed transfer pricing methodology and details of information and analyses supporting that methodology, *e.g.* identification of comparable prices or margins and expected range of results etc.;

f)   The assumptions underpinning the proposal and a discussion of the effect of changes in those assumptions or other events, such as unexpected results, which might affect the continuing validity of the proposal;

g)   The accounting periods or tax years to be covered;

h)   General description of market conditions (*e.g.* industry trends and the competitive environment);

i)   A discussion of any pertinent ancillary tax issues raised by the proposed methodology;

j)   A discussion of, and demonstration of compliance with, any pertinent domestic law, tax treaty provisions and OECD guidelines that relate to the proposal; and

k)   Any other information which may have a bearing on the current or proposed transfer pricing methodology and the underlying data for any party to the request.

The rest of this section discusses some of the most important items from the above list in more detail.

C.3.4   Comparable pricing information

40.   The taxpayer should include a discussion of the availability and use of comparable pricing information. This would include a description of how the search for comparables was carried out (including search criteria employed), what data relating to uncontrolled transactions was obtained and how such data was accepted or rejected as being comparable. The taxpayer should also include a presentation of comparable transactions along with adjustments to account for material differences, if any, between controlled and uncontrolled transactions. In cases where no comparables can be identified, the taxpayer should demonstrate, by reference to relevant market and financial data (including the internal data of the taxpayer), how the chosen methodology accurately reflects the arm's length principle.

C.3.5   Methodology

41.   The MAP APA proposal should provide a full description of the chosen methodology. In cases involving associated enterprises, the chosen methodology should also respect the guidance found in the Guidelines on applying the arm's length principle of Article 9 of the OECD Model Tax Convention. It is stated at paragraph 2.10 of the Guidelines that "further, any method should be permitted where its application is agreeable to the members of the MNE group involved with the transaction or transactions to which the methodology applies and also to the tax administrations in the jurisdictions of all those members." That guidance on use of transfer pricing methods is particularly relevant in the context of a MAP APA, because of the opportunity to obtain advance agreement on the method to be used. The

application of the methodology should be supported by data which can be obtained and updated over the period of the MAP APA without imposing too great a burden on the taxpayer, and which can be reviewed and verified effectively by the tax administrations.

42.   The taxpayer should, to the extent possible, provide an analysis of the effect of applying the chosen methodology or methodologies during the proposed period of the agreement. Such an analysis necessarily will have to be based on projected results and so details of the assumptions on which those projections were made will be needed. It may also be helpful to illustrate the effect of applying the APA methodology or methodologies to the periods immediately before the APA period. The usefulness of this analysis, even as an illustration, will depend on the facts and circumstances surrounding the transactions in question being comparable to those applying to the prospective transactions contemplated under the proposal.

C.3.6   Critical assumptions

43.   In entering into a MAP APA relating to the arm's length pricing of controlled transactions that have not yet occurred, it is necessary to make certain assumptions about the operational and economic conditions that will affect those transactions when they take place. The taxpayer should describe in the proposal the assumptions on which the ability of the methodology to accurately reflect the arm's length pricing of future transactions is based. Additionally, the taxpayer should explain how the chosen methodology will satisfactorily cope with any changes in those assumptions. The assumptions are defined as "critical" if the actual conditions existing at the time the transactions occur could diverge from those that were assumed to exist, to the extent that the ability of the methodology reliably to reflect arm's length pricing is undermined. One example might be a fundamental change to the market arising from new technology, government regulations, or widespread loss of consumer acceptance. In such a case, the divergence may mean that the agreement would need to be revised or cancelled.

44.   To increase the reliability of the MAP APA methodology, taxpayers and tax administrations should attempt to identify critical assumptions that are, where possible, based on observable, reliable and independent data. Such assumptions are not limited to items within the control of the taxpayer. Any set of critical assumptions needs to be tailored to the individual circumstances of the taxpayer, the particular commercial environment, the methodology, and the type of transactions covered. They should not be drawn so tightly that certainty provided by the agreement is jeopardised, but should encompass as wide a range of variation in the underlying facts as the parties to the agreement feel comfortable with. In

general, however, and by way of example only, critical assumptions might include:

a)   Assumptions about the relevant domestic tax law and treaty provisions.

b)   Assumptions about tariffs, duties, import restrictions and government regulations.

c)   Assumptions about economic conditions, market share, market conditions, end-selling price, and sales volume.

d)   Assumptions about the nature of the functions and risks of the enterprises involved in the transactions.

e)   Assumptions about exchange rates, interest rates, credit rating and capital structure.

f)   Assumptions about management or financial accounting and classification of income and expenses; and

g)   Assumptions about the enterprises that will operate in each jurisdiction and the form in which they will do so.

45.   It may also be helpful to set parameters for an acceptable level of divergence for some assumptions in advance, in order to provide the necessary flexibility. These parameters would need to be set individually for each particular MAP APA and would form part of the negotiations between the competent authorities. Only if the divergence from the prediction exceeded the parameter would the assumption become "critical" and action considered. Any action to be taken might also depend on the nature of the assumption and the level of divergence.

46.   If the reliability of the proposed transfer pricing methodology is known to be sensitive to exchange rate fluctuations, it would seem sensible to design a methodology that was capable of accommodating a certain degree of expected fluctuation, perhaps by providing for prices to be adjusted to take into account exchange rate movements. Also it could be agreed in advance that movements in either direction of up to X% would require no action, that movements greater than X % but less than Y% would trigger a prospective review of the methodology to make sure it remained appropriate, whilst a movement of more than Y% would mean that a critical assumption had been breached and it would be necessary to prospectively re-negotiate the MAP APA. These parameters would need to be set

individually for each particular MAP APA and would form part of the negotiation between the competent authorities.

C.3.7   Unexpected results

47.   A problem may arise when the results of applying the transfer pricing methodology agreed in the MAP APA do not fulfil the expectations of one of the parties, as that party may question whether the critical assumptions, and the methodology which they support, are still valid. The resolution of such questions may take a considerable amount of time and effort, thereby negating one of the objectives of the whole process. One possible solution to this problem is to include enough flexibility in the proposal to cope with likely changes in the facts and circumstances so that unexpected results are less likely to occur so that there is less risk that the MAP APA agreement based upon the proposal will need to be renegotiated. The proposal must still, of course, conform to the arm's length principle.

48.   One way of achieving the above objective is to design a methodology that appropriately takes into account likely changes in facts and circumstances; for example, some variation between projected and actual sales volume can be built in to the pricing methodology at the outset by including prospective price adjustment clauses or allowing pricing to vary with volume. The allowable level of deviation should be set by reference to what would have been accepted by independent parties.

49.   Another possible way of achieving the objective of increasing certainty, is to agree an acceptable range of results from applying the method of the MAP APA. In order to conform with the arm's length principle, the range should be agreed by all affected parties in advance, thereby avoiding the use of hindsight, and based on what independent parties would have agreed to in comparable circumstances (see paragraphs 3.55-3.66 for discussion of the range concept). For example, the quantum of an item, such as a royalty, would be accepted so long as it remained within a certain range expressed as a proportion of the profits.

50.   If the results fall outside the agreed range, the action to be taken would depend on what had been negotiated in the proposal in accordance with the wishes of the parties. Some parties may not wish to take the risk that the results will be significantly different from what they expected. Accordingly, they would use the range concept simply as a means of determining whether a critical assumption had been breached as described in paragraph 46. Other parties may place more emphasis on certainty of treatment than on avoiding unexpected results and so may agree that the MAP APA should contain a mechanism for adjusting the results so that they fall within the range agreed in advance.

C.3.8   Duration of the MAP APA

51.   By its nature, an APA applies to prospective transactions and so one issue to be decided is how long it will last. There are two sets of conflicting objectives that affect the negotiation of the appropriate term. On the one hand, it is desirable to have a sufficiently long period so as to grant a reasonable degree of certainty of treatment. Otherwise, it may not be worth making the initial effort of resolving potential transfer pricing problems in advance, as opposed to tackling problems only when they arise through the normal audit or tax return examination procedures. On the other hand, a long period makes the predictions as to future conditions on which the mutual agreement negotiations are based less accurate, thereby casting doubt on the reliability of the MAP APA proposals. The optimal trade-off between these two sets of objectives will depend on a number of factors, such as the industry, the transactions involved and the economic climate. The term should therefore be negotiated between the competent authorities on a case-by case basis. Experience to date has shown that a MAP APA might, on average, last for 3-5 years.

D. Finalisation of the MAP APA

D.1   Introduction

52.   The success of the MAP APA process, as an alternative to relying solely on traditional audit or examination techniques, depends to a large extent on the commitment of all the participants. The ability of the relevant competent authorities to reach agreement in a prompt manner will be determined both by their actions and importantly by the willingness of the taxpayer(s) to provide all the necessary information as promptly as possible. The usefulness of the process, both for taxpayers and tax authorities, will be significantly diminished if the MAP APA is not agreed until the period proposed to be covered in the taxpayer's request has nearly expired. Such delay may also make it more difficult to avoid the use of hindsight when evaluating the proposal because the results of applying the methodology will be known for most of the period proposed by the MAP APA. Understandably, given the relatively early stage in the evolution of the MAP APA process, the goal of prompt prospective resolution has not always been met in the past. To some extent, of course, some delay in the process is inevitable; MAP APAs tend to deal with large taxpayers, complex fact patterns, and difficult legal and economic issues, all of which require time and resources in order to understand and evaluate.

53.   Tax authorities are encouraged, where possible, to devote sufficient resources and skilled personnel to the process to ensure that cases are settled promptly and efficiently. Some tax authorities may wish to improve the efficiency of their MAP APA programmes by setting informal goals for the length of time taken to complete the process and by publishing the average completion time. Particular treaty partners may also agree to set informal goals for completion of their bilateral negotiations. Given the often complex and difficult fact patterns, the possible need for translations and the relative novelty of such arrangements, it is not felt desirable to set more specific or binding targets for concluding MAP APAs at this stage. However, it will be appropriate to set more specific targets for completion time in the future, once more experience with the MAP APA process has been gained.

54.   Once a taxpayer's proposal has been received by the tax administrations, they should mutually agree on the co-ordination of the review, evaluation and negotiation of the MAP APA. The MAP APA process can conveniently be broken up into two main stages; a) fact finding, review and evaluation and b) the competent authority discussions, each of which is discussed in further detail below.

D.2   Fact finding, review and evaluation

D.2.1   General

55.   In reviewing the MAP APA proposal, the tax administrations may undertake whatever steps they deem appropriate in the circumstances to conduct the mutual agreement procedure. These include, but are not limited to: requests for further information deemed relevant to review and evaluate the taxpayer's proposal, the carrying out of fieldwork (*e.g.* visits to taxpayer's premises, interviews with staff, review of financial or managerial operations, etc.) and the engaging of necessary experts. Tax administrations may also have recourse to information collected from other sources, including information and data on comparable taxpayers.

56.   The aim of this stage of the MAP APA process is for the participating competent authorities to have all relevant information, data, and analyses they need for the negotiations. Where one tax administration obtains additional information from the taxpayer relevant to the subject of the MAP APA, for example at a meeting with the taxpayer's staff, both the taxpayer and the tax administration should ensure the information reaches the other participating tax administration(s). The relevant competent authorities should arrange, amongst themselves and the taxpayers, for an

appropriate mechanism to corroborate the completeness and details of documents and information supplied by the taxpayer(s). The requirements of the participating competent authorities should be respected. For example, many jurisdictions require that not only is the same factual information provided to all participating competent authorities but that it should, as far as is practicable, be made available at the same time.

57.   The prospective nature of a MAP APA often involves the provision by the taxpayer of commercial information relating to forecasts which is likely to be even more sensitive to disclosure than information supplied after the event. Accordingly, in order to ensure that taxpayers have confidence in the MAP APA process, tax administrations should ensure that taxpayer information provided during the course of the MAP APA process is subject to the same secrecy, confidentiality and privacy safeguards of the relevant domestic law as any other taxpayer information. Further, where information is exchanged between competent authorities under the terms of the tax treaty, that information can be disclosed only in accordance with the specified terms of the treaty, and any exchange must comply with the exchange of information article(s) of the relevant treaty.

58.   Generally, the competent authorities would conduct simultaneous, independent reviews and evaluations of the taxpayer's proposal, assisted in this task, where necessary, by transfer pricing, industry, or other specialists from elsewhere in their tax administration. However, it may be more efficient in appropriate cases to have some degree of joint fact finding. This could take a variety of forms ranging from an occasional joint fact finding meeting or site visit, to the preparation of a joint report by delegated caseworkers.

D.2.2   Role of taxpayer in the fact finding, review and evaluation process

59.   In order to expedite the process, taxpayers should take responsibility for ensuring that the competent authorities, before they start to negotiate, are in possession of the same facts, have all the information they need and have a thorough understanding of the issues. This can be achieved by the taxpayer routinely making information requested by one tax administration available, at broadly the same time, to the other tax administration, preparing and transmitting notes of fact finding meetings by one tax administration to the other tax administration and where logistically and economically practical, facilitating joint fact finding meetings. The taxpayer should also arrange for any necessary translations to be made and ensure there is no undue delay in responding to requests for further relevant information. The taxpayer should also be entitled to confer with its tax

administrations when mutually appropriate and convenient while the proposal is undergoing review and evaluation, and should be kept informed of progress.

D.3   Conduct of Competent Authority discussions

D.3.1   Co-ordination amongst the Competent Authorities

60.   Many countries prefer to be fully involved in the process as soon as it commences and wish to work closely with the other competent authorities. Other countries prefer to confine their involvement to reviewing and commenting upon the MAP APA proposals as they near completion. However, the involvement of all participating tax administrations in the process at an early stage is recommended, subject to resource constraints, as this should maximise the efficiency of the process and help forestall unnecessary delays in concluding the mutual agreement.

61.   The competent authorities should conduct the mutual agreement discussions in a timely manner. This requires the devotion of sufficient resources and appropriately skilled personnel to the process. It is desirable that the competent authorities discuss and co-ordinate an appropriate plan of action with regards to such matters as: designating authorised officers, exchanging of information, co-ordination of the review and evaluation of the proposal, tentative scheduling of dates for further consultations, negotiation and conclusion of a suitable agreement. The level of input and resources required should be tailored to the individual requirements of the case.

62.   Experience has also shown that early and frequent discussion between the competent authorities as problems arise can be helpful and can avoid unpleasant surprises during the process. Given the nature of MAP APAs, there will often be significant issues which cannot be resolved simply by exchange of position papers and so more formal exchanges, such as face to face meetings between the competent authorities may be required. Use of conference calls or video conferencing may be helpful.

D.3.2   Role of the taxpayer in Competent Authority discussions

63.   The role of the taxpayer in this process is necessarily more limited, than in the fact finding process, given that the finalisation of a MAP APA is a government to government process. The competent authorities may agree to have the taxpayer make a presentation of the factual and legal issues before the discussions themselves commence, when the taxpayer would leave. It also may be helpful to arrange to have the taxpayer

available, on call, to answer any factual questions that may arise during the discussions. The taxpayer should avoid presenting new factual information or making supplementary representations at this meeting. The tax authorities will require time to review such matters and this will necessitate a postponement of a final decision on the proposed MAP APA. Such information should have been supplied prior to the commencement of the discussions.

D.3.3   Withdrawal from the APA process

64.   The taxpayer or tax administration may withdraw from the MAP APA process at any time. However, withdrawal from the process, especially at a late stage and without good cause, should be discouraged because of the inevitable waste of resources caused by such action. When a MAP APA request is withdrawn neither the taxpayer nor the tax administrations should have any obligations to each other, and any previous undertakings and understandings between the parties would be of no further force and effect, unless otherwise required by domestic law (*e.g.* APA user fee may not be refundable). If a tax administration proposes to withdraw, the taxpayer should be advised of the reasons for such action and given an opportunity to make further representations.

D.3.4   Mutual agreement document

65.   Participating competent authorities should prepare a draft mutual agreement when they have agreed on the methodology and other terms and conditions. It may be that, despite the best efforts of the competent authorities, the proposed mutual agreement does not completely eliminate double taxation. The taxpayer(s) should therefore be given an opportunity to say whether such a draft MAP APA is acceptable before it is finalised; there can be no question of imposing such an agreement in advance without the taxpayer's consent.

66.   The MAP APA will be in the form of a written document and the content, layout etc. will be decided by the participating competent authorities. In order to achieve the objective of providing a clear record of the mutual agreement and for the agreement to be effectively implemented, the mutual agreement should contain the following minimum information or should refer to where this information is provided in the MAP APA proposal documentation:

a)   The names and addresses of the enterprises that are covered by the arrangement;

b) The transactions, agreements or arrangements, tax years or accounting periods covered;

c) A description of the agreed methodology and other related matters such as agreed comparables or a range of expected results;

d) A definition of relevant terms which form the basis of applying and calculating the methodology (*e.g.* sales, cost of sales, gross profit, etc.);

e) Critical assumptions upon which the methodology is based, the breach of which would trigger renegotiation of the agreement;

f) Any agreed procedures to deal with changes in the factual circumstances which fall short of necessitating the renegotiation of the agreement;

g) If applicable, the agreed tax treatment of ancillary issues;

h) The terms and conditions that must be fulfilled by the taxpayer in order for the mutual agreement to remain valid together with procedures to ensure that the taxpayer is fulfilling those terms and conditions;

i) Details of the taxpayer's obligations to the tax administrations as a result of the domestic implementation of the MAP APA (*e.g.* annual reports, record keeping, notification of changes in critical assumptions etc.); and

j) Confirmation that, in order to secure the confidence of taxpayers and competent authorities in a MAP APA process in which information is exchanged freely, all information submitted by a taxpayer in a MAP APA case (including the identity of the taxpayer) will be protected from disclosure to the fullest extent possible under the domestic laws of the respective jurisdictions and all information exchanged between the competent authorities involved in such a case will be protected in accordance with the relevant bilateral tax treaty and applicable domestic laws.

D.4 Implementation of the MAP APA

D.4.1 Giving effect to the MAP APA and providing confirmation to the taxpayer

67.   Once the MAP APA has been finally agreed, the participating tax authorities need to give effect to the agreement in their own jurisdiction. The

tax administrations should enter into some kind of a confirmation or agreement with their respective taxpayers consistent with the mutual agreement entered into by the participating competent authorities. This confirmation or agreement would provide the taxpayer with the certainty that the transfer pricing transactions covered by the MAP APA would not be adjusted, so long as the taxpayer complies with the terms and conditions of the mutual agreement, as reflected in the domestic confirmation or agreement and has not made materially false or misleading statements during the process, including statements made in annual compliance reports. The terms and conditions would include certain assumptions which, if not met, might require an adjustment to be made or the agreement to be reconsidered.

68.   The way this confirmation or agreement is given will vary from country to country and the exact form will depend on the particular domestic law and practice. In some countries the confirmation or agreement will take the form of an APA under the relevant domestic procedure. To implement the mutual agreement effectively, the domestic confirmation or agreement must be consistent with the MAP APA and give the taxpayer, as a minimum, the same benefits as negotiated in the mutual agreement. Additionally, where it was not possible to completely eliminate double taxation, it is open to one of the participating jurisdictions to give unilateral relief from the remaining double taxation in its domestic confirmation procedure. Also, that confirmation or agreement may cover additional matters to those contained in the MAP APA, for example the domestic tax treatment of other or ancillary issues, additional record keeping or documentation requirements and the filing of reports. Care should be taken to ensure that none of the additional terms of the domestic confirmation or agreement conflict with the terms of the MAP APA.

D.4.2   Possible retroactive application ("Roll back")

69.   Neither the tax administrations nor the taxpayer are in any way obliged to apply the methodology agreed upon as part of the MAP APA to tax years ending prior to the first year of the MAP APA (often referred to as "rolling back"). Indeed, to do so might be impossible if a different fact pattern then prevailed. However, the methodology to be applied prospectively under the MAP APA may be instructive in determining the treatment of comparable transactions in earlier years. In some cases, the transfer prices may already be under enquiry by one tax administration in accounting periods prior to the MAP APA period and that tax administration and the taxpayer may wish to take the opportunity to use the agreed methodology to resolve the enquiry, or, pursuant to domestic law requirements, the tax administration may choose to make such an

adjustment even without the taxpayer's request or agreement. If the taxpayer wants certainty of obtaining relief from double taxation, the consent of the other affected tax administration(s) to the "roll back" would be needed. The ability to "roll back" will also depend on the relevant domestic law and the treaty, for example with regard to time limits.

E. MAP APA monitoring

70.   It is essential that the tax administrations are able to establish that the taxpayer is abiding by the terms and conditions on which the mutual agreement is based, throughout its duration. As the mutual agreement is made between the tax administrations and the taxpayer is not a party to such arrangements, the tax administrations have to rely on the domestic confirmation or agreement procedure described above in order to monitor the taxpayer's compliance. If the taxpayer fails to abide by the terms and conditions of the MAP APA, then it no longer need be applied. This section therefore focuses on the aspects of the domestic procedures necessary for the successful implementation of the MAP APA and on the necessary measures to ensure the taxpayer's compliance with all of its terms and conditions.

E.1   Record keeping

71.   The taxpayer and the tax administrations should agree the types of documents and records (including any necessary translations) that the taxpayer must maintain and retain for the purposes of verifying the extent of the taxpayer's compliance with the MAP APA. The guidance in Chapters IV and V of the Guidelines should be followed in order to avoid the documentation requirements becoming overly burdensome. Provisions regarding the retention period and the response time for producing the documents and records may also be included.

E.2   Monitoring mechanisms

E.2.1   Annual reports

72.   For each tax year, or accounting period, covered by the MAP APA, the taxpayer may be required to file, in addition to its tax return, an annual report describing the taxpayer's actual operations for the year and demonstrating compliance with the terms and conditions of the MAP APA, including the information necessary to decide if the critical assumptions, or other safeguards, have been met. This information should be made available

by the taxpayer to the tax administration with which it has concluded the domestic confirmation or agreement, in the manner provided for under the relevant domestic law or procedure.

E.2.2 Audit

73. A MAP APA applies only to the parties specified in the agreement and in respect of the specified transactions. The existence of such an agreement would not prevent the participating tax administrations from undertaking audit activity in the future, although any audit of transactions that are covered by the MAP APA would be limited to determining the extent of the taxpayer's compliance with its terms and conditions and whether the circumstances and assumptions necessary for the reliable application of the chosen methodology continue to exist. The affected tax administrations may require the taxpayer to establish that:

a) The taxpayer has complied with the terms and conditions of the MAP APA;

b) The representations in the proposal, the annual reports and in any supporting documentation, remain valid and that any material changes in facts or circumstances have been included in the annual reports;

c) The methodology has been accurately and consistently applied in accordance with the terms and conditions of the MAP APA; and

d) The critical assumptions underlying the transfer pricing methodology remain valid.

E.3 Consequences of non compliance or changes in circumstances

74. In general, the consequences of non compliance with the terms and conditions of a MAP APA, or the failure to meet a critical assumption, will turn on a) the terms of the MAP APA, b) any further agreement between the competent authorities as to how to deal with such non compliance or failure, and c) any applicable domestic law or procedural provisions. That is, the MAP APA itself may explicitly prescribe procedures to follow, or describe the consequences that will arise, in situations of non compliance or failure. In such situations, the competent authorities may, at their discretion, enter into discussions of what action to take on a case by case basis. Finally, domestic law or procedural provisions may impose consequences or obligations on the taxpayer and affected tax administration. The following paragraphs provide suggested guidelines similar to

procedures that have been adopted in some jurisdictions and which have, on the whole, proved workable. It should be emphasised, however, that some tax administrations may wish to adopt different procedures and approaches.

75.   If the tax administrations determine that any requirement of the MAP APA has not been met, they may nevertheless agree, based on the terms and conditions of the MAP APA, to continue to apply it, for example where the effect of the failure to comply is not material. If they do not agree to continue to apply the MAP APA, there are three options that a tax administration could take. The nature of the action to be taken is likely to depend on the seriousness of the non compliance.

76.   The most drastic action is revocation, which has the effect that the taxpayer is treated as if the MAP APA had never been entered into. Less serious is cancellation, which means the taxpayer is treated as if the MAP APA had been effective and in force but only up to the cancellation date and not for the whole of the proposed period. If the MAP APA is cancelled or revoked, then for those tax years or accounting periods for which the cancellation or revocation is effective, the relevant tax administrations and taxpayers will retain all their rights under their domestic laws and treaty provisions, as though the MAP APA had not been undertaken. Finally, the MAP APA may be revised, which means that the taxpayer will still have the benefit of the MAP APA for the whole of the proposed period, albeit that different terms apply before and after the revision date. Further details are provided below.

E.3.1   Revoking a MAP APA

77.   A tax administration may revoke a MAP APA (either unilaterally or by mutual agreement) if it is established that:

a)   There was a misrepresentation, mistake or omission that was attributable to the neglect, carelessness, or wilful default of a taxpayer when filing the MAP APA request and submission, the annual reports, or other supporting documentation or in supplying any related information; or

b)   The participating taxpayer(s) failed to materially comply with a fundamental term or condition of the MAP APA.

78.   When a MAP APA is revoked, the revocation is retroactive to the first day of the first tax year or accounting period for which the MAP APA was effective and the MAP APA will no longer have any further force and effect on the affected taxpayer(s) and the other tax administration. Because of the serious effect of this action, the tax administration proposing to revoke a MAP APA should only do so after a careful and thorough

evaluation of the relevant facts and should inform and consult with the affected taxpayer(s) and other tax administration(s) on a timely basis.

E.3.2   Cancelling a MAP APA

79.   A tax administration may cancel a MAP APA (either unilaterally or by mutual agreement) if it is established that one of the following situations has arisen:

a)   There was a misrepresentation, mistake or omission that was not attributable to the neglect, carelessness, or wilful default of a taxpayer when filing the MAP APA request and submission, the annual reports, or other supporting documentation or in supplying any related information; or

b)   The participating taxpayer(s) failed to materially comply with any term or condition of the MAP APA; or

c)   There was a material breach of one or more of the critical assumptions; or

d)   There was a change in tax law, including a treaty provision materially relevant to the MAP APA; and it has not proved possible to revise the agreement (see paragraphs 80-82 below) to take account of the changed circumstances.

80.   When a MAP APA is cancelled the date of cancellation will be determined by the nature of the event that led to the cancellation. This may be a specific date, for example if the event giving rise to the cancellation was a material change in tax law (although the MAP APA may still provide for there to be a period of transition between the date of change in the law and the cancellation date). In other cases, the cancellation will be effective for a particular tax year or accounting period, for example where there was a material change in one of the critical assumptions which could not be ascribed to a particular date in that tax year or accounting period. The MAP APA will no longer have any further force on the affected taxpayer(s) and the other tax administration from the date of cancellation.

81.   The tax administration may waive cancellation if the taxpayer can show reasonable cause, to the satisfaction of the tax administration, and if the taxpayer agrees to make any adjustment proposed by the tax administration to correct the misrepresentation, mistake, omission or non-compliance, or take into account the changes in critical assumptions, tax law

or treaty provision relevant to the APA. Such action may give rise to the revision of the MAP APA (see below).

82.   The tax administration proposing the cancellation should inform and consult with the affected taxpayer(s) and the other tax administration(s) in a timely manner. This consultation should include an explanation of the reasons for proposing that the APA be cancelled. The taxpayer should be given an opportunity to respond before any final decision is taken.

E.3.3   Revising a MAP APA

83.   The validity of the transfer pricing methodology is dependent on the critical assumptions continuing to apply for the duration of the MAP APA. The MAP APA and any domestic confirmation or agreement should therefore require the taxpayer to notify the affected tax administrations of any changes. If, after evaluation by the tax administrations, it is established that there has been a material change in conditions noted in a critical assumption, the MAP APA may be revised to reflect the change. As discussed above, the MAP APA may also contain assumptions, which although falling short of being critical to the validity of the MAP APA, nevertheless warrant a review by the affected parties. One result of such a review may again be a revision of the MAP APA. However, in many cases the terms and conditions of the MAP APA may be sufficiently flexible to account for the effects of such changes without the need for revision.

84.   The taxpayer's notification to the tax administrations that such a change has taken place should be filed as soon as practicable after the change occurs, or the taxpayer becomes aware of the change, and in any event no later than the date for filing, if required, the annual report for that year or accounting period. Early notification is encouraged in order to give the affected parties more time to try to reach agreement on revising the MAP APA, thereby reducing the likelihood of cancellation.

85.   The revised MAP APA should state the date from which the revision is effective and also the date on which the original MAP APA is no longer effective. If the date of the change can be precisely identified, then normally the revision should take effect from that date but if a precise date cannot be identified, then normally the MAP APA would be revised with effect from the first day of the accounting period following the one in which the change took place. If the tax administrations and the taxpayer cannot agree on the need for a revised MAP APA or how to revise the MAP APA, the MAP APA will be cancelled and will no longer have any further force and effect on the participating taxpayers and tax administrations. The determination of the effective date of the cancellation of the MAP APA will

normally follow the same principles as applied to determine the date of revision.

E.4   Renewing a MAP APA

86.   A request to renew a MAP APA should be made at the time prescribed by the participating tax administrations, bearing in mind the need for sufficient lead time for the taxpayer(s) and tax administrations to review and evaluate the renewal request and to reach agreement. It may be helpful to commence the renewal process well before the existing MAP APA has expired.

87.   The format, processing, and evaluation of the renewal application would usually be similar to those for an initial MAP APA application. However, the necessary level of detail may be reduced with the agreement of the participating tax administrations, particularly if there have not been material changes in the facts and circumstances of the case. Renewal of a MAP APA is not automatic and depends on the consent of all parties concerned and on the taxpayer demonstrating, among other things, compliance with the terms and conditions of the existing MAP APA. The methodology and terms and conditions of the renewed MAP APA may, of course, differ from those of the previous MAP APA.

Annex to Chapter VI

Examples to Illustrate the Guidance on Intangible Property and Highly Uncertain Valuation

The following three examples illustrate the application of the principles concerning arm's length pricing when valuation of transferred intangible property is highly uncertain at the time of the transaction. See paragraphs 6.28-6.35.

The adjustments and assumptions about arm's length arrangements in the examples that follow are intended for illustrative purposes only and should not be taken as prescribing adjustments and arm's length arrangements in actual cases or particular industries. While they seek to demonstrate the principles of the Sections of the Guidelines to which they refer, those principles must be applied in each case according to the specific facts and circumstances of that case.

Example 1

1.   Manufacturing and distribution rights for an established drug are licensed between associated enterprises under an agreement that fixes the rate of royalty for the three-year term of the agreement. Those terms are found to be in accordance with industry practice and equivalent arm's length agreements for comparable products, and the rate is accepted as being equivalent to that agreed in uncontrolled transactions based on the benefits reasonably anticipated by both parties at the time the agreement is executed.

2.   In the third year of the agreement, it is discovered that the drug has capabilities in another therapeutic category in combination with another drug, and the discovery leads to a considerable increase in sales and profits for the licensee. Had the agreement been negotiated at arm's length in year three with this knowledge, there is no doubt that a higher royalty rate would have been agreed to reflect the increased value of the intangible.

3.   There is evidence to support the view (and the evidence is made available to the tax administration) that the new capabilities of the drug were unanticipated at the time the agreement was executed and that the royalty rate established in year one was adequately based on the benefits reasonably

anticipated by both parties at that time. The lack of price adjustment clauses or other protection against the risk of uncertainty of valuation also is consistent with the terms of comparable uncontrolled transactions. And, based on analysis of the behaviour of independent enterprises in similar circumstances, there is no reason to believe that the development in year three was so fundamental that it would have led at arm's length to a renegotiation of the pricing of the transaction.

4.   Taking all these circumstances into account, there is no reason to adjust the royalty rate in year three. Such an adjustment would be contrary to the principles set out in Chapter VI because it would represent an inappropriate use of hindsight in this case. See paragraph 6.29 of the Guidelines. There is no reason to consider that the valuation was sufficiently uncertain at the outset that the parties at arm's length would have required a price adjustment clause, or that the change in value was so fundamental a development that it would have led to a re-negotiation of the transaction. See paragraphs 6.30-6.31.

Example 2

5.   The facts are the same as in the previous example. Assume that at the end of the three- year period the agreement was re-negotiated between the parties. At this stage it is known that the rights to the drug are considerably more valuable than they had at first appeared. However, the unexpected development of the previous year is still recent, and it cannot reliably be predicted whether sales will continue to rise, whether further beneficial effects will be discovered, and what developments in the market may affect sales as competitors piggyback on the discovery. All these considerations make the re-evaluation of the intangible rights a highly uncertain process. Nevertheless, the associated enterprises enter into a new licensing agreement for a term of ten years that significantly increases the fixed royalty rate based on speculative expectations of continuing and increasing demand.

6.   It is not industry practice to enter into long-term agreements with fixed royalty rates when the intangible involved potentially has a high value, but that value has not been established by a track record. Nor is there evidence that, given the uncertainty in valuation, any projections made by the associated enterprises would have been considered adequate by independent enterprises to justify an agreement with a fixed royalty rate. Assume that there is evidence that independent enterprises would have insisted on protection in the form of prospective price adjustment clauses based on reviews undertaken annually.

7.   Assume that in year 4 sales increased and the royalty rate established under the ten-year agreement is regarded as appropriate under the arm's length principle. However, at the beginning of year 5, a competitor introduces a drug that has greater benefit than the first drug in the therapeutic category in which the first drug, in combination, unexpectedly had provided benefits, and sales of the first drug for that use rapidly decline. The royalty rate fixed at the outset of the ten-year agreement cannot be regarded as arm's length beyond year 5, and it is justifiable for the tax administration to make a transfer price adjustment from the beginning of year 6. This adjustment is appropriate because of the evidence, mentioned in the preceding paragraph, that in comparable circumstances independent enterprises would have provided in the agreement for a price adjustment based on annual review. See paragraph 6.34 of the Guidelines.

Example 3

8.   Assume that Company X licenses the rights to produce and market a microchip to Company Y, a newly established subsidiary, for a period of five years. The royalty rate is fixed at 2 percent. This royalty rate is based on a projection of benefits to be derived from the exploitation of the intangible, which shows expected product sales of 50 to 100 million in each of the first five years.

9.   It is established that contracts between independent enterprises dealing with comparable intangibles in comparable circumstances would not consider the projections sufficiently reliable to justify a fixed royalty rate, and so would normally agree upon a price adjustment clause to account for differences between actual and projected benefits. An agreement made by Company X with an independent manufacturer for a comparable intangible under comparable circumstances provides for the following adjustments to the rate:

Sales	Rate
Up to 100 million	2.00%
Next 50 million	2.25%
Next 50 million	2.50%
In excess of 200 million	2.75%

10.   In fact, although sales by Y in year 1 are 50 million, in subsequent years sales are three times greater than projected figures. In accordance with the principles of this section, for these subsequent years the tax administration would be justified in determining the royalty rate on the basis

of the adjustment clause that would be provided in a comparable uncontrolled transaction such as that between Company X and the independent manufacturer. See paragraphs 6.30, 6.32-6.33 of the Guidelines.

Appendix

Recommendation of the Council on the Determination of Transfer Pricing between Associated Enterprises [C(95)126/Final]

As amended on 11 April 1996 [C(96)46/FINAL], 24 July 1997 [C(97)144/FINAL], 28 October 1999 [C(99)138], 16 July 2009 [C(2009)88] and 22 July 2010 [C(2010)99]

The COUNCIL,

Having regard to Article 5(b) of the Convention on the Organisation for Economic Co-operation and Development of 14th December, 1960;

Having regard to the Declaration of 21st June, 1976 adopted by the Governments of OECD Member Countries on International Investment and Multinational Enterprises and the Guidelines annexed thereto [C(76)99(Final)];

Having regard to the Report on the Transfer Pricing Guidelines for Multinational Enterprises and Tax Administrations, hereafter referred to as "the 1995 Report" [DAFFE/CFA(95)19 and Corrigendum I] adopted on 27 June 1995 by the Committee on Fiscal Affairs, as supplemented by the report on intangible property and services adopted on 23 January 1996 by the Committee on Fiscal Affairs [DAFFE/CFA(96)2] and incorporated in Chapters VI and VII; by the report on cost contribution arrangements adopted on 25 June 1997 by the Committee on Fiscal Affairs [DAFFE/CFA(97)27] and incorporated in Chapter VIII; by the report on the guidelines for monitoring procedures on the OECD Transfer Pricing Guidelines and the involvement of the business community [DAFFE/CFA/WD(97)11/REV1], adopted on 24 June 1997 by the Committee on Fiscal Affairs and incorporated in the Annexes; by the report on the guidelines for conducting Advance Pricing Arrangements under the mutual agreement procedure adopted on 30 June 1999 by the Committee on

Fiscal Affairs [DAFFE/CFA(99)31] and incorporated in the Annexes; by the report on the transfer pricing aspects of business restructurings, adopted by the Committee on Fiscal Affairs on 22 June 2010 [CTPA/CFA(2010)46] and incorporated in Chapter IX; revised by the report on comparability and profit methods, adopted by the Committee on Fiscal Affairs on 22 June 2010 [CTPA/CFA(2010)55], which replaced Chapters I-III; modified by an update of Chapter IV which was adopted by the Committee on Fiscal Affairs on 6 June 2008 [CTPA/CFA(2008)30/REV1]; by an update of the Foreword and of the Preface which was adopted by the Committee on Fiscal Affairs on 22 June 2009 [CTPA/CFA(2009)51/REV1]; and by an update of the Foreword, Preface, Glossary, Chapters IV-VIII and Annexes which was adopted by the Committee on Fiscal Affairs on 22 June 2010 [CTPA/CFA(2010)47];

Having regard to the fundamental need for co-operation among tax administrations in order to remove the obstacles that international double taxation presents to the free movement of goods, services and capital between Member countries;

Considering that transactions between associated enterprises may take place under conditions differing from those taking place between independent enterprises;

Considering that the prices of such transactions between associated enterprises (usually referred to as transfer pricing) should, nevertheless, for tax purposes be in conformity with those which would be charged between independent enterprises (usually referred to as arm's length pricing) as provided in Article 9 (paragraph 1) of the OECD Model Tax Convention on Income and on Capital;

Considering that problems with regard to transfer pricing in international transactions assume special importance in view of the substantial volume of such transactions;

Considering the need to achieve consistency in the approaches of tax administrations, on the one hand, and of associated enterprises, on the other hand, in the determination of the income and expenses of a company that is part of a Multinational Enterprise Group that should be taken in to account within a jurisdiction.

I.   RECOMMENDS to the Governments of Member countries:

I.1.   that their tax administrations follow, when reviewing, and if necessary, adjusting transfer pricing between associated enterprises for the purposes of determining taxable income, the guidance in the 1995 Report, as amended – considering the integrity of the Report and the interaction of the different chapters – for arriving at arm's length pricing for transactions between associated enterprises;

I.2. that tax administrations should encourage taxpayers to follow the guidance in the 1995 Report, as amended and to that end that they give the 1995 Report as amended publicity in their country and have it translated, where necessary, into their national language(s);

I.3. that they develop further co-operation between their tax administrations, on a bilateral or multilateral basis, in matters pertaining to transfer pricing.

II. INVITES the Governments of Member countries:

II.1. to notify the Committee on Fiscal Affairs of any modifications to the text of any laws or regulations that are relevant to the determination of transfer pricing or of the introduction of new laws or regulations.

III. INSTRUCTS the Committee on Fiscal Affairs:

III.1. to pursue its work on issues pertinent to transfer pricing and to issue the additions to the guidelines referred to in the 1995 Report as amended;

III.2. to monitor the implementation of the 1995 Report as amended, in cooperation with the tax authorities of Member countries and with the participation of the business community and to recommend to the Council to amend and update, if necessary, the 1995 Report as amended, in the light of this monitoring;

III.3. to report periodically to the Council on the results of its work in these matters together with any relevant proposals for improved international cooperation;

III.4. to develop its dialogue with non-Member countries, consistently with the policy of the Organisation, with the aim of assisting them to become familiar with the 1995 Report as amended, and where appropriate encourage them to associate themselves with the 1995 Report as amended.

IV. DECIDES to repeal the Recommendation on the Determination of Transfer Prices between Associated Enterprises issued on the 29th May 1979 [C(79)83(Final)].

OECD PUBLISHING, 2, rue André-Pascal, 75775 PARIS CEDEX 16
PRINTED IN FRANCE
(23 2010 09 1 P) ISBN 978-92-64-09033-0 – No. 57511 2010

LaVergne, TN USA
26 October 2010

202361LV00002B/8/P